ISLAM
Beliefs and Observances
Sixth Edition

Caesar E. Farah, Ph.D.
University of Minnesota

IN MEMORY OF MY PARENTS

All inquiries should be addressed to:
Barron's Educational Series, Inc.
250 Wireless Boulevard
Hauppauge, NY 11788
http://www.barronseduc.com

International Standard Book No. 0-7641-1205-8

Library of Congress Catalog Card No. 99-73279

PRINTED IN THE UNITED STATES OF AMERICA
9876

Table of Contents

Preface to the Sixth Edition

THE MUSLIM WORLD continues to experience some agonizing convulsions as is so sadly evident in the recent events affecting the Muslim Kosovars of Yugoslavia. Turmoil in India as a result of Hindu hostility towards Muslims, growing Indonesian intolerance of non-Muslim minorities, Europe's insistence on keeping Muslim Turkey out of its Union, the branding of Islam by its detractors and politicians in America as a religion promoting terrorism, increasing hostility among certain Muslim leaders towards the United States for its unflinching support of their enemies at home and abroad—all such manifestations and trends do not bode well for promoting harmony, tolerance, and understanding when they have become most needed for the sake of world peace.

In this edition I have sought to make emendations and to update the data, especially in the later chapters, to provide a fuller understanding of what has transpired in the Muslim world since the fifth edition was published in 1994.

I am grateful to the readers of *Islam* for their continuing interest in what this book has to offer by way of promoting better understanding and appreciation for Muslims and their societies in these turbulent and unsettled times, in the hope that the coming millennium will witness greater harmony and mutual respect for the Muslim world by a distrustful West.

Minneapolis, Minnesota
October 1999

Caesar E. Farah

Preface to the First Edition

IN THE INTEREST of making the precepts and motivation in the religion of Islam better appreciated by a larger segment of the reading public this presentation has been limited specifically to the religious aspect of Islam. The sociopolitical and cultural aspects have been treated only to the extent that they materially influenced the fundamentals and observances of the faith.

It is the author's wish that the reader will acquire a more accurate perspective of what Islam stands for today as a mainspring of human action for hundreds of millions in a large segment of the world. To help him towards that end, a conscious attempt has been made to simplify as much as is reasonable the most important ingredients of the Islamic religion and to show the range of their impact on the lives of its adherents.

In citing translations of the Qurʾānic verses used herein, I have depended very frequently on the versions of authors whose rendition has been deemed expressive not only of the word but also of the spirit of the Arabic original. M. M. Pickthall's *The Meaning of the Glorious Koran* is most useful in this regard.

Transliterations from the Arabic follow the linguistically preferred method with slight modifications introduced where called for. A full listing of the terms used in the body of the text can be found in the Glossary with explanations oriented towards the context wherein they were cited. The list of recommended reading is designed to help the reader pursue his study of Islam in still broader detail than afforded in the presentation herein made.

I should like to express my appreciation to my family for their patience and understanding and their support in the preparation of this book.

Bloomington, Indiana
March, 1967

Caesar E. Farah

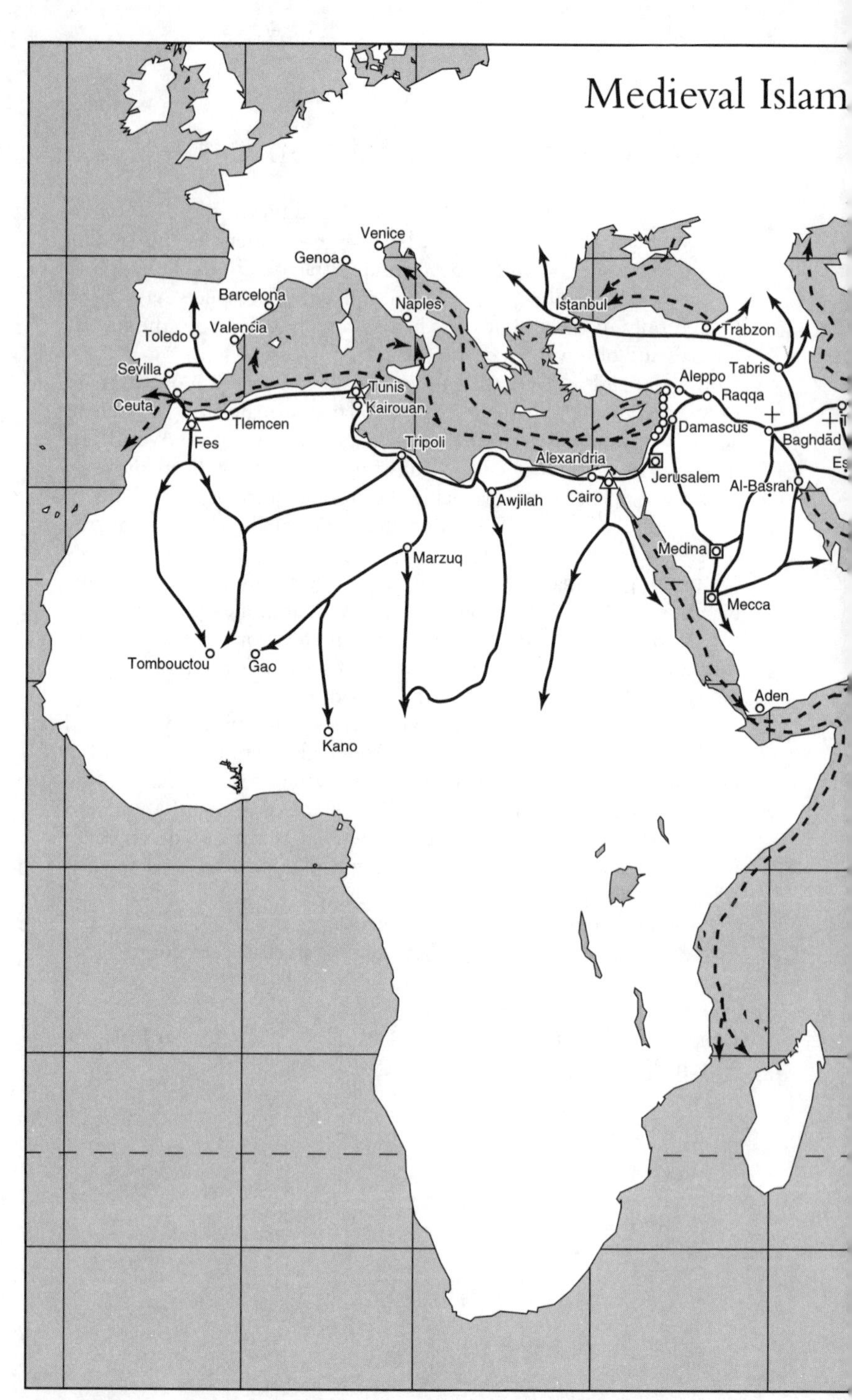
Medieval Islam
Venice
Genoa
Barcelona
Naples
Toledo
Valencia
Sevilla
Ceuta
Tunis
Kairouan
Tlemcen
Fes
Tripoli
Istanbul
Trabzon
Tabris
Aleppo
Raqqa
Damascus
Baghdād
Alexandria
Jerusalem
Al-Basrah
Cairo
Awjilah
Marzuq
Medina
Mecca
Tombouctou
Gao
Kano
Aden

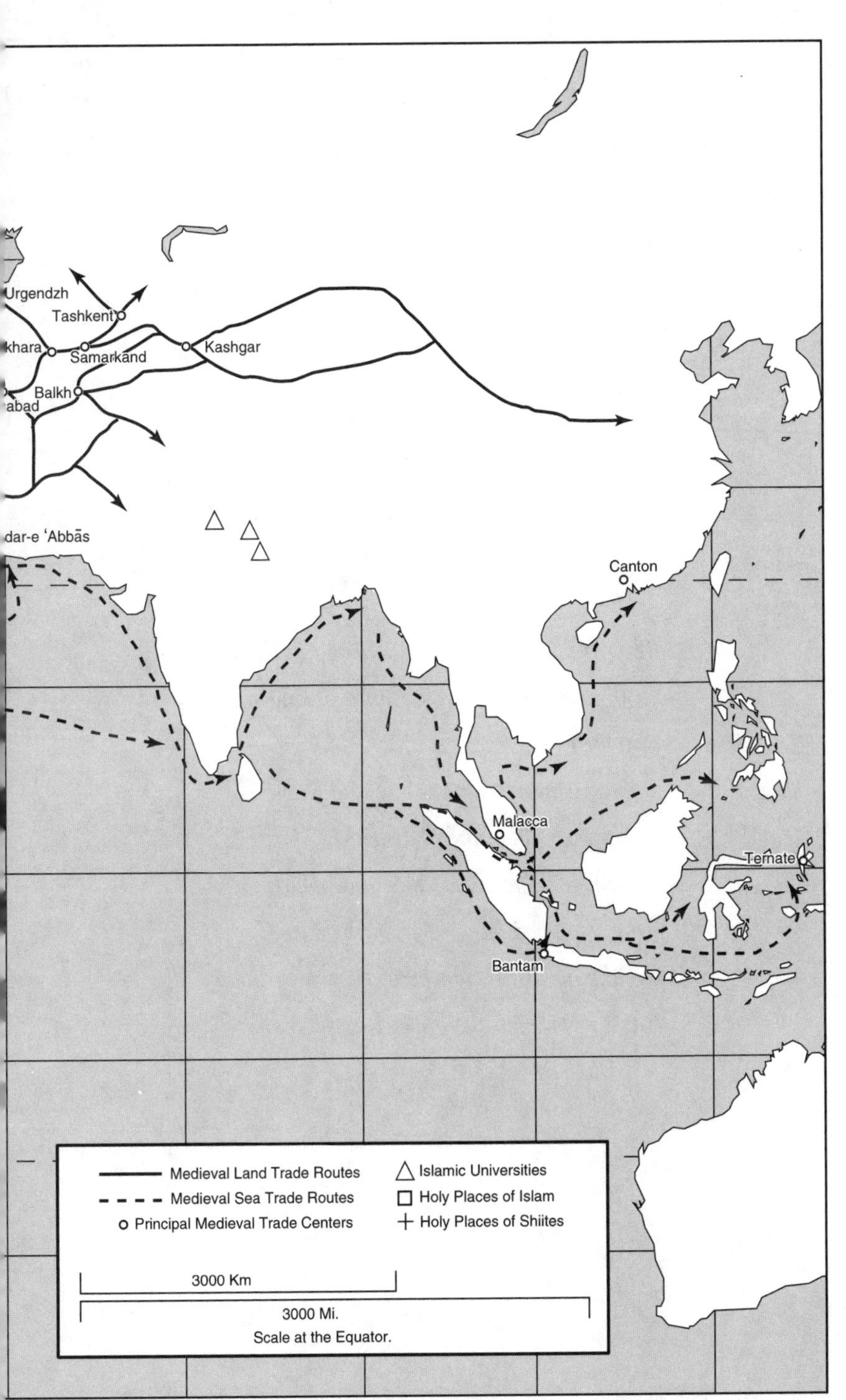
Urgendzh
Tashkent
khara
Samarkand
Kashgar
Balkh
abad
dar-e ʻAbbās
Canton
Malacca
Ternate
Bantam
Medieval Land Trade Routes
Medieval Sea Trade Routes
Principal Medieval Trade Centers
Islamic Universities
Holy Places of Islam
Holy Places of Shiites
3000 Km
3000 Mi.
Scale at the Equator.

"Say (O Muslims): We believe in Allah
and that which is revealed unto us and that
which was revealed unto Abraham,
and Ishmael, and Isaac, and Jacob,
and the tribes, and that which Moses
and Jesus received, and that which
the Prophets received from their Lord.
We make no distinction between any of them,
and unto Him we have surrendered."

QUR'ĀN 2:136

CHAPTER 1

An Introduction to Islam

WHEN WE SPEAK of Islam we are concerned not only with a religion akin to the other monotheistic religions, Judaism and Christianity, but with a way of life, a system that encompasses the relationships of the adherents to each other and to their society from birth until death.

The religion of Islam provides a strong bond that brings together Muslims regardless of race or nationality in a fellowship constructed upon faith in the one God. When considered in this context, Islam has much in common with both Christianity and Judaism. To the extent, however, that Islam stresses communal solidarity, as measured in terms of successes encountered in this area, it has more in common with Judaism than with Christianity.

In the thirteen and a half centuries of its existence, Islam the religion fostered the growth of a political commonwealth and of a distinct culture. At one time it commanded the allegiance and following of diverse peoples incorporated into a vast fraternity which stretched from the Pyrenees in Western Europe to the Philippines in the Western Pacific. Within such wide territorial reaches Muslims, formerly of varying creeds and cultural backgrounds, forged a common culture drawing on the precepts of their religion and expressing itself through the medium of the Arabic language. Muslims evolved basic philosophical and religious concepts that shaped the fundamentals of Islam and added luster and richness to their way of life. Unrestrained by dogmatism, Muslims readily engaged themselves in the pursuits of philosophy, literature, science, mathematics, and astronomy, converting their chief cities from Spain to Central Asia into the foci of a brilliant civilization when Europe for the most part was experiencing a period of cultural arrestation.

Hence in projecting our study of Islam we cannot achieve a meaningful understanding of the religion without giving some consideration to its institutional and cultural facets. All three aspects of Islam shaped what may be termed "the system of Islam" and assured the triumph and efflorescence of the faith. The study also requires relating the forces which for centuries had a molding effect on the religion as it evolved from a simple set of elementary beliefs to an all-encompassing complex framework of theological reference. It is equally necessary for us to draw attention to powerful forces of attraction which enabled Islamic society to cohere and withstand disruption under strong pressure. Pride in belonging to a unifying faith coupled with the spirit engendered thereby contributed to the social solidarity and cultural development of the believers in Islam.

But this commonly shared pride did not always succeed in safeguarding the socioreligious solidarity of the Muslims. Such breaches as disrupted the cohesiveness of Islam will be given due consideration as we follow the fluctuations in its historical career through alternating phases of accomplishment and decline.

For a number of centuries the Muslim East and the Christian West confronted each other across the length and breadth of the Mediterranean basin. Sometimes their relations were characterized by peaceful and fruitful exchanges; quite often both sides viewed each other with antipathy and indifference punctured by frequent conflicts. Generally, neither the Muslim nor the Christian world appeared to be aware of the fundamental religious precepts they shared in common, derived as they were from the common fount of Judaic and Hellenic beliefs. Not many Christians today, for instance, are aware of the fact that Muḥammad, the messenger of Islam, believed Jesus and Moses to be the most important bearers of God's one hallowed message to His people as enshrined in the Testaments and the Torah. Indeed, to millions of Christians for hundreds of years Muḥammad was an object of contempt; certainly in no way did he command the respect which his followers accorded Jesus, whose position of deference in the holy book of Islam is permanently assured.

Until recent scholarship began to strip Islam of the prejudicial views surrounding it, the Western world, at the very best, had contented itself with a distorted understanding of one of mankind's significant living religions. In his two brilliant works, *Orientalism* and *Covering Islam*, Edward Said provides ample proof of such distortions and what underlies them. Geographical proximity and frequent exchanges notwithstanding, the Christian accused the Muslim of worshiping a "false prophet." To the follower of Christ the follower of Muḥammad was a blasphemer who would not figure in God's great design, or in the salvation reserved for the faithful believers in Jesus. Indeed, in the eyes of the Christians Islam was synonymous with "Mohammedanism," with its false implication of being a system of belief founded upon the worship of the person "Mohammed" (Muḥammad). Yet nothing is more repugnant to the devout Muslim than to be called a "Mohammedan"; from the point of view of his religion, to accord devotional respect to any being other than Allah, God of the Worlds, of Christians and Jews, is to commit the major unpardonable sin.

The term *Islam* in the lexicon of the Arabs means "Submission." The religion of Islam is the religion of submission to the will of the omnipotent and omniscient Creator, the only God, who admits of no associates in the worship of Him. In the eyes of the believers, Muḥammad, like Abraham, Moses, and Jesus, is a prophet of God. But unlike the Christian conception of Jesus, Muḥammad is not regarded as divine; to the believers in him he is a mortal who was called upon by God to deliver His eternal message to the unbelieving Arabs, as Moses had delivered it to the Hebrews and Jesus to the rest of mankind.

Muḥammad lived, preached, and died in the full light of history. Countless millions since the time of his death in 632 have paid homage to him as they journey far and wide to reach his burial place in Medina.

Distortions prejudicing the Western conceptions of Islam may be dated to the earliest centuries, but particularly from the period of the Crusades, when Christian Europe's hostility for the people and their religion crystallized. The church fathers treated Islam as a heresy; Muslims were infidels; Muḥammad a "renegade bishop," an "impostor," who rebelled against the central mission of Christ. Dante ranked the prophet of Islam low among the ill-fated occupants of the Inferno. Christian authors in subsequent times held him in no better regard. In his *Vie de Mahomet* (Life of Muḥammad), published at the end of the seventeenth century, Prideaux held Muḥammad up as a mirror to "unbelievers, atheists, deists and libertines." To the irreligiously inclined Voltaire, the prophet of Deism, Muḥammad was the fount of fanaticism. The more generous Abbé Maracci regarded Islam as a distorted extension of Christianity while he begrudgingly conceded in his Latin translation of the Qur'ān (Koran), the sacred book of Islam, that "this religion contains many elements of natural truth evidently borrowed from the Christian religion, which seems to be in accordance with the law and light of nature."[1]

Early attempts to place Islam and its messenger in a more objective framework of reference were few and far between. Late in the eighteenth century, a Dutch professor of theology at the University of Utrecht came to the conclusion that "no religion has been more calumniated than Islam." The noted English scholar George Sale spent long arduous hours translating the Qur'ān into English, seeking to obtain a deeper insight into the real meaning of the message of Islam. In the preliminary discourse he brought out the point that "there is no false doctrine that does not contain some truth."

With such scholars paving the way, systematic attempts aimed at casting light upon the falsities surrounding the Christian view of Islam were in full evidence by the 1830s. Henceforth scholars, mostly German Orientalists, began to examine Islam from a detached point of view shorn of preconceived notions and assumptions.

That these scholars were inclined to view Islam in a more favorable light is evident in the testimony of Professor Weil: "In so far as he brought the most beautiful teachings of the Old and New Testament to a people which was not illuminated by one ray of faith, he may be regarded, even by those who are not Mohammedans, as a messenger of God."[2] Other reputable Orientalists—de Perçeval, Lammens, Caetani, Muir, Nöldeke—pioneered works on Muḥammad and Islam that have since their time become classical for their authoritativeness. It was largely through their efforts that we witness the gradual lifting of the veil of tendentious fiction and emotional bias that had blurred the European's vision of Islam. This trend towards an objective understanding of Islam in its multiple facets has persisted, both in Europe and the United States, up to the present time.

Major breakthroughs in the area of communications have drawn the peoples of the world into closer contacts. There is more interest today in the cultural values and institutional beliefs of non-Westerners. To be sure a great deal of this interest derives from a superficial observation, largely through sightseeing tours of the exotic cities of Islam—Cairo, Tangier, Baghdad, Damascus, Istanbul; but a lot of it is engendered also by need. The oil of Arabia is as alluring to the Western companies that exploit and market it as the bazaars of Cairo are to the American tourist. The entire history of the post-World War II era is replete with incidents that have focused attention on the strategic importance of the Muslim world, particularly in the East-West struggle. Scholars, technicians, diplomats, and the average citizens of the Western world, all from their varying points of interest, have demonstrated the need for a more positive understanding of the vital significance of the Islamic world, its peoples, institutions, and beliefs.

As curiosity arouses interest and interest leads to inquiry, and as the scholar begins to examine more closely the whole posture of Islam in its historical and environmental contexts, the Western reader begins to appreciate the reasons for a systematic study of Islam.

In the first place there are over a billion people today who adhere to the religion of Islam. Not only do they represent all the known races of mankind, but they inhabit a nearly contiguous stretch of land from the shores of the Atlantic in the West to the confines of China and Malaysia in the East. Geographically, the followers of Muḥammad are concentrated in North Africa, the regions of the Near and Middle East, Russia, Central Asia, China, the Malayan peninsula, northern and central India, Indonesia, and the Philippines. In more recent decades the Muslims have gained a wide following south of the Sahara in the very heart of black Africa. In the Balkans and Western Europe there are nearly ten million Muslims. To this might be added a nearly equal number in the Americas. One out of every six human beings today subscribes to the faith of Islam; he lives within a social structure largely the product of Islam, and he is guided in his daily life by norms and precepts forged in the caldron of Islam.

Secondly, the role of Islam in regulating the affairs of the believer cannot be overlooked. On an average the Muslim invokes the name of Allah (God) no less than twenty times a day. No other known prophet of a monotheistic religion receives as much mention in prayer as the Prophet of Islam. More children bear Muḥammad's name than any other name popular to mankind. No known body of sacred literature is as thoroughly and systematically committed to memory, or is recited as frequently, as the holy book of Islam. At certain prescribed times of the day from atop a minaret in the towns, hamlets, and cities of Islam, the voice of the muezzin rings out in clear melodious Arabic the call to prayer. Spontaneously, devotees everywhere turn in the direction of Mecca, birthplace of Islam and its perpetual shrine, to perform the ritual prayer as established in the days of Muḥammad. If by some magical flight an outsider could transplant himself into the midst of the faithful during the noon-hour prayer on the day of congregation in any given mosque, he would behold lines upon lines of Muslims representing the major races of mankind performing in unison, and according to prescribed form, the same prostrations and genuflections and uttering the same prayer to Allah, in Arabic, regardless of their native tongues.

Thirdly, it would be difficult to observe a more thorough manifestation of devotion to God than is evinced by the followers of Islam. No other religion appears to inculcate as much dependence on God in the trivia of daily life; nor does God figure so centrally among other religious groups in the ups and downs of ordinary living. Indeed, no task, commitment, performance, journey, or repose, however minute or momentous, pleasurable or unpleasurable, is undertaken without first invoking the name of Allah. No blessing or bounty of any sort is received except through the grace of Allah. Until recently Muslims tended to accept their lot trusting in God for redress. Today one witnesses a surge against leadership that has not abided by the decrees of the faith on social justice and amelioration. Misfortunes are no longer endured with passivity and resignation. Islam enjoins against oppression and sanctions the use of force to eliminate oppressors as Allāh wills, albeit He still has the prerogative to bestow or withhold as He sees fit.

When over three million pilgrims continuously stream to Arabia on the annual pilgrimage, they observe for themselves the strong bonds at work in gathering them together from all parts of the world. These are the bonds of Islam, equating all Muslims regardless of race or nationality, economic or social status. As a symbol of their equality in Islam, the believers shed the attire of daily life for a plain white linen cloth worn by all preparatory to entering the sanctuary of Islam in a state of ritual purity. This manifestation of egalitarianism can be attributed to the sense of unity in faith for which the religion of Islam is directly responsible. The leveling force of Islam has not ceased to attract to the faith the downtrodden of humanity with the same power of appeal that gained it the loyalty of Arabians and non-Arabians alike in earlier centuries. Through conversion abetted by the expansion of the polity, Islam grew steadily in stature until it came to enjoy the rank of a major world religion that still attracts converts to its fold.

Unity in belief accounts for the unusual display of solidarity in Islamic society and for the dynamism which propelled the faith forward. Pride in faith explains the accomplishments of the believers not only in religion, but in the areas of political and cultural endeavors as well. The historical development of Islam in all of its facets reflects its power of appeal; this appeal has been decisive in winning over to the religion the inhabitants of Africa in the face of strong competition from Christianity.

The growth from modest and obscure beginnings in a barren segment of Arabia to the status of a great world empire is the historical testimony to the zeal with which Islam infused its believers. This growth was occasioned less by a conscious effort to spread the faith than by the exemplary conduct of the conquerors as manifested in their personal lives. Military conquest, to be sure, created the polity, but the society molded by the polity was buttressed by values imparted to it by the Islamic faith. The bonds which caused Islamic society to cohere reposed in the tenets of the faith. These in turn nurtured the forces that made for the unity of Arab, Persian, Turk, Indian, Berber, and Spaniard on the basis of adherence to a common religion, not nationality.

Molded into a coherent community by the tenets of Islam, Muslim society succeeded in weathering the political disintegration of the polity when localized dynasties inherited the great Islamic empires. Although Islam the religion and Islam the polity have not been coterminous since the first Muslim century, it is noteworthy to remark that with the exception of the Iberian peninsula, Islam the religion has remained firmly implanted in the soil that once gave it political sanctity.

The triumph of the principle of nationality and the concomitant growth of nationalism in certain parts of the Muslim world resulted in the supplanting of the theocracy by political entities presently enjoying the ramifications of sovereign rule. Among them may be listed such national states as Turkey, Iran, Pakistan, Indonesia, Syria, Iraq, the United Arab Republic, the Kingdom of Jordan, Saudi Arabia, Libya, Sudan, Tunisia, Algeria, Morocco, and a number of oil-producing emirates on the Persian Gulf: Kuwait, Qatar, the United Arab Emirates, Oman, and Yemen, all on the Arabian peninsula. In addition, there are the recently created republics of Kazakhstan, Uzbekistan, Tajikistan, Azerbaijan, Kirgistan, and Turkmenia, and strong enclaves of Muslims in China, Myanmar, Malaya, India, the Philippines—not to mention African states like Somalia, Chad, Tanzania, Niger, Nigeria, and a number of West African states.

The dissolution of colonial and imperial domination over Muslim lands in the aftermath of World War II left in its wake numerous secular national states that diluted Islamic solidarity. Secularism to be sure has posed a rival claim for the allegiance of Muslims. But the ties based on religion, which continue to transcend national boundary lines, have not been seriously impaired. Indeed, the Western observer becomes aware of a pattern of challenge and response within the fragmented polity of Islam that is strikingly Muslim. Unifying institutions, such as those centered on mosque or bazaar, persist in Islamic countries in spite of their ethnical heterogeneity and continue to be reflected in the practices which they still share in common.

While focusing attention on the historical forces that enhanced the religion when the polity had disappeared, one can not ignore the role of philosophical contentions impacting the evolution of Islam and contributing both to orthodoxy and heterodoxy in the shaping of an Islamic identity. Cultural trends, like social trends in general, were shaped by the precepts of Islam and, in turn, played a constructive part in the career of Islam as a civilizing force. When Christian Europe was experiencing its "Dark Ages," the cities of Islam in Spain, North Africa, and the East were alive with cultural creativity. Within the framework of tolerance provided by Islam, Muslim scholars in Toledo and Cordova, Cairo, Baghdad, and Damascus were feverishly adding new dimensions to our knowledge of philosophy, the sciences, mathematics, and astronomy. In the arts and crafts, in commerce, agriculture, and navigation innovations introduced by Muslims had a lasting effect in the shaping of our Western traditions; traces of such contributions prevail in numerous technical terms derived from the Arabic and surviving in Western languages. While these specific aspects of Islam's growth fall outside the purview of this work, to the extent that they contributed to the image of Islam they become germane to our understanding of this religion.

Scholarship and learning in general went on relatively unhampered by dogmatism or religious injunctions. The fact that Islam boasts of no organized clergy similarly made the task of adaptation to modern life relatively easy. Indeed, the absence of such an institution is one of the unique features of Islam, which only serves to bring out the remarkable capacity of Islamic society to cohere. Coherence was achieved not by the guiding hand of a clerical institution, but by the volition of the adherents, resulting from reasoned individual and communal interests.

The institution of the caliphate was designed originally to rally the believers and centralize their loyalties; but the caliph by the exercise of his will or the force of his personality alone did not always succeed in maintaining the political solidarity of Islam. In the last analysis the solidarity engendered by Islam stems not from a rallying institution or figure, but from *pride of belonging.* This does not necessarily mean that such pride of belonging was successful in preventing schismatic movements. Islam did develop its schisms, but these stemmed mostly from political differences which later became religiously oriented. The overwhelming majority of Muslims until today have remained loyal to the orthodox or Sunni sect of Islam.

According to the historical record, Islam was not able to foster a political coherence commensurate with the religious. Some scholars believe that had Islam succeeded in resolving the problem of successorship to the lay authority of the Prophet Muḥammad in the earlier decades, political solidarity might have become more firmly established. But the trend favoring national determination in Muslim lands is not necessarily a modern phenomenon. As early as the second century of Islam, the conquered Iranians resented the refusal of the conquering Arabs to accord them the full social equality ordained by Islam. The challenge to caliphal authority equated with Arab hegemony resulted frequently from such resentment. The nature of the challenge often took on the form of "ethnicism," a movement spearheaded by ethnical elements desirous of asserting their avowed cultural superiority over their Arab overlords even though the basic tenets of Islam opposed the show of preference outside the bond of religion. If from the point of view of Islamic dogma the Muslim must assert his individual identity, he would have to justify this in terms of his superior piousness, not his ethnical heritage.

But repugnant as ethnicism was to the dogmatist, in his religious and philosophical disputations the ethnicist provided an important medium for the cultural enhancement of Islam. To him accrues a good part of the credit in the "internationalization" of the religion and in making it a substantial cultural as well as a religious, social, and political force. By successfully challenging the authority of the self-styled dogmatist to control the realm of the intellect, or even to dictate to it, partisans of the non-religious sciences seized upon philosophy as a weapon of liberation. Soon there developed a rational school of thought spearheaded by Aristotelianism and epitomized by Averroës (Ibn Rushd). Much of the contribution of Islam in the realm of ideas that inspired the Scholastic movement in late medieval Europe resulted from the disputations of the Muslim Platonists and Aristotelians, culminating in the reconciliation of reason and faith in Islam before Medieval Catholicism and Judaism were able to achieve the same end.

European interest in Islamic scholarship in the Upper Middle Ages was not restricted merely to the influence of Averroism on the Scholastic philosophers, such as Magnus, Abelard, and Aquinas. Advanced concepts in medicine as embodied in the famous *Canons* of Avicenna, in mathematics as articulated by al-Bīrūni or astronomy as enhanced by al-Majrītī—all of whose works were translated into Latin in the twelfth century—were equally sought by budding European scholars. Frederick II Hohenstaufen surrounded himself with Muslim savants in his semi-Islamized court at Palermo. The abbots at the monastery of Cluny in France, center of the earliest reform movement in the thirteenth century, actively availed themselves of Muslim scholarship. Peter the Venerable busied himself with a translation of the Qur'ān into Latin late in the twelfth century. Muslim learning provided an impetus for the revivification of independent thinking in southern Europe in the Upper Middle Ages leading into the Renaissance.

Contacts of this nature in the late Middle Ages led to one of those rare periods of productive exchange between Islam and Christianity when the sword was subordinated to the pen. The courts of Toledo, Cordova, and Palermo attracted Christian scholars in the waning years of the Middle Ages with as much appeal as the riches of Syria attracted Christian warriors in the days of the Crusades. Through such intellectual contacts Christian scholars not only acquired an appreciation of Muslim scholarship but also came to appreciate the heritage of the classical age of Greece and of an Aristotle whom Muslim intellectuals regarded as their "first teacher."

But this period of fruitful exchange which contributed to the subsequent general awakening of Europe, and from which Europe became the principal beneficiary, left no immediate imprint on the world of Islam. Europe's rise to prominence—intellectually, politically, commercially, and militarily—coincided with general arrestation in Muslim lands. Indeed, with the exception of the military prowess displayed by the Ottomans in the creation of the last important Muslim empire, the Muslim world for the most part began to experience its own medieval period. During this age, which lasted approximately from the sixteenth to the nineteenth century, the torch of learning was dimmed; creativity slowed down to a trickle; the posture of the Muslim world became defensive and weakened; and wealth hitherto acquired by Muslim control of transient trade diminished when the Portuguese succeeded in diverting such trade from its sources in the farther East. Gradually the enfeebled petty dynasties of Islam either vanished or were overcome by a revitalized Europe. Finally, in the course of our present century, European powers succeeded in imposing their political hegemony—and substantially their cultural—over a much weakened and strife-torn Muslim world.

But out of defeat victory may yet emerge. Modernism in its Western context appears to have kindled in the Muslims not only a fiery resentment of the West, but also a general disposition to investigate the secret of the West's success. There is sufficient evidence to point to a general revivalism in the making, conspicuous recently not only in the political sphere but in the realm of ideas as well.

Contacts with the West in recent decades have set in motion trends that are bound to transform, if not remold and enhance traditional Islamic values. We are on the threshold of witnessing an Islamic version of Europe's "Renaissance" and "Reformation." The Islamic world has the advantage of being able to draw on the wealth of technological advances today to lift itself into the twenty-first century and avoid the pitfalls into which Europe stumbled while traversing the same course.

Present religious reformist movements in Islam, while lacking uniformity and sustained momentum, envisage a bootstrap operation that will revitalize Islamic society and tailor the religious ideal to present-day needs. The religiously oriented reformers propose to bring this about by dipping into the reservoir of Islam's accumulated values and beliefs, many of which are valid still for Islam's posture in the modern world. The secularly oriented modernists, on the other hand, believe that they must depend considerably on the accumulated experiences and tools of the West. They have been losing ground lately.

The area of conflict between these groups centers on the question whether a general Islamic renaissance can be produced without jeopardizing the fundamental tenets of the religion. The streamlining of religious concepts appears to be the *sine qua non* of modernization in Islam. There are movements today concerned with ways and means to reinterpret Islam. Current efforts seek to plow through the deadweight of medieval accretions back to the puritanical ideals of the Prophet and his Companions. Muslim reformers believe they can eliminate these accretions without compromising the essence of the Islamic faith. In this regard such efforts are reminiscent of the Protestants and of the task confronting them in the period of the Reformation.

As Islam girds itself for the twenty-first century and prepares to adjust itself to the demands of a modern civilization heavily tinged by the material bounty of a triumphant technology, it must be equally prepared to fight off the competition of rival ideologies. Atheistic communism and secular nationalism had been its principal rivals. Communism is no longer a contender, but secular nationalism, however much weakened, still contends for the loyalties of Muslims in a manner which the Islamists interpret as opposed to the basic precepts of their religion. But the gains made by Islam in the face of such competition among African Americans, in the

U.S., in Europe, and in Africa attest to its dynamism, even at this crucial state of its transition.

The study of Islam in those facets which explain its prominence as a religious force will provide us with an insight into the sources of its strength in its meteoric rise to the status of a major world force today. The remarkable spirit awakened by the preachings of Muḥammad provided the base of this strength and contributed to the dynamism which has not ceased to manifest itself even in times of misfortunes. Such resilience as Islam was able to muster in the face of adverse experiences enabled the religion to gain followers while lacking the external power to withstand the political encroachment of the West. It is probable that the vitality which at one time permeated all levels of Islamic society will still enable Muslims to maintain a religious solidarity notwithstanding the assaults of a powerful secular nationalism and a materialism fueled by unprecedented advances in technology that strive to submerge the Muslim's identity in an ocean of national distinctiveness. But be he a Nigerian or a Pakistani, an Egyptian or an Iranian, his historical heritage still favors pride of identity inside the pale of Islam over pride of adherence to nationality. This becomes increasingly evident when the Muslim's loyalty is put to the test.

The secret of Islam's powerful appeal lies in the fact that it is not only a religion regulating the spiritual side of the believer, but also an all-embracing *way of life* governing the totality of the Muslim's being. For this reason no study of Islam can be complete without a commensurate study of the non-religious forces unleashed by it; these, however, can not be treated sufficiently in a study of this nature.

Muslims today actively working to preserve the richness of their faith can count on powerful support in the dynamism characteristic of Islam in the early stages of its evolution. The forces that enabled the religion to surmount earlier crises may serve Islam well as it passes through its own "Reformation" and prepares itself for the role it can play in the general revitalization of the Islamic world. Already in the last few decades enlightened Muslims have wrought changes in attitudes that had stubbornly refused to respond to new stimuli for nearly half a millennium. Very recently the most famous theological center of Islam, the Azhar University—once the fount of conservatism in the realm of ideas upsetting to traditional religious concepts—has begun to bestir itself into new fields of knowledge hitherto regarded as heretical. The Azhar may become the principal agent in the streamlining of the faith, and in accommodating Islam to the exigences of the modern age. Other active groups in Egypt, Turkey, and Pakistan have propounded their own solutions, each predicated on a different set of premises. The puritanical movements that have multiplied across the Muslim world increasingly stress what they regard as the only logical cure for social, economic, and political ailments, namely to revert to a literal observance of the injunctions of the Qurʾān, which can be done only with the restoration of the Islamic republic first created by the Prophet Muḥammad himself.

That some sort of reform will result is beyond a doubt; what is crucial for the future of Islam is the question of whether such reform as will ensue can accommodate traditional concepts and at the same time charter a course for it in an age overrun by technology.

CHAPTER 2

The Setting in Arabia

TO SOMEONE CONVERSANT with the setting in Arabia on the eve of Islam it would have been inconceivable to believe that within the short lifetime of a contemporary of Muḥammad the land should provide the stage for a revolutionary transformation of religious and social values. Considering the geography, topography, ethnical structure, cultural level of development and the religious, social, and political institutions then prevailing, one had little reason to anticipate that out of a land so characterized by sharp and conflicting contrasts there would emerge a powerful force for uniformity and unity generated by a newly ordained system of religious, social, and political concepts. It would have been difficult to envisage that the inhabitants inspired by Islam could shortly be fired by a powerful zeal that would carry them out of the confines of Arabia on a course of conquest leading to their acquiring an empire larger than anything suggested by their wildest imaginations.

The Land

The Arabian peninsula, shaped into a rectangle spanning twelve hundred by nine hundred miles at its extreme measurements and consisting of a little over one million square miles, is set off from the neighboring world by natural barriers: water on three sides—Persian Gulf, Arabian Sea, Indian Ocean, and Red Sea—and the Syrian Desert on the fourth. One can understand why its inhabitants would refer to it as "the island" (*al-Jazīrah*). No foreigner who had set foot in Arabia was able to give us a description of the land until most recent times. A study of its topography reveals why it was so uninviting to outsiders, and also why the inhabitants migrated when the opportunities presented themselves.

The land consists mainly of barren volcanic steppes interspersed by nearly impenetrable sandy wastes—al-Rubʿ al-Khāli (the empty quarter) in the south and al-Nufūd in the north—with hardly any surface water except for a few rivulets on the western coast which run dry most of the year, a limited number of underground pools which sustain the few oases on the plateau of Najd, and the rains of spring and late summer which benefit mostly Yemen in the southwest and the Tihāmah plain along the Red Sea littoral. Because of such topographical handicaps, Arabia during most of its history was unable to sustain a population commensurate with its size.

The sharp divisions and contrasts in its topographical features are no less evident in Arabia's inhabitants. A certain dichotomy characterizes not only the racial structure of the people but their modes of existence as well. The predominant racial strain is Caucasian. Arabians subscribe either to the Alpine substratum—prevalent in the south and extreme north—or to the Mediterranean—mostly in the central and northern parts of the peninsula. Geographical barriers and topographical contrasts have contributed to the confinement of the population to less than twenty million in a land nearly a third of the size of the United States.

The People

Contrasts of this nature also account for the sharp division of Arabs into settled and nomadic groups. The division is echoed in their inherited traditions which attribute their descent to

"Yamani" (southern) or "Qaysi" (northern) origins. According to biblical and Qur'ānic testimony, the Arabs are descendants of Shem, oldest son of Noah, hence the appellation "Semite." This kind of kinship can apply only to a commonly shared linguistic and cultural heritage, as anthropologically there is no racial unity among them.

Distinguishing characteristics are evident also in the language: the southerners spoke a dialect partly surviving today in the Ethiopic or Amharic, the result of early South Arabian colonization of Ethiopia, while the northerners spoke Arabic, the language of Muḥammad and the Qur'ān and the prototype of the Arabic spoken today by nearly two hundred and fifty million people. The watered mountain terraces of Yemen and the Tihāmah, also the hillsides and plain of Oman, encouraged the development of agricultural settlements which nurtured the rise of the early civilizations, while the bleak plateaus and steppes in west-central and northern Arabia favored a preponderantly nomadic existence and provided no incentive for the rise of civilizations before Islam.

The impact of climatological and topographical limitations on the type of life led by the Arabian and on the historical evolution of his traditional values is not to be underestimated. Indeed, no real appreciation of the full range of the transformation wrought by Islam can develop without knowledge of the traditions and values of pre-Islamic Arabia. Where a settled mode of life was permitted, in the southwest corner of the peninsula—the *Arabia Felix* ("Fortunate Arabia") of the ancients—there evolved the earliest civilizations associated with the land: the Minaean, Sabaean, and Himyarite. From the second millennium b.c. until the beginnings of the Islamic era in the seventh century a.c. these civilizations thrived mainly on agriculture and trade. The theocratic-aristocratic concept of government evolved by the Arabians established a tradition with which early Islam did not break.

Another tradition, that of emigration, is also deeply rooted in the history of Arabia. In periods of drought or when the delicate irrigational system broke down—as it did following the alleged fatal breach of the great dam at Ma'rib around 535 B.C.—large segments of the inhabitants tended to emigrate and to strike out northward into the fertile valleys of Mesopotamia and the Syrian littoral in search of new means of subsistence. From the third millennium B.C. onward, and at nearly five-hundred year intervals, mass emigrations from Arabia accounted for the rise of the earliest civilizations in Syria and Mesopotamia: Amorite, Akkadian, Canaanite, Phoenician, Aramaean, Hebrew, Nabataean, Ghassānid, and last, but not least, the Muslim Arab, which has survived until the present time.

The deep-seated cleavage between the northern and southern Arab was carried over into Islam and tended to distract from the unity of the believers in times of acute crises. The appellation *Arab* is traditionally said to derive from the little town of Araba in the southeast district of the Tihāmah where, according to legend, settled Yaʿrab the son of biblical Joktan—the eponymous father of the original Arabs—thus imparting his name to the locality and, by extension, to the entire peninsula and its inhabitants. More appropriately, the term *Arab* derives from the Semitic word root referring to "nomad." But as the tribes multiplied and wandered far and wide over the steppes and sandy wastes of the land, they chose to believe that they were descendants either of Qaḥṭān (Joktan) or ʿAdnān from a common ancestor: Ismāʿīl (Ishmael) son of Abraham and Hagar. The Qaḥṭānis, also known as "Yamanis," regarded themselves as the pure Arabs and looked upon the ʿAdnānis or Qaysis as foreigners domiciled in the land or accepted by the indigenous Arabs. With the Qaḥṭānis we associate the rise of the earliest known civilizations in Arabia. But it is largely with the ʿAdnānis that Islam triumphed. Such cleavages were not eradicated totally with the later claim of Islam on the loyalties of both.

Tradition

Another important factor which contributed to the outlook of the pre-Muslim and later Muslim Arab is the role into which he was cast either as an intermediary or as a pawn in the life and death struggle of clashing imperial interests. From earliest times Arabia occupied a medial position geographically between the great ancient centers of civilization in the Mesopotamian, Nile, and Indus valleys, the western Indian littoral, and the Ethiopian highlands. This strategic position encouraged its southwest inhabitants to build thriving civilizations as middlemen in the transit of trade, particularly when some of the best utilized trade routes of ancient times were those which traversed the peninsula along the west coast from south to north terminating on the Mediterranean, or in the lower Nile and Mesopotamian valleys. But the land on the whole did not rise to pivotal importance because of its natural limitations and divided peoples. Only with Islam did the peninsula become united in faith and hence able to strike out on an imperial course of its own.

In the period immediately preceding the birth of Islam, tribal states north of the peninsula were drawn into the struggle between the Sasānid and Byzantine empires. The Ghassānids, protégés of Byzantium, had left south Arabia following the collapse of the Ma'rib dam and settled in the Ḥawrān region in southern Syria. Their rivals, the Lakhmids, protégés of Persia, settled in lower Iraq around al-Ḥīrah. Both were active in trade, and they developed prosperous societies in which Hellenic and Persian influences were pronounced. But their primary utility to their Byzantine and Persian overlords was as buffers against marauding kinsmen from the peninsula. Shortly before the emergence of Islam, the rulers of these buffer states had become discontented with the growing intolerance of their Perso-Byzantine masters, particularly when these overlords cut off the subsidies which their protégés had been receiving from them. Harsh suppressive measures undertaken against them drove the Ghassānids and Lakhmids into the arms of their surging Arabian kinsmen who under the banner of Islam afforded them the opportunity to avenge themselves by participating in the destruction of both empires.

The south Arabians were no less prone to being drawn into the Perso-Byzantine rivalry. Prodded by Byzantium, Christian Abyssinia waged war on the Ḥimyarite state which was suspected of having close ties with rival Sasānid Persia. When the last Ḥimyarite ruler, dhu-Nuwās (d. 525), began to persecute the Christians of neighboring Najrān and to compel his subjects to convert to Judaism, in a "plague-on-both your houses" attitude, Abrahah, the Abyssinian general, crossed the Red Sea with his armies, overran the Ḥimyarite kingdom, then struck out northward to attack the Persians in their own sanctuary. But he was able to reach only the outskirts of Mecca because, according to the testimony of the Qur'ān, his army was pestered by pebble-throwing birds which prevented Abrahah from reaching Mecca. His son, however, held on to the land until 570 when the Persians reduced it to a satrapy—only a few months before the birth of Muhammad, whose followers soon regained the south and consolidated the whole Arabian peninsula under Islam.

Trade

Another tradition of important consequence to the birth and shaping of Islam is trade. South Arabians from earliest times engaged in trade. Bedouin tribes served as carriers and middlemen, as did the northerners who built their efflorescent principalities at Petra, the rock-hewn city in southern Jordan, and Palmyra in northern Syria whose Zenobia was hailed as "Queen of the East" until the Romans carried her off in golden chains to Rome in 273. Another key town astride the important artery of trade was Mecca in the Ḥijāz in west central Arabia. Here around the year 400 an impoverished segment of Kinānah, once a member of the Kinda confederation, the only such association known to have existed in central Arabia before Islam, renounced its nomadism and settled down in one of the bleakest of surroundings where agriculture was impossible. Since trading was about the only means of survival available to them, these once scattered migrating kingroups found common ties as middlemen. Henceforth they are known to history as the "Quraysh."[1]

Muḥammad was a member of an important family of the Quraysh. The extent of their dependence on trade and the fear of being deprived of the special advantages they enjoyed as middlemen and entrepreneurs is reflected in their violent opposition to the preachings of Muḥammad against an order that gained them power and prosperity. Yet in their rise to economic, political, and social prominence, the Quraysh unwittingly paved the way for Islam.

At first the Quraysh merely traded with transient caravans; next they entered the main markets of neighboring settlements and soon gained control over them. Through a series of shrewd maneuvers, the Quraysh extended their trade connections from Syria to Abyssinia and became the dominant force in the commerce of western Arabia. Mecca, their home base, rose with them to pivotal importance in the economy of the entire peninsula. To finance such vast trade investments, Qurayshites of all walks of life—men, women, clients, and associates—reached into their private purses and extended credit in return for a commensurate share of the profits. Khadījah, the first wife of Muḥammad, was a prosperous trader; it was as a dependable leader of her caravans north into Syria that Muḥammad caught her fancy.

Values

Even more than the traditions, the values of village cultures and their nomadic antecedents left an undeniable impact on Islam; indeed, it may be shown that the values shaped the core of Islamic tenets and supplied the believers with a good many of their mainsprings of action, if not their dynamism. Mobility, the struggle for survival, a rugged individualism, a strong sense of loyalty to family and tribe, hospitality, simple concepts of religion, and aggressiveness are among the principal traits which the nomadic Arab carried over into Islam with him.

The need for mobility, dictated by a constant search for the means of livelihood, accounts basically for the Arab's nomadic existence. Roaming the broad lonely steppes seeking pasture and water holes for his flocks, he was afforded at best a life of austerity. The Bedouin subsisted on a limited diet of dates, milk, and occasionally camel flesh; a tent made of camel or goat hair served as his habitat; a few easily transportable implements and weapons provided for his needs; and his closest companions next to his kin were the camel and the horse which he made famous. He tolerated nothing that impaired his mobility because without it his survival would have been in jeopardy.

He battled both nature and man to survive; but however much he cherished personal freedom and the ingrained individualism that accompanied it, he perceived the necessity of banding with related families and clans to form tribes, and sometimes tribal alliances, for the purpose of defense. A typical tribe consisted of the *shaykh* (chief) and his family, other free families, certain protected clients not related by blood, and slaves. Sometimes kinship was acquired through designated rituals, particularly when noble ancestry figured prominently in determining status; this explains why the Arabs even after they were assimilated by Islam maintained a strong fondness for genealogy.

The simple institutions cultivated by the tribe, and which infused the early Islamic polity with a strong democratic spirit, were likewise decreed by mobility. The only elective office was that of the *shaykh,* who was chosen from the male membership of the tribe on the basis of experience and unusual personal leadership qualities topped by ability and wisdom—the exact criteria applied in the choice of the first four caliphs of Islam. The *shaykh* was invested with no executive or legislative functions and enjoyed no special privileges. His voice was heard in council, but in the settlement of disputes the daily assemblies held for that purpose heard equally the recommendations of the wise man or woman, priest, or seer. Not organized law but custom provided guidance; and in the execution of justice the aggrieved party himself served as the instrument. This practice frequently resulted in vendettas, particularly when the *dīyah* (blood money) payment was not enforceable.

The duties of the *shaykh,* like those of the early caliphs of Islam, outweighed his privileges. He was responsible for the care of the poor, of widows and orphans, for hospitality to strangers and wayfarers, for the payment of *dīyah,* and for the maintenance of order within the tribe. His supreme task was to lead the tribe into battle, a very common occurrence in pre-Islamic Arabia.

Mobility impaired the development of concrete social organization. In the absence of established political institutions and a defined legal system, blood ties substituted for law in determining the loyalty of the tribesman. With the triumph of Islam, religion served the same end. Hence the Arabian version of "patriotism" was his *ʿaṣabīyah* (clannishness). Kinship became the mark of "citizenship" for the tribe; and once this was established, a member could command the protection and support of the entire tribe. This principle, in Islam, substitutes communal responsibility towards the believer for the former tribal responsibility towards a member of the tribe. The pagan Arabian tribesman was entitled to no rights outside the bonds of the tribe any more than the Arabian Muslim could depend on any rights outside Islam. The same applied to obligations. Such relationships of the individual to the group account for tribal solidarity, a phenomenon consecrated in Islam. Solidarity to tribal, and later Muslim, Arabia was the *sine qua non* of survival and, in time of growth, of power. The pagan Arab, like his Muslim successor, recognized that his individual fortunes were intertwined with and inseparable from the fortunes of the whole community.

As war was an important means of survival for the tribe, the razzia,[2] or raiding, became the instrument of economic need. Moved predominantly by the same consideration, Arabian tribes, united in Islam, struck out on a series of extended raids which netted them an empire greater than Rome's at its zenith. Although booty was a main goal of tribal raids, often the tribes warred upon each other for a variety of reasons such as to defend their honor, to carry on an established vendetta, to exact vengeance for spilled blood when *dīyah* was denied, or just for the sportiness of war. According to the law of the desert, blood called for blood; and often wars of revenge and counter revenge became long drawn out affairs, attested by the celebrated *Ayyām al-ʿArab*.[3] But more often than not, intertribal warfare resulted from quarrels over water holes, oases, and flocks: the necessities of economic survival. The tribes also raided the caravans of townsmen to supplement their needs, particularly when townsmen refused to purchase protection.

It is important to observe here that in the Ḥijāz on the eve of Islam the line of demarcation between tent-dweller and town-dweller was not clearly drawn. The nomad could just as readily lead a life of quasi-urbanity as the settled Arabian could indulge in semi-nomadism. The tendency on the whole for both sides was to achieve a *modus vivendi* because of their basic interdependence: the townsman purchased the Bedouin's milk products, meat, and wool, and the Bedouin in turn acquired in the town's market such essentials as weapons, cloth, and other finished commodities. The Islamization of Arabia reduced tribal warfare but did not compromise this basic relationship of nomad and settler.

Being a creature of the desert, the Arab naturally developed such personal qualities and habits as would comport with the exigences of his environment. He led an exacting life which called for tenacity and endurance, self-reliance and egoism; hence only the virtues which stressed manliness (*murū'ah*) could appeal to him. He acquired a rugged individualism which in turn nurtured his democratic leanings. The life of exertion to which he was subjected required no discipline. The Bedouin, consequently, never developed an instinct to obey authority. He jealously guarded his rights, but he did not shun his tribal obligations lest he become an outcast. His egotism reinforced his self-confidence and permitted him to accept a status inferior to none in the tribe. He had strong aristocratic tendencies, evident in his mores and in his pride of lineage; to him the Arab nation was "the noblest of nations" (*afkhar al-umam*).

All in all, the values of the Arab, nomad or settler, were measured in terms of purity of blood as it flowed in the veins of a long line of noble ancestors, in the eloquence of his tongue, in the power of his sword-wielding arm, and in the speed of his mount.

Such was the makeup of the Arab whom the Caliph ʿUmar I (634–644) regarded as the "raw material" of Islam and whose values supplied Islam with the vigor and dynamism in the period of rapid growth and expansion without which its triumph would scarcely have reached the unprecedented limits recorded by history.

Rhetorical oratory and poetry constituted for the Bedouin a dearly cherished source of aesthetic pleasure. He was easily swayed by the power of speech and rhythm and aroused beyond compare by the eloquence of his tongue. Hence poetry and oratory provided the best incitement to valorous deeds on the battlefield. The Qurʾān preserves the rhetorical wealth of the Arab's pre-Islamic heritage; indeed, rhetorical oratory proved itself a strong energizing force in times of war. He who commanded the right word at a crucial moment could bring victory to his tribe. Poetry served as a weapon of "psychological warfare" aimed at demoralizing the enemy through derision. But such powers of eloquence were not for all to share and employ: they were gifts of the spirits (*jinn*).[4]

Cultivated as an art, poetry had the effect of strengthening the Arab's consciousness of a separate identity attributed to a lofty ancestry that transcended tribal affiliations. In this context, a properly uttered poetic expression served as a rallying force in an otherwise divided society. Poetic contests were held during the month of truce, which prevailed over Arabia, when thousands of tribesmen converged on the fair of ʿUkāz at Mecca, not only to barter their ware but also to match poetic wit. Each vied with the other for the prize of having his poetic composition adjudged the best, as this meant that it would be suspended from the side of the Kaʿbah (Kaaba).[5] This deep reverence for the powers of speech can be vividly traced in the mass of literary works of all types produced by the cultural efflorescence of Islam. Indeed, the reader would be hard put not to find poetic verse embellishing the pages of a scientific treatise or a historical narrative.

Religion

Most relevant to any study of Islam in its essential function as a religious force is to trace its relations to the religion, or religions, of pre-Islamic Arabia. Islam, like Judaism and Christianity, is indebted for certain basic conceptual, institutional, and ritualistic ideas and practices to the rudiments of the Semitic religion that evolved in the steppes and settlements of the Arabian peninsula. As an established authority on pre-Islamic Semitic religions has observed, "No positive religion that has moved men has been able to start with a *tabula rasa,* and express itself as if religion were beginning for the first time . . . A new scheme of faith can find a hearing only by appealing to religious instincts and susceptibilities that already exist in its audience . . ."[6]

Certain deities and cultic rituals associated with the simple animistic, then daimonic, worship of the early inhabitants survived in a transformed and highly sophisticated version in the three great monotheistic religions. Tribal deities like Allah and Jehovah, sanctified stones and springs such as the Blackstone of the Kaʿbah, the well of Zamzam, Bethel of the Old Testament, the ritual prayer, the offering of blood sacrifices to the deity, the pilgrimage, and numerous rites—not all of which were absorbed—were popular in the period of Arabian history before Islam, which the Muslims term "*Jāhilīyah*,"[7] and became consecrated in Islam and its kindred religions.

The idea that the deity may reveal itself to the select, as Jehovah revealed himself to Jacob in a dream at Bethel, Jesus to Paul on the road to Damascus, and Allah to Muḥammad through the intermediation of Gabriel in a cave outside Mecca, is familiar to earlier Semites. As a matter of fact, in the anthropomorphic state of worship revelation was indispensable to the formalization of relationships between man and his god, as was the cementing of ties ensuing therefrom by a sacrificial ritual. The concept of blood ties, of man to man and man to his god, whereby tribal affiliation is sanctified and the deity assumes the status of patron and ancestral lord to the tribe, developed from such premises. And as the deity was believed to favor the locality where it revealed itself, the tribe converted the place into a sanctuary and instituted a pattern of periodic revisitation to offer homage. The Kaʿbah in Mecca eventually became the supreme sanctuary in pre-Islamic Arabia, and Muḥammad preserved its status in Islam as well.

The tribes of Arabia selected for their deities those which best reflected their distinguishing characteristics and aspirations; the Semites, whether of the desert or town variety, literally created their gods in their own images. The mood and temperament of the god was a reflection of the worshiper's attitude. There were hundreds of such deities in pagan Arabia; the Kaʿbah alone at one time housed three hundred and sixty-seven of them. Of all those mentioned in the Qur'ān, four appeared to be most popularly revered on the eve of Islam: al-ʿUzzah (power),[8] al-Lāt (the goddess),[9] and Manāh (fate):[10] all three female deities, popularly worshiped by the tribes of the Ḥijāz, were regarded as the daughters of Allah (the god) who headed the Arabian pantheon when Muḥammad began to preach.

Allah, the paramount deity of pagan Arabia, was the target of worship in varying degrees of intensity from the southernmost tip of Arabia to the Mediterranean. To the Babylonians he was "*Il*" (god); to the Canaanites, and later the Israelites, he was *"El"*; the South Arabians worshipped him as "*Ilāh*," and the Bedouins as "*al-Ilāh*" (the deity). With Muḥammad he becomes *Allah,* God of the Worlds, of all believers, the one and only who admits of no associates or consorts in the worship of Him. Judaic and Christian concepts of God abetted the transformation of Allah from a pagan deity to the God of all monotheists. There is no reason, therefore, to accept the idea that "Allah" passed to the Muslims from Christians and Jews.

Jewish Settlements

Muḥammad was in contact with Jews in Yathrib (Medina) with whom he disputed theologically but later broke for political reasons. During this brief period of exchanges he acquired a number of ritualistic concepts from them, but the influence of strictly Jewish beliefs is still under debate.

Although the presence of Jewish tribes in Arabia dates back to 1200 B.C.—when the Rachel tribes spent their wandering years in Sinai and al-Nufūd,[11] it was not until the first Christian century following the second unsuccessful uprising against the Romans in 132–135 after Christ that an influx of Jewish tribes and some proselytizing among Bedouins brought them into the Ḥijaz. On the eve of Islam they had acquired some of the best land in the oases of Taymā', Khaybar and Yathrib; in Yathrib alone they constituted nearly one half the population.

Knowledge of superior agricultural techniques, monopoly over important commodities of trade, like iron (used in making arms, coats of mail, and agricultural tools), resulted in their dominance in the rich oases and at the important trade fairs of Taymā' and Yathrib. To secure this dominance, they played upon the rivalries among the Aws and Khazraj. Both tribes had engaged in a long feud with them for control of the palm-tree plantations in the neighboring oases. It was to resolve their perennial dispute that they invited Muḥammad to come to Yathrib and serve as mediator; this, as we shall see, was of important consequence to the development of the Islamic polity and crystallization of Islamic institutions.

Although the presence of the Jewish settlements in Arabia did not materially influence the development of Islamic concepts, it did, on the other hand, affect the political destiny of the Ḥimyarites. It was allegedly a certain abu Kārib As'ad Kāmil, king of Yemen during Ḥimyarite rule, who first adopted the Jewish faith early in the fifth century A.D. His last successor dhu-Nuwās embarked on the policy of forcible conversion which led to the Abyssinian invasion and ended the possibility of Judaism becoming firmly rooted in this important corner of Arabia at a time when Muḥammad was about to preach the religion of submission to Allah.

Christian Elements

The Christian settlements in Arabia during this crucial period left perhaps less of an impact on the development of Islam, principally because the chief Christian centers were on the periphery of the peninsula: in Najrān north of Yemen, in Syria, and Ḥīrah in lower Iraq. There was a minor settlement in Mecca consisting of caravan leaders, monks, merchants from Syria, curers, healers, doctors, dentists, smiths, carpenters, scribes, Christian women married into the Quraysh, and slaves from Mesopotamia, Egypt, Syria, and Byzantium sold in the market place of the town.[12]

Bedouins of the Ḥijāz on their caravan journeys to Syria and other Christian centers undoubtedly carried back with them a superficial knowledge of Christian beliefs and customs. Dissident Christian sects, mostly of the Monophysite confession, and numerous monks turned ascetics had their retreats in the steppes of north Arabia along caravan routes. As a caravan leader, Muḥammad is said to have befriended a Christian monk, Bahīra and to have worn tunics which were the gifts of other Christian monks. Two Christianized Arab tribes, Judham and ʿUdhra, roamed the Ḥijāz. According to local tradition, there were even Christian religious artifacts in the Kaʿbah at Mecca.

It is not unlikely that Muḥammad may have exchanged religious views with monks, even with Christians who possessed some formal knowledge of Christian theology. Jacobites and Nestorians are known to have conducted active missionary activities among the pagan tribes of Arabia; indeed, priests and deacons were assigned to each tribe, and in Najrān the Monophysites had established churches which, when persecuted by dhu-Nuwās, invited Abyssinian intervention. Monasteries astride caravan routes were open day and night to traveling caravans and roaming Bedouins. Here, besides receiving food and shelter, they undoubtedly had occasion to observe such practices as praying, fasting, and alms giving—three of the five basic injunctions of Islam. The Nestorians had established schools and some churches in many of the towns frequented by Arab tribesmen of the Ḥijāz.[13]

When Muḥammad began his summons to Islam, Christians were involved in deep theological disputes, not the least of which was over the use of icons, a dispute which culminated in the celebrated iconoclastic controversy in Christianity. Some Christians in South Arabia were accused in the Qurʾān of having departed from the basic tenets of their faith.[14] Such dissensions, coupled with the fact that the Bedouin Arabian, even in the judgment of the Qurʾān, was notoriously inclined to irreligion,[15] could not have disturbed materially the few religious convictions of the Arabs before the preachings of Muḥammad.[16]

Evidence of Transformation

Be that as it may, socioeconomic trends long current in Arabian society appeared to converge in the Ḥijāz, and specifically at Mecca, when Muḥammad emerged on the scene. The mustering of economic power through control of transit trade and the housing of pagan deities in the Kaʿbah under their supervision gave the Quraysh an enviable position of influence and contributed to their rising status. Mecca had become the center of pilgrimage and the hub of economic life in West Arabia.

To encourage the flow of pilgrims and trade, the Qurayshites concluded pacts with various tribes securing the inviolability of transients and pilgrims. The Kaʿbah and the area surrounding it were declared *ḥarām* ("forbidden," i.e., to warfare); within a general mile radius from it no blood might be spilled. With their economic power ever on the increase, the Qurayshite oligarchy ruling Mecca deliberately kept extending the *ḥaram* to assure the stability of social relations in a zone crucial to trade; and in order to enhance the inviolability of their area, Meccan traders ringed the Kaʿbah with the idols of other tribes.[17]

The rise of "Allah" to prominence in the pantheon at Mecca was commensurate with the rising status of the Quraysh. The pagans in and around Mecca at an earlier date had already considered him the supreme deity. The attributes associated with "Allah" before Islam, namely his being regarded as creator of the world and lord guardian of contractual obligations, of the wayfarer and fate, were preserved in the Islamic conception of him. That he enjoyed a high status during this period is evident in the deference accorded him by certain Christians[18] and non-Christians, like the Ṣābians[19] and the Magians,[20] who regarded Allah as a deity and even implored their indigenous gods to intercede with him on their behalf. The Ṣābians not only made ritualistic sacrifices to Allah and sent offerings to the Kaʿbah, but even regarded their astral gods as "Companions of Allah." Perhaps it is owing to this recognition of Allah that the Muslims later extended their protection to both Ṣābians and Magians even though they did not strictly qualify as possessors of scriptures in the same context as Christians and Jews.

What is of significance to the mission of Islam is the trend toward socioreligious centralization in Meccan society on the eve of the advent of Muḥammad. While laboring to establish and safeguard their economic ascendancy, the merchant oligarchy of

Qurayshites ruling Mecca brought about a transformation of values, most important being the establishment of security under *law* in lieu of *kinship.* Thus when Muḥammad preached social unity and solidarity on the basis of Islam, he was exploiting a trend already in evidence. In the area of the *ḥaram* a stranger was afforded protection because of the sanctity it enjoyed. The support of a native patron would be called upon only when an injustice was perpetrated against the stranger. To be born or to sojourn in the sanctified environment of the Kaʿbah gave non-Qurayshite Arabs precedence over others.

Such extra privileges as were obtainable in Mecca encouraged Arab tribesmen to forsake their local shrines for the Kaʿbah in Mecca, thus contributing to the growing centralization of worship there. What was happening in effect is that an increasing number of Arabs were discarding tribal ties as a means of protection for the *jiwār* (protection) of the Kaʿbah where Allah reigned supreme. As more and more non-kin Arabs banded in the *jiwār* of the *ḥaram,* the prestige of Allah as patron grew concomitantly; so did his functions and responsibility toward his followers "as the guardian of faith and the avenger of treason"; in his name tribesmen were to "fulfill their contracts, honor their relatives by oath, and feed their guests."[21]

Of paramount importance to the development of the central socioreligious function of Allah in Islam as an equalizer and a force of solidarity was this pre-Islamic institution in Mecca. When rights and obligations, hitherto unrecognized outside membership in the tribe, became extra-familial or extra-tribal in the *jiwār* of the *ḥaram,* it was the prerogative, if not indeed the responsibility, of Allah to serve as imposer and guarantor. When Muḥammad called upon all Qurayshites to forsake the idols and place all their faith in Allah, it was not the novelty of the preaching as much as the fear of economic loss from having to abandon guardianship over the Kaʿbah, home of the idols of pagan Arabia and the target of the profitable pilgrimage as well as an all-round stimulant of trade, that impelled them to resist him, even by force.

What is of relevance to our understanding of the new socioreligious bonds constructed by Islam is the fact that the commercial development accruing from the centralization of worship caused the transformation of Meccan society from a social order determined primarily by kinship and ethnic homogeneity of origin into an order in which the fiction of kinship served now to mask a developing division of society into classes characterized by considerable ethnic diversity.[22]

As the Quraysh amassed wealth and gained power, the economic gulf separating its component clans widened. Eventually the clans of Makhzūm and Umayya, who later were very instrumental in the spread of Islam, came to the forefront and occupied the "inner city" around the Kaʿbah; the other eight and poorer clans dwelt in the outskirts—Muḥammad belonged to one of them, the Banū Hāshim.

When the function of the clan no longer served the economic ambitions of the Quraysh, they placed their destiny in the hands of an oligarchy of rich merchants who with their immediate families and dependents controlled political power in Mecca and dominated its economic and religious life. They decided on general policy, concluded alliances as needed, and entered into formal trade agreements with the courts of Abyssinia and Persia.

As the reorientation of Meccan society on the eve of Islam began to crystallize, it reflected increasingly the growing distinctions which we associate with class gradations rather than those formerly attributed to tribal affiliations. In this new Meccan society "class" distinction played a more determinative role, a phenomenon unknown to pastoral tribes. The dependent population of Mecca reflected the gradations of its society into slaves, missionaries, merchants in charge of caravans, middlemen like ʿUmar who became the second caliph, those who became dependents through usury, wage-earners, and finally, clients *(mawāli)*.

But the organization of power among the aristocracy of Quraysh was not complete because their council of oligarchs lacked legislative force and the means to execute decisions without having to resort to traditional methods, such as refusing protection to a recalcitrant. In a society now organized around functional classes rather than tribal membership, the threat of a blood feud or a protracted vendetta was no longer an effective weapon of social restraint when friction developed within the society. If restraint existed, it was due largely to fear of repercussions from antagonizing the controlling clans of the "inner city."

But in this crucial period of Mecca, when traditional socioreligious values were giving way to new ones, the evolving system was not free from injustices; otherwise Muḥammad would have lacked the wherewithal for his preaching of a new socioreligious system based on submission to one God. The discriminatory and exploitative policies of the "inner Quraysh" toward the "Quraysh of the outskirts" (clients and slaves), gained for Muḥammad an audience, the earliest target of his preachings, and provided him with a core of early followers. Obnoxious practices instituted by the oligarchy, such as wage payment and debt slavery, contributed to the growing unrest directed against them. Some clients escaped exploitation because of the nominal backing of patrons to whom they were tied by some kin-ritual, but those without such backing and other unaffiliates were exposed to attack or even unobstructed killing in a blood feud.[23]

Mecca at the birth of Muḥammad was in a state of fermentation, aggravated by social injustices that had resulted from discontent with the system of privilege benefiting those with the right connections. And while the trend toward religious unity was pronounced, the social order was lacking because of the widening gap between the privileged and underprivileged.

The need for modification and change, such as was portended in the message soon to be offered by Muḥammad was both unavoidable and timely. In this respect, his role was indeed preordained.

CHAPTER 3

Muḥammad the Prophet

HISTORY RELATES OF MEN who distinguished themselves by deeds and left permanent imprints on their societies; of prophets who delivered the message of the true God to their peoples; of statesmen who excelled in the service of their nations; of authors who left monumental additions to the literary wealth of mankind; of conquerors who led their followers to victories, wealth, and renown; and of those who by force of personality or unusual calling succeeded in transforming values or completely revamping the societies into which they were born.

The Role

Muḥammad, the prophet of Arabia, has fulfilled for his people a role that combines the functions of a distinguished prophet, statesman, author, and reformer. He has earned for himself as a consequence the respect and reverence of countless people, Muslim and non-Muslim everywhere.

By vocation Muḥammad was a prophet in the true biblical sense with a message for his people, a message anchored in religious belief but aiming at the realization of fundamental social, economic, and political reform. The religion he founded was hampered by no wrangling creed or barrier to man's relations with God or to his fellow man. He succeeded, both as prophet and as reformer. The fact that Muḥammad's mission was accomplished in his lifetime is a living testimony "to his distinctive superiority over the prophets, sages, and philosophers of other times and countries."[1]

While our knowledge of men who filled similar roles from Moses to Zoroaster to Jesus is shrouded with legend, often incomplete and frequently colored, and while the accounts of Muḥammad's life and deeds contain their share of incompleteness and coloring, the fact remains that he was the first to live and preach in the full light of history. We have more information relating to his career than we have of his predecessors. His life by and large is not wrapped in mystery, and few tales have been woven around his personality.[2]

For biographical information on Muḥammad we are dependent on the work of ibn Isḥāq (d. 767) as preserved in the recension of ibn Hishām (d. 834) and the *Maghāzī* of al-Wāqidī (d. 822/23). Ibn Saʿd (d. 845), a noted historian, compiled an encyclopaedic work on the Prophet and his followers which contains valuable information on the life and preachings of Muḥammad. But no source or work can yield more dependable information on the genius of Muḥammad or provide a greater insight into his personality and accomplishments than the Qurʾān, the sacred book of Islam.

While the Qurʾān in Islamic theology conveys strictly the word of God, it remains in respect to the message contained therein a true mirror of Muḥammad's character and his accomplishments. Complementary information is obtainable also in the sayings and deeds of the Prophet that have been amassed in voluminous quantities but carefully scrutinized by scholars of the early Islamic centuries. These non-canonical texts, which contain eyewitness accounts of Muḥammad, fall under the category of *ḥadīth* (utterances) and *sunnah* (observed conduct).

The life and preachings of Muḥammad are in marked contrast with what Arabian society had ordained for his fellow Meccans. The established facts of his life have been subjected to much less variance of interpretation than those of preceding prophets. This is due to the circumspection of available sources.

He was born about 570/71, the posthumous son of ʿAbdullāh and Āminah. On his father's side he descended from the impoverished house of Hāshim, adjudged by the Quraysh the noblest of the dominant aristocracy; on his mother's, from the Najjār branch of Khazraj, a major tribe of Yathrib, his adoptive city.

His grandfather, ʿAbū al-Muṭṭalib was a *ḥakam* (arbiter), a position of high regard, and in the early youth of Muḥammad, the custodian of the Kaʿbah, indeed the virtual head of the Meccan commonwealth. He took charge of Muḥammad's upbringing upon the death of his mother when Muḥammad was only six years old. When the grandfather died, the care of the child was entrusted to his paternal uncle Abu-Ṭālib.

Most of his youth was evidently uneventful as the lack of biographical information on Muḥammad's early life suggests. The most important landmark in his youth prior to the prophetic call is his marriage to Khadījah, a wealthy Qurayshite widow who was impressed by Muḥammad's personality and virtues when he served as a factor in her caravan trade with Syria. He was twenty-five at the time and she allegedly fifteen years his senior. The marriage lasted until her death, over fifteen years later. During this period Muḥammad would have no additional woman for a wife, an unusual disposition for the times when polygamy was widely practiced by his fellow Arabs. Yet these were the years that afforded him the happiness which escaped him as an orphaned youth.

Khadījah bore him two sons, who died in infancy, and four daughters. Two of the daughters married the future second and fourth caliphs of Islam. His daughter Fāṭimah married his first cousin ʿAli, the son of Abu Ṭālib, whom he had taken under his wing and raised as an act of gratitude when Abu Ṭālib, Muḥammad's uncle, died.

The mission of Muḥammad began after a careful period of soul-searching and spiritual reassessment lasting over fifteen years. When the call to prophecy came at last, there was no turning back. He hesitated but he did not fail to respond.

Muḥammad was a mature man of forty when he received the first revelation. It came to him as he was contemplating in a cave on Mt. Ḥirā', above Mecca, to which he habitually withdrew. The injustices permeating all levels of Meccan society in his days undoubtedly weighed heavily on his mind and caused him much anguish. The wealthy lorded it over the poor; the helpless were at the mercy of the strong; greed and selfishness ruled the day; infanticide was widely practiced by Bedouins who lacked adequate means of sustenance, and there were numerous other practices prevailing on all levels of Arabian society that had the effect of widening the gulf between the privileged aristocracy and the deprived multitudes of Mecca. With such considerations preying on his mind, Muḥammad found himself confronted by a twofold crisis: spiritual and social.

In his early life he had understood only too well what it meant to be an orphan and poor. Now he had time to do something about both. It is important to note here that Muḥammad's preaching of monotheism and of social reform went hand in hand. Indeed, no other message is so thoroughly underscored in the revelations received from Allah than the stress on equal treatment and social justice. To Muḥammad these constituted a vital concomitant of worship. The revelations of the one and only God enjoin consistently the exercise of mercy and benevolence as the necessary adjuncts of belief in Him.

This dual role of Muḥammad as preacher and reformer is largely evident in his life and career. What he sought was the cohesion of Arabian society through uniform beliefs and a unified faith. He knew this could be accomplished only through the worship of the one God alone and through laws authorized by the sanctity of divine command. With such laws Muḥammad would bind the hitherto scattered ends of Arabia.

He preached belief in the one God, God of Abraham, Moses, and Jesus, and the brotherhood of all Arabs in *islām,* or "submission" to God.

In preaching monotheism at this time Muḥammad had before him the failure of the *ḥanīfs* (monotheists) who had preceded him by a century or two, as evidenced in the inscriptions left behind. Judging by the standards of his time, his undertaking was fraught with risks and great obstacles.

Muḥammad himself was overwhelmed when he awakened to the awesome realities of the task he was being charged with. "No incipient prophet," said Edward Gibbon, "ever passed through so severe an ordeal as Muḥammad." Indeed, as the commandments of Allah became increasingly manifest in the revelations that were descending upon him, Muḥammad undertook to show that the whole organization and institutional beliefs of pagan Arabia were not in conformity with the divine will. The voice of Muḥammad amidst the strong chorus of opposition was indeed a lone voice. Yet he persistently challenged the moral and social norms governing Arabia, and particularly the values and institutional practices of Mecca, the hub of Arabia, under the powerful leadership of the Qurayshite oligarchy. The values he found repugnant centered around the pantheon sanctified by the Kaʿbah which had become symbolical of disunity and unbelief. He set for himself the task of eliminating this symbol and substituting for it what would make for unity and the true faith as it was revealed unto him.

His Ministry

The facts relating to his ministry have been treated in almost every narrative concerning Muḥammad's mission. While the launching date is not exactly fixed, it is commonly accepted that revelation was received by Muḥammad in a dream one night during the month of Ramadān as he secluded himself in the cave on Mt. Ḥirāʾ. The deliverer of the revelation and all subsequent ones was held to be Gabriel the archangel. Gabriel brought to Muḥammad the command of God:

> Read in the name of thy Lord who created, who created man of blood coagulated. Read! Thy Lord is the most beneficent, who taught by the pen, taught that which they knew not unto men.[3]

Muḥammad recounted to his wife the facts of his experience and was seriously perturbed over the prospects of being possessed, like the soothsayers of his day, by the *jinn*. Khadījah reassured him of his sound judgment; so did her cousin Waraqa ibn Nawfal, a blind man known to his associates as a *ḥanīf.*[4] Waraqa was familiar with the scriptures of the Jews and Christians; he detected in Muḥammad the signs of prophethood and predicted hardships for his mission. "They will call thee a liar," said he to Muḥammad, "they will persecute thee; they will banish thee, and they will fight against thee."

The gravity of his portended mission gave him much reason to pause and reconsider. It is probable that during this critical period of soul-searching he became particularly receptive to Judaic and Christian concepts of monotheism. For some time before, and probably through the proddings of Waraqa, he had become strongly inclined in that direction. Indeed, the Qur᾿ān suggests this in the verse:

> And if thou art in doubt concerning that which we reveal unto thee then question those who have read the scripture before thee. Verily thy Lord hath caused His truth to descend upon thee. So be not of those who waver.[5]

Some time lapsed before the next revelation descended. But with the assurance of Allah propelling him forward, Muḥammad no longer doubted that he was being commissioned for a serious mission. All hesitation vanished and the Angel once more spoke to him while he lay with his limbs wrapped in a mantle:

> Oh thou enwrapped dost lie! Arise and warn, and thy Lord magnify, and thy raiment purify, and the abomination fly.[6]

This was the most critical point in Muḥammad's career. It was the climax of a long beginning which stretched back into his youth. As a five-year-old boy, while being cared for by a Bedouin nursemaid, Ḥalīmah, he was supposed to have had his inwards cleansed by "two men in white garments," echoed in the Qur᾿ān: "Have We not opened thy breast for thee?"[7] When he was twelve he had accompanied his uncle Abu Ṭālib to Syria, and it was near Busra that the Christian monk bearing the legendary name Baḥīra is alleged to have seen in him the markings of a true prophet. Still while a lad, he was upbraided by Zayd ibn ʿAmr, an outcast of Mecca because of his monotheistic beliefs, for making offerings to the idols. After that episode, and according to tradition, Muḥammad never knowingly stroked one of their idols nor did he sacrifice to them until God honored him with His apostleship.

Contacts with Waraqa, Jews, and Christians must have given him some familiarization with existing versions of monotheism, although Muḥammad's narration of events attributed to the Scriptures shows that this familiarization could not have been the result of interaction with anyone who had an educated knowledge of the sacred texts.

The call to prophecy was not a unique occurrence among Semitic peoples; indeed the details concerning Muḥammad's role as a *nabi* (prophet), *rasūl* (messenger) and *nadhīr* (warner) have parallels in the Old and New Testaments. Pagan Arabs before Muḥammad's time were not as familiar with a *nabi* as they were with the *shāʿir*[8] who made his ominous predictions through the medium of rhymed prose, a form of expression preserved in the Qurʾān.

When Muḥammad preached the worship of God and God only, the earliest believers consisted of his wife Khadījah, Abu Bakr, the popular and respected merchant of Mecca who became the first caliph, his cousin ʿAli, and his adopted son Zayd ibn Ḥāritha. His uncle Abu Ṭālib, who defended him against all his foes and stood by him during the most critical period of his prophethood, never accepted the message of Islam; nor did he, on the other hand, insist that his nephew stop preaching the religion of Allah.

After three years of rather quiet and earnest preaching in his home city in the shadow of the Kaʿbah, Muḥammad succeeded in converting altogether thirty individuals; most of them came from the deprived classes. The Quraysh, who had profited from the existing economic and social order in Mecca based on the worship of the idols, were skeptical of Muḥammad's message and contemptuously unreceptive. Their indifference to his preachings soon turned to anxiety when Muḥammad decided to abandon the quiet and unobtrusive approach for a bolder public appeal, calling upon his fellow Meccans to desist from their worship of the idols. But such attempted inducements as promising them the bounties of Allah or threatening them with the consuming fires of *Jahannam* (hell) appeared to yield no positive results. His audience remained largely unconvinced; indeed, many were beginning to believe that he was beside himself, if not possessed by the evil *jinn*.

Failing to win over his fellow Meccans, Muḥammad began to work on traders and other individuals who frequented Mecca during the season of the annual pilgrimage. He excited his listeners to heed the call of God and to learn the lesson of those who had fallen; those who had disobeyed God's ordinance: "Set not up with Allah any other God (O man) lest thou sit down reproved, forsaken."[9]

The prophet was becoming increasingly a warner, stressing the inevitable doom awaiting the skeptics and disbelievers on the day of reckoning. "Who so desireth that (life) which hasteneth away, We hasten for him therein that We will for whom We please. And afterward We have appointed for him hell; he will endure the heat thereof, condemned, rejected."[10]

If he gained converts, it was due less to the threats of eternal fire than to the strong justice and egalitarian principles embedded in his message of submission to God. The promise of sharing with the "haves" had a particular appeal to the "have-nots" of Mecca. The aristocracy of the Quraysh did not hesitate to remind him, "Why is it that thou art followed only by the most abject from our midst!"

Opposition

Prudence soon moved the aristocracy of the Quraysh to take firmer steps than public derision of Muhammad, especially when they could not prevent his message from gaining a wider following on account of its appeal to fairness and dignity.

> O ye who believe! Let not a folk deride a folk who may be better than they (are), nor let women (deride) women who may be better than they are; neither defame one another, nor insult one another by nicknames. Bad is the name of lewdness after faith. And whoso turneth not in repentance, such are evil-doers.[11]

The message had another force of attraction in its strong democratic spirit.

> O mankind! Lo! We have created you male and female, and have made you nations and tribes that ye may know one another. Lo! The noblest of you, in the sight of Allah, is the best in conduct. Lo! Allah is Knower, Aware.[12]

The Quraysh could perceive from the spirit and text of such preachings that Muḥammad was in effect undermining the entire structure of their society, founded as it was on a system of privilege. They concluded that the message could have only one enduring effect: the loosening of their political, religious, and commercial grip on Mecca.

The Quraysh, therefore, made the decision to take all necessary steps and adopt all feasible means to wipe out Muḥammad and his followers. Each family of the Quraysh accordingly was charged with the responsibility of stamping out the new belief. This was often accomplished by harsh methods. Muḥammad escaped such treatment because he enjoyed the honor and immunity of Hāshim, his immediate clan and largely because of his uncle's prestige among the oligarchs. Moreoever, Abu Ṭālib consistently refused to coerce his nephew-protégé into abandoning his mission.

When fearing for Muḥammad's life, his uncle pleaded with him to give up his mission, the nephew replied with conviction: "I will not forsake this cause until it prevails by the will of God or I perish instead, no not if they (the Quraysh) would place the sun on my right hand and the moon on my left!"[13]

A delegation headed by ʿUtbah also failed to dissuade him from continuing his preaching through such promises as "we are willing to gather for you a fortune, larger than what is possessed by any of us; to make you our chief, and if you desire dominion we shall make you our king, and if the demon which possesses you cannot be subdued we will bring you doctors and give them riches to cure you." To them Muḥammad replied with the words preserved in the Qurʾān:

> Good tidings and a warning, But most of them turn away so that they hear not.[14]

> Say (unto them O Muḥammad): I am only a mortal like you. It is inspired in me that your God is One God, therefore

take the straight path unto Him and seek forgiveness of Him. And woe unto the idolaters.[15]

Persecution intensified and became unbearable. Muḥammad advised those of his followers who could not depend on the protection of their kinsmen to seek refuge in the Christian kingdom of Abyssinia. And so in the year 615 about eleven to fifteen families, followed later by eighty-three individuals, male and female, arrived in Abyssinia where the Negus took them under his wing and refused to surrender them to the Quraysh. Muḥammad and his small party of staunch followers remained in Mecca to continue the struggle against overwhelming odds.

One traditional but not well attested account of this period, an account given notoriety by Salman Rushdie's book *The Satanic Verses*, underscores Muḥammad's privation and the strong pressure upon him to conform to the beliefs of the Quraysh. It was during a prayer session at the Kaʿbah that, in a moment of weakness, he referred to the three female deities, al-Lāt, al-ʿUzzah and Manāh, "...as the most exalted cattle egrets (*gharānīq*, mistaken for cranes)" and stated: "Verily their intercession is to be hoped for." The Quraysh were pleasantly surprised; and while they did prostrate themselves before Allah as Muḥammad called upon them to do, they still were unwilling to submit to His worship alone.

Muḥammad, however, was reportedly rebuked by Gabriel for including words in the revelation not transmitted from Allah who "...abolishes that which Satan proposes...(and) establishes His revelations."[16] After he had repented for having yielded to temptation in a moment of trial, God spoke again to Muḥammad and the idolatrous verses were expunged from the Qurʾān; in their place was substituted the verse, "Shall yours be the male and his the female?[17] This were then an unjust division! They are naught but names which ye and your fathers have named."[18]

His recantation evoked all the more the anger of the oligarchs who stepped up their persecution of Muḥammad's followers and even plotted his death. Besides, the Muslims had for some time boldly and openly carried on their worship of Allah in the environs of the sacred Kaʿbah. The Quraysh now retaliated by ostracizing their Hāshimite cousins who had pledged themselves to defend their Muslim kinsmen and secluded them in a *wādī* (vale) outside the city where for more than two years they suffered extreme hardships. Still they would not deliver Muḥammad to his persecutors.

Prudence decreed that Muḥammad take precautions to safeguard the lives of his followers. Threatening his kinsmen with the wrath of Allah and eternal damnation seemed to make no imprint on them. Pagan Arabians, moreover, had no preconceptions of a life hereafter, or of rewards and punishments in such a life. They had looked upon such notions with ridicule and were not restrained by fear of judgment from pursuing their persecution of the believers.

The Qurayshite oligarchy in another respect had looked upon Muḥammad's claim to prophethood with skepticism because they had been convinced that if Allah really wanted to appoint a messenger, surely He would have chosen one from their midst! Were they not, after all, the leaders of Mecca and the custodians of the sacred shrine wherein He dwelt and was revered?

Their skepticism of Muḥammad's mission manifested itself in another way. If Muḥammad were truly sent, so they argued, why did he refuse to produce a sign in testimony of his declared mission or perform a miracle like other prophets before him?[19] Why did he insist, as he did time and again, that he was not sent by God to work miracles? Was it sufficient to argue that the only miracle he was capable of was to point to God's power as manifested in His divine word and in His creation round about them?

The only miracle attributed to Muḥammad by the believers in him is the Qur'ān. That so illiterate an Arab was capable of such rich utterances was truly miraculous in their eyes. And when the outside observer ponders the powerful impact he wrought on pagan Arabia in a decade of work, he is indeed overwhelmed by the miracle Muḥammad performed.

In the midst of the crisis, death carried off both his faithful wife and the uncle who had been his benefactor and protector. The loss was somewhat mitigated by the conversion to Islam of the future caliph, ʿUmar ibn al-Khaṭṭāb, a man of strong will and conviction who contributed materially to the strengthening of the Islamic faith and the community.

Muḥammad remained the target of ridicule; his opponents accused him of sorcery and fraudulent lifting of ideas from Christians and Jews. But to be berated and slandered apparently was the normal fate of prophets. The reception accorded his predecessors among Jews and gentiles had not been milder.

> If they deny thee, even so the folk of Noah, and (the tribes of) 'Ād and Thamūd, before thee, denied (Our messengers); and the folk of Abraham and the folk of Lot; (and) the dwellers of Midian. And Moses was denied; but I indulged the disbelievers a long while then I seized them, and how (terrible) was My abhorrence! [20]

The Hijrah

When he first considered seeking outside assistance, Muḥammad went to Ṭā'if, a town sixty miles east of Mecca; but the inhabitants turned him back after he had spent a month among them fruitlessly endeavoring to win them over to the new faith. Two years later a delegation of twelve arrived from Yathrib to perform the pilgrimage. Muḥammad met with them. They believed that he could solve the intertribal discord of the Aws and Khazraj—the two powerful tribes whose rivalry for control of the rich oases of Yathrib and its lucrative trade was rupturing the social fabric of Yathrib. They accepted his message and returned to Yathrib to join the small coterie of Muslims won over by the Prophet earlier. Next year, in 622, an emissary sent by the Prophet returned from Yathrib accompanied by seventy-three men and two women who extended Muḥammad a formal invitation to come to Yathrib.

Shortly thereafter, about one hundred Muslim families slipped out of Mecca and headed for Yathrib where they were warmly received. The Meccans, now fearing an alliance between Muḥammad and the hostile tribes of Yathrib, seriously contemplated killing him. But accompanied by Abu Bakr his cousin and followed by his cousin 'Ali, he eluded his would-be assassins and reached the city by a round-about route on September 24, 622. This year became subsequently the first year of the Muslim calendar,[21] popularly referred to as the "Hegira" (Hijrah).[22] It is a significant date in Islamic history, because it heralded the dawn of a new era, the Islamic era, and the end of the "Age of Ignorance" (Jāhilīyah).

The migration to Yathrib introduced a new phase in Muḥammad's struggle with his kinsmen among the Quraysh. They were angered by his abandonment of folk and home city; the desertion of kin in pre-Islamic Arabia was tantamount to committing suicide. The Quraysh implored their deities "to bring the woe upon him who more than any among us has cut off the ties of kinship and acted dishonorably."[23]

In Mecca Muḥammad had preached a predominantly ethical doctrine anchored in justice and equality under God, whose worship alone would bring this about. But in Yathrib he acquired a new role, that of arbiter in the feuds of the Yathribites and of a statesman providing leadership to the Muslims who broke the ties of kinship and organized themselves as a separate community wherein Islam was substituted for blood ties.

This new role changed the character of Muḥammad's preachings. He had become the head of an organized society. The role of the statesman accedes to his role as prophet. Muḥammad became increasingly an organizer, and the statesmanship in him emerged. Allah came to his rescue and obligingly caused the appropriate revelations to descend upon him as the occasion called for them.

The citizens of the city, which after his death was referred to as "*Madīnat al-Rasūl*" (the city of the messenger) or more popularly, "*Madīnah*," "Medina," consisted of three basic groups: (1) those who helped bring Muḥammad to Yathrib, the *Anṣār* (supporters); (2) those who emigrated from Mecca at his behest, the *Muhājirūn* (emigrants), and (3) Jewish clients of Aws and Khazraj and those branded *Munāfiqūn* (hypocrites) in the Qur'ān. To weld all parties together into a uniform administrative social unit and at the same time to provide them with freedom of internal government, Muḥammad entered into a *ḥilf* (pact) with the *Anṣār* from among the Aws and Khazraj and their Jewish clients defining the rights and obligations of each side. Thus was established the first *ummah* (community), secular in its structure but theocratic in its governance, in that "Allah and Muḥammad were designated as its ultimate source of arbitration."[24]

The Commonwealth

In this manner the prophet-statesman established under the aegis of Islam the first polity in the history of the Muslim world. Faith and society were merged. Islamic hegemony emerged. Though predominantly non-Islamic in its structure, Islam nevertheless became the commonwealth's guarantor. The believers were committed to safeguard the rights of all citizens governed by the commonwealth's laws, be they Muslim or Jewish. The fact that the inhabitants adhered to a variety of religious and non-religious convictions and were willing to accept Islamic leadership is a tribute to the statesmanship of Muḥammad. It is also a measure of Islam's capacity for tolerance. This strengthened their receptiveness to the new ideas propagated by Muḥammad in spite of the presence in their midst of a strong Jewish faith, which presumably had predisposed them beforehand towards monotheism. As a noted scholar points out: "from a religious standpoint paganism in Medina was dead before it was attacked; none defended it, none mourned its disappearance. The pagan opposition to Muḥammad's work as a reformer was entirely political . . ."[25]

Having reconciled the disputing factions, introduced law, and restored order through skillfully transferring the center of power from the tribes to the community represented by the commonwealth, Muḥammad earned the respect of all statesmen familiar with the obstacles he overcame in the process of transferring power. The Prophet was now ready to square off with his antagonists in Mecca. He was not seeking revenge; he was moved rather by the same sense of mission which had impelled him from the start to gain his kinsmen's acceptance of Allah as the only God.

Some scholars are of the opinion that he was moved also by economic necessity. Muslims in Medina had been experiencing considerable hardships because of their poverty. For some two years, moreover, the Quraysh and *Muhājirūn* had been clashing. The latter had been attacking the caravans of the former to compensate for losses they incurred by forced emigration to Yathrib, and the Quraysh retaliated by acts of sabotage directed against fruit trees in the oases around Medina and by theft of flocks belonging to the Muslims.

Mounting opposition came also from many of the Jews who in the two years of theological debate with the new prophet became convinced that he was not exactly the Messiah they had been awaiting. For some time they had been turning against him, and had often sided with his enemies. This not only incurred for them the animosity of Muḥammad, but served also to reinforce his growing conviction that any accommodation of sweeping Jewish beliefs and practices in Islam would dilute its appeal and weaken its role as a dynamic force possessing a strong message of its own. Jews had falsified their scriptures to conceal the foretelling of his mission as the prophet of God when they questioned his role. He also accused them of deviating from the true worship of God, as attested in numerous verses in *sūrahs* ("the Cow") of the Qurʾān. The final break with the Jews came when formal hostilities broke out between the Meccans and the Medinans.

The Struggle with the Quraysh

In January of 624 a Meccan army led by Abū Jahl headed for Medina. Though lacking in adequate resources for defense and outnumbered three to one, the Muslims were determined to stand their ground at the wells of Badr. This was a new experience for the Muslim community. The believers, furthermore, were not sure whether Allah would give them permission to defend themselves. Surely He would not suffer the believers in Him to perish at the hands of His enemies. He spoke, and Muḥammad relayed the message:

> Allah defendeth those who are true…sanction is given unto those who fight because they have been wronged… Those who have been driven from their homes unjustly only because they said: Our Lord is Allah…[26]
>
> Fight in the way of Allah against those who fight against you, but begin not hostilities. Lo! Allah loveth not aggressors.

> And slay them wherever ye find them, and drive them out of the places whence they drove you out, for persecution is worse than slaughter.[27]

In the encounter that ensued, Allah granted victory to the believers even though their enemies were more numerous and had fought bravely. The so-called "battle of Badr," a skirmish by modern standards of warfare, provided the "day of decision," as Muḥammad termed it and as echoed in the Qur'ān:

> There was a sign for you in the two hosts which met: one army fighting in the way of Allah, and another disbelieving...[28]
>
> Lo! Herein verily is a lesson for those who have eyes. Ye slew them not, but Allah slew them...[29]

As for the effect of victory on the Muslim community, it represented a turning point in its future development. All eyes now turned to Muḥammad whose temporal power had received a boost by a military victory. The Prophet's career was enhanced: first preacher, then administrator, and now military commander. This *was* a miracle, though not exactly the kind of miracle which the Quraysh had so often sought from their kinsman and now experienced in an unpleasant manner.

Muḥammad had humbled the mighty of Mecca. Skeptical Bedouins flocked to the faith, the faithful were strengthened in their belief, and the disaffected had grounds for fear.

But the Quraysh struck back in the following year, defeating the Muslims and nearly killing the Prophet at the battle of Uḥud when the archers left their positions of defense and allowed the enemy's cavalry to surround the defenders, who were outnumbered 3000 to 700. Fortunately for the Muslims, the Quraysh did not follow up their victory with the occupation of Medina. Again the community was saved.

The Break with the Jews

The main Jewish tribes, Qurayzah, Banū al-Naḍīr, and Qaynuqā', though signatories of pacts with Muḥammad, which essentially granted protection to those who committed no crimes and provided for mutual assistance against aggression, chose not to abide by their commitment. Moreover, the Banū Qaynuqā' turned to ridiculing the Muslims and challenging their fighting abilities. Muḥammad besieged them in their quarters for fifteen days following which they evacuated Medina for the borders of Syria. They had sided with Muḥammad's enemies in open violation of the terms of the charter, and their protector ibn 'Ubayy failed in convincing the Prophet to grant them protection. The Banū al-Naḍīr were quick to perceive that Jewish positions in Medina were no longer tenable. Efforts at reconciliation failed, particularly when the "Hypocrites" supported their position against Muḥammad. A military showdown was inevitable. It took place in 626 with Muḥammad launching the assault by laying siege to the stronghold of the Banū al-Naḍīr. After fifteen days of being hemmed in, they requested and were granted permission to leave Medina with their movable property; their holdings in land and appurtenances were turned over to the *Muhājirūn*. This was a precedent set for the disposal of property gained in warfare in the future. The Banū Qaynūqā' had been banished from Mecca earlier, before the showdown with Banū al-Naḍīr.

From both religious and political considerations, the commonwealth of believers had to eliminate disruptive forces and consolidate its defenses against the real threat to its independence and existence, regardless of whether the threat was from within or from without.

In the two or three years following the setback of Uḥud, the Muslims were preoccupied with the task of repelling the forays of nomadic tribes against their possessions. But in the meanwhile, the Qurayzah, another Jewish tribe that had entered into a pact relationship with the commonwealth of Medina, were induced by the dispossessed Banū al-Naḍīr and the "Hypocrites" to join the Quraysh in a new assault on Medina. This group was being organized and led by Abu Sufyān, the chief oligarch of Mecca.

The "Confederates" (al-Aḥzāb), as they were called, invested the city in 627 and presented the Medinans with the most serious threat to date. But on the advice of a Persian convert, the defenders dug a trench across the access to the beleaguered city.

Revolted by such unwarlike tactics, the assailants, who took pride in the tribal methods of warfare, withdrew after a month of fruitless siege and minimal losses to both sides. Cold weather and disunity in the ranks of the assailants contributed to the decision to withdraw.

Angered by the betrayal of the Banū Qurayzah in the violation of their oath, Muhammad submitted them to trial by the chief of the Aws whom they had requested to pass judgment upon them. Saʿd ibn Muʿādh, the chief, decreed all fighting men of the Banū Qurayzah be put to death. This was in keeping with Jewish law (Deuteronomy 20:12), which decrees the killing of every male in such situations. He was convinced that they would have meted out similar judgment on the Muslims had they and their allies triumphed instead. None but four would forsake Judaism for Islam as a price of survival.

Next Muḥammad embarked on an expedition to encircle Mecca and subdue the neighboring tribes who usually allied themselves with the Quraysh. Having accomplished this mission, he next set out with fourteen hundred of his followers on a pilgrimage to the city in 628.

The Quraysh at first were determined to block his entry into the city. But the diplomatic genius of Muḥammad again turned an adverse situation into a victory. At al-Ḥudaybīyah, leaders of the Quraysh concluded an agreement with the Muslims that granted them permission to perform the pilgrimage in the following year provided Muḥammad would accept a ten-year truce. This was an important gain for the Muslims, as the conclusion of a pact with the Quraysh was tantamount to their being recognized as equals. The pact went further by permitting those who wished, to accept Islam. Many did.

Only one more obstacle remained: Jewish control over Khaybar and the neighboring areas of Fadak and Taymāʾ in the rich agricultural areas to the north. Muḥammad and his followers believed they could never exert full political power in Arabia until the power of the Jews in the whole land was eliminated. Quite clearly the hostility here displayed was over political and economic, not religious differences. The Muslims invested the strong fortifications at Khaybar for days; numerous engagements took place before the Jews finally succumbed to superior Muslim forces. The Jews had fought bravely by Muslim accounts, losing both military commanders in battle. Muḥammad made peace with them, allowed them to maintain control over their agricultural lands provided they paid half of the yield to the Muslims. Muḥammad took one of their women, Ṣafiyah, "the lady of Banū Qurayzah and Banū al-Naḍīr" for a wife. Zaynab, the daughter of al-Ḥārith and wife of Sallām, both of whom had fallen in battle in leading Jewish resistance against Muḥammad at Khaybar attempted to poison him and his followers in revenge. While records are uncertain about her fate, they do show that Muḥammad realized that Muslims and Jews could not share Arabia politically or economically. On religious grounds he did not challenge their beliefs, indeed he returned to them all the Torahs captured at Khaybar, even allowed some to return to Medina and trade; but it was only a matter of time before they would exit the land.

In 629, accompanied by two thousand followers, Muḥammad went on a pilgrimage to Mecca. In accordance with the truce terms the city was vacated of its inhabitants to accommodate the Muslims during their three-day visit to their former homes. It was at this time that the Muslims gained two important converts—ʿAmr ibn al-ʿĀṣ and Khālid ibn al-Walīd. Both men during the next decade were to write a valorous record in the annals of Islamic conquests.

On returning to Medina, Muḥammad dispatched a force of three thousand men under the leadership of his adopted son Zayd to exact retribution from the Ghassānid prince who had murdered a Muslim envoy sent earlier by the Prophet to solicit the conversion of Ghassānid Arabs to Islam. A year before, in 628, the Prophet had dispatched envoys to the Byzantine Emperor Heraclius and the Sasānid "king of kings," Chosroes Parvis, asking them to accept Islam. The Byzantine emperor politely declined the invitation, but the Persian Chosroes tore up Muḥammad's invitation in a rage and insulted the envoy. When the Prophet learned of the results, he was prompted to state "and thus will the empire of Chosroes be torn to pieces"; as indeed came to pass, and at the hands of the Prophet's followers, seven years later.

The encounter with the Ghassānids proved disastrous to the Muslim force which suffered the loss of Zayd, the son, and Jaʿfar, a cousin of Muḥammad. The Muslim force was spared complete annihilation thanks to the ingenious maneuvers of Khālid who succeeded in withdrawing the remnants of the expedition to Medina. But the Muslims avenged this defeat a month later when al-ʿĀṣ forced a number of hostile tribes to submit to the new faith, restoring in the process the prestige which the Muslims had lost during their previous encounter in the borderland separating Syria from Arabia.

The Submission of Mecca

The final episode in the career of Muḥammad and his crowning achievement was the submission of Mecca to Islam, accomplished in the year 8 of the Muslim calendar (630). At the instigation of the Quraysh, the Banū Bakr violated the truce of Ḥudaybīyah by attacking the Banū Khuzāʿah, allies of the Muslims, and killing a number of them. "And if they break their pledges after their treaty [e.g., with you, Muḥammad] and assail your religion, then fight the heads of disbelief..."[30]

Muḥammad resolved to end, once and for all, the resistance of the Quraysh. He gathered together a force of ten thousand men and set off for Mecca on January 1, 630. When still a day's journey from the city, a delegation of the Quraysh headed by the chief oligarch Abu Sufyān met the Prophet and offered to submit to the new faith. Muḥammad was spared thereby the unpleasant task of forcibly entering Mecca. Instead, the faithful entered the city in peace. The Prophet's mission was rapidly nearing completion.

Mecca and its inhabitants were treated with magnanimity. Only four criminals, condemned according to prevailing laws, suffered execution. This show of clemency was not unrewarded, however, as thousands of Meccans now formally adopted Islam. In the Kaʿbah Muḥammad personally destroyed three hundred and sixty idols with his staff as he proclaimed "God is great!

Truth has come. Falsehood has vanished!" Henceforth Allah was to be the sole dweller of the Kaʿbah which was now made into the principal shrine of Islam. "He only shall tend Allah's sanctuaries who believeth in Allah and the Last Day and observeth worship and payeth the poor-due and feareth none save Allah."[31] With the destruction of the idols Muḥammad destroyed the symbol of wealth and power of pagan Arabia, and the Meccans witnessed for themselves how powerless their idols really were.

The destruction of the idols was followed by a sermon to the swollen ranks of the assembled multitudes in which Muḥammad proclaimed: "Verily the true believers are brethren; wherefore make peace among your brethren; and fear Allah, that ye may obtain mercy."[32] The pagans of Mecca submitted to Islam as had been ordained in Allah's words:

> When victory and triumph are come from God and thou seest hosts of people embrace the religion of God, ye will then praise the glory of your Lord and implore His pardon, as He is ever ready to welcome penitence.[33]

The new converts pledged to adore no other deity save God and to abstain from theft, adultery, lying, and backbiting when they offered their submission to the Lord of the Worlds.

While still in Mecca, Muḥammad dispatched emissaries to all parts of Arabia for the purpose of preaching Islam to the tribes. Temples dedicated to pagan worship were torn down. The two major tribes of Thaqīf and Ḥawāzin had to be subdued by force, and Muḥammad's followers were victorious but not without an initial serious setback. He was much more magnanimous in his treatment of the Thaqīf and Ḥawāzin than perhaps they deserved or expected. They turned consequently to Islam and embraced the faith with an ardent zeal.

This was in the ninth year of the Hijrah, which witnessed an upward trend in the fortunes of Islam. It was a year of decisive triumph, when all of Muḥammad's enemies, the Quraysh, Thaqīf, and Ḥawāzin, submitted to him. Christian and Jewish tribes on the periphery of Arabia reached amicable agreements with the Prophet of Islam, who in return for his promise of protection received from them a consideration in a form of payment later termed *jizyah.* Muḥammad made no attempt to convert them to Islam, as both peoples already had received the Scripture from Allah; Muḥammad, moreover, had been specifically commissioned by Allah to bring the message to non-believers in Him.

This did not eliminate possible conflict with Christians and Jews. A part of Muḥammad's role was also to set straight those who had formerly received the Scripture but later deviated.

> Fight against such of those who have been given the Scripture as believe not in Allah nor the Last Day, and forbid not that which Allah hath forbidden by His messenger, and follow not the religion of truth, until they offer tribute on the back of their hands bowing low.[34]

In its pronouncements concerning Christians and Jews, the Qurʾān refers to their having succumbed to what Islam regards a deadly sin, namely *shirk* or association in worship; this in itself would justify the visitation of the wrath of Allah at the hands of the Muslims.

> The Jews say Ezra is the son of God while the Christians say Christ is the son of God.... They say this with their own mouths imitating the saying of those who disbelieved of old. May God fight them, how perverse they are! They have taken as lords besides Allah their rabbis and their monks and the Messiah, son of Mary, when they were bidden to worship only one God. There is no God but He! Be He glorified by those they associate with Him as partners; He it is who sent His messenger with guidance and the true religion that He may cause it to prevail over all religion, however much disbelievers are averse![35]

Yet in spite of such strong statements concerning the "deviation" of other Scripturists, Islam still permitted Christians and Jews, wherever they were to be found in lands under Muslim domination, to retain their religious practices unrestrained.

The Submission of Arabia

The year 631 is also known as the "year of delegations" (*Sanat al-Wufūd*) when the tribes of Arabia sent their representatives to Mecca to offer their submission to Allah and their fighting men to Muḥammad. They paid taxes as enjoined upon them, a novel experience for them. Those who once ridiculed and satirized the Prophet now outrivaled one another in their laudatory praise of a man from the Quraysh who had triumphed in the name of Allah over every obstacle placed in his path. Muḥammad had thus become a hero of Arabia, the first and the last Arab to accomplish so much from a very inauspicious start.

Following the submission of the tribes, Muḥammad sent out his representatives to the various parts of Arabia to teach the precepts of the new religion, enjoining them to "deal gently and be not harsh." The Prophet's messengers were to bring cheer to the converts and good tidings to those who believed that the key to heaven is "to bear witness to the divine truth and do good."

Muḥammad had now successfully fulfilled his mission. In ten short years after his flight from Mecca, he had gained over to Islam the whole of Arabia, a land that had never before united under any set of ideals or beliefs. Now they came from all over to proclaim their submission to God and loyalty to Muḥammad.

Idolatry was destroyed; spirituality now superseded superstition, cruelty, and vice. A land hitherto torn by intertribal warfare in pursuit of plunder and material gain was now united in purpose by ties that made one Arab a brother to every other Arab in submission to the one God and His apostle Muḥammad. *Blood* ties were now subordinated to the kinship of *faith*. Ideals hitherto measured in terms of worldly gains were lifted to heights the skeptical Arab would never have accepted ten years before: an afterlife with rewards and punishments meted out to the deserving on a day of judgment. Such injunctions from Allah pertaining to charity, goodness, right-doing, acting justly, observing peace, all would have been deemed unacceptable outside the confines of tribal society before Muḥammad began to preach. These precepts were now made a condition of belief for all those who professed Islam.

The Farewell Message

In February of 632 Muḥammad set out once more with a large contingent of his followers to perform what turned out to be a farewell pilgrimage to Mecca. The city had been purged of all traces of idolatry during the preceding year when Muḥammad had decreed that none but the believers should perform the pilgrimage rite. Before the ceremony was completed, Muḥammad addressed the Muslims from atop Mt. ʿArafāt, a short distance from the city, in a speech which has figured in the pilgrimage ritual ever since. To the assembled multitudes he proclaimed:

> O believers harken unto my words as I know not whether another year will be permitted unto me to be amongst you. Your lives and possessions are sacred and inviolable (and so you must observe) the one toward the other, until ye appear before the Lord, as this day and month is sacred for all; and remember you will have to present yourselves to the Lord who will demand that you give an account of your deeds...Listen to my words and harken well. Know ye that all Muslims are brothers. Ye are all one brotherhood; and no man shall take ought from his brother unless it is freely given to him. Shun injustice. And let those here assembled inform those who are not of the same who when told afterwards may remember better than those who now hear it.[36]

Muḥammad concluded his sermon with the remarks: "O Lord! I have fulfilled my message and accomplished my task," to the echo of the assembled: "Verily thou hast." He ended with the words "O Lord! I beseech Thee to bear witness unto it."

The eleventh year of the Hijrah and the last of his life was spent in Medina. At this time Muḥammad integrated the tribal and provincial communities that had professed Islam and dispatched deputies to all parts of Arabia to teach the injunctions of the new religion to converts, to administer justice, and to collect tithes.

A new military expedition against the Byzantine prefect who had killed Zayd, Muḥammad's envoy, was in the process of departing when news of the Prophet's illness leaked out. Some anxiety followed and a number of impostors, or pretenders,[37] rose to share the prophetic role with Muḥammad.

The last few days of his life Muḥammad arranged to spend with his wife ʿĀʾishah, the youngest daughter of Abu Bakr. Though he had grown weak and feeble, he continued to lead the faithful in public prayer up to the third day prior to his death. In his last sermon to the believers he stated: "O Muslims! If I have wronged any of you, I am here to make amends; if I owe ought to any of you, all that I possess belongs to you." He prayed to God for mercy, then enjoined the faithful to observe religious duties and lead peaceful lives, reminding them of Allah's promise: "Abode in paradise We shall grant unto those who seek not to exalt themselves on earth or do wrong; a happy issue will attend the pious."

In a final gesture, an eloquent testimony to the role which he faithfully carried out to the end, Muḥammad told all those near him: "I have made lawful only that which God hath ordained and I have prohibited only that which God so commanded in His Book." Then turning to his daughter Fāṭimah and aunt Ṣafiyah for the last time he said to them: "Work ye both that which will gain thee acceptance with the Lord; for verily I have no power to save thee in any wise." He then rose and returned to ʿĀʾishah's dwelling where he died a few hours later, on June 8, 632 in the arms of his young wife.

> "Thou shalt surely die (O Muḥammad)
> And they also shall die!"

He was buried on the very spot in ʿĀʾishah's home where later a mosque was erected. Abu Bakr faced up to the task of announcing the Prophet's death addressing the faithful assembled outside:

> "O Muslims! If any of you has been worshiping Muḥammad, then let me tell you that Muḥammad is dead.
>
> But if you really do worship God, then know ye that God is living and will never die!"

CHAPTER 4

Muḥammad the Man

MUḤAMMAD RATES as one of the truly great personalities of history. Muḥammad's success in accomplishing his mission within ten short years is a tribute to his faith and to his superior moral qualities. His life and his work are a living testimony to his genius. That he towered over contemporaries, many of his predecessors and successors alike, is evident in the radical transformation of fundamental values and mores he wrought for a people who hitherto had excelled in their uncontrollable individualism and insatiable egoism.

The Genius in Him

Muḥammad's insecure early youth wherein misery often prevailed apparently had awakened in him the instincts which in later years relentlessly drove him on and instilled in him the determination to accomplish clearly stated goals: unity in worship and a coherent society for the Arabs. Stimulated by the social injustices he himself experienced, and which reached deep into his youth, Muḥammad preached religion. By means of religion he sought to accomplish certain important aims, involving a complete social transformation as revolutionary in nature and extent as any of the modern crusading socialistically motivated ideologies.

The idea of religion serving to bring about social revolution was not alien to Semitic societies. From the times of the Pharoah Ikhnaton to the times of Moses and the ethical prophets of Israel; from Zoroaster to Jesus to Muḥammad, when social conditions became intolerable and grew increasingly lacking in equity, in righteousness, and in the fundamental principles of morality, religion not ideology provided the incentive for change.

The success of Muḥammad's mission, based on other-worldly precepts, rests in no small measure on his own worldly gifts. He was thoroughly practical and master of both individual and mass psychology, as is attested by the near fanatical devotion of his Companions to him and to the message he preached. Muḥammad's teachings were tailored to the mundane wants of his audience as can be seen in his earthly depiction of rewards and punishments for the skeptics and unbelievers. His message reflected the clairvoyance of his understanding in relation to his milieu and the needs of Arabian society in his time.

He never forgot himself even in the highest moment of triumph, remaining just and temperate in the exercise of authority which, had he chosen, could have been absolutely dictatorial. Had he been lacking in sincerity and genuineness, this side of him would have manifested itself upon his conquest of Mecca. As our sources acknowledge, the city was treated with the magnanimity that doubtlessly he himself would not have received had the Quraysh triumphed instead. There was nothing to prevent him in this moment of victory from gratifying his own ambition and satisfying a sense of lust or revenge if it had been at all present.

His capacity for achievement is evident in the success of his mission. His cardinal aim to assert the worship of one God, and that God alone, was attained, and with it a doctrine that would insure its perpetuation. A new ritual and a new cult were born. The old system of belief based on idolatry was abolished, by force when peaceful persuasion failed. Commensurate with the triumph of Allah was the erection of a new society based on submission to Him, a society which recognized the universal brotherhood of all Muslims. First the Arabs of Arabia and later, with the expansion of Islam outside of Arabia, all those who submitted to Allah in Islam were looked upon as rightful members of this vast fraternity.

At first, and by his own admission, Muḥammad had no intention of founding a new religion. He merely wanted his fellow Arabs to worship one God, the only God, as worshiped by their neighbors, the Christians and the Jews.

> Say, we believe in Allah and in what has been revealed to us, in what was revealed to Abraham, Ishmael, Isaac, Jacob, and the tribes; in what was given to Moses and Jesus, and in what the prophets received from their Lord: we make no distinction between any of them.[1]

Muḥammad did not consider his mission as superseding those of his predecessors, the former prophets of Allah from Abraham to Jesus; he looked upon his mission rather as serving to complete and revitalize these earlier religions and to set straight misconceptions associated with them.

Nor did he look upon himself as superior to any of the former prophets; he was one of them, but the last to be commissioned by Allah to deliver the same message previously delivered by his former colleagues.

Beside reminding his people of Allah's command that they should worship none other but Him, Muḥammad also drew attention, especially where called for, to deviations by other worshipers of the same God from the true worship established by Him. Indeed, it is also to Muḥammad's credit that at the height of his religious and political authority he did not insist that Jews and Christians should renounce their version of monotheism for that which he preached.

It was out of respect for all those who worshiped God alone, Muslim and non-Muslim, that Muhammad made himself available to them for guidance and comfort. The destitute, the sick, and those in need of hospitality had access to him. Muḥammad made no distinction between them on the basis of their worship of the true God. He looked upon himself as the liberator and protector of the other religions.

This strong protective instinct was manifest in his extensive legislation to define and safeguard the rights of women. He enforced puritanical injunctions clearly unheard of before his time, such as banning intoxicating beverages, the gratification of illicit sex relations, and the like. He conceived it his sacred duty to promote the moral and material welfare of his people. Some authorities in subsequent decades have advanced the claim that Muḥammad did not propose the establishment of a formal code of law since, from their point of argument, he only volunteered rules of conduct and ritual when they were extorted from him by questioning. There might be some truth to this argument; at least it would help explain the absence of a well laid out system of law for political conduct. The absence of a defined system of law had drastic consequences, following the death of Muḥammad, for political solidarity in the Islamic commonwealth.

The study of Islam reveals the eclectic nature of Muḥammad's preachings. This eclecticism, however, did not prevent it from acquiring an identity of its own stamped by Muḥammad's personality and mirroring the basic precepts which guided his life. Islam is the religion of Allah.

The last revelation from God gave the religion its official name:

> This day have I perfected your religion for you and completed My favor unto you, and have chosen for you as religion AL-ISLAM.[2]

Faith was perhaps the strongest moving force behind Muḥammad's personality. And the central repository of this faith was his conception of the will of God as it finally came to be expressed in the Qur'ān. The strength of his faith did indeed write one of the most dramatic chapters in the history of mankind. The strong and powerful appeal which the Qur'ān has held over the hearts and minds of hundreds of millions during the past thirteen centuries attests the strength of Muḥammad's convictions.

When we consider that the Qur'ān mirrors the heart and mind of an Arab principally illiterate and unschooled in any formal knowledge, we cannot but admire the faith which moved, and indeed conditioned, the man Muḥammad. While he emphatically denied his ability to perform miracles, arguing all along that God alone was the miracle worker; when considering the effects wrought by the Qurʾān on Muḥammad's people, and when pondering the magnitude of its impact on Arabs and non-Arabs alike, we cannot deny that this was indeed one of the greatest miracles ever performed by one who insisted he was a mortal like everyone else. This was the miracle of the nonmiracle worker.

By a fortune somewhat unusual Muḥammad, while preaching the worship of God alone, became the founder not only of a religion but also of a nation which later evolved a distinct culture of its own. Circumstances beyond his anticipation transformed Muḥammad from a religious teacher in Mecca to ruler and legislator in Medina, "but for himself he sought nothing beyond the acknowledgment that he was Allah's apostle."[3]

Above all he served as the transmitter of a text which is a poem, a code of laws, a book of common prayer, and a bible in one, reverenced to this day by a sixth of the whole of the human race, as a miracle of purity of style, of wisdom and of truth.[4]

While the establishment of Islam as the religion of Arabia and the foundation of its government and society is Muḥammad's supreme achievement, the subsequent development of a coherent commonwealth guided by the precepts of the new faith and the rise of a nation out of the heterogeneous tribes separated by clear geographical and ideological barriers is no less important for our understanding of the full range of Muḥammad's work. The radical transformation of values achieved in the Bedouin Arab, regarded as singularly egotistical in his skepticism and antipathy to change, is perhaps another miraculous achievement.

The Qurʾān provides a contrast between the life and mores of the Arabs in the shade of Islam and their values in pre-Islamic times. Not only did Muḥammad abolish and nearly uproot the institution of blood feuds, the most evil of the institutions governing social relationships in pre-Islamic Arabia, he almost reversed this institution by insisting that rivals engaged in mortal conflict should embrace and accept brotherhood in Islam. He urged upon all true believers a real union of hearts.

The essence of Muḥammad's socioreligious message is embodied in the Qurʾānic text:

> O ye who believe! Observe your duty to Allah with right observance, and die not save as those who have surrendered (unto Him);
>
> And hold fast, all of you together, to the cable of Allah, and do not separate. And remember Allah's favour unto you: how ye were enemies and He made friendship between your hearts so that ye became as brothers by His grace; and (how) ye were upon the brink of an abyss of fire, and He did save you from it. Thus Allah maketh clear His revelations unto you, that haply ye may be guided,
>
> And there may spring from you a nation who invite to goodness, and enjoin right conduct and forbid indecency. Such are they who are successful.
>
> And be ye not as those who separated and disputed after the clear proofs had come unto them. For such there is an awful doom.[5]

His Personal Assets

The question comes to mind: what kind of a person was Muḥammad to cause such a deep and lasting stir in the wastes of Arabia? What kind of a personality did he have?

From what we know, he appears to have been a humble and unpretentious being, if not outrightly austere in his habits and manner of living. He dwelt in a very simple abode in unaffected surroundings. An ambassador to the Quraysh, an outsider who had contact with Muḥammad in the period of exile once stated in this regard: "I have seen the Persian Chosroes and the Greek Heraclius sitting upon their thrones; but never did I see a man ruling his equals as does Muḥammad."

Muḥammad possessed a gentle disposition, and his temperament rarely gave way to anger. He was endowed with high moral standards and qualities of trustworthiness to such a degree that his contemporaries were prompted to call him *al-Amīn* (the trusted one) long before he embarked upon his mission. Indeed, it was his high moral qualities that induced the Yathribites to solicit his mediation in their internecine disputes. Muḥammad was exceedingly loyal to his friends and those near him. His biographer relates the story of the Christian slave Zayd who after a period of association with Muḥammad was given the opportunity to return to his father, but Zayd chose instead to remain with Muḥammad. For this act of devotion Muḥammad subsequently awarded Zayd his freedom and formally adopted him as his son.

The dignity of his personal habits, his stately and commanding stature, tact, equilibrium, and self-control made of Muḥammad a natural leader of men. A patriarchal simplicity permeated his life. He was self-reliant to a rare degree, personally delivering alms into the hands of petitioners, tying up cattle, mending his own clothes, cobbling his sandals, and aiding generally in the household duties of his wives. He never rejected an invitation; he disliked to say no, and he was "more bashful than a veiled virgin," proclaimed his witty wife ʿĀʾishah. He had the unique faculty of making each guest feel that he was the favorite. He exuded joy to those who were happy and tender sympathy to the afflicted and bereaved. Generous and magnanimous, Muḥammad shared his food with the hungry and when he died he left all his modest belongings to the faithful.

Marital Life

Further insight into his personality and character can be derived from a glance into his domestic life. This is one facet of Muḥammad where authorities concede he set an example of virtue emulated by so many millions of believers in subsequent times.

While it is not the aim of this study to make an apologetic presentation of Muḥammad's attitude toward the opposite sex or to narrate his marital indulgences, it suffices for us to state here that the revelations bearing celestial injunctions have often provided his critics with much unwarranted fodder for ridiculing his claim to prophethood. In these, "the latter-day saints" of Christian Europe found cause for dubbing Muḥammad a sensual man who was reportedly guided to ecstatic visions through the favors bestowed upon him by the opposite sex. Scholars in more recent times have found appropriate answers to such early charges.

Those who have referred to his plural marriages as evidence of his sensual nature made little mention of the fact that in the prime of his youth and adult years Muḥammad remained thoroughly devoted to Khadījah and would have none other for consort. This was in an age that looked upon plural marriages with favor and in a society that in pre-biblical and post-biblical days considered polygamy an essential feature of social existence. David had six wives and numerous concubines,[6] and Solomon was said to have had as many as 700 wives and 300 concubines.[7] Solomon's son Rehoboam had 18 wives and 60 concubines.[8] The New Testament contains no specific injunction against plural marriages. It was commonplace for the nobility among Christians and Jews to contract plural marriages. Luther spoke of it with toleration.

Muḥammad's marriages after Khadījah's, yielding about eleven wives in all, were due partly to political reasons and partly to his concern for the wives of his Companions who had fallen in battle defending the nascent Islamic community. In spite of the calumnies heaped upon him by his detractors who, among other things described him as a voluptuary and wife-hungry, a study of Muḥammad's marital inclinations reveals that, besides the political considerations for acquiring more than one wife following the death of Khadījah, pity and elementary concern prompted him in later years to take on wives who were neither beautiful nor rich, but mostly old widows. The wives of companions fallen in battle had to be looked after, and Muḥammad married them in order to offer them shelter and care.[9] His marriage to Zaynab, wife of his adopted son, was the result of her unhappy marital relationship with Zayd. Both she and her family, the noble of Hāshim and Quraysh, frowned upon a marriage to a freed slave. Muḥammad, however, was determined to establish the legitimacy and right to equal treatment of the adopted in Islam. Nevertheless, this marriage did occasion considerable criticism of the Prophet, and his concern over such criticism earned him the rebuke of Allah:

"And ye feared men when God had the greater right that ye should fear Him."[10]

In these post-Khadījah marriages, he is known to have dearly loved ʿĀʾishah, daughter of his most trusted companion Abu Bakr, and the only virgin wife he ever married. This fact was recognized by his other wives who gave him permission to consort with her without concern for themselves.

His Status as Prophet

An important facet of Muḥammad's character relates to his role as prophet and, specifically, to the question whether he was genuine. Many of his ill-wishers had insisted that he was a "false prophet." The issue here revolves around his sincerity. Certain writers have alluded to his being subject to epileptic seizures, psychic tension, and other abnormal physical manifestations, all of which, it has been argued, inspired Muḥammad to receive revelations from God.[11]

> ...If epilepsy is to denote only those severe attacks which involve serious consequences for the physical and mental health, then the statement that Mohammed suffered from epilepsy must be emphatically rejected.[12]

What is germane to the discussion is the product, not the means. Many personalities before Muḥammad who were considered "psychologically sound" had less to offer to posterity even when they were accorded the dignity of being official spokesmen for God. We have an example in the Hebrew prophets who preached that the Israelites should return to the worship of *Yhwh* (Jehovah), as Muḥammad called to the worship of Allah.

Like Jesus, Moses, and the prophets in between, Muḥammad was genuinely convinced of his prophetic role. The triumph of Islam as first the religion of Arabia and later of hundreds of millions of non-Arabians thirteen centuries later would not have been assured, the might of the Islamic imperium notwithstanding, were it not for the powerful appeal of Muhammad's message. The Qurʾān clearly attests to the magnitude of this message's impact, so strong that only a person endowed with superior qualities of insight could achieve it.

What is relevant for us to note is the fact that Muḥammad did not announce his mission until after a protracted period of reflection and hesitation. He had advanced well into mature life when he proclaimed his mission to the Arabs at the age of 40. Muḥammad, unlike his predecessors, grew accustomed to believing that the ideas emanating from the depth of a mature soul and a rational mind attributed to the divine will, herein equated with God, must be made known and must gain acceptability.

This was his conviction; this conviction impelled him to act. The role of Gabriel as the intermediary between God and Muḥammad is only symbolic of the process by which Muḥammad became conscious of the mature concepts that we find subsequently enshrined in the Qurʾān, and draped with utmost sanctity. The intent was to insure veracity by means of sanctity, which only the association of Godhood could impart to it. Muḥammad never doubted that these concepts embodied in revelations actually represented the command of that all-pervading will, the will of God.

"Prophecy" is an old and well utilized concept among Semitic peoples. "The role of a prophet to the pagan Arab was filled by the *shāʿir*; to the older Canaanites and their religious protégés, the Hebrews, he was a *nabi* (one who foretells). While the function of the prophet was familiar to most primitive peoples in one form or another, the more sophisticated elucidation of the role, which regards the prophet as the anointed mouthpiece of the deity, was left to the Hebrews to develop.

Muḥammad's treatment of his predecessors, the biblical prophets, and his image of himself in the general hierarchy of prophets merit consideration. In the manner of his carrying out the requirements of prophecy, Muḥammad followed in the tradition of the other Hebrew prophets, manifesting all the signs attending the role—impassioned utterances, use of rhyme in speech, intense preoccupation with God and moral issues, and a sense of urgency to declare the will of God.[13]

As a result of his intensified disputes with the Jews of Medina and the subsequent theological rift with them, Muḥammad acquired a clearer vision of his own place in the hierarchy of prophets. Of all the preceding prophets starting with Adam, who in the eyes of Muḥammad was the very first, Abraham through his son Ishmael, the eponymous father of the Arabs, becomes the patriarchal prophet. Muḥammad also brought into the picture of prophethood certain individuals who do not occur in the Jewish or Christian scriptures; nevertheless it is the biblical prophets who play the central role as the annointed agents of God. These are accorded full recognition in the Qurʾān:

> Say (O Muslims): We believe in Allah and that which is revealed unto us and that which was revealed unto Abraham, and Ishmael, and Isaac, and Jacob, and the tribes, and that which Moses and Jesus received, and that which the Prophets received from their Lord. We make no distinction between any of them, and unto Him we have surrendered.[14]

Muḥammad considered himself a prophet in the true biblical line, but subsumed no extra prerogatives. God, in the Qurʾān, regarded him as the "Seal of the Prophets." In the testimony of the Qurʾān:

> Muḥammad is but a messenger, messengers (the like of whom) have passed away before him.[15]
>
> Muḥammad is not the father of any man among you, but he is the messenger of Allah and the Seal of the Prophets; and Allah is Aware of all things.[16]

Muḥammad believed he was called to deliver the message of God to his own people and also to set straight distortions in the Scriptures grafted on the message of God by Jews and Christians. Again as preserved in the Qurʾān:

> And the Jews say the Christians follow nothing (true), and the Christians say the Jews follow nothing (true); yet both are readers of the Scripture. Even thus speak those who know not. Allah will judge between them on the Day of Resurrection concerning that wherein they differ.[17]

This point receives considerable emphasis in the Qurʾān, as for example:

> And the Jews will not be pleased with thee, nor will the Christians, till thou follow their creed. Say: Lo! the guidance of Allah (Himself) is Guidance. And if thou shouldst follow their desires after the knowledge which hath come unto thee, then wouldst thou have from Allah no protecting friend nor helper.[18]

The sensitive nature of the Prophet's task is in juxtaposition to the official view of the Scriptures; this is partially evident in the Qurʾānic verse:

> Those unto whom We have given the Scripture, who read it with the right reading, those believe in it. And whoso disbelieveth in it, those are they who are the losers.[19]

Muḥammad was quite serious over the message he brought to his people and would not tolerate seeing it mocked or derided. "Take not those for friends who make a jest and sport of your religion from among those who were given the Book before you, and the disbelievers…"[20] On a number of occasions he rebuked the Jews when they chided his message with the words of the Qurʾān:

> Say: O, People of the Scripture! Do ye blame us for aught else than that we believe in Allah and that which is revealed unto us and that which was revealed aforetime, and because most of you are evil-livers?[21]

He disputed less with the Christians because he had less contact with them. There were relatively few Christians in his part of Arabia while the Jewish tribes were quite numerous in the environs of Medina where his doctrine of Islam was being molded. He appeared, however, to be equally distrustful of Christians, as stated in the Qurʾānic verse:

> O ye who believe! Take not the Jews and Christians for friends. They are friends one to another. He among you who taketh them for friends is (one) of them. Lo! Allah guideth not wrongdoing folk.[22]

Versatility of the Message

In the socioreligious injunctions and ordinances imposed on the believers and preserved in the Qurʾān, we have a measure of the versatility of Muḥammad's message. He preached to the pagans. When they became converted, he organized them into a separate community. He legislated for this community, then led it through the most trying period of its existence.

In turning statesman he never forgot his principal role as the messenger of God. While the Qurʾān abounds with legislation for the organized community, the strong ethical rejoinders are never lost sight of. Time and again Muḥammad enjoins the faithful to do rightly by the Lord and His creation, to fight for the faith, to perform commendable deeds, and to refrain from what is objectionable in the sight of God.

> ...thine God is one God so submit ye all to Him. And give thou glad tidings to the humble, whose hearts are filled with fear when God is mentioned, and who patiently endure whatever befalls them, and who observe prayer and give generously of what We have provided them.[23]

The ethical message is strongly intertwined with the social. The full extent of his social legislation encroaches on the civil and ceremonial codes of Islam and is beyond the range of this present study. Much of the revelation enjoining social legislation for the nascent community of Islam belongs to the period of Muḥammad's preaching in Medina. Most of the ordinances and canonical laws of a developed Islamic society in the centuries following Muḥammad's death can be traced to these legislative revelations.

Revelations pertaining to women, their rights and obligations, their status in society and in the family, have been carefully recorded and often portrayed in vivid and realistic terms. Other revelations dealing with slaves, their treatment and liberation; with orphans, minors, the needy and destitute of all sorts, have provided the cornerstone for the social structure of Islam.

While we endeavor to focus attention on Muḥammad's religious and social achievements, we must also take notice of the moral forces awakened by him in forging a coherent nation out of a most unwieldy conglomeration of tribes and systems of belief. "Half Christian and half Pagan, half civilized and half barbarian, it was given to him in a marvelous degree to unite the peculiar excellences of the one with the peculiar excellences of the other."[24]

By moral persuasion, and by coercion when called for, Muḥammad won Arabia over to the worship of the one and only God. He instilled in its wild tribes the will to fraternize rather than to continue their fratricidal wars and vendettas; to cohere rather than to pull apart when there was no precedent for cohesion in Arabia outside the tribe, and to abandon long established and hallowed practices and beliefs when until his advent they experienced none other.

A partial testimony to the type of change wrought by Muḥammad's message is preserved in the apocryphal statement attributed to his cousin Ja'far, the son of Abu Ṭālib, in his address to the Negus of Abyssinia when the early Muslims had sought refuge there:

> Jāhilīyah people were we, worshiping idols, feeding on dead animals, practicing immorality, deserting our families and violating the covenant terms of mutual protection, with the strong among us devouring the weak. Such was our state until Allah sent unto us a messenger from amongst ourselves whose ancestry we know and whose veracity, fidelity and purity we recognize. He it was who summoned us to Allah in order to profess Him as one and worship Him alone, discarding whatever stones and idols we and our forbears before us worshiped in His stead. He moreover commanded us to be truthful in our talk, to render to others what is due them, to stand by our families and to refrain from doing wrong and shedding blood. He forbade committing fornication, bearing false witness, depriving the orphan of his legitimate right and speaking ill of chaste women. He enjoined on us the worship of Allah alone, associating with Him no other. He also or-

> dered us to observe prayer, pay *zakāh* [alms] (*sic*) and practice fasting.[25]

Muḥammad brought to his people what men of faith construe the commandments of God, as Moses and Jesus had brought similar commandments to their peoples before him. These commandments are eloquently enshrined in the Qurʾān in such verses as:[26]

> Set not up with Allah any other god (O man) lest thou sit down reproved, forsaken.
>
> Thy Lord hath decreed, that ye worship none save Him ...(that ye show) kindness to parents...and lower unto them the wing of submission through mercy, and say: My Lord! Have mercy on them both as they did care for me when I was little.
>
> If ye are righteous, then lo! He is ever Forgiving unto those who turn (unto Him).
>
> Give the kinsman his due, and the needy, and the wayfarer, and squander not (thy wealth) in wantonness.
>
> And let not thy hand be chained to thy neck nor open it with a complete opening, lest thou sit down rebuked, denuded.
>
> And come not near unto adultery. Lo! It is an abomination and an evil way.
>
> Slay not your children, fearing a fall to poverty, We shall provide for them and for you. Lo! The slaying of them is great sin.
>
> And slay not the life which Allah hath forbidden save with right.
>
> Come not near the wealth of the orphan save with that which is better till he come to strength; and keep the covenant.
>
> Fill the measure when ye measure, and weigh with a right balance; that is meet, and better in the end.
>
> (O man), follow not that whereof thou hast no knowledge. Lo! The hearing and the sight and the heart—of each of these it will be asked.
>
> And walk not in the earth exultant. Lo! Thou canst not rend the earth, nor canst thou stretch to the height of the hills.

Other verses selected at random equally portray the essence of Islam's commandments as revealed unto Muḥammad and taught by him:[27]

> Fear ye the Lord who from a single soul ye didst create ...and therefrom its mate...
>
> And give to the orphans their due...to the women their dowries.
>
> Devour not possessions amongst yourselves by means unlawful...
>
> And covet not that whereby Allah hath shown distinction for some over others... Ask Allah of His bounty...
>
> And show kindness to parents and to kindred, and orphans, and the needy, and the neighbor...
>
> Approach not prayer when you are not in full possession of your senses...nor when you are unclean.
>
> Verily Allah commands you to make over trusts to those entitled to them and that...ye judge justly between men.
>
> O ye who believe! Obey Allah, and obey His messenger and those who are in authority among you.
>
> Whatever of good befalleth thee it is from Allah, and whatever of ill befalleth thee it is from thyself.
>
> Fight, therefore, in the cause of Allah...and urge on the believers...

The Qur'ān explicitly enjoins the believer to avoid "the evil of all that is hateful in the sight of thy Lord."[28] Muḥammad is reminded that "this is (part) of that wisdom wherewith thy Lord hath inspired thee..." and commanded to "set not up with Allah another God, lest thou be cast into hell, reproved, abandoned."[29]

Muḥammad in his lifetime faithfully carried out what he regarded the will of God. Millions of Muslims never doubted that he was genuinely commissioned by Allah to deliver His commandments to those who believed in Him. Yet for a long time, well through the Middle Ages and up to the Age of the Enlightenment, Muḥammad's prophethood and message remained the object of suspicion and controversy. In his biography of Muḥammad Prideaux treated the Prophet's life as "a mirror to unbelievers, atheists, deists, and libertines." Nearly a century earlier a prominent Orientalist when using the name of Muḥammad felt impelled to qualify it with the statement: "at the mention of whom the mind shudders...[30]

In his *Vie de Mahomet* published posthumously, the Count de Boulainvilliers went to the opposite extreme and attempted to "portray Moḥammed as a wise and enlightened lawgiver, who sought to establish a reasonable religion in place of the dubious dogmas of Judaism and Christianity."[31] Two decades later Savary published a translation of the Qurʾān in which he treated Muḥammad "as one of those unusual personalities occasionally appearing in history, who remake their environment and enlist men in their triumphant train."[32] When at about the same time Voltaire attacked the Qurʾān and Muḥammad in his *Mahomet ou le fanatisme,* he was not motivated by Christian disdain for Islam and its prophet but rather by his intense dislike of fanaticism of which Muḥammad in his eyes was a good example.[33] Later in his *Essai sur les moeurs,* Voltaire tones down his judgment and grants recognition to the accomplishments of Muḥammad upon which his claim to fame rests. In 1840 when he delivered his second lecture on "Heroes and Hero-Worship," Thomas Carlyle stated the prevalent view of Muḥammad as "an impostor, an incarnation of falsehood, and that his religion was a combination of charlatanism and stupidity." But he hastened to mention that "such a view is a reflection upon ourselves." "For countless people," he argued, "Mohammed's words have been the guiding star of their lives. Can it be possible that so many creatures, created by God, have lived and died for something which must be regarded as a tragic fraud?"[34] Yet to this day the name of the Prophet Muḥammad is evoked by nearly a billion faithful only with the qualifying phrase, "peace be upon him." The same respect is accorded by Muslims to all the other prophets. It is only proper that peace should be with him given his legacy both as a leader and a prophet.

CHAPTER 5

Foundations of Islam: The Qur'ān

AT THE CORE of Islam lies the Qur'ān, the Word of God. To a religion that has no ecclesiastical organization, mystical ritual, a body of saints whose aid the troubled soul may invoke (unless he subscribes to a mystical or sufi order), the way Christians do, the Qur'ān remains the principal inspiration and refuge for the Muslim. More than representing the supreme embodiment of the sacred beliefs of Islam, its bible and its guiding light, the Qur'ān constitutes the Muslim's main reference not only for matters spiritual but also for the mundane requirements of day to day living.

The Qur'ān is more widely read than any other sacred text; indeed, more portions of it are committed to memory than those of any other similar body of sacred writings. The Muslim's extensive dependence on the Qur'ān makes of it the principal recourse both in the performance of religious duties and in the acquisition of basic knowledge. To him the Qur'ān has profound historical and literary meaning besides serving as his manual of prayer, code of religious and ethical well-being, his guide to social behavior and daily living, and a compendium of useful definitions and maxims of practical value. It is a repository of historical knowledge as unfolded by God and revealed unto the believers as a reminder. It is also the basic textbook for all Muslim youth studying the Arabic language in its present form.

As a magnificent piece of rhymed prose, it yields not only aesthetic contentment but provides also much philosophic truth. It is a valuable tool to the lexicographer seeking to perfect the language, to the scientist probing for clues concerning the existence of man and of the world, to the historian seeking understanding of the purpose of life as ordained by God for mankind, and to the theologian who regards the Qurʾān as the ultimate unchallengeable recourse for all religious knowledge. The Muslim jurist finds in the Qurʾān the basic laws governing Islamic society. Indeed no book, sacred or non sacred, has served, and continues to serve, so utilitarian a function to so many millions as the Qurʾān, Allah's gift to the Arabs through His messenger Muḥammad.

Conception

The term "*Qurʾān*" in a literal sense means "recitation," "readings," that is, of a prototype, a "concealed book" or a "well-guarded tablet" which in Muslim theology is supposed to rest in the Seventh Heaven. The Qurʾān more specifically refers to the body of these "readings." Perhaps one may refer to it as a "lectionary," of the type known to the ancient Aramaeans. The Arabs often refer to it as "*al-Kitāb*" (the book), that is, of Allah. Each chapter in the Qurʾān is termed "*sūrah*" (literally, series). Those who studied the Qurʾān called these *sūrahs* "revelations"; indeed, the term *revelation* is more appropriate in describing the process by means of which Muḥammad received the Qurʾān from God.

The sanctity of the Qurʾān lies in the Muslim consideration of the text as the official word of God and of Muḥammad as the appointed mouthpiece of God. Muḥammad is said to have received the *sūrahs* from the archangel Gabriel, the go-between. The manner of transmission is known as "*tanzīl*" (literally, causing to descend), that is, from heaven, bits by bits, readings from the "prototype of scriptures," the original word which Jews and Christians previously had received through the aegis of prophets who like Muḥammad had been commissioned to deliver God's sacred message to mankind.

This series of readings for which Muḥammad was called upon by Gabriel to deliver to the Arabs, who hitherto had lacked a body of sacred text, was to be in Arabic, "the language of the angels," as verified by the Qurʾān:

> We have made it an Arabic Qurʾān that we (Arabs) may see the truth. And it is truly in the mother of books (scriptures) with Us (preserved), most exalted and wise.[1]

The text was revealed to Muḥammad piecemeal over a span of two decades as the occasion required. The orthodox theologians in the century following Muḥammad's death advanced the premise that the Qurʾān is uncreated, being as it were the word of God. A school of rationalist thinkers in the third century of the Hijrah boldly proclaimed the opposite view, namely, that it was created. Modern deconstructionists, mainly European scholars, have boldly stated that the Qurʾān should be treated as a historical document subject to modern notions of critical analysis as has the Bible in recent times.[2]

Perhaps one reason for the differing conceptions of the Qurʾān's background lies in the seeming contradictions to the untrained eye. The orthodox theologians had insisted that the duty of the faithful was to accept it literally and not to question the tenor or meaning of the revelations. In the twenty-three years of Muḥammad's prophethood, revelations were received as the occasion merited. Chronology was not the factor, and what appeared out of focus at first was usually set in perspective by further revelation at a later date. Many of the revelations were recorded in the Prophet's lifetime, often under his own supervision, albeit the final recension of the Qurʾān was made after his death. Henceforth, the only avenue left for further clarification was exegesis. While the wording of the verses was important, Muḥammad stressed content instead. Indeed, it has been alleged that he himself often determined the order of verses during prayer sessions, relayed later by his followers and immediate companions. Western scholars who point to the role of exegesis as an indication of incomplete wording often neglect to mention that it resulted more often from lexical and philological discrepancies than from confused wording.

Arrangement

Those unfamiliar with the historical evolution of the Qur'ān find the arrangement difficult to understand. The ordering of the *sūrahs* follows no particular chronological or contextual pattern. Those reading the Qur'ān for the first time are struck by the apparent disjointed fashion in which the *sūrahs* are arranged and by the rather "odd headings" selected for each. In the choices available for arranging the content of the Qur'ān, a system of classification according to substance was impracticable because of the variety of subjects treated under any one heading. A chronological system, however welcome it may have been, was out of the question because the date of the earlier revelations was imperfectly known, and because a number of passages belonging to different dates had been joined together.

This has led Western observers to see stylistic inconsistencies in the arrangement of chapters and verses. At first the individual revelations were distinguished from each other only by the superscription: "In the name of God the compassionate the Most merciful."[3] Headings and numbering of verses were absent in the original codices and still form no integral part of the holy script. Those Western scholars found it relevant for understanding the content that attention be paid to both the time and circumstance of revelation.

We have, by way of example, revelations recognizing the two pagan deities, al-ʿUzzah and al-Lāt as the daughters of Allah; we have also revelations rescinding the same. This suggests a much different time frame. To Muḥammad there was no contradiction here because if Allah is absolute and arbitrary, why should there be any restraint on what He commands and forbids? Allah may vary His ordinances at pleasure, prescribing one set of laws for the Jews, another for the Christians, and still another for Muslims.

The total *sūrahs* of the Qurʾān number 114. They vary in length from 287 verses ("*al-Baqarah*") to 3 ("*al-Naṣr*" and "*al-Kawthar*"). The verses themselves are of very unequal length; some consist of two words,[4] while others run for nearly half a page.[5] Each, treated as a separate chapter or contextual unit, focuses on a particular subject, often carrying over into another unit.

Since an arbitrary mode of arrangement was unavoidable, it is not surprising that the redactors should adopt the one prevailing, arraying, in descending order, the longer ones first and the shorter *sūrahs* at the end. The exceptions most noticed are the very last two which contextually appear to lack continuity with the main body of the text. Similarly and by reason of its contents, *Sūrah I* (the "Fātiḥah") is placed at the beginning, partly because it praises Allah in the same vein that Psalm I praises the righteous man and largely because it gives classical expression to important articles of faith.

The longest *sūrahs*, which come first, relate to the period of Muḥammad's role as head of the community in Medina; the shorter ones, embodying mostly his ethical teachings came earlier, during his prophethood in Mecca; yet in the order followed by the Qurʾān, they are to be found mostly in the latter part. Some of the verses betray clearly traces of amalgamation, fused together for a variety of reasons at the time of the Qurʾān's codification even though they are the result of distinct occasions of revelation.

Each *sūrah* usually ends with the epitaph "Meccan" or "Medinan" to indicate the place of revelation. In the case of the composite *sūrahs*, segments thereof belong to entirely different periods, overlapping in terms of place as well as time of revelation.

Some Western scholars have regarded this arrangement as motivated purely by mechanical considerations. This on the surface may be the case; but actually were we to observe closely the closing lines of some *sūrahs* and the opening lines of those immediately following each, we would detect some sort of continuity. In the "*Fātiḥah,*" for instance, the believer invokes God to point the right path to Him; immediately following, in the chapter termed "*al-Baqarah*" (the cow) the first six verses provide the principal points of "the path," or what can be described as the embodiment of the cardinal doctrine of Islam. The same type of continuity in trend of thought can be seen in the chapter "*al-ʿImrān*" (the family of ʿImrān) which ends with injunctions carried over into the following chapter, "*al Nisāʾ*" (the women).

The manner of dividing or providing breaks in *sūrahs* varies from version to version. Each *sūrah* usually received a title based on the occasion that might have invoked the revelation. The process of titling dates back to the second Muslim century.

Since the Qurʾān was intended for oral recitation, the *sūrahs* were organized into seven sections each called a "*ḥizb*" or "*manzil*." This arrangement is said to have taken place at the insistence of the Prophet himself in order to facilitate the reading of the whole Qurʾān in one week's time. Those who relayed this information use it as proof of the Prophet himself having a hand in the editing and completion of the holy text's organization in his lifetime.

Dividing the Qurʾānic text in subsequent times into four, eight or thirty parts is for the practical purpose of committing the Qurʾān to memory.

Style

The style of expression underlying the Qurʾān is a curious blend of poetic rhymed prose and a lyrical flow, familiar modes of expression to the pre-Islamic Arab. Whether owing to accident or design, the sacred text was particularly adaptable for oral recitation, a carry over from the Jāhilīyah when this method of expression was most popular in Arabia. Stylistically the Qurʾān shows the strong predominance of *sajʿ* (rhymed prose), a form of rhyme which adheres to no meter, but was popularly utilized by the soothsayers of pagan Arabia.

The choice of modes of expression available to Muḥammad was limited; for precedent he had either rhymed prose without meter or poetry (*shiʿr*) with meter. The latter he consciously rejected because of his strong antipathy for the pagan poet who utilized this style and who was allegedly in league with the *jinn*, by whom he was supposed to be inspired, while Muḥammad took pains to dissociate himself from being in league with any other spirit but Allah's. His antipathy to the poet is reflected in the Qurʾān: "It is indeed the saying of a noble messenger and not of a poet little of which you will believe."[6]

Some say Muḥammad disdained the poet because he felt himself lacking in poetical talents; others say it was the person of the poet he found repugnant but not his style. Understandably he who considered himself divinely guided could not identify himself with someone moved by the *jinn,* inferior creatures created by Allah. "And as for the poets, it is the erring ones who follow them; dost thou not see them wandering aimlessly in every vale preaching that which they do not believe."[7]

While the Prophet vehemently denounced the *shāʿir* (poet) and dissociated himself from him, his unconscious affinity with the poet shows up in certain *sūrahs*, which for all practical purposes are "charms against magic and diablerie."[8]

> Say, I seek refuge in the Lord of the dawn, from the evil He has created, from the evil of the night when it overspreads…from the evil of one who envies…[9]
>
> Say, I seek refuge in the Lord of mankind…from the evil of the sneaking whisperer, who whispers into the hearts of men, who is of the jinn and of man…[10]

This affinity is seen also in the solemn imprecation whereby the Prophet invokes the visitation of destruction upon his own uncle ʿAbd al-ʿUzzah (servant of ʿUzzah, the female pagan deity) whom the nephew referred to as "Abu Lahab" (father of flame):

> Perish the hands of Abu Lahab and perish he!
> His wealth shall avail him naught, nor what he hath gotten in fee
> Burned in blazing fire he shall be!
> And his wife, the faggot-bearer, also she.[11]

Neither *sajʿ* nor *shiʿr,* on the other hand, can explain the full style adapted to the text of the Qurʾān. In many of the non-Meccan *sūrahs* there is a flowing lyrical style which is characteristically the Prophet's; it represents his own contribution, and lacks a precedent in the earlier rhetoric used.

Neither form nor style necessarily follows a haphazard arrangement. The utility seen in both lies in the fact that the Qur'ān was intended to leave an impact on the *listener,* which could be achieved only by means of oral recitation. The motive is somewhat psychologically conceived. His audience being principally illiterate, the word they appreciated most was the oral. Hence by design more than accident, the target of Muḥammad's preachings became sensitized to the power of the rhymed word of Allah which, like the rhetorical utterances of the *shāʿir* in yesteryears, was to light his aesthetic soul in an era when rhyme reigned supreme in the environs of ʿUkāz.

Biblical Affinities

A Jew or Christian familiar with the contents of the Biblical, Apocryphal, Talmudic, or Midrashic literatures would be struck by the extent of the Qur'ān's dependence on them. With the exception of a few narratives purely Arabian in origin, namely, the stories referring to ʿĀd, Thamūd, and Luqmān, and two alluding to dhu 'l-Qarnayn (the two-horned one or Alexander the Great), and the "Seven Sleepers," all other such narratives have their biblical parallels.

What would be obvious to the Jew or Christian is the discrepancy between the Biblical-Midrashic and Qur'ānic version of the same narrative. It is clear to the expert that concern was less with the details of these accounts than with the moral underlying them. Such narratives in the Qur'ān aimed at reinforcing points that God wished to emphasize in revealing them to Muḥammad. His was a didactic approach; and like his predecessors among the prophets of the Semites, he illustrated his themes forcefully and convincingly.

Muḥammad's interest in the sacred literature of Christians and Jews may reflect his own conception of the Islam he preached as the perfection of that religion which God had ordained for Jews, Christians, and now Arabs submitting to Him in Islam. Muḥammad made it amply clear that the religion he preached was the same religion God willed for Abraham, Moses, and Jesus. If Islam were indeed the perfection of God's religion, then the prophets of God, encompassing nearly all those cited in the Testaments, become of singular importance to Muḥammad's mission and his role as a prophet. If Christianity and Judaism, however imperfect they may have appeared to Muḥammad, were expressions of earlier religions willed by Allah, then Muḥammad must show Islam's ties therewith; otherwise from the point of view of basic principles and personalities instrumental in shaping these earlier religions of Allah, Muḥammad's mission would have been deemed redundant and unwarranted.

Hence by force of necessity Muḥammad considered it essential to the credibility of his mission that he set straight the erroneous interpretations given by Jews and Christians to Allah's religion and, more important, to justify his break with his Jewish adversaries when the occasion called for it. This would also account for the frequent occurrence in the Qur'ān not only of biblical themes, but of biblical narratives and personalities as well.

The inconclusive manner in which these narratives survive in the Qur'ān, moreover, often in vague and sometimes in erroneous confusion, for example where Muḥammad mistakes Miriam, Moses' sister for Mary, Jesus' mother, suggests that he derived his knowledge of these accounts and personalities either from uninformed sources or from informants, perhaps Monophysite Christians, whose views of their religion did not comport with the orthodox version of the same. The motive, nevertheless, clearly shows through his narration of these accounts: to illustrate more forcefully the main theme of God's great design for man, namely, to reward the righteous and punish the wicked. Although his knowledge of the Scriptures was not as deep as that of the experts, it enabled him, at least to his own satisfaction, to meet the criticism of his Jewish adversaries in Medina; criticism which lapsed so strongly into derision that he could eliminate it only by uprooting the Jews from the city and its environs.

Muḥammad's conception of Islam's role in the cosmic order ordained by the great architect may have resulted in the incorporation of biblical themes into the sacred text. The Qur'ān endorses the story of the creation of Adam and the angels' worship of him. We find in it biblical narratives relating to the flood and the role of Noah; the patriarchate of Abraham and his deliverance from the fire which Nimrod made to destroy him; the stories of Cain and Abel, Joseph and his brothers, Jacob and the tribes, David and Solomon, and numerous others connected with the Old Testament prophets. New Testament accounts, such as the role of Jesus, his "virgin birth," his childhood, denial of the crucifixion, and how Jesus foretold the coming of Muḥammad are also integrated into the Qurʾān. There are narratives on Mary, John the Baptist, and Zachariah.

These personalities and accounts are mustered into the Qurʾān in order to illustrate the purport of his mission; to explain and justify his position in God's design for mankind as it will be revealed on the Day of Judgment. The numerous stories and legends created "were added for homiletic purposes or to demonstrate the supernatural origin of his knowledge."[12]

The biblical narratives and tales of wrath suited Muḥammad well in his capacity as *nadhīr* (warner) battling to win over to Allah his Meccan and his Medinan opponents, whether they were pagan or Jewish. He fought them often with their own weapons, turning the testimony of the Scriptures against the Jews as supporting evidence of Allah's predictable wrath if the unbelievers should persist in their obstinacy, resistance, persecution, or derision of the believers in Him. There were ample supporting tales of vengeance in the Old and New Testaments; also varied samples of the destruction visited upon the disbelievers of earlier times and the persecutors of God's children such as the Egyptians, the "people of Lot," of Noah, ʿĀd, and Thamūd.

The main purport of the Qurʾān in the context of its historical evolution is two-fold: a call to belief in the one God, the supreme repository of all moral law and ethical guidance and, secondly, the establishment of the practical guides and precepts necessary for organizing the believers into a coherent community that would assure the triumph of the religious force that called it into being in the first instance.

This dual aim falls into a sequential order: the pre-Hijrah period, which was devoted to the task of making converts; and the post-Hijrah decade dedicated to organizing the community of believers. A study of the revelations received during both periods, taking into account the overlaps, clearly supports this observation.

The Meccan Period

In the Meccan period of the evolution of the Qur᾿ān, Muḥammad preoccupies himself with persuading his skeptical listeners to turn away from their idol gods and worship the one God. Regardless of how he uses his arguments or orients his discourse, the aim is the same; so is his target. He resorted to reason, logical proof, and fair exhortation in his attempts at persuasion just as often as he resorted to threats of impending doom. The central theme plays up the greatness, goodness, and righteousness of God as manifested in nature, history, and His revelations to Muḥammad. God is depicted in most exalted terms. His omnipotence and omniscience are continuously stressed.

There is no god but Allah. Muḥammad is His messenger, the Qur᾿ān His word. Idolatry and all deification of created beings are imposingly condemned.

> Say, God is one; God who liveth on without father and without son, and like unto whom there is none.[13]
>
> They surely disbelieve who say God is the third of three. There is no God but He. And if they desist not from what they say, a painful punishment lies for the blasphemer in bay.[14]

The joys of heaven and the pains of hell are portrayed in most vivid sensuous terms, as is also the fear and terror which will seize mankind on that awesome day, "When the sky shall be severed, and the stars shivered, and when the seas to mingle shall be suffered, and the graves uncovered."[15] This day of reckoning will bring man before his Creator, "A Day when one soul shall not obtain anything for another soul, but the command on that Day shall be with God alone."

It is then that "A soul shall know that which it hath deferred or delivered" and it will be asked "… what beguiled thee against thy gracious Master to rebel, who created thee and fashioned thee right...?" Then comes the confrontation, "Nay, but ye disbelieve in the Ordeal (last judgment)" and the judgment "Surely the pious in delight shall dwell, and the wicked shall be in Hell, burning there on the Day of Ordeal, and evermore Hellfire they shall feel!"

Such are samples of the Meccan *sūrahs*; they are shorter but more numerous than the Medinan *sūrahs*, and executed for the most part in a different strain, forming practically a distinct group from the latter.

Not much can be learned about the date of their revelation as we lack reliable traditions on the subject. Indeed, our knowledge of the whole period preceding the Hijrah is insufficient to provide insight into the time and circumstance of the revelation of Meccan *sūrahs*. These, however, encompass moral legislation, the various stories and legends attributed to Christian and Judaic sources which Muḥammad must have derived from oral narrators, the legends which were adapted to Qur'ānic cosmogony, and the colorful depiction of God's design for man and the world.

The Prophet in the opinion of certain authorities[16] often expressed himself with "utmost vehemence," even allowing himself to be carried away emotionally. The words "seem rather to burst from him," in the fashion of the old soothsayer's utterances. The *sūrahs* resemble, according to the same view, oracles in their brevity: short crisp sentences in relatively constant but frequently changing rhyme. The oaths with which some begin also follow the pattern of expression used by the soothsayers.

But not all the *sūrahs* of this period are so vividly expressed. The older ones appear to reflect the calmer moods of the Prophet, yet still it is not possible for us to date them chronologically. One may surmise, however, that the increasing passion of expression was the result of obstinate resistance to the message; otherwise it would be difficult to account for the terrible threats thundered out by Muḥammad against those who ridiculed the preaching of the unity of God, of the Resurrection, and of the Judgment. When his uncle Abu Lahab rudely repelled him, he immediately consigned him and his wife to hell in a brief special *sūrah* with which Allah obliged Muḥammad.

In vividly portraying the everlasting bliss of the pious and the torments awaiting the wicked, the lyrical, abrupt, and moving nature of these *sūrahs* left a strong impact on the imagination of simple men who had not been conditioned in their youth by strong religious preconceptions. While the earlier Meccan *sūrahs* reflected more the fiery and enthusiastic imagination of Muḥammad and less his ideas and abstract thought on which exact reasoning depends, the later ones were more mundane, animated, and prosaic in tone. The periods are drawn out, the revelations longer; the histories of the earlier prophets, briefly related in the first period, are now more fully detailed.

The first *sūrah* of the Qur'ān, the Muslim equivalent of the Lord's Prayer, belongs to this intermediate Meccan period; it is simple in wording but full of meaning and implication for the faithful.

> In the name of God, the compassionate, the most merciful.
> Praise is to God, Lord of the worlds.
> The compassionate, the most merciful
> Master of the Day of Judgment.
> Thee alone we worship and thee alone for help we pray.
> Show us the right path,
> The path of those whom Thou hast favored;
> Not of those who have incurred Thine wrath
> Nor of those who have gone astray.

This simple prayer is the most often repeated of all, no less than twenty times a day, by every Muslim who performs his daily ritual prayers with its emphasis on the compassionate nature of God as *al-Raḥmān*. Indeed, so much did Muḥammad refer to God as *al-Raḥmān* that it was a matter of conjecture for a while whether he would not formally adopt *al-Raḥmān* for the proper name of God.

The *sūrahs* of the later Meccan or third period form a large part of the Qur'ān. They are almost entirely in prose; both the revelations and the verses are somewhat longer. The practical fieriness of the earlier *sūrahs* is considerably toned down. The Prophet's proclivity for the sermonizing effect is much more accentuated. This may be due to the fact that the message's effect had been largely achieved and the propagation of Islam through these later Meccan *sūrahs* was much more successfully assured.

The Medinan Period

It is in the revelations received in Medina that the historical message of Islam as embodied in the Qur'ān becomes easier to perceive. We are able now to trace the event which occasioned the revelation. These *sūrahs*, by and large, are much easier to assimilate because they allude to accomplished facts and events.

They are more prosaic in style. They also abound in legislative injunctions. Since these *sūrahs* reflect the triumphant establishment of the religion and of the Muslim community, they are more assured in tone, more aggressive and conquering. It is now the voice of the chief that speaks, the voice of the lawgiver and statesman who is detailing rules of conduct for the believers in God.

These revelations are much more heterogeneous in derivation and practical in nature as they are tailored to meet the sociopolitical needs of an organized community, the community of believers in Medina. The style resembles that of the later Meccan *sūrahs*: pure prose enriched occasionally by rhetorical embellishments. In them can be detected the injunctions and impressive proclamations of Allah to the faithful.

It is in the Medinan *sūrahs* that we find the Qur'ān's contextual affinity with biblical themes. We noted earlier parallels between a number of narratives and interpretations given in the Qur'ān and in biblical texts. We also observed that a goodly number of these parallel Judaic sources. Only a few seem to show connection with Christian topics. The reason for this lies in the relative absence of Christian dwellers in Medina and its environs at the time of Muḥammad's leadership there.

There are certain scholars,[17] however, who believe that concepts and notions of Judeo-Christian religious themes were sufficiently established in the principal cities of the Ḥijāz to enable someone interested in them to acquire some sort of a frame of reference. But the historical record, which points to sharp resistance to Muḥammad's preachings, coupled with minimum conversions to Islam of non-pagan tribesmen, does not uphold the theories of such scholars.

Nevertheless, similarities in doctrinal and cultic concepts are too strong and numerous not to suggest some sort of affinity, most probably derived from oral sources close to Muḥammad, like his wife Khadījah's cousin Nawfal. Muḥammad in his youth, long before he saw himself a prophet in the making, had occasions to come in contact with Christians knowledgeable in the workings of their faith, like the monk Baḥīra, perhaps during his caravan journeys north into Syria where the Christian sects were numerous and the monks ready to discuss the principles of their beliefs with listeners. It would be farfetched, however, to accept the views of those who state that Muḥammad may have attended meetings in which a miscellany of missionaries representing Christian sects and other preachers recounted biblical topics and a mass of Judeo-Christian lore deriving not immediately from the Scriptures but from the post-canonical periphery—Aggada, Targum, Midrash of the Jews, and the apocryphal, patristic, homilitical, and liturgical literature of the Christians.

Affinity with the Scriptures

It is interesting to observe here that during the first period of his mission when Muḥammad took for granted the support of those already believing in the Scriptures, he saw no reason or need to scrutinize the obvious discrepancies between the revelations he received and those already recorded by Christians and Jews through earlier messengers. When the resistance of the Jews mounted during the Medinan period, and when Muḥammad became disappointed for not being acknowledged by the "People of the Book" as a messenger in his own right after he had acknowledged the validity of their scriptures, he was impelled to defend his mission by distinguishing between the *true* content of the Scriptures and what the Jews and Christians claimed them to be.

A consequential development of this rejection of Muḥammad by those with whom he displayed spiritual kinship was the Arabization of Islam. While he did not renounce cultic rituals and rites already adopted, he did give them often a peculiarly Arabian orientation. Instead of Jerusalem, Mecca becomes the primary home of Islam and the Kaʿbah its most sacred shrine; Friday, not Saturday or Sunday becomes the equivalent of the Sabbath though officially it is not a day of rest; the faithful are called to prayer by the voice of the muezzin, not by bells, trumpets, or gongs; and Jesus, not Moses, becomes the second most important prophet.

Having despaired of winning over the Jews he referred to the Christians as Jews who believed: *Naṣārah*, or "*Anṣār Allāh*" (partisans of Allah), hoping they would be less hostile to and more receptive of the message even though in the early years he had far less contact with them than he had with the Jews of Medina. Still he did not absolve the Christians of error when thematic or doctrinal conflict arose; they were accused also of having corrupted the Scriptures.

The substance of the Prophet's early utterances shows a broadly derivative and eclectic nature, which suggests that the frame and structure of the early *sūrahs* may have consciously emulated Christian prototypes. It is not unlikely that later, when the Prophet in Medina faced the problems of legislating for an independent community predicated on entirely new norms and mores, Muḥammad sought relevant prototypes. Facing new issues involving law, cult, ritual, affairs of state and church, and the overriding necessity for immediate and decisive action consonant with the exigencies of the moment, Muḥammad may well have found in related precedents (ordained previously by the same deity to peoples so privileged) the supporting aids he needed to gain credence for his message.

The fundamental similarity in the concepts of the Bible and the Qurʾān show not only the integral relationship and basic kinship of both, but reveal also the conscious identification of the Qurʾān with God's basic design that began on the day of creation of the world and of Adam, and which shall continue until that day, the Day of Judgment, when the Lord's unfoldment of history shall end.

The Allah of the Qurʾān is the Lord, Jehovah and God of the Bible. As He previously entered into personal relationships with those who formerly had believed in Him, so does He again establish ties with those who seek Him out, even though it was necessary for Him to send the "reminder" once more. He is the one and same creator who governs the worlds and the affairs of men, His dependent creatures. As ruler of the universe He rules history; hence rewards and punishments are His way of settling accounts on a day of reckoning, when the dead are resurrected, body and soul together, to await that Last Day, the Judgment Day.

While no man can question His will and while His acts are not always in accordance with our desires, He is still the compassionate, most merciful and just, the one and only God.

So far the Qurʾān and Bible tally in their view of God; but there is an important difference: the God of Muḥammad does not come to man in incarnate form. Therefore, there are no intermediaries between Him and man; no interceders either. Man's account is directly with his Lord. There is no reference to Him as "father"—He was not begotten nor does He beget. He is detached from the petty annoyances and worries of man.

The concept of divine government reminds us of the Bible. All comes to pass by the decree of God. Notions of preordainment, or predestination or bondage of the will are likewise familiar. God both in the Bible and the Qurʾān plays a determinative role in the unbelief of man, in lending substance to the idea that some beings are led astray with God's knowledge, if not by His will. All is part of His great design for man and the world, which no one has the right to question.

Muḥammad's conception of his prophetic role is also familiar. The doctrine of revelation has both Semitic and Aryan antecedents, the schema may differ but the essence and purport are identical: Revelation is brought by an angel or a spirit, the chosen messenger speaks for God not himself when delivering the message, and as the Bible testifies, "The ego of the prophet disappears before the Higher ego (God)." The idea of the revelation being a transcript of the original preserved in the highest heaven and constituting a rule of faith and a prescription for life are identical in the sacred texts of Christians, Jews, and Muslims.

We see this close identity also in the common usage of terminology referring to the process of worship. Terms like *ṣalāh* (prayer), *sabbiḥ* (praise), *tazakka* (was purified), *ʿabd* (servant), *mathal* (parable), *iqraʾ* (recite), *malāʾikah* (angels) are the same in Islam, Christianity, and Judaism.

With language come ideas: what is meant by a prophet, a holy book, revelation, prayer, praise, angels, demons, heaven, and hell. These were known to Muḥammad, mostly indirectly through various media, through poets, monks, *ḥanīfs*, and traders from the *Ḥijāz* who alighted at Christian places of worship on caravan stops, and other such contacts.

Muḥammad's Logic

Credit must be given also to the powers of logical thinking within a predetermined framework of reference but emanating from the genius of the Prophet himself. Once you accept the premise "there is no god but God" who is the sole creator and ruler of the destiny of man; who points out the path to life everlasting for those who acquit themselves on the day of reckoning, then the doctrinal and cultic route to salvation, with the exception of detail, assumes a logical pattern. The religion of one God must per se resemble those that preceded it in accepting this premise. One God means one holy scripture, distortions and perversions notwithstanding. If the Christian Bible and the Jewish Torah should contain material that does not conform to the logic of the Prophet's conception of revelation, then the Qurʾān must serve as the final recension of God's testament.

Aids to assist man in his quest for life everlasting are important not because Jews and Christians already had them, but because it is God's desire that they should constitute an essential accompaniment of man on his journey to Him. Fasting was ordained for the believers in Medina after the Hijrah, and presumably following Muḥammad's brief association with Judeo-Christian cultic practices. Prayer likewise serves an important role, not because monks were observed to pray regularly, but because prayer according to a fixed and prescribed formula would serve a needed disciplinary role once the wild-spirited Bedouin was tamed for Allah and Islam. The promise of rewards was an inducement, the threat of Hell a deterrent; these too figured in Muḥammad's strategy for taming the pagan. The pilgrimage was to serve as a reminder of their common brotherhood; the tithe was to remind them of their obligations towards their less fortunate brethren. The stress on the absolute unity of God was to provide no excuse for the new converts to associate any of their rejected idol deities with Allah, and thus to eliminate a source of disunity and its attending strife, the evils of which precipitated the prophethood of Muḥammad.

Codification

The one hundred and fourteen *sūrahs* of the Qur'ān were revealed over a period of two decades. Many of the revelations were committed to memory upon their "descent." Numerous *sūrahs*, on the other hand, were recorded on various bits of parchment, palm leaves, smooth stones, and similar objects. Being principally illiterate, the Prophet himself did no writing; he had entrusted most of what had been recorded to his aide, Zayd ibn Thābit.

When Muḥammad died there existed no singular codex of the sacred text. While the memorizers were numerous, no one of them knew the whole. The revelations were scattered and were threatened with being lost. Oral transmission, moreover, was an unreliable method of preserving the Qur'ān because it left the door open sometimes to deliberate, but often to inadvertent, alterations. Disputations over the substance of the sacred text obviously could not be permitted, and the need for a uniform codex was soon in evidence.

Shortly after the death of Muḥammad, his father-in-law successor Abu Bakr (632–634) was compelled to reconquer Arabia for Islam. In the fighting that ensued, a good number of the Prophet's Companions, especially the *ḥuffāẓ* (sing. *ḥāfiẓ*: memorizer) among them, were killed. The short, but sanguinary, campaign in 633 against the false prophet or pretender Musaylimah also took its toll of the Companions. Abu Bakr was prevailed upon by ʿUmar, who later succeeded him as caliph (634–644), to undertake a formal codification of the Qurʾān.

Abu Bakr gave the twenty-two-year-old Zayd, aide to the Prophet, native of Medina where most of the revelations were to be found, the responsibility of codifying the revelations. Zayd proceeded to assemble the text from scattered sources but chiefly "from the breasts [memory] of men [the Companions]" as he put it. His efforts yielded the first assembled copy of the Qurʾān, which he handed over to the caliph. Abu Bakr at his deathbed bequeathed the codex to his successor ʿUmar who later turned it over to his daughter Ḥafsa, one of Muḥammad's widows.

This first redaction of the sacred text of Islam had no canonical authority, and the format pursued in arranging the revelations is not known. The Muslims had no access to it and not many could recite much of this official version from memory. Furthermore, serious quarrels soon erupted among the Muslim levies from the various districts of conquered lands over the true content of the Qurʾān, owing to a number of interpretations made possible by lexical difficulties.

It was especially during a serious military engagement, the battle of Nehavand in 650–51, that Ḥudhayfah, commander of the Muslim forces, became acutely aware of the serious consequences such disputations over the content of the holy text could have for future campaigns. It was he who prevailed upon the caliph ʿUthmān (644–656) to produce one authoritative universal version of the Qurʾān.

Once again the task was entrusted to Zayd. Assisted by a commission of three leading Qurayshites, Zayd assembled all available copies of the text and proceeded to dictate to the scribes the contents of the final redaction. The work was done in 657, twenty-five years after Muḥammad's death, the year when the caliph pronounced the text the official codex for all Muslims. The main copy was kept in Medina while three others were sent to the principal Muslim encampments at Baṣra and

Kūfa in Iraq and Damascus in Syria. All other copies were ordered destroyed.

Scholars have lamented the destruction of these non-authorized versions of the Qurʾān, a grave loss in their eyes from the point of view of textual criticism. The version established by ʿUthmān for all time is not complete according to certain critics who point to the fragmentary nature of some passages in support of their attestations. It is probable that a few detached pieces were left out of the final redaction when they had been a part of the earlier codex. It is not easy to prove, on the other hand, that Zayd willfully left out passages embarrassing to certain important converts once staunch opponents of Muḥammad. Nor can we tell whether he had been encouraged by the first three caliphs involved in the redaction of the Qurʾān to interpolate.

It is quite possible that Zayd in assembling the revelations did not have access to all previous versions. There is also the possibility of simple inadvertent clerical errors in the process of recording. Skeptics are of the opinion that Zayd prudently introduced some slight alterations to the wording of the revelations not readily detected. They have accused him also of permitting some "extras" to find their way into the official codex immediately preceding the final revision. These extras are said to ante-date both the Hijrah and, in the view of the extremists, even the Meccan period of Muḥammad's preachings.

Since no devout Muslim would willfully attempt to tamper with the word of God, we must assume that, by and large, the final codex is a faithful reproduction of the earlier version. Critics generally agree that the redaction sponsored by the caliph ʿUthmān contains none but genuine elements even though their arrangement is in disarray.

The content was fixed, but additional problems engendered by the use of the Arabic alphabet remained. These merit some attention if we are to appreciate the full range of the Qurʾān's textual history.[18] There were many words which could be read in different ways and persons who chose could read into the text what they looked for. There were discrepancies not only in the reading of the script, but also in pronouncing it.

Dialectical license in grammatical forms, which had not then been restricted, posed an additional problem. The sense of the words may not have varied, but readings did. Eventually seven possible readings of the Qurʾān became possible as a result of divergences, but with the passing of time they were reduced to two. When vowel signs, diacritical points, and other orthographic signs were invented to distinguish between similarly formed consonants, proper vocalization ensued and arbitrary conjecture on the part of the reader was virtually ended.

Yet the correct recitation of the Qurʾān was not necessarily enhanced thereby. This remains until today an art which even those most fluent in the Arabic language can not readily master. Recitation of the Qurʾān, even today, is aided by a semi-musical modulation which differs from one school to another of those concerned with the study of the Qurʾān.

Exegesis

Owing to the numerous obscurities inherent to the Qurʾān's format, it was very soon after the death of Muḥammad that certain individuals began to apply themselves to the task of interpreting these vague sections. Not all of those who set out on this important undertaking were qualified or honorable in intent. Indeed, even Ibn ʿAbbās, a first cousin of the Prophet and the earliest of the exegetes, gave currency to a number of falsehoods; some of his students appear to have followed his example. He and his students were less concerned with the exegesis of individual words than with the exposition of the meaning of whole passages.

With philology as a tool in later times, understanding the Qurʾān was simplified, and when with the lapse of time knowledge of the old language declined, more and more effort was expended on the explanation of vocables. Very few results of the hermeneutical efforts invested in the first two centuries of the Hijrah survive. This was the period when not only the opportunists, but also philologists, grammarians, and even philosophers set themselves to the task of explaining the difficulties in the Qurʾān.

One of the fullest and earliest of the important commentaries is Ṭabari's (839–923), executed in thirty parts.[19] This commentary contains elaborate data not only on canonical law but also on the circumstances of each revelation. While not all hopes were realized with this commentary, still in this conservatively faithful work we have the summation of all Qur'ānic knowledge of the first three centuries following the death of Muḥammad.

Another well known commentary is the *Kashshāf* of Zamakhshari[20] (1074–1144) which represents a more progressive tendency than Ṭabari's, but is equally respectful of the Qur'ānic text. Zamakhshari was an adherent of the Muʿtazilite or rationalistic school of philosophy and therefore less concerned with the accumulation of traditions than with the rational interpretation thereof. Zamakhshari delighted in uprooting traces favorable to determinism, anthropomorphism, intervention of the *jinn,* and in making distinctions between the *essence* and the *attributes* of God. Zamakhshari has been praised for his great insight and still greater subtlety but criticized for his aptness to read his own scholastic ideas into the Qur'ān.

Fakhr-al-Dīn al-Rāzi (d. 1209) was an anti-Muʿtazilite who inserted his own literary dissertations, philosophic and juridic, in what resembles less an exegesis and more a series of monographs. Still he was the last in the great line of exegetes. Later commentators like Bayḍāwi (d. 1286), who bequeathed us a most useful exegesis[21] even though it was but an abridgment of Zamakhshari's work, al-Maḥalli (d. 1495), and al-Suyūṭi (d. 1505) continued the work of exegesis by producing their own versions.

Numerous other commentaries have been written, some quite prodigious in size; Muslim and non-Muslim scholars disagree on their worth compared to earlier ones, yet they provide us with useful hints for a fuller understanding of the Qur'ān.

Translation

Officially the Qur'ān was not to be translated into other languages because Allah declared to Muhammad: "We have revealed unto thee an Arabic Qur'ān." By this the faithful understood that

Arabic was to be the sole language of the Qur'ān, particularly because it is a copy of the archtype preserved in heaven. Moreover, Arabic was the language in which the archangel Gabriel revealed the Qur'ān to Muḥammad and in which it was subsequently to be preserved. So for centuries the faithful, regardless of their native tongue, were taught to recite their Qur'ān in Arabic.

Unauthorized translations have since come into being in forty-three different languages including the interlinear free translations by Muslims into their respective native languages—Persian, Chinese, Urdu, Javanese, Maratti, Bengali[22] are among the few. The earliest translation was done into Latin by Peter the Venerable, Abbot of Cluny ca. 1141. The *'ulamā'* (ulema) officially accepted a Turkish rendition and in more recent times have managed to tolerate an English translation, that of Muḥammad Marmaduke Pickthall, but under the title "*The Meaning of the Glorious Koran.*"[23] Since then there have been a number of direct literal translations and even one (Dawood's) with rearranged *sūrahs*.

The earliest unauthorized English translation was from the French of Sieur Du Ryer. But perhaps the most highly regarded for a time was the extremely paraphrastic rendition of Gorge Sale (1734). Rodwell's translation (1861) represented a brave attempt to give the revelations in chronological order. Palmer wisely chose to retain the traditional arrangement in his translation (1880). Since then we have had translations by Bell (1937–39); Arberry (1955); Yūsuf Ali, which possesses a considerable amount of explanations; and Thomas Irving, which has marginal notations to guide the reader in locating a topic.

The more recent translations attempt a critical rearrangement of the *sūrahs* and are more abreast of modern scholarship. None, however, are entirely faithful to the letter of the original because of certain idiosyncrasies of the Arabic language which the most literate of Arab philologists can not always render with exactitude.

But the need for proper understanding of the holy word of Allah required meticulous and careful study. All relevant tools—philology, grammar, lexicography—were enlisted in the service of hermeneutics. The faithful in the succeeding centuries acquired, as a consequence, a whole body of literature bearing on the sacred text. There are books on the spelling and the right pronunciation, on the beauty of its language, its verses, words, letters, pertaining not only to philological but also to historical disciplines. Indeed, Arabic philology came into being as the handmaiden of the Qurʾānic text, being intimately connected with its recitation and exegesis.

"To exhibit the importance of the sacred book for the whole mental life of the Moslems would be simply to unite the history of that life itself," wrote the eminent German scholar Theodore Nöldeke. "The unbounded reverence of the Moslems for the Qurʾān reaches its climax in the dogma that this book, as the divine word, i.e., thought, is immanent in God, and consequently *eternal* and *uncreated*."

All Muslims with the exception of the Muʿtazilah accepted the dogma of *iʿjāz al-Qurʾān* (uncreatedness of the Qurʾān). No combination of man or supernatural forces can reproduce a fragment thereof, as it is a work existing from all eternity and unequaled.

This dogma of the uncreatedness of the Qurʾān may have been influenced by Christian sources. Some Muslim theologians did indeed protest against it, particularly when the rationalist school in Islam was strong during the caliphate of al-Maʾmūn (813–833), who was one of them. But the strong distinctions and sophisms propagated by Muʿtazilite theologians failed to override the view that came to prevail.

CHAPTER 6

The Fundamentals of Islam: Beliefs

MUSLIM THEOLOGIANS have postulated that Islam the faith is anchored in two fundamental conceptions: *īmān* (expression of faith) and *iḥsān* (right-doing). When *īmān* and *iḥsān* are buttressed by manifest acts of worship, *ʿibādāt,* the essentials of the religion of submission to Allah are enunciated.

The "Shahādah"

The one prerequisite for becoming a Muslim is to profess the *shahādah* (open testimony): *la ilāha illa ʾl-Lāh* [Allah] ("there is no god but God") with the essential concomitant that God is the sole and unassisted author of creation.[1] This holds validity not only for Islam, but also for all similarly revealed religions.

The open profession of belief in one God "who begotteth not nor was begotten" is accompanied by the second important pronouncement in the *shahādah: "wa Muḥammadan rasūlu ʾl-Lāh"* ("and Muḥammad is the messenger of God"). By uttering the first part of the *shahādah* one becomes a *muslim,* submitter to God; but when he pronounces the second part of the same, he becomes a *Muslim*, an adherent to the religion of Islam. The *shahādah* is the most frequently recited testimony in the daily life of the faithful.

To be a *practicing* Muslim, the adherent is obligated to acknowledge and apply the two basic fundamentals: Beliefs and Acts. Both are absolutely necessary for the establishment of one's faith as a Muslim. In partaking of Islam the believer acknowledges his dependence on God, his creator, sustainer and guide, and his solidarity with fellow believers.

By a combination of will and design inspired by an uncompromising belief in Allah, Muḥammad succeeded in reducing the essence of the doctrine and cultus that gave form and expression to Islam to the believer's level of comprehension and credibility. He inculcated his followers with the will to abide by the ordinances and injunctions of Allah and molded out of their profession of faith a community unified by belief in Allah and cohering through the common observance of prescribed acts of devotion. He preached complete submission, *islām*, to Allah.

"Al-Islām"

"Al-Islām" signifies the total submission to the will of God. The religion took on the title of "Islam" because Allah decreed it in the Qurʾān:

> Lo the religion with Allah is *al-Islām* (the Surrender) to His will and guidance.[2]

He who professes adherence to the faith is a "Muslim" (Submitter).

> He hath named you *Muslimūn* (Muslims)...of old time and in this (Scripture) that the messenger may be a witness against you, and that ye may be witnesses against mankind.[3]

Referring to a Muslim as "Mohammedan" is the result of a false analogy with "Christian," a worshiper of Christ. Muslims do not worship Muḥammad as Christians worship Christ.

Indeed, in Islamic doctrine the worship of anyone other than God is *shirk,* or association in worship, and constitutes the major unpardonable sin, *kabīrah.*

Since Allah prescribed the religion of Islam for the Arabs through His messenger Muḥammad, Islam becomes a divinely revealed religion like Judaism and Christianity. It is the same religion which Allah had previously revealed unto Abraham, who is considered the "first Muslim" after Adam.

> He hath revealed unto thee (Muḥammad) the Scripture with truth confirming that which was (revealed) before it, even as He revealed the Torah and the Gospel.[4]
>
> We gave it unto Abraham against his folk... And We bestowed upon him Isaac and Jacob; each of them We guided, and Noah did We guide aforetime; and of his seed (We guided) David and Solomon and Job and Joseph and Moses and Aaron... And Zacharia and John and Jesus and Elias. Each one (of them) was of the righteous...and We chose them and guided them unto a straight path... Those are they unto whom We gave the Scripture and command and prophethood. But if these disbelieve therein, then indeed We shall entrust it to a people who will not be disbelievers therein.[5]

The official view of Islam, as derived from the Qur᾽ānic verse "But if these disbelieve therein" is that Jews and Christians erred in their interpretation of Allah's Scripture, making it necessary for Allah to send "the Reminder."

Muḥammad's mission was thus foreordained on two counts: first, to set straight the tenets of the Scriptures; and second, to bring the true Scripture to the Arabs, descendants of Abraham, the first Muslim, but who were not aware of Allah's command to their forefather.

In another respect, Muḥammad's role was to fulfill the mission of his predecessors among the prophets and to eliminate the deviations that had set in. The aim of his own mission was not to replace but rather to complement the mission of his predecessors. With this understanding of his mission, Muḥammad called upon Christians and Jews to recognize his prophetic role and to accord him the consideration and respect accorded his predecessors.

> Say: O people of the Scripture! Come to an agreement between us and you: that we shall worship none but Allah, and that we shall ascribe no partner unto Him, and that none of us shall take others for lords beside Allah.[6]

Unlike his predecessors who had forecast the advent of successors, Muḥammad considered himself the last officially commissioned by God, the "Seal" (*khātimah*) even though, like them, he had served to bring "the Reminder."

> Lo! it is naught but a Reminder to (his) creatures. And they measure not the power of Allah its true measure when they say: Allah hath naught revealed unto a human being. Say (unto the Jews who speak thus): Who revealed the Book which Moses brought, a light and guidance for mankind, which ye have put on parchments which ye show, but ye hide much (thereof), and by which ye were taught that which ye knew not yourselves nor (did) your fathers (know it)? Say: Allah. Then leave them to their play of cavilling. And this is a blessed Scripture which We have revealed, confirming that which (was revealed) before it, that thou mayst warn the Mother of Villages[7] and those around…[8]

The fact that Muḥammad had not chosen a title for the message he was preaching until after the conquest of Mecca in 631 is significant. It is quite possible to see in this delay of over a decade some consideration of the extent to which he identified the basic tenets of the religion he preached with those he formally acknowledged to be divinely ordained. Indeed, it is commonly accepted by scholars that the verse imparting title to the faith he preached in his prophetic career is the very last in order of descent. It was during his "Farewell Pilgrimage" to Mecca and specifically his last formal address to the faithful at ʿArafāt, when all Arabia had embraced Islam, that Allah spoke to Muḥammad for the last time:

> This day are those who disbelieve in despair of (ever harming) your religion; so fear them not, fear Me! This day have I perfected your religion for you and completed My favor unto you, and have chosen for you as religion AL-ISLAM.[9]

Allah

A most crucial point in Islamic doctrine is the stress on Allah's absolute oneness. The Qur'ān is replete with the seriousness of the consequences awaiting those who ascribe any other entity to Allah.

> He unto Whom belongeth the sovereignty of the heavens and the earth, He hath chosen no son nor hath He any partner in the sovereignty.[10]

The orthodox Muslim (Sunni) conception of God may be summed up as follows: God is one; He has no partners; Singular without any like Him; Uniform, having no contrary; Separate, having no equal; Ancient, having no first; External, having no beginning; Everlasting, having no end; Ever-existing, without termination; Perpetual and constant, with neither interruption nor ending; Ever qualified with the attributes of supreme greatness; nor is He bound to be determined by lapse of ages or times. He is both the Alpha and the Omega, the Manifest and the Hidden. He is real.[11]

He is omnipresent, too exalted to be contained in any one place and too holy to be determined by time; for He existed before He created time and place, and He is now as he always existed. There is nothing like Him in His essence nor is there of His essence in any other besides Him. His holiness makes Him impervious to change and He is beyond contingencies. But He abides through all generations with His glorious attributes, free from all imperfection.

While Muslim theology takes pains to describe what God is, it conversely specifies what God *is not*:

> God is not a formed body; nor a measurable substance; neither does He resemble bodies, either in their being measurable

or divisible. Neither is he a substance, nor do substances exist in Him, neither is he an accidental form, nor do accidentals exist in him.

Allah in His essence is one, as He is in His attributes and acts; He is the all-mighty, judge of the universe and master of the Day of Judgment. He knows, sees, and hears everything. He is the creator of heaven and earth, of life and death. His knowledge is perfect, His will is beyond challenge, and His power is irresistible. All these qualities are manifest in His creation. While everything needs Him, He depends only upon things originated by Him. Allah is not identifiable with man, with whom His only connection is the fact He created him. All that which Allah created will return unto Him.

The principal elements of worship in Islam entail belief in God, His angels, scriptures revealed to believers in Him, the messengers, destiny (*gadar*), and the Day of Judgment. Recognition of God is the supreme manifestation of faith; indeed, over 90 percent of Muslim theology is concerned with Allah as the one real God who is indivisible in nature.

> Say! He is Allah, the one! Allah the eternally besought of all! He begotteth not nor was begotten. And like unto Him there is none!"[12]

The role of God as creator is heavily emphasized:

> Lo! your Lord is Allah Who created the heavens and the earth in six days, then mounted He the Throne. He covereth the night with the day, which is in haste to follow it, and hath made the sun and the moon and the stars subservient by His command. His verily is all creation and commandment. Blessed be Allah, the Lord of the Worlds![13]
>
> He hath created the heavens and the earth with truth. High be He exalted above all that they associate (with Him).
>
> He hath created man from a drop of fluid, yet behold! he is an open opponent.
>
> And the cattle hath He created, whence ye have warm clothing and uses, and whereof ye eat;

And wherein is beauty for you, when ye bring them home, and when ye take them out to pasture.

And they bear your loads for you into a land ye could not reach save with great trouble to yourselves. Lo! your Lord is Full of Pity, Merciful.

And horses and mules and asses (hath He created) that ye may ride them, and for ornament. And He createth that which ye know not.

And Allah's is the direction of the way, and some (roads) go not straight. And had He willed He would have led you all aright.

He it is Who sendeth down water from the sky, whence ye have drink, and whence are trees on which ye send your beasts to pasture.

Therewith He causeth crops to grow for you, and the olive and the date-palm and grapes and all kinds of fruit. Lo! herein is indeed a portent for people who reflect.

And he hath constrained the night and the day and the sun and the moon to be of service unto you, and the stars are made subservient by His command. Lo! herein indeed are portents for people who have sense.[14]

The omniscience of Allah is equally emphasized:

He is the Knower of the invisible and the visible, the Great, the High Exalted.[15]

And with Him are the keys of the invisible. None but He knoweth them. And He knoweth what is in the land and the sea. Not a leaf falleth but He knoweth it, not a grain amid the darkness of the earth, naught of wet or dry but (it is noted) in a clear record.[16]

The sovereignty of Allah is related to His omnipotence, and both are conceived of in equal terms:

Say: O Allah! Owner of Sovereignty! Thou givest sovereignty unto whom Thou wilt, and Thou withdrawest sovereignty from whom Thou wilt. Thou exaltest whom Thou wilt and Thou abasest whom Thou wilt. In Thy hand is the good. Lo! Thou art Able to do all things.

> Thou causest the night to pass into the day, and Thou causest the day to pass into the night. And Thou bringest forth the living from the dead, and Thou bringest forth the dead from the living. And Thou givest sustenance to whom Thou choosest, without stint.[17]

His attributes distinguish Him from His creatures. These Attributes of Allah are clearly distinguished from His essence; they too are adumbrated in the Qurʾān:

> Allah's are the fairest names. Invoke Him by them. And leave the company of those who blaspheme His names. They will be requited what they do.[18]

According to the renowned theologian al-Ghazāli,[19] Allah has ninety-nine beautiful names (*al-asmāʾ al-ḥusna*); these are frequently repeated by the faithful whose "rosary" consists of a like number of beads, but often reduced to thirty-three for convenience of recitation. The attributes most pronouncedly stressed are Allah's might and majesty:

> He is Allah, than whom there is no other God, the Sovereign Lord, the Holy One, Peace, the Keeper of Faith, the Guardian, the Majestic, the Compeller, the Superb, Glorified be Allah from all that they ascribe as partner (unto Him).
>
> He is Allah, the Creator, the Shaper out of naught, the Fashioner. His are the most beautiful names. All that is in the heavens and the earth glorifieth Him, and He is the Mighty, the Wise.[20]

Allah's omnipotence is mitigated and tempered with justice because He is equitable. He has complete knowledge of every good deed of man however insignificant, and Allah will take cognizance of it on the day of reckoning. Being transcendent does not preclude Allah's consciousness of all that takes place and He will not suffer the smallest injustice to befall anyone "...and they will not be wronged even the hair upon a datestone."[21]

God rewards and punishes, yet He is also the Merciful, Guardian of His servants, Defender of the orphan, Guide of the wrongdoer, Liberator from pain, Friend of the poor, generous and ready-to-forgive Master.

> And, O my people! Ask forgiveness of your Lord, then turn unto Him repentant; He will cause the sky to rain abundance on you and will add unto you strength to your strength. Turn not away, guilty![22]

God is the Merciful (*al-Raḥmān*) and the compassionate (*al-Raḥīm*); these are basic to His attributes, as attests the Qurʾān in every *sūrah*. He is forgiving and reassuring to the sinner who repents; and although God can overtake with His punishment anyone He wishes, His mercy "encompasses everything" because He Himself has commanded that mercy shall be an unbreakable law. "Mercy is a pillar of Islam and an attribute of God."[23]

God makes Himself known to men through (1) scriptures and (2) prophets. As He had given to the Jews the Law (*Tawrāt*) (Torah) and to the Christians the Gospel (*Injīl*) so He revealed to Muḥammad the Qurʾān. Each time a revelation is made, God sends it with a messenger, apostle or prophet to each people. He started the process with Abraham and ended it with Muḥammad.

Muḥammad's task was to remind men of Allah's decrees. When he met opposition, he was compelled to turn warner, and ultimately teacher, guide, and ruler, though he had been commissioned at first as messenger. When through the exercise of his natural faculties Muḥammad convinced very few of his fellow Meccans, he announced the doctrine of God's election.

Cosmology

Allah created the world in six days. Everything therein is the work of Allah. Beside Himself there are only two other uncreated beings: (1) the prototype of the Qurʾān, "mother of the Book" which was transcribed on a "preserved tablet" (*lawḥ maḥfūz*)[24] and (2) the throne (*kursi*) upon which Allah is seated in the Seventh Heaven surrounded by angels, pure, sexless beings, some of whom bear the throne while others are engaged in praising Him continually.

Angels also serve as His messengers who are sent to fight with the believers against the heathen. Some of them, known as *jinn*, are guardian angels of man accompanying him constantly at close range to watch over his deeds and keep a record thereof to be produced on the day of reckoning. Other angels are watchmen of hell, whose duty it is to usher in the condemned and make sure they do not escape. There are other types, like the "mediate being" between Allah and man, referred to as the "word" (*amr*) from which derives the "spirit" (*rūḥ*) or "holy spirit" (*rūḥ al-qudus*). Another manifestation of Allah to the believers only is the "glory" (*sakīnah*).

Allah creates each new life by breathing into it a soul. Hence man consists of both soul and body. This duality is maintained, even unto death and resurrection. Every man according to Muslim belief is possessed with a good and bad impulse. The fall of Adam was the work of *Iblis*, one of the *jinn*. Adam by his fall lost the grace of God, which was restored to him only by the gracious choice of God.

Men are separated from the angels by the *jinn*,[25] male and female, inhabitants of the desert, created from smokeless fire. Before Muḥammad's time they used to roam the heavens spying; but in the time of the Prophet they could learn no more of its secrets. Indeed, some of the *jinn* were converted by his teachings.

Lowest of creation in Allah's estate is the devil (*Shayṭān*) or Satan, who at one time was himself an angel but expelled from heaven for refusing to bow to Adam and the Lord's command.

The "Commandments"

Since what we term "commandments" is not specifically spelled out in any one document, we must learn of the do's and don'ts of Islam only through perusing the contents of the Qurʾān. From this we can adduce the following injunctions:

1. *Acknowledging there is no god whatsoever but God—*
   "Thy Lord hath decreed, that ye worship none save Him..."
2. *Honoring and respecting parents—*
   "And lower unto them the wing of submission through mercy, and say: My Lord! Have mercy on them both as they did care for me when I was little."
3. *Respecting the rights of others—*

"Give the kinsman his due, and the needy, and the wayfarer.…But if thou turn away from them, seeking mercy from the Lord, for which thou hopest, then speak unto them a reasonable word."

4. *Being generous but not a squanderer—*

"…squander not (thy wealth) in wantonness. Lo! the squanderers were ever brothers of the devil, and the devil was ever an ingrate to his Lord.

"And let not thy hand be chained to thy neck nor open it with a complete opening, lest thou sit down rebuked, denuded. Lo! thy Lord enlargeth the provision for whom He will, and straiteneth (it for whom He will)."

5. *Avoiding killing except for justifiable cause—*

   "Slay not the life which Allah hath forbidden save with right. Whoso is slain wrongfully, We have given power unto his heir, but let him not commit excess in slaying."

6. *Committing not adultery—*

   "And come not near unto adultery. Lo! it is an abomination and an evil way."

7. *Safeguarding the possessions of orphans—*

   "Come not near the wealth of the orphan save with that which is better till he come to strength; and keep the covenant. Lo! of the covenant it will be asked."

8. *Dealing justly and equitably—*

   "Fill the measure when ye measure, and weigh with a right balance; that is meet, and better in the end."

9. *Being pure of heart and mind—*

   Your Lord is best aware of what is in your minds. If ye are righteous, then lo! He was ever Forgiving unto those who turn (unto Him)."

10. *Being humble and unpretentious—*

    "And walk not in the earth exultant. Lo! thou canst not rend the earth, nor canst thou stretch to the height of the hills…and follow not that whereof thou hast no knowledge. Lo! the hearing and the sight and the heart—of each of these it will be asked."

And generally the Qurʾān enjoins Muslims to avoid "The evil of all that is hateful in the sight of thy Lord." It also stresses that "This is (part) of that wisdom wherewith thy Lord hath inspired thee (O Muḥammad)."[26]

Eschatology

The Islamic belief in the hereafter is traceable to the earlier *sūrahs* of the Qurʾān. The Resurrection, Last Judgment, Paradise, and Hell are all described.

At death the body again turns to earth while the soul sinks to a state of sleep or unconsciousness. At a time unknown to all but Allah and decreed by Him as "the Hour" (*al-Sāʿah*) or the "Day of Resurrection" (*Yawm al-Qiyāmah*), and the "Day of Judgment" (*Yawm al-Dīn*), an angel of the Lord will sound the clarion. At this moment the earth will be rent asunder and the body will issue forth to rejoin its soul. A period of protracted waiting will follow. Allah will then appear on His throne surrounded by the angels. The Qurʾān is replete with descriptions of that day:

> A day on which no soul hath power at all for any (other) soul. The (absolute) command on that day is Allah's.[27]
>
> The day when the Trumpet is blown. On that day We assemble the guilty white-eyed (with terror).[28]
>
> And when the trumpet shall sound one blast
>
> And the earth with the mountains shall be lifted up and crushed with one crash,
>
> Then on that day will the Event befall.
>
> And the heaven will split asunder, for that day it will be frail.
>
> And the angels will be on the sides thereof, and eight will uphold the Throne of their Lord that day above them.
>
> On that day ye will be exposed; not a secret of you will be hidden.[29]

The object of the Resurrection is to judge the deeds of men for the purpose of rewarding the faithful and punishing the guilty. Not only mankind but also the *jinn* and irrational animals will be judged.

Judgment does not immediately follow the Resurrection.

Mankind resurrected must wait a long time during which period anxiety and suspicion will torment those in doubt. Men will resort to their respective prophets for intercession that they may be redeemed from the painful situation and be called upon for trial.

> On that Day no intercession availeth save (that of) him unto whom the Beneficent hath given leave and whoso He accepteth.[30]
>
> (On that day) neither the riches nor the progeny of those who disbelieve will aught avail them with Allah. They will be fuel for fire.[31]

At the given time the great book in which the deeds of mankind have been recorded will be opened and a list of each one's deeds will be given, to the good in his right hand and to the evil, in his left.

> And the Book is placed, and thou seest the guilty fearful of that which is therein, and they say: What kind of a book is this that leaveth not a small thing nor a great thing but hath counted it! And they find all that they did confronting them, and thy Lord wrongeth no one.[32]

A balance will be present to weigh the deeds of all, and sentence will be passed depending on how the scales are tipped. He whose balance is laden with good works will be saved; he whose balance is light will be condemned.

> Thou seest the wrong-doers fearful of that which they have earned, and it will surely befall them . . .[33]

There will follow a period of mutual retaliation when those who were made to suffer unjustly will have satisfaction. The injurer will be made to yield a measure of his good works to the injured proportionate to the injury. This could spell the difference between Hell and Paradise.

Brutes will be made to pay the penalty for cruelty. Then God will command that they be turned into dust. The wicked, however, are destined to protracted suffering in Hell where they will cry out "would that we were also turned to dust."

When the trial is over those destined to Hell or Paradise will be made to pass over a narrow bridge to their respective destinations. The bridge is so fashioned that the favored will cross with ease and facility while the condemned will tumble off into Hell.

As for the idolators, the *jinn* will testify against them and they will be condemned to eternal damnation. But those who had embraced the revelations of Allah, even if they had sinned, will spend a term in Hell proportionate to their sins. They will be delivered therefrom upon expiating their sins by the right amount of punishment. The Sunni Muslim, however, insists that no infidel who denied the existence of God or any person who did not believe in the unity of God shall ever be redeemed. While, on the other hand, no one who acknowledged the existence and unity of God will be made to suffer eternal fire.

The Qurʾān goes into considerable detail to portray the nature of punishments and rewards. The righteous will gain eternal peace and joy in the garden of Allah, studded with trees, flowing water, and all the niceties of earthly dwelling which the desert Arabian considered the chief attractions of an ideal paradise.

> And hath awarded them for all that they endured, a Garden and silk attire;
>
> Reclining therein upon couches, they will find there neither (heat of) a sun nor bitter cold.
>
> The shade thereof is close upon them and the clustered fruits thereof bow down.
>
> Goblets of silver are brought round for them, and beakers (as) of glass
>
> There serve them youths of everlasting youth, whom, when thou seest, thou wouldst take for scattered pearls.
>
> Their raiment will be fine green silk and gold embroidery. Bracelets of silver will they wear. Their Lord will slake their thirst with a pure drink.
>
> (And it will be said unto them): Lo! this is a reward for you. Your endeavour (upon earth) hath found acceptance.[34]

The wicked condemned to eternal damnation will be cast into the fiery ditch *Jahannam* (Hell) where pains of body and soul are united.

They will abide therein for ages.
Therein taste they neither coolness nor (any) drink
Save boiling water and a paralysing cold:
Rewards proportioned (to their evil deeds).
So taste (of that which ye have earned). No increase do We give you save of torment.[35]

The rewards of Paradise and punishments of Hell vary in degree, depending on earned merits or demerits. Yet as seen in the verses of the Qur'ān, if taken literally, both types of rewards are depicted in sensual and material terms with body and soul together being subjected to them.

Still there is a greater joy than those expressed in mundane terms; indeed, the greatest joy of all to the happiest soul is to "...see the face of his Lord, night and morning, a felicity which will surpass all the pleasures of the body, as the ocean surpasses a drop of sweat."

Rewards will exceed the measure of man's good deeds, but punishment will be in proportion to his evil work.

> For those who do good is the best (reward) and more (thereto). Neither dust nor ignominy cometh near their faces. Such are rightful owners of the Garden; they will abide therein.
>
> And those who earn ill deeds, (for them) requital of each ill deed by the like thereof; and ignominy overtaketh them—They have no protector from Allah—as if their faces had been covered with a cloak of darkest night. Such are rightful owners of the Fire; they will abide therein.[36]

The type of sin a Muslim may commit is defined in the Qur'ān in terms of the judgment to be passed thereon. The greatest sin, known as the *kabīrah*, which earns the perpetrator eternal fire, is committed by those who associate others with God in the worship of Him.

> Lo! Allah forgiveth not that a partner should be ascribed unto Him. He forgiveth (all) save that to whom He will. Whoso ascribeth partners to Allah, he hath indeed invented a tremendous sin.[37]

> ...We shall expose them to the Fire. As often as their skins are consumed We shall exchange them for fresh skins that they may taste the torment....[38]

Another major sin is causing the death of an innocent being. "The guerdon of an ill-deed is an ill the like thereof...."[39]

The category of lesser offenses (*ṣaghāʾir*) cover all other types of sinning. While the *sūrahs* of the Qurʾān do not definitely specify, a number of them assert that Allah in His omnipotence can deliver the damned if He so wills; other revelations seem to imply that, for Muslims, hell is only temporary.

> If Allah afflicteth thee with some hurt, there is none who can remove it save Him; and if He desireth good for thee, there is none who can repel His bounty. He striketh with it whom He will of his bondmen. He is the Forgiving, the Merciful.[40]

Predetermination and Free Will

The question of the "bondage of the will" or "free will" preoccupied Muslim theologians as it had their Christian counterparts. By and large all Muslim sects do not agree on this crucial element of Islamic dogma. The one important principle of agreement held by all, however, is that Allah in His divine justice allows man the freedom of those actions upon which he will be judged. From this point of view man *does* possess free will. The notion that man is totally dependent in all aspects of belief and deeds on God as the author of virtues and vices, crimes and punishments is beginning to be discarded by recent Muslim theologians. The modernists among them have reverted to the idea of placing responsibility for man's actions upon man's own conscience.

The path to Allah is open to everyone, even the wrongdoers should they seek to tread it. Allah grants all of His creatures the powers to do good deeds and shun evil. He welcomes the one who seeks Him on his journey to Him even though the underling may commit some mistakes along the way. Man will earn his rewards on the basis of his faith and good deeds because of God's mercy and benevolence. The one who does not occupy himself with good deeds will be left alone. God may not stretch His arm towards him, but at the same time He will not be the one who puts him on the evil path.

Certain authorities consider belief in predestination a pillar of the faith. The Qur'ān appears to lend credence to this concept in the verses:

> All things have been created after a fixed decree....[41]
>
> No soul can ever die except by Allah's leave and at a term appointed....[42]
>
> Thy God hath created and balanced all things, and hath fixed their destinies and guided them . . .[43]
>
> Say: Naught befalleth us save that which Allah hath decreed for us. . .[44]
>
> ...nor is there anything not provided beforehand by us or which We send down, otherwise than according to a foreknown decree.[45]
>
> ...He hath created everything and hath meted out for it a measure.[46]

The sayings of the Prophet are replete with his insistence on God's role as preordainer and determiner of all that takes place. On one occasion Muḥammad told his listeners that God had said to him: "I have created this family for Hell; and their actions will be like unto those of the people of Hell." To Adam God had said the opposite: "I have created this family for Paradise, and their actions will be like unto those of the people of Paradise." But the servant of God from the Muslim theological point of view will have control over his actions from the time of birth until his death. "When God createth His servant for Paradise, his actions will be deserving of it, until he dies [*sic*] when he will enter therein; and when God createth one for the fire, his actions will be like those of the people of Hell, 'til [*sic*] he dies, when he will enter therein."[47]

The tendency of the Bedouin Arab to allow his "predetermined role" to come in the way of the fulfillment of his moral and religious obligations as a convert to Islam was curbed by the Prophet. Muḥammad insisted that the righteous will do good works and obey the word of God, while the wicked will perform evil deeds.

> To him who giveth alms and feareth God, and yields assent to the excellent creed, to him We will make easy the path to happiness. But to him who is worldly, and is indifferent, and who does not believe in the excellent creed, to him We will make easy the path to misery.

According to the sayings of Muḥammad: "The first thing which God created was a (divine) pen, and He said to it, 'Write'; it said, 'What shall I write?' And God said: 'Write down the fate of every individual thing to be created,' and accordingly the pen wrote all that was, and that will be, to eternity."

When pressed, Muḥammad stated: "God hath predestined five things to his servants; their duration of life, their actions, their dwelling places, their travels, and their portions."

To the debates and inquiries aroused by belief in predestination, Muḥammad would answer with the injunction to his followers: "Your forefathers were undone through debating about fate and destiny. I conjure you not to argue on those points."

The official orthodox view concerning the essence of the doctrine of predestination is summed up in the statement:

> A Muslim should believe in his heart, and confess with his tongue, that the most exalted God hath decreed all things; so that nothing can happen in the world, whether it respects the conditions and operations of things, or good or evil, or obedience or disobedience, or sickness or health, or riches or poverty, or life or death, which is not contained in the written tablet of the decrees of God. But God hath so decreed, good works, obedience and faith, that He ordains and wills them, that they may be under His decree, His salutary direction, His good pleasure and command. On the other hand, God hath decreed and does ordain and determine evil, disobedience and infidelity; yet without His salutary direction, good pleasure and command; but only by way of temptation and trial. Whosoever shall say, that God hath not indignation against evil and unbelief, he is certainly an infidel.[48]

The apparent contradictions ensuing from belief in predestination have posed as much a psychological problem for the believing Muslim as they have for the devout Christian. Muslim theologians have attempted to resolve such a contradiction by the explanation that man is not acquainted in this life with anything of what God has predestined for him. The lack of this knowledge, it is argued, allows him personal freedom of choice and action, which are in no way affected by his ignorance, and which ought not interfere in his fulfilling the normal obligations attending his belief. Bondage of the will in such a situation is not recognized. From this point of view the Muslim is free to act to make an intelligent choice, the choice of the agent, a choice plainly in contrast with the mechanical determination governing the physical world.

If what God has willed for man is concealed from him, the will of God is made manifest to him periodically through messengers, God's prophets, who familiarize man with duties to perform and injunctions to respect, so no act of disobedience can be justified on the plea of ignorance of what man is supposed to do or not to do, or the pretext that he was actuated to disobey or to sin by divine decree. Man is not cognizant of what he was predestined to do until the act is committed, by his own choice and free will, of which he is quite conscious. It is then and only then that he realizes that the act committed was preordained. By such an argument faith in divine predestination can neither require denial of human consciousness of freedom of will nor eliminate the factor of individual responsibility from human conduct.

Man's ignorance of his fate is deliberately presaged by God. If he knew from the beginning of his consciousness that he was doomed to perdition, he might naturally make no effort to resist his destiny or to attempt progress; or seeing that he was predestined to salvation, he might not attempt to earn it. By having no foreknowledge of his destiny, man's duty would be to adhere to the law ordained by God and revealed unto man by His prophets. Man's intelligent free action, it is agreed, must simply respect God's eternal decrees and have faith in them.

Hence belief in God, His oneness, His role as the sole Creator and absolute Disposer is dictated by reason and logic, not by blind faith. As the cultivator can not rightly claim to be the creator of his own harvest, so man cannot rightly claim to be the author of his own actions.

> Lo! Allah enjoins justice and good deeds, and that ye be kind to kinfolk as He condemns indecency, illicit deeds and all wrong.[49]
>
> Say, my prayers, my offerings, my life and my death are for God, Lord of the Worlds Who has no partner with Him. This I have been ordered (to believe), and I am the first to submit (unto Him).[50]

It is also argued that belief in predestination prevents fortune or misfortune to sway the believer from the "right path." Inasmuch as good and bad have been predetermined and decreed by God, no amount of human effort can hold back the inevitable. Hence the Muslim submits himself with resignation to all trials with the knowledge that this is a part of God's design.

> And We shall try you with fear and hunger, and loss of property and life and blessings; (therefore, O Prophet) give good tidings to those who are patient, who when misfortunes befall them say: Verily we belong to God, and to Him we shall verily return. Those (the patient) are they, on whom blessings and mercy from their Lord (will descend), and those are the followers of the right path.[51]

Being alive to the purpose of divine will enables a believing Muslim to accept cheerfully his fate and to endure conditions of hardship and misfortune without loss of faith. Reliance on fate under such circumstances may have its salutary side: it allows him to perceive that which enabled the world of Islam collectively to weather the misfortunes of periods of sharp decline and to preserve a sense of solidarity in the face of surging political and ideological pressures from a Western world that was simultaneously on the ascendancy.

The omnipotence of God does not prevent man from enjoying freedom of will. Muḥammad did not dispute the right of man to make a choice between good and evil. The Qur'ān is strong on this matter of free choice:

> Say the truth is from your Lord, whosoever wisheth he may believe; and whosoever wisheth he may disbelieve.[52]

By pointing what path man should follow in Islam, the Qur'ān clearly enunciates that (1) God has determined the destiny of man from the foreknown character of those whose fate He determined and because it is in conformity with His own will—a fundamental concept shared by both Judaism and orthodox Christianity; (2) man is directly responsible for his own actions so long as he is master of his free choice. God has endowed man with intellect and revelation, and left him with a vast sphere of human activity where he enjoys freedom of control and direction. For that reason man will be held accountable for the right or wrong exercise of his faculties. Hence it is a matter of serious concern that man should ascertain the right way to guide him in his conduct. "And show us the right path, the path of those thou hast favored and not of those who have strayed," appeals the Muslim daily to God.

By the aid of his intellect and God's guidance, the Muslim is expected to work out his moral and spiritual endeavors in his dealings with the Creator and the created. It is the Muslim's theological view that human intellect is susceptible to error resulting in the violation of human or divine laws and necessitating direct guidance and injunctions from God to compensate for such frailties of reason.

In obeying the laws enjoined by the Creator, the believer is better equipped to carry out his duties and attain the right path to Him. God, however, does not compel him to do so.

"Verily, We have shown to man the right path; he may be grateful or ungrateful." The lack of compulsion is further evident in the Qur'ānic verse "Verily this is a reminder to all people, for those of you who wish to take the right course." Man's freedom of choice stems from God's will. "It is for Allah only to furnish strong proof, for if He so willeth He would have guided ye all."

One of the strong points of Islam's beliefs is that God has entrusted to man the moral freedom that enables him to master himself. This moral freedom exalts him over the rest of God's creations. It is for man either to reap the benefits of a righteous act or earn condemnation for evil deeds.

CHAPTER 7

The Fundamentals of Islam: Obligations

THE QUR'ĀN specifically reminds the believer: "Lo! those who believe and do good works and establish worship and pay the poor-due, their reward is with their Lord and there shall no fear come upon them neither shall they grieve."[1]

Obligations in Islam are of two types: moral and ceremonial. Under the category of moral falls the concept of *Iḥsān* or right-doing. Fundamental Islamic law has elaborately defined the precepts of right-doing as embracing categories relating to man's relations with man and man's relations with God.

Moral Obligations

Right-doing entails morally acceptable works, the responsibility of which reposes with both the individual and society. In the area of personal morality much emphasis is placed on *selflessness* as a form of *gratitude* towards God. "And feed with food the needy wretch, the orphan and the prisoner, for love of Him, (Saying): We feed you, for the sake of Allah only. We wish for no reward nor thanks from you."[2]

Man's gratitude constitutes an element of *love for Allah,* an article of the Muslim's faith. "Say, (O Muḥammad, to mankind): If ye love Allah, follow me; Allah will love you and forgive you your sins. Allah is Forgiving, Merciful."[3]

Obedience to Allah and His messenger, Muḥammad, is equally stressed. "Say: Obey Allah and the messenger. But if they turn away, lo! Allah loveth not the disbelievers (in His guidance)."[4]

Kindness is decreed and boastfulness condemned. "Lo! Allah loveth not such as are proud and boastful, who hoard their wealth and enjoin avarice on others, and hide that which Allah hath bestowed upon them of His bounty…"[5] Having been orphaned early in his childhood, Muḥammad was particularly sensitive to Allah's decree, "And We have commended unto man kindness towards parents" and the Muslim's prayer, "Arouse me that I may give thanks for the favour wherewith Thou hast favoured me and my parents, and that I may do right acceptable unto Thee."[6] Allah insists, "If one of them or both of them do attain old age with thee, say not 'Fie' unto them nor repulse them, but speak unto them a gracious word."[7]

Consideration for others, namely the destitute, the orphan and the needy, is eloquently taught as an integral part of the Muslim's beliefs and his religious duties. In the words of the Qur᾽ān:

> Hast thou observed him who belieth religion?
> That is he who repelleth the orphan,
> And urgeth not the feeding of the needy.[8]
> …but righteous is he who…giveth his wealth, for love of Him, to kinsfolk and to orphans and the needy and the wayfarer…[9]
> …(Show) kindness unto parents, and unto near kindred, and orphans, and the needy, and unto the neighbour who is of kin (unto you) and the neighbour who is not of kin, and the fellow-traveller and the wayfarer and those whom your right hands possess….[10]
>
> Give unto orphans their wealth. Exchange not the good for the bad…[11]
>
> And when kinsfolk and orphans and the needy are present

> at the division (of the heritage), bestow on them therefrom and speak kindly unto them.[12]

Dreadful punishment awaits those who choose the opposite path.

> Lo! Those who devour the wealth of orphans wrongfully, they do but swallow fire unto their bellies, and they will be exposed to burning flame.[13]

Chastity and restraint are decreed for women, who are enjoined to be decent and modest and to display their charms only to their husbands or very near relatives. Men, on the other hand, must treat their wives kindly and be gentle with them, just and considerate.

Other decrees command the faithful to be *honest* in their dealings with others, *true* to their commitments, *loyal, humble* and *peace-loving.*

> The (faithful) servants of the Beneficent are they who walk upon the earth modestly, and when the foolish ones address them answer: Peace.[14]

Social morality in Islam requires one to place *duty* before *right.* Duties in Islam are incumbent on all the faithful, regardless of status in society. Indeed, Islam recognizes no social gradation, though in reality it may exist. In this regard the Qurʾān specifically states: Verily there is no preference for any of you except by what ye enjoy in good health and your deeds of righteousness.

In no other religion besides Judaism is the leveling process so strong. The wealthy are obligated by a precept of the faith's fundamental concepts to aid the poor as a *duty,* not a privilege. To be helpful and kind are recurrent themes in the Qurʾān. The establishment of a fair and just society was one of the strongest motivations in Muḥammad's mission. The faithful are urged to be *just* and fair-minded in their transactions.

> O ye who believe! Be ye staunch in justice, witnesses for Allah, even though it be against yourselves or (your) parents or (your) kindred, whether (the case be of) a rich man or a poor man, for Allah is nearer unto both (than ye are)....[15]

In several instances the Qur'ān stresses the need to deal justly, and the *Sharī'ah*[16] has made of justice one of the inviolable precepts of social morality. Justice in this content provides guarantees for rights, reinforced by ordinances enjoying the full sanctity of the faith. To be equitable is a duty that stems from brotherly relations.

> O ye who believe! Be steadfast witnesses for Allah in equity, and let not hatred of any people seduce you that ye deal not justly. Deal justly, that is nearer to your duty....[17]

Justice underlies also the stress on fraternity and equality in Islam. The *Sharī'ah* treats believers as brethren, regardless of their nationality or place of abode. As a member of a fraternity reposing in faith and buttressed by it, the Muslim has the right, and commensurately an obligation, to respect freedom, protection, security and the loyalty of his fellow Muslim. With justice as his guiding precept, the Muslim's duty is to weigh in an equitable balance between Muslim and non-Muslim.

> ...and let not hatred of any people seduce you that ye deal not justly .[18]
>
> ...Allah commandeth you...if ye judge between mankind, that ye judge justly...[19]
>
> ...And if ye give your word, do justice thereunto, even though it be (against) a kinsman; and fulfill the covenant of Allah....[20]

To be *beneficent* is another duty of each Muslim who respects the commandments of his religion. In its broader application beneficence (*birr*) obligates the faithful to act rightly in all circumstances: comfort the poor with material gifts, be truthful in his transactions, good in his communal relations, and constantly mindful of God's will in every aspect of his dealings, all of which must conform to the principle of right-doing. It is the duty and the privilege of the one who has to give to him who has not. "And in their wealth the needy and the deprived have due share," states the Qur'ān.[21]

Ostentation and vulgar display are frowned upon, if not forbidden. The leveling forces of Islam were to work through two powerful media: the decrees of the *Sharīʿah* and the conscience of the individual. Islam, like Christianity, denies the blissful life in the hereafter to those who deny the needy a fair share of the provisions of this life. Indeed, the conscience of the true believer would not rest were he to "eat, dress and make merry while his neighbors and relatives were unable to earn a living."[22]

The Muslim is not to be subjected to derision on account of poverty. While Islam depends partly on the believer's faith and respect of decency to take positive measures for mitigating the circumstances of the poor, the *Sharīʿah* nevertheless empowers the community to appropriate from the excess wealth of the individual when necessary what is required to satisfy the needs of his less fortunate brother. As a matter of fact, the Qurʾān threatens:

> ...They who hoard up gold and silver and spend it not in the way of Allah, unto them give tidings (O Muḥammad) of a painful doom,
>
> On the day when it will (all) be heated in the fire of hell, and their foreheads and their flanks and their backs will be branded therewith (and it will be said unto them): Here is that which ye hoarded for yourselves. Now taste of what ye used to hoard.[23]

Islam also condemns usury.

> Those who swallow usury cannot rise up save as he ariseth whom the devil hath prostrated by (his) touch...Allah will blot out usury, and causeth charity to prosper.[24]

To be *respectful* of a fellow believer's welfare in the society of Islam is another article of faith.

> ...They are the loyal. Those who entered the city and the faith before them love those who flee unto them for refuge, and find in their breasts no need for that which hath been given thee, but prefer (the fugitives) above themselves though poverty become their lot....[25]

Qurʾānic verses strengthen the notions making for solidarity between the individual and society.

> The believers are naught else than brothers. Therefore make peace between your brethren…[26]
>
> And the believers, men and women, are protecting friends one of another; they enjoin the right and forbid the wrong…[27]

The strongest concomitant of solidarity is abiding by individual and communal responsibilities as ordained by the religion and the canonical law of Islam. "Help your brother whether he is the doer of wrong or wrong is done to him," decrees the Prophet of Allah. The individual is the cornerstone of Islamic society; "he perfects it and is perfected by it, he gives to it and receives from it, and he protects it and is protected by it."[28] Both the conscience of the individual and of society collectively are held to account.

"Everyone of you is a shepherd and everyone of you will be questioned about those under him," said the Prophet. "Unto me it has been revealed that you should be humble that ye may not be proud over others."

Personal morality is as important as social morality; indeed, the one may not be realizable without the other. The Prophet and the Qur'ān stressed the need for purifying the individual's moral character as the *sine qua non* of achieving individual and collective responsibility. Allah in the Qur'ān addresses Muḥammad: "Lo! thou art of sublime morals." The qualities enshrined in the character of Muḥammad are those which God commands the Muslims to respect. Foremost among these are: truthfulness, "…in truth they give not thee (Muḥammad) the lie, but evil-doers give the lie to the revelations of Allah."[29]

Courage is another important quality stressed, and acts of bravery performed by the believers in nascent Islam contributed to its rise and spread. The Muslim is taught to fear not death, as his life is in the hands of the Creator who directs it to life eternal if dedicated to the fulfillment of Allah's will. Hence numerous deeds of martyrdom attest to the courage inculcated in the true believer.

Qualities making for sociability are equally emphasized. A properly trained Muslim youth is "well-mannered, sociable, faithful and sincere because such traits are essential for the perfection of his faith…"[30] Concomitantly, the true Muslim "does not deceive, cheat, or swindle."[31]

Unrestrained individualism had been the major blight of pre-Islamic Arabia. Muḥammad the messenger of Allah was armed with revelations to curb it and to destroy bigotry and false pride, evils accompanying such individualism.

> O Mankind! Lo! We have created you male and female, and have made you nations and tribes that ye may know one another (and be friends). Lo! the noblest of you, in the sight of Allah, is the best in conduct.[32]

Instead of manifesting their individualism, Allah through Muḥammad decreed that the faithful show *brotherly love* towards one another. This was indeed a strange decree, for the Arabs hitherto had gloried only in chauvinistic clanishness (*ʿaṣabīyah*) and considered it beneath their dignity to fraternize with those whom they looked upon as inferiors. Early in his mission he was derided, as was Noah before him, with the words of his detractors: "We see thee but a mortal like us, and we see not that any follow thee save the most abject among us, without reflection."

This type of solidarity between the individual and society is the basis of its health; it is the means whereby social ills are resisted and reforms are achieved. Islam through the decrees of God that prod the believer's consciousness stresses this responsibility of the individual to the community in almost a filial and beneficent vein and the community's towards the individual in a motherly and protective attitude.

> And the believers, men and women, are protecting friends one of another; they enjoin the right and forbid the wrong...[33]
>
> And there may spring from you a nation who invite to goodness, and enjoin right conduct and forbid indecency. Such are they who are successful.[34]

The practice of mercy is perhaps one of the most stressed injunctions of the message of Islam and the rock upon which right-doing rests. Indeed, in the view of a knowledgeable devout Muslim "the entire Islamic law (*Sharīʿah*) does no more than elucidate, sanction, order, or prohibit that which does or does not constitute righteous action."[35]

Mercy is not only strongly enjoined, but it is regarded also as an essential characteristic of God. In the early days of Muḥammad's preachings he stressed *raḥmah* (mercy) and *Raḥmān* (the merciful) so much that his listeners believed he was calling upon them to worship a god called *al-Raḥmān*.

The *Ḥadīth* stresses the all-encompassing mercy of God.

> When God had perfected creation, He wrote in the book which He kept near Him: 'My mercy triumphs over my anger.' God divided mercy into one hundred parts; He kept ninety-nine of them for Himself and released one for the world, from that alone comes all the grace which mankind enjoys.[36]

The Qur'ān contains numerous revelations on mercy ending invariably with the words "Allah is Forgiving, Merciful."[37]

> ...My mercy embraceth all things, therefore I shall ordain it for those who ward off (evil) and pay the poor-due, and those who believe Our revelations.[38]
>
> And We reveal of the Qur'ān that which is a healing and a mercy for believers...[39]
>
> It was by the mercy of Allah that thou wast lenient with them (O Muḥammad)...[40]
>
> There hath come unto you a messenger (Muḥammad) of yourselves, unto whom aught that ye are overburdened is grievous, full of concern for you, for the believers full of pity, merciful.[41]

The stress on mercy has had a strong effect on Muslims everywhere whose every move and each little act is "in the name of the most Merciful" (*al-Raḥmān al-Raḥīm*), and who greet one another with "may peace and the mercy of God be upon you." To them it is the foundation of society and progress. Hence the practice of mercy is a duty of every believer.

Muḥammad's preaching of mercy was undoubtedly founded also on practical considerations. Mecca was a city given to extremes of wealth and poverty, particularly in the area of social relations where the old Arab custom of meeting the social needs of the member of a family or a tribal affiliate did not apply to those who had no family or tribal ties. Numerous Meccans, accordingly, had no status but sought protection in the *jiwār* of the Kaʿbah, or the *ḥaram* area.

> And when it is said unto them: Spend of that wherewith Allah hath provided you, those who disbelieve say unto those who believe: Shall we feed those whom Allah, if He willed, would feed?[42]

The fact that the general standard of living in West Arabia was pitifully low by any method of comparison and that the Bedouins, like the poor of the city, were subsisting at near famine level, did not rule out the major inducement for preaching mercy. Pious gifts preached in Islam are partly for accumulating stores with Allah and partly for "cleansing" the soul of the believer.

The effect of solidarity was not lessened by low subsistence levels, nor was the motive for displaying benevolence entirely religious. The old tribal acceptance of the social practice of helping one's own is reinforced in Islam but not by religious conviction. The Arab's reputation for charity was not to be diminished when Islam upended the mores of pagan Arabia. Charity in Jāhilīyah Arabia was a mark of nobility; in Islamic Arabia it becomes a precept of the faith, albeit restrained and circumscribed.

> Give the kinsman his due, and the needy, and the wayfarer, and squander not (thy wealth) in wantonness. Lo! the squanderers were even brothers of the devils, and the devil was even an ingrate to his Lord.[43]

Ceremonial Obligations

Ceremonial obligations play a special role in drawing the faithful nearer to God and in helping them fulfill their duty to Him. They also have certain disciplinary effects in curbing the excess desires of the believers, in teaching them to do things together for the welfare of the group and for the purification of their souls.

Manifest acts of common worship strengthen the awareness of one Muslim for the other in times of success or of adversity. In many respects they serve to cement communal bonds by stimulating the individual's sense of belonging. Meeting the devotional requirements of the faith is the basic prerequisite of being a Muslim.

Shahādah

The most important and oft repeated act of faith among the Muslim's ceremonial duties is his testimony to the unity of God *la ilāha illa ʾl-Lāh*, "there is no god but God," commonly termed *al-Shahādah* (bearing witness). The *Shahādah* is more of a necessary reminder than it is a prescribed religious duty. When fully uttered the two-fold formula of Islam reads: (1) *ashhadu anna la ilāha illa ʾl-Lāh*, (2) *wa anna Muḥammadan rasūlu ʾl-Lāh*, (1) "I bear witness that there is no god (whatsoever) but God, (2) and that Muḥammad is the messenger of God." The mere uttering of this phrase, properly witnessed, makes a Muslim of the reciter. The "doctors" of Islamic jurisprudence have confirmed the fact that the title "Muslim" is due him who pronounces the *Shahādah*.

It is the first few words spoken in the ears of a newborn babe and the last on the lips of the dying. The *mujāhid*, fighter for Islam in the holy war, becomes a *shahīd* ("ultimate witness"), or martyr for the faith, if he falls in battle. No words are more often uttered than these; they are repeated by the average believer no less than twenty times daily. They constitute the basic part of the muezzin's call to prayer from the top of a minaret.

Ṣalāh

Of the five ceremonial duties incumbent on the Muslim, *Ṣalāh*, or the ritual prayer, is an essential obligation of Muslim worship and the supreme act of righteousness. Without rendering it, the Muslim in fact ceases to be one in practice.

Muḥammad placed greater importance on prayer than on any other religious duty. Prayer in Islam is not the same as in Christianity as it "does not mean the conversation of the heart with God,"[44] but resembles rather public worship with readings from the Qurʾān, already committed to heart, commencing with the "*Fātiḥah*," followed by other short verses and the confession of faith (*shahādah*) and of the benediction or petition for the Prophet, and of brief praises. At prescribed moments in the *ṣalāh* there is room for personal invocation of God's aid and His guidance in what the Muslims call *duʿāʾ*.

The act of prayer is not left to the whim of the believer to perform; it constitutes rather a well-defined ritual, faithfully executed according to a prescribed pattern. Five times a day, at dawn, midday, midafternoon, sunset, and nightfall the muezzin mounts the balcony of slender minarets throughout the world of Islam and intones in the melancholy modulation of a resounding voice the call to prayer: "God is great (four times). I bear witness that there is no god but God (twice). I bear witness that Muḥammad is the messenger of God (twice). Come to prayer (twice). Come to contentment (twice). There is no god but God." During the call at dawn the muezzin reminds the faithful that "prayer is better than sleep."

The believer may perform the prayer ritual wherever he finds himself at the prescribed time, although city dwellers usually gather in mosques[45] for praying. The only time he is obligated to pray with his fellow Muslim is at the noon service of Friday,[46] the Muslim's sabbath but not really a day of rest. According to the Qurʾān:

> O ye who believe! When the call is heard for the prayer of the day of congregation, haste unto remembrance of Allah and leave your trading....
>
> And when the prayer is ended, then disperse in the land and seek of Allah's bounty,...[47]

In every mosque there is a semi-circular recess called the *miḥrāb* that sets the direction of prayer, which is always towards Mecca. All worshipers face the direction of Mecca as they pray. At this given moment in the Muslim world, the rendering of the devotional requirement would project the image of Mecca and the sacred Kaʿbah at the middle with concentric circles of believers around the world focusing their sights towards the middle.

In the mosque the faithful stand in straight lines facing the *miḥrāb* that points to Mecca; and up front with his back to the first row stands the *imām*, the leader in prayer. The procedure is supposedly modeled on that used by the Prophet who provided the broad outlines for it; details were worked out later, after considerable haggling by jurists, as were the five distinct and independent orisons per day. In Mecca during the early years of nascent Islam, only two seemed to have been prescribed.

> Establish worship at the going down of the sun until the dark of night, and (the recital of) the Qurʾān at dawn.[48]

Later, in the Medinan period, a third was added, presumably in keeping with the Jewish tradition of praying three times a day. This addition took place during the early period of rapport between Muḥammad and the Jewish community. The number of five daily prayer performances evidently was affixed by the jurists as a compromise reportedly between this number and forty which Allah allegedly asked of Muḥammad when he visited the Seventh Heaven on that night of the journey (*miʿrāj*).

> Glorified be He Who carried His servant by night from the Inviolable Place of Worship[49] to the Far Distant Place of Worship[50] the neighborhood whereof We have blessed, that we might show him of our tokens!

The time of performance is fixed as follows:

fajr—when the sky is filled with light but before actual sunrise
zuhr—immediately after midday
ʿaṣr—sometime between three and five o'clock in the afternoon
maghrib—after sunset but before the onslaught of darkness
ʿishāʾ—any hour of darkness

The worshiper is enjoined to approach this sacred duty in a state of legal purity or ceremonial cleanliness, *ṭaḥārah*.

> O ye who believe! Draw not near unto prayer when ye are drunken, till ye know that which ye utter, nor when ye are polluted, save when journeying upon the road, till ye have bathed. And if ye be ill, or on a journey, or one of you cometh from the closet, or ye have touched women, and ye find not water, then go to high clean soil and rub your faces and your hands (therewith)....[51]

As seen from this revelation the Muslim must be also free of every defilement (*ḥadath*), great or small. For the prayer to be valid, the believer must approach it with purity of body, which implies purity of soul, and of dress and place. Ablutions prepare the believer for prayer; no other restrictions exist as "neither priests nor sacrifices nor ceremonies are needed to lift the heart of man towards his creator."[52]

Ablution is of two types: *ghusl,* a general form, and *wuḍū'* or the limited type. *Ghusl* is necessary after acts of great defilement (*janābah*) such as sexual intercourse; *wuḍū'* after small defilements arising from satisfying the calls of nature, from sleep, simple contact with the opposite sex, etc. The *wuḍū'* is the most commonly performed, either in the private dependencies of the Muslims or in the court itself of the mosque.

The process entails the use of legally pure water with which the worshiper washes first his face, then his hands and forearms to the elbows; the right hand next passes over the head, followed by the washing of the feet, all in this order. Cleanliness in this sense also prohibits the worshiper from performing the ritual prayer while wearing a garment stained with blood, excrement, and other such defilements; the efficacy of the prayer is immediately destroyed if such defilement takes place in the midst of it.

After having readied himself for prayer, the worshiper selects a *templum* or an immediate sanctuary where he takes up position facing Mecca, center of the shrine, the *qibla*[53] of Islam, after making sure that the ground he has taken up is not defiled, and preferably delineated by some visible object; hence the use of a "prayer rug."

The ritual is begun with the Muslim standing erect, his repeating the call to prayer (*iqāma*), and next putting into words his intention (*nīyah*) to undertake so many bowings (*rakʿāt*, sing. *rakʿāh*). This intention is important to the validity of the prayer as it represents the conscious will of the worshiper. Then raising his open hands to the level of the shoulder, the worshiper utters the *takbīr* (lit. "magnification") or the formula: *Allāhu akbar* which signifies the beginning of his dissociation for the duration of the prayer with all earthly affairs. The insertion at this point of any word or gesture foreign to the ritual immediately cancels the prayer, as such distractions interrupt the union of the worshiper with God. Muslim jurists laid so much stress on this formula that they called it *takbīr al-iḥrām* (the *takbīr* of sanctification).

The principal postures assumed in executing the prayer ritual are:[54]

1. From standing position, left hand placed in the right, worshiper recites the first chapter of the Qurʾān or the "*Fātiḥah*" followed by a few other verses usually from Sūrah CXII: "Say, God is One, the eternal God, begetting not and unbegotten; none is equal to Him."

2. Upper part of body is next inclined forward from the hips, and another *takbīr* is recited while the palms of the hands rest on the knees in an obeisance or *rukūʿ* and the performer recites the words "(I extol) the perfection of my Lord the Great."

3. Erect posture (*iʿtidāl*) is resumed while the worshiper utters the words "*Allāhu akbar.*"

4. Next follows the posture of greatest surrender to God, *sujūd* (prostration), the high point of the prayer, with the worshiper uttering the same words over again.

5. Kneeling on the ground follows; then with hand outstretched in front of him the worshiper touches the ground with his brow at the base of nose.

6. He raises his body and sits on the base of his heels while still in a kneeling position and his hands stretched along his thighs in a *julūs* or *quʿūd* (sitting) position.

7. He prostrates himself for the second time preceded and followed by the *takbīr.*

8. Back to a *julūs* position, the *shahādah* is repeated, the intercession for Muḥammad, "*ṣalla-ʾl-Lāhu ʿala sayyidina Muḥammad,*" follows, then the ending with the worshiper turning his head first over his right shoulder then over the left pronouncing the *taslīm*: "*al-salāmu ʿalaykum wa raḥmatu ʾl-Lāh.*"

Having followed through uninterruptedly from the recitation of the "*Fātiḥah*" to the second prostration, the worshiper is said to have completed a *rakʿah.* A full complement of daily prayers contains a ritual number of *rakʿāt.* The *zuhr, ʿaṣr,* and *ʿishāʾ* have four, the *fajr* has two, and the *maghrib* has three.

The Friday Prayer or *ṣalāt al-jumʿah* is performed in the mosque wherever feasible and when forty or more have assembled, hence the application of the term *jāmiʿ* (place of assembly) to the place of worship. The leader in prayer (*imām*) has no special religious function, and no ecclesiastical status or religious authority to issue injunctions as "there is no priesthood in Islam."

The *imām* may come rather from any walk of life; he is chosen by his coreligionists to lead them because of his reputation for knowledge of the faith and piety.

The prayer is followed immediately by the central function of the ritual, namely a *khuṭbah* (sermon) delivered by an *imām khaṭīb* and consisting of a general eulogy, according to a nearly fixed formula (*khuṭbat al-naʿt*), and pious exhortations (*khuṭbat al-waʿẓ*) in which the *khaṭīb* (deliverer of the sermon) can display his eloquence. He ends the *khutbah* by invoking the blessings of Allah upon the community and its heads.

In the early days of Islam the caliph either in person or through his representative presided over the solemn Friday Prayer; later for protection purposes he prayed within an enclosure of wood (*maqṣūrah*). In the days of Muḥammad, women attended mosque prayers standing behind men. Later they too prayed behind the *maqṣūrah*; and with the passing of time, fewer of them came to the mosque (*jāmiʿ*) because, according to a prophetic tradition, it was preferable that they pray at home.

What is most striking in observing the faithful carrying out their prayer obligations is the marvelous simplicity and sobriety of the Qurʾānic ritual "which leaves the maximum of freedom in respect of the most elevated of spiritual functions."[55]

> The utmost solemnity and decorum are observed in the public worship of the Muslims. Their looks and behaviour in the mosque are not those of enthusiastic devotion but of calm and modest piety…they appear wholly absorbed in the adoration of their creator; humble and downcast, yet without affected humility, or a forced expression of humility.[56]

The peaceful and serene manner in which the worshiper carries out his prayer in congregation with others has a certain advantage. In the first instance the prescribed formula for the ritual has a disciplinary effect on the Muslim. It develops in him a greater awareness of his equality with the Muslim next to him and a stronger consciousness of solidarity. Praying in congregation promotes in the worshiper a sense of fraternal kinship with the one beside him, so lacking in pre-Islamic days when the only tie recognized was that of *blood* not *belief.*

The ceremony attending worship concentrates the thoughts of the worshiper "beyond the realm of the body, and enables him to express his devotion and to render thanks for divine bounties in the most profound manner."[57] "By bringing all Muslims together in the same ritual of humility and submission to the Lord, it makes them feel that they are all His creatures and thus brothers."[58] Following the *imām* in prayer gives the worshiper a real experience in discipline and obedience. Facing in the direction of Mecca provides him a constant reminder of the birthplace and mainspring of his faith, and of the center around which his religious sentiments hover.

Establishing worship may serve the moral elevation and purification of body and mind—"Surely, prayer preserveth one from lewdness and iniquity..."[59] But in the final analysis neither the permanence of prayer nor the offering of sacrifices to God can alone endear the Muslim to God; "...it is your righteousness that reacheth Him."

Zakāh

Invariably referred to as the "poor tax" or "poor-due" and "almsgiving," the *zakāh* literally means giving back to Allah a portion of His bounty as a means of avoiding the sufferings of the next life, and as an "expiation" or "purification" of what the Muslim retains for himself of material possessions.

While the *zakāh* may be regarded as an act of beneficence, a precept of right-doing and a charitable act in a moral sense, *zakāh* is less of a voluntary and more of a required religious observance; indeed, it is a fundamental of the faith.

> Establish worship and pay the poor-due and obey the messenger, that haply ye may find mercy.[60]

At the beginning of Islam, the *zakāh* was rendered as an act of piety and love; with the passing of time it took on more and more a legal connotation until it became obligatory, a ritual act, a legal duty. It was levied either in currency or in kind—cattle, grain, produce, or commodities.

> Lo! those who give alms, both men and women, and lend unto Allah a goodly loan, it will be doubled for them, and theirs will be a rich reward.[61]

It was in the days of the Prophet that the habit of bringing alms to the leader of the community began. From this habit was engendered the process that transformed it into a permanent type of taxation. In due time the Muslim community appointed officials to gather the poor-due from the communicants of the faith.

The Qurʾān specifies for whom the *zakāh* is due:

> The alms are only for the poor and the needy, and those who collect them, and those whose hearts are to be reconciled, and to free the captives and the debtors and for the cause of Allah, and (for) the wayfarers, a duty imposed by Allah.[62]

The distribution of alms is prescribed in the Qurʾān according to fixed categories of utilization:

1. First and foremost to the poor and needy *(fuqarāʾ)*; then

2. Officials (*ʿamalah*, sing. *ʿāmil*) who gathered the *zakāh*;

3. "Those whose hearts are to be reconciled"—in early Islam these were the recalcitrant Meccans whose hostility often had to be bought off;

4. Slaves to purchase their freedom;

5. Paying back debts incurred as a consequence of acts of benevolence;

6. Arming the *mujāhidūn* (sing. *mujāhid*, fighter) engaged in a holy war (*jihād*) against infidels;

7. Supporting institutions dedicated to the service of God *(fī sabīl ʾl-Lāh*, in the way of Allah), and for

8. Aiding poor travelers.

The exact amount was never spelled out; but the average was usually between 2 and 3 percent of earnings or possessions. Later on, both the percentage levied and the mode of payment were worked out according to carefully laid down and specifically defined rules. Products of the soil, chattel and precious metals and merchandise become liable to *zakāh* when such items attain a certain minimum value called *niṣāb*. It is paid in kind; but when values exceed the *niṣāb,* then it is subject to fluctuation; when levied on harvests or fruits, the amount is between one-tenth (hence the *ʿushr*) and one-twentieth. There are set rules as to when cattle, precious metals, and manufactured products become liable to *zakāh*. The basic rule is that they must remain in the hands of the same owner for one year.

Both obligatory (*zakāh)* and non-obligatory (*ṣadaqah*) taxes were assessed and collected by a functionary called *ʿāmil* in the early period of Islam. In addition to determining and levying the precise amount, the *ʿāmil* arranged also for its transport to the depots where he personally was responsible for its safekeeping.

The *zakāh* or statutory alms was supplemented by the *ṣadaqah*, voluntary or non-obligatory alms. These were not defined or delimited; the faithful volunteered them as his proclivity for doing good or acquiring merits when Allah moved him. Today they are paid at the end of the month of fast at designated centers.

Ṣawm

Ṣawm, or fasting, is another prerequisite of faith, also decreed by the Qurʾān:

> O ye who believe! There is prescribed for you the fast, as it was prescribed for those before you, that ye may ward off (evil)...[63]

"Those before you" alludes to other devotees of Allah, such as the Jews who fasted on the Day of Atonement, but more probably to the Eastern Christians, who fasted for thirty-six days. Ritual fasting was not known to Arabia before Islam. The fast is to be observed "in the month of Ramaḍān in which was revealed the Qurʾān...and whosoever of you is present, let him fast the month, and whosoever of you is sick or on a journey, (let him fast) the same number of other days."[64]

The month of fast varies constantly because the lunar calendar followed by the Muslims may move Ramaḍān through the whole course of the solar year.[65] The day of fast accordingly can be unusually long and, in a thirty-year cycle, it may coincide with the longest day of the year. Under such circumstances fasting can be an occasion of severe mental and physical strain for the faster.

During the fast the Muslims may not partake of any food or drink; nor may they smoke, or have sexual intercourse with the opposite sex, from the time when a white thread can be distinguished from a black one before sunrise until sunset.

> ...Then strictly observe the fast till nightfall and touch them not, (i.e., opposite sex), but be at your devotions in the mosques...[66]

If a Muslim is able to fast and does not, he may make up for it by feeding a poor man; but "if ye fast it is better for you." If the believer in full control of his health and faculties (*ʿāqil, bāligh*) does not accomplish his fast obligations as prescribed, then he must give expiatory alms (*fidya*). If the sexual prohibition is violated, then he must free a slave or fast two months or feed sixty persons.

The validity of the fast is determined by the *nīyah* (intention) of the Muslim. "But whoso doeth good of his own accord, it is better for him..."[67] Mosques are well attended during Ramaḍān, and the *rakʿāt* accompanied by recitations from the Qurʾān and interspersed after each four by meals may well last the whole night.

The fast is broken immediately after sunset with a *fuṭūr* (light meal). The faster may "eat and drink until the white thread becometh distinct to you from the black thread of the dawn."[68] This culminates with a *suḥur* (dawn meal), the time when it may be taken at the latest is announced by a crier in towns called the *muwaqqit* (time determiner) or *musaḥḥir* (dawn determiner). Special calendars today give in advance the precise time.

The beginning of the month of fast is determined by the appearance of the new moon. The end is likewise determined by a similar astronomical observation. If atmospheric conditions do not permit proper determination, the *qāḍi* or another religious authority of the locality may make the decision. The period of the fast may last from 28 to 30 days.

The fast ends on the first day of the month of Shawwāl with a great feast termed *ʿĪd al-Fiṭr* in the Eastern lands and *al-ʿĪd al-Ṣaghīr* in the Western lands of Islam. The feast of breaking the fast calls for a solemn prayer, *Ṣalāt al-ʿĪd*. On this day the statutory alms marking the end of the fast (*zakāt al-fiṭr*) are given and the head of each household gives to the poor a prescribed quantity of the customary food of the country as an act of piety.

The feast is an occasion for festivities lasting three full days during which time Muslims rejoice and exhibit their new clothes and exchange embraces. This feast of Ramaḍān is one of the most warmly and strictly observed holidays of Islam. Those who seek to avoid it incur severe approbation from their brethren.

Ḥajj

The fifth religious duty of the Muslim is the pilgrimage or *ḥajj* to the sacred monuments of Mecca, at least once in a lifetime for those who are physically able or can afford to perform it. The pilgrimage takes place during a certain period of the Muslim year, namely the first ten days of dhu 'l-Ḥijjah. As an institution the pilgrimage is a carry-over from the pre-Islamic period. It was practiced by ancient Semites as a farewell to the harsh effects of the burning sun so characteristic of this part of the world.

The trek to Mecca "*al-Mukarramah*" (the Highly Honored) is more or less constant. Pilgrims from the remotest corners of Asia, Africa, the western hemisphere, and Europe work their way by every conceivable mode of transportation known to man, from airplanes to camel backs, to the birthplace of Islam and to "the Greatly Illuminated City," by which Medina is known.

The Muslim may perform either the *ḥajj*, the major pilgrimage, or the *ʿumra*, the lesser. Muḥammad referred to them by these terms in 630 when he negotiated with the Qurayshites to enter Mecca. While the revelations received in Mecca make no mention of the *ḥajj*, we have no reason to doubt that Muḥammad prayed to Allah before the Kaʿbah in the early years of his mission as later.

A number of sites are the target of the pilgrimage, and to understand the ritual performed round about them a note of explanation is necessary. Nature condemned most of central and west central Arabia to aridity. Violent thunderstorms, rare but furious, lash the surface with raging waters, very little of which furrow through to yield the few permanent springs upon which the inhabitants of this land depend.

The well of Zamzam is one such a spring. Indeed, it was around it, a stopping place of the caravan trade from Yemen to Syria along the Red Sea, that Mecca was built. According to Muslim legend, it was here that Abraham's wife Hagar and their son Ishmael were abandoned and where the angel Gabriel answered their plea for water by causing the spring of Zamzam to leap forth at the spot where Ishmael kicked his heels after his mother had run desperately back and forth between two hills. Abraham, according to the same tradition, came later to Zamzam and with the help of his son Ishmael rebuilt the Kaʿbah, the House of God (*Bayt al-Lāh*) on the very spot where Adam had built it before it was swept away by the Great Deluge of biblical lore.

The most important monument is the Kaʿbah (literally the cube), located in the middle of a square enclosure surrounded by a wall. It measures 36 x 30 at the base and is 18 feet high. There is nothing special about it as a structure. The façade is of undressed stone covered by the *kiswa* (vesture), made usually by the sovereign of the leading Islamic state. Egypt in the past led in presenting the *kiswa,* which is of a woven green cotton material inset with gold silk girdled by a black band two thirds up, on which are inscribed verses of the Qurʾān. The *kiswa* was carried annually to Mecca and the Kaʿbah during the pilgrimage season in the *maḥmal* (planquin). Today it is made in Mecca itself, largely by Muslims from Bokhara who settled there.

At the southeast corner of the Kaʿbah is the Black Stone; not far from it at the northern side is the door which is opened on fixed days of the year to the faithful. Surrounding the Kaʿbah is the ellipsoidal roadway *(maṭāf)* on which the pilgrims make the ritual circuits *(ṭawāf)*. Opposite the Black Stone, on the other side of the *maṭāf,* is the little mosque of Zamzam surrounded by the great courtyard (*ṣahn*) measuring 300 x 180 feet and bounded with galleries punctured by twenty-two gates.

The shrine of Mecca and the city's environs to the extent that the light of the sanctuary can be seen from beyond the city, which limit is marked off by pillars on all sides, constitute the *ḥaram* or the hallowed grounds. This concept was known to pre-Islamic Arabia. Within this ground, consecrated to the gods of the pagan Arabs beasts grazed in peace, the yield of the soil was respected, and none but those in a state of ritual sanctity could enter. Islam placed an interdiction on all non-Muslims, barring their entry to the sacred city.

Every able-bodied Muslim must perform this important religious duty once in a lifetime provided he has the means to undertake the long journey entailed should he live far from Mecca.

"And pilgrimage to the House (*Kaʿbah*) is a duty required by Allah from those (of you) who can find a way thither."[69]

A woman may also undertake the *ḥajj* if the husband permits it, and if she is accompanied either by him or by another person serving as protector. In some cases the performance of the pilgrimage may be delegated to a substitute who will undertake it for him. In this eventuality he would still get credit for it.

Should a believer die without having performed the pilgrimage when he could have and should have, arrangements may be then made for it to be done postmortem on his behalf by his heirs, who would thereby be performing a pious act subject to rewards on the Day of Judgment. In some cases bodies are sent to Mecca for burial.

The act of pilgrimage is attended by certain ritual ceremonies commencing from the moment the faithful declares his intention to undertake it; but it is on the borders of the *ḥaram* that it truly begins, although it is at certain prescribed stations called *mīqāt* (plural *mawāqīt*) along the route approaching the *ḥaram* that he performs the rites which prepare him to enter the sanctuary. It is here that he sheds his daily clothing and dons two seamless wrappers, one around the loins reaching to just above the knees (*izār*) and the other about the shoulders (*ridāʾ*) after ablution and prayer. With the exception of two pieces of leather soles (*naʿl*) strapped to his feet, he goes without head cover or shoes. After these necessary preliminary preparations, he enters the *ḥaram* and does not thereafter shave, trim his nails, or anoint his head during the entire ceremonial period.

Highlighting the ceremony of the *ḥajj* are the following encumbrances: a visit to the *Masjid al-Ḥarām* (the sacred mosque), kissing the Black Stone, circumambulating the Kaʿbah seven times *(ṭawāf)* three times at a run and four at a quick pace, a visit to *Maqām Ibrāhīm*, where there is a sacred stone upon which Abraham allegedly climbed while laying the upper courses of the Kaʿbah. There is also the ascent to Mount Ṣafa whence the pilgrim runs to Mount Marwa seven times, then to Mount ʿArafāt, on the ninth day of the pilgrimage. The *wuqūf* at ʿArafāt, "station before Allah" as it is called, constitutes the culminating point of the pilgrimage without which the ceremony would be null and void.

The *wuqūf* takes place in the afternoon of the ninth day. The pilgrim stands erect before Allah and recites pious formulae under the leadership of an *imām* who also gives a solemn *khuṭbah*, one of the four ritual *khuṭbahs* of the entire pilgrimage. Then immediately at sunset the pilgrims proceed to another valley, Muzdalifah, situated between ʿArafāt and Mina. Here they spend the night of the tenth day, the last of the pilgrimage, which culminates at sunrise. At Mina the final ceremonies of the *ḥajj* take place.

The *wuqūf* at Muzdalifah is followed, like that of ʿArafāt, by a "flight" (*ifāḍah*) that brings the pilgrims back to Mina at sunrise. Here at the edge of a steep slope (*ʿaqaba*), where the road to Mina starts, and before a stone stele with a sort of large basin in front of it the pilgrim casts seven little pebbles picked up at Muzdalifah while reciting *Bism ʾl-Lāhi, Allāhu akbar* (in the name of God, God is great). The casting of the seven pebbles is in commemoration of Abraham's escape from Satan, when tempted by him at this spot, by his throwing seven stones at him. The stele is referred to popularly as *al-Shayṭān al-Kabīr* (the great Satan).

The ceremony ends with the sacrifice of an animal at Mina, usually a sheep or goat, which the pilgrim had consecrated during the *ḥajj*. Part of it is eaten by the owner, or owners; the remainder is distributed to the poor of Mecca. A few pieces dried in the sun are carried back by the pilgrims, while the rest of the carcass is processed and canned by the Saudi government for distribution to the poor and needy. The pilgrims continue to live at Mina for a few days more.

This sacrifice on the 10th of dhu-'l-Ḥijjah is one of the most important feasts of Islam, although it is not considered as significant as the *wuqūf* at ʿArafāt in the ceremony of the *ḥajj*. On this day throughout the Muslim world the head of each family sacrifices an animal in the same ceremonial manner followed at Mina. The feast is invariably known to the Arabs as the *ʿĪd al-Aḍḥā* (feast of the offerings) or *ʿĪd al-Qurbān*; to the Turks as *Būyūk Bayram*; and to the Muslims of North Africa as *al-ʿĪd al-Kabīr* (the great feast).

At the end of the sacrifice ritual the pilgrim has his head shaven and nails cut. The waste is carefully buried at Mina. Henceforth he is in a state of partial desanctification (*taḥallul al-ṣaghīr*). Full desanctification occurs only after the pilgrim scurries back to Mecca and performs at the Kaʿbah the *ṭawāf al-ifāḍah*. At this point he has fulfilled the ceremonies of the pilgrimage (*manāsik al-ḥajj*) and is entitled to be called "*Ḥājj*," or "*Ḥājji*" to the Turks.

After a few days more at Mecca, the *Ḥājj* departs for home with a strong sense of accomplishment as he has just fulfilled the crowning act of his religion and acquired an enviable reputation among fellow believers who have no claim to the title. More important, he is instilled with a keener awareness of the power of Islam which can bring together each year men and women of so many different nationalities and races. This is one of the strongest forces working for solidarity among Muslims devoted to their faith. The pilgrimage is the "plenary assembly as well as the fair of Islam."[70]

A visit to Medina is the next step; it is here as he stands before the tomb of the Prophet that the believer is moved most deeply. Some might visit also Jerusalem, site of the *Miʿrāj*[71] and home of so many prophets, especially ʿIsa (Jesus). Upon reaching home, the pilgrim performs the same ceremonies which he underwent on departure. He also distributes souvenirs, water of Zamzam, and pieces of the *kiswa*, to relatives and friends.

CHAPTER 8

Solidarity Through Institutional Unity

A MEANINGFUL UNDERSTANDING of the unifying powers of Islam the religion can be derived from a perusal of the institutions it sired. The full impact of the religion can not be fully appreciated without some knowledge of its political, social, and cultural ramifications.

The doctrinal requirements of Islam, together with the obligations imposed by the Qur'ān and the traditions that developed therefrom, gave rise to institutions and usages which transformed a primitive religious community into a highly organized sociopolitical society cohering through the forces engendered by its religion and in turn strengthening the sentiment of belonging among Muslims. Islam in this respect served as the catalytic force that induced the formation of a distinct identity among the believers in the first few centuries which centrifugal forces in later centuries could not break down, not even in more recent times when the concept of nationality differences gained sway in Muslim lands.

The revelations to Muḥammad as enshrined in the Qur'ān and his exemplary conduct as reflected in the *Ḥadīth* provided the framework and the legislative basis of Islamic society, reaching into almost every aspect of individual and group life in this society with emphasis on duties and obligations. Such legislation gave rise to a variety of institutions and practices which, with the passing of time, shaped the pattern and norms governing Islamic society in its multifarious aspects.

The Accident of Circumstance

Circumstance played an equally important role in the first century of Islam's existence. Sustained military probes on the periphery of Islamic Arabia, resulting from a carry-over of the razzia institution from pre-Islamic times and encouraged by ineffective resistance to these probes, culminated within a short century in the establishment of an extensive empire. Islam had banned internecine warfare but it could not subdue the militant zeal of the desert Arabian; indeed, his newly acquired beliefs served to strengthen rather than lessen his zeal for gain and, if he should fall in battle, for martyrdom. Raids in search of gain led to campaigns, campaigns led to wars of conquest, and these ultimately to the establishment of an Islamic empire.

Islam undoubtedly provided the moving force, although one can not state that the zeal to convert non-Muslims to Islam was the major inducement. Far from being destructive, the desert Arabian as conqueror under the banner of Islam exhibited strong qualities of restraint and discipline in his relationships with the conquered peoples, who represented a variety of ethnic and sectarian groups with strongly differing cultural backgrounds. The credit for such restraint belongs to the tenets and precepts of Islam as clearly enunciated in the Qur'ān. Indeed, under the influence of Islamic injunctions, the conqueror was duty-bound to respect and protect the conquered, especially those who already acknowledged their belief in Allah in Christianity and Judaism. Not by the sword, but by the exemplary conduct of these zealous Muslims and gains anticipated therefrom, did so many of the conquered—pagan, Christian, Shaman, Zoroastrian, Hindu, and Jew—convert to Islam, faith of the conqueror, and adopt for their own the values sustaining this faith.

Contrary to hitherto accepted judgment, it was not by force but by the appeal of his readily comprehensible faith and the example of personal and communal living that the Arab in Spain or Turkistan turned into a magnet for Islam, not a repellent.

Islam in many instances gained from the conversion of those peoples who had evolved a more distinct culture than that of the conqueror. The conquered first as clients and later as a dominant force in Islamic society continued to acquire and utilize the products attending Islam, namely, the language as well as cultural and social norms. The resultant interaction of Islam, the religion, and its medium of expression, the Arabic language, with the cultural background of the converts—Persian, Hellenized Syrian, and Egyptian—abetted both the "internationalization" of Islam and its acquiring a distinct culture of its own.

The Arab supplied the broadened Islamic fraternity with Islam and the Arabic language, the two principal media of coherence, together with a broad spirit of tolerance through a deliberate policy, carefully defined, of non-interference in the communal affairs of the conquered. In the resultant diversity Islam found its greatest enrichment, and to the religious nurture of unity and solidarity a new dimension, the cultural, was added.

The survival of indigenous cultural values introduced by converts to Islam, while imparting to the faith a local coloring tolerated by it, did not transgress or compromise the prerequisites of belief as defined by the *Sharīʿah*, the fundamental law of Islam; nor did the acceptance of them override the exigencies of communal solidarity which the Islamic theocracy imposed on all believers.

Not by force of arms nor by administrative fiat did the Arab Muslim, by far the minority element in the lands conquered, impart cohesion and solidarity to the society of converts. By a combination of magnanimity tempered with justice and exemplary conduct, the soldier in earlier centuries like the merchant later, opened up wedges for the expansion of Islam into southeast Asia and sub-Saharan Africa, areas where the force of Islamic arms was never felt. While valor and example played significant roles in the spread of Islam, we cannot discount the impact of Qurʾānic legislation and the qualities of leadership exhibited by the caliphs and those close to Muḥammad in his lifetime. Legislative fiat and circumstance combined to create, assimilate, and consolidate a monolithic Islamic society.

To understand the range of the religious impact on the growth and consolidation of the organized Islamic community and on the institutional structure of this cohering body before transformation set in during the period of decline, and more recently when modernism began to cause radical changes in institutional beliefs and practices, a perusal of the fundamental structural basis must be made.

The Caliphate

We noted that the Qur'ān played a vital role in defining the path of growth followed by the religion. The Qur'ān and Sunnah together shaped the institutions attending the rise of Islam to sociopolitical as well as religious heights of attainment. Among the earliest and most germane to the rise of Islam is the institution of the caliphate.

When Muḥammad ruled the destinies of the faithful, Allah assisted him generously with properly timed revelations which enabled him to attend to the basic administrative needs of a nascent community that looked to itself for the means of coherence and development. Muḥammad served in all capacities as minister, judge, and ruler. He made all important decisions and was the ultimate recourse for all. Upon his death the faithful in democratic council elected the much respected Abu Bakr successor (*khalīfah* or caliph) to Muḥammad's temporal but *not* spiritual authority. Thus began an important institution that lasted until April of 1924 when it was abolished by Kemal Ataturk of modern Turkey.

The caliph was not only ruler but also *amīr al-mu'minīn* (commander of the faithful) and the *imām* (guide) of the community. To the Sunni orthodox Muslim the office was elective; but with the first Umayyad caliph Mu'āwiyah (661–680) it became hereditary in his line and continued that way until the end.

The Shiʿites, however, have insisted on legitimacy, namely, that the *imām* must come from Muḥammad's line through his daughter Fāṭimah and her husband ʿAli, the Prophet's first cousin and his closest associate, with full unchallengeable authority due him as God's successor on earth. This "divine right kingship" notion reflected the old Persian theory and was not unfamiliar to the Byzantines. The Persians today are the largest Shiʿite group in Islam.

The caliphate in its heyday was a powerful instrument working for solidarity and coherence in Islam. The caliph enforced legal decisions, safeguarded the divinely revealed restrictive ordinances, maintained the armies and guarded the community of Islam from external attack, enforced order and security, meted out justice, received and distributed the *zakāh* and other alms, maintained the Friday services and public institutions, decided between disputants, served as supreme judge in matters bearing legal claims, married minors who had no guardians, distributed booty gained in war, and generally catered to a variety of needs brought before him by the faithful. Later in the ʿAbbāsid period of the caliphate, particularly from the ninth century onward, under mounting Persian influence, the caliph became more withdrawn from public accessibility. With the creation of a bureaucratic machine, his functions were whittled away gradually, until finally the caliph became a mere ceremonial figure.

The first caliphs were elected from amongst the Companions of Muḥammad. They faithfully carried on the tradition established by him and ministered to the needs of the community along lines set by the Prophet himself. For this they were titled by historians as *al-khulafā' al-rāshidūn* (the rightly guided caliphs). Even though the community expanded militarily under ʿUmar I with the conquest of Syria and Egypt from Byzantium (636–641) and the Persian Empire from its Sāsānid rulers (637–640), the first three caliphs took no active part in war. They regarded themselves primarily as custodians and enforcers of the *Sharīʿah*,[1] canon law with which they had been charged. By and large, they were pious men who followed the Prophet's example of austere living and personal accessibility to the faithful.

The Umayyad caliphs[2] who succeeded them were more interested in acquiring and enjoying the benefits of this life and its material enrichments. With them the caliphate became more nearly a form of kingship and lost much of its spiritual orientation. This materialistic orientation notwithstanding, the Umayyad caliphs were careful to safeguard the temporal interests of the Muslim community and to organize it formally into a state administered by an expanding bureaucratic machinery that reflected the strong influences of the assimilated conquered peoples and their traditions of government.

The ʿAbbāsid successors[3] to the Umayyads had forcibly usurped their caliphal authority under the pretext of restoring the pure and pious traditions of the Prophet to caliphal rule. But they were also heirs of the Sāsānid "King of Kings" and of the traditions associated with him. Now under the influence of Persian advisers and courtiers they began to emulate Persian ways and their love of pomp and splendor, familiar to the reader of the tales popularized by the *Arabian Nights*. The caliph no longer regarded himself as the *primus inter pares* of the community, the *imām* who led by personal example the faithful along the righteous path. He was now an absolute sovereign served by all the prerogatives due the despot; unlimited powers were at his disposal; he was beyond reach of the public, and fully capable of exercising such powers at will.

But a bureaucracy, ever on the increase since Umayyad days, eventually appropriated for itself most of the powers which the caliph once held in his hands. An *imām* took over leadership of the Friday prayer and delivered the important *khuṭbah; a qāḍi* dispensed justice as decreed by the Qurʾān and embodied in the *Sharīʿah*; a *ʿāmil* was in charge of gathering taxes, and an *amīr* commanded the army and often the administration in the various far-flung provinces of the caliphate. The numerous decrees issued in the name of the caliph were drawn up by *kuttāb* (sing. *kātib*) al-*sirr* (scribes, secretaries) constantly multiplying in numbers.

With the ʿAbbāsids the institution of vizierate entered the scene, and the vizier, who enjoyed no special function at first other than that of a general aide-de-camp and confidant to the caliph, now took charge of a whole hierarchy of viziers constituted as a sort of "cabinet" and began to exercise powers not much unlike those of the most developed modern cabinet systems.

There came into being also the office of the *ḥājib*[4] (chamberlain) who served as a screen between the caliph and his subjects. When the Seljuk Turks appeared on the scene in the tenth century, the much abused and incapacitated caliph found himself under the tutelage of his rescuers upon whom he gratefully bestowed the title of *amīr al-umarā*ʾ (the prince of princes) and then *sulṭān* (sultan—possessor of supreme authority), an office which detracted from the caliphal image of authority and prevented the caliph from exercising full power.

The gradual whittling away of caliphal authority rendered the caliph almost totally powerless towards the end of the ʿAbbāsid era. He was now no more than a ceremonial figure, isolated from his subjects, and little aware of their problems. He fell prey as a consequence to the exploitation of powerful local *amīrs* who acknowledged only nominally the caliphal office.[5] The effect was to decentralize the empire and give vent to *shuʿūbīyah*[6] movements with their strong centrifugal tendencies. Indeed, one observes that such a tendency was the unavoidable consequence of the caliph's withdrawal from the public exercise of the prerogatives of his office and his retreat, often voluntary, from the active display of his powers.

The result is that regions which possessed a geographical and independent historical personality before Islam began to assert themselves again under some sectarian adhesion in Islam like Fāṭimid Egypt, Umayyad Spain, Shīʿite Persia, Khārijite Oman, Sharīfian Morocco. The dynastic structure and control of such and similar countries by the nineteenth century maintained very loose ties, when at all, with the Ottoman caliph in Istanbul.

The story of how decentralization took place and how influential it was in creating schismatic movements in the Islamic polity constitutes a separate study. Our concern here is with those institutions that have had a centralizing and binding effect; some of which have not ceased to do the same until today. The Qurʾān and the traditions associated with Muḥammad, his Companions, and the Orthodox caliphate are among them. The ideals persisting from pre-Islamic tribal society with emphasis on loyalty, kinship ties, and the pilgrimage also served to bind together the polity and cement solidarity.

Jihād

Jihād has two connotations: greater and lesser. The greater is the function of the individual who must strive constantly to live up to the requirements of the faith. The lesser is primarily a community function and thus, an obligation. The idea of *jihād* in a military context with its emphasis on the notion of continuous struggle against non-believers in God tended to keep alive the spirit of solidarity in the community over and against outsiders. While the Qur'ān does not make of *jihād* in the "holy war" context an article of faith, it is the *Ḥadīth* which renders it into a formula for "active struggle" that invariably tended toward a militant expression. The incentive for *jihād* lies in its two-fold benefits: booty for this life and martyrdom with its immediate promise for a blissful eternal hereafter for those killed in battle, the *shuhadā'* (sing. *shahīd*: martyr).

The exercise of *jihād* was the responsibility of the *imām*, or the caliph when the powers of the office were still in his hands; the territory of sanctioned war, *dār al-ḥarb*, invariably was on the frontier of *dār al-Islām* (abode of Islam). The yearly raids against the Byzantines by the 'Abbāsids, and later the Turkish thrusts into Byzantine holdings in Asia Minor, which ended ultimately in the destruction of the empire altogether, were sanctioned by *jihād*, as were the raids into Hindustān by the Ghaznawids in the tenth and eleventh centuries.

Jihād in a militant context did not affect non-Muslim subjects and residents. The governing institutions of Islam affected directly the communicants and only superficially non-communicants whose residence among Muslims was accepted, tolerated, and indirectly regulated.

The conquerors permitted full juridical and administrative control to Christian and Jewish communities whose protection the Qur'ān enjoins and who are known as *ahl al-dhimmah* or *dhimmis* (dimmis), in exchange for the *jizyah*, a sort of personal tribute-tax levied on all those capable of paying it. Their social and religious status with few exceptions[7] was respected. The bishop, rabbi, or the head of the protected community was directly responsible for its affairs and welfare to the Muslim caliph, and later, sultan.

In the principal cities of Islam where strong pockets of tributaries survived, *dhimmis* filled important offices and professional positions. The ruler's physician invariably was a Christian or a Jew; they engaged freely in a number of professions, practiced banking, carried on trade, indulged in scholarly pursuits, enjoyed authority, and led relatively prosperous lives, which sometimes made them the target of mobs incited by the *dhimmis'* more fanatical Muslim neighbors. Non-Muslim foreigners in Muslim lands, increasingly more numerous from the eighth century onward as members of foreign missions, traders, and the like, enjoyed *amān* (formal safety) in keeping with the ancient Arab custom of granting *jiwār* (quarter) to outsiders. While they were still looked upon as *kuffār* (sing. *kāfir*: infidel), they nevertheless acquired the status of protégés and came to enjoy the same privileges extended to dimmis.

The *Sharīʿah* sanctioned the residence of Muslims in non-Muslim lands provided they were permitted to carry on their religious duties unencumbered. In the twelfth century, Syrian Muslims lived under the jurisdiction of Frankish Crusader and non-Crusader princes in the Norman kingdom of Sicily. They dwelt in relative safety of person and possessions and were not treated as "colonials," as were their coreligionists during the Spanish regime of the Reconquista. Today no less than three hundred million Muslims in China, Southeast Asia, India, and Europe live under predominantly non-Muslim jurisdiction.

The Sharīʿah and Fiqh

The *Sharīʿah* encompasses legislation derived from the Qurʾān and the *Ḥadīth*. Tradition and the juridical consolidation of life molded under the stimuli of the Qurʾān and the *Ḥadīth*, with no distinction between spiritual and temporal law, served to rally the believers throughout the Muslim world. Only in recent times did decisions sustained by the *Sharīʿah* begin to affect the institutions and livelihood of Muslims, supplemented and sometimes supplanted by modern legal practices.

The *Sharīʿah*, unlike laws developing from the precedents established by Roman law, stresses individual cases. Through the use of analogical reasoning, a doctrinal point resting on the *Sharīʿah* can apply by extension to like points without following any carefully defined formula for such extended use. The jurist could almost always find one case from the multitudinous accumulation over the centuries that would provide him with the proper precedent for a given legal matter. This is what kept the *Sharīʿah* alive and functional in pulling Islamic society together.

The *Sharīʿah* is Islam's constitution. The function of evolving useful effectual legal principles from the *Sharīʿah* gave rise to the *Fiqh* (jurisprudence), without differentiation between the spiritual and the secular. The process of evolving *Fiqh* started when Muḥammad first began to adjudicate for the nascent Muslim community in Medina. While Allah provided him with revelations suitable for certain cases, often the Prophet drew on the customary law or usages of Arab tribes, and sometimes of Jewish tribes, in and around Medina as long as elements of the faith were not compromised thereby.

Thus the eclectic nature of legal development in Islam can be said to have been predetermined in the lifetime of the Prophet. With the exception of frequently recurring subjects pertaining to inheritance, marriage, enactments concerning children, the treatment and emancipation of slaves, laws dealing with murder and theft, property and commercial matters, where more careful attention to detail is given, Muḥammad was content to treat "legal problems" on their individual merits with no conscious effort to build up a uniform system or code.

Hence, upon his death the faithful inherited a few specific prescriptions in the Qurʾān and a mass of recorded decisions of the cases he handled. Specifically, Muḥammad had left behind his particular use of what would be analogous to common law, equity and legislation, and to enactments and recordings based thereon. The death of Muḥammad may be considered to have ended constitutional legislation in orthodox Islam. What we note instead in subsequent years is the exposition and systematization of Islamic law deriving from the *Sharīʿah* through *Fiqh*.

At first the *fuqahāʾ* (sing. *faqīh*: jurist) followed entirely practical precedents. When confronted with a problem, the Qurʾān was their first recourse; if no satisfying answer was found therein, they resorted next to the specific decisions made by Muḥammad himself. If this procedure proved unsatisfying, the jurist had the choice of following Muḥammad's precedent by consulting the common law of Medina. Should this also fail to yield a proper precedent, then the *faqīh* was empowered to follow his personal judgment or, as another recourse, to use equity as a standard of decision.

The Sunnah

The *Sunnah* (literally, path) relates to the body of tradition associated with the conduct of Muḥammad in his discharge of prophetic responsibility and to the manner in which he handled himself as guide, judge, and ruler of the organized Muslim community *when not specifically directed by Allah.*

To emulate the way of *the man* as well as *the prophet* becomes exceedingly important in later decades for successors and jurists unable to find specific revelations coping with the demands of an expanded and more complex society. The study and adaptation of Muḥammad's *sunnah* to rising needs became a considerable enterprise. But in the meanwhile there had come into being literally hundreds of thousands of *ḥadīth* or sayings attributed to Muḥammad, but not all verifiable. Before this vast corpus could enjoy official sanctity, it had to be carefully screened and the genuine traditions ascertained.

In the course of time the *Sunnah* acquired special merits for a variety of purposes. It was useful to Muslims who sought to justify dissenting views over important doctrinal interpretations. The traditions, and particularly the sayings of Muḥammad, served to bolster a variety of causes ranging from personal ambitions to complex doctrinal and institutional decisions. These were more often in situations that would have incurred for Muslims embarked on a course of deviation the approbation rather than the approval of Allah and the Prophet.

The evolution of the *Sunnah* as an important legal corpus had its start with the Companions of Muḥammad. These associates of the Prophet were dedicated men who found in his conduct and sayings much to emulate. Hence they made careful mental notations of Muḥammad's life and deeds. To follow in his footsteps was the desired end, the end which every properly brought up young Muslim does not cease to strive after.

Muḥammad to the believers was a mortal like themselves who lived a life pleasing to God and served his fellow Muslims well. Thus his sayings and doings, manners and customs, his answers to questions on religious life and faith and, above all, his decisions in legal disputes became a source of important reference for the layman and the jurist, the philosopher and the theologian, the rebel and the law abider, the respectful of tradition and the innovator, according to a process of challenge and response that gained much validity for the Islamic society in the stage of its development and institutionalization.

The *Sunnah* in later centuries, when confronted by Western ideals and institutions that challenged Islamic traditional beliefs and usages, lent much support to the traditionalists seeking to combat foreign influences on all levels of Islamic society. This resistance has been particularly evident in very recent times. Such concern for tradition gave rise to the extensive literature termed *Ḥadīth* in Islam, the study of which preoccupied Muslim scholars for generations.

Specific schools came into being in the ninth century for assembling and categorizing the sayings of Muḥammad in support of all sorts of arguments and disputes. Theologians and jurists made of these a legal system of reference for passing decisions on important theological and juridical questions. Liberal thinkers in the ninth century were less concerned with *Ḥadīth* arguments than they were with rational or speculative theories to support their contentions. The conflict that ensued between these "rationalists" and their antagonists the "traditionalists" accounts for much of the philosophical and theological studies of Islam in the heyday of its cultural development.

When the conquests brought Muslim jurists in contact with Roman law in the provinces they, like the Muslim administrator, found much of value and practical utility in it. As long as local customs and usages did not conflict with the basic tenets of the *Sharīʿah*, they tried to avail themselves of them. The presence of Roman legal terminology in Arabic legal nomenclature attests the influence of Roman codes on Islamic legalism. When Muslim law permits the *qāḍi* to exercise his *raʾy* (personal judgment) we are reminded of the use of "equity" in Anglo-Saxon law. The use of *istiḥsān*[8] (preference) as a legal principle, even when the analogy of the code decreed another course, represents another concession to a non-doctrinaire approach. Resorting to *istiṣlāḥ*,[9] deciding on that which would bring the greatest benefit to the community at large, is another nontraditionalistic recourse.

But in the heated controversy that ensued over such principles of legal decision, liberty of opinion was in the end narrowed to *qiyās*, use of analogy, the nearest the Muslim *Sharīʿah* came to the principle of "legal fiction" as applied by Western jurists.

The Umayyad caliphate ended the somewhat pious theocratic empire of the Orthodox caliphs. In the following eras, public life tended to exhibit with few exceptions far less religious sentiment; indeed, the pious said that it was "godless." Law was still needed, but in its development it became more speculative and opportunistic. The study of *sunnah* and *ḥadīth* passed into the hands of private individuals noted for their personal piety. The result was that interpretation of the *Sharīʿah* became more idealistic and less in keeping with the realities of Islamic society, and that *Ḥadīth* with, until now, its handmaiden *Fiqh* came to a parting of the ways. Students of *Ḥadīth* gathered traditions for their own sake with the idea of providing prophetic guidance and dicta for the details of life as they faced them, on the assumption that any caliph, *amīr* or responsible individual who went beyond the patriarchal form developed at Medina was of this world "imperiling his soul at every turn."

The subscribers of *Ḥadīth* were seeking to apply it to the details of human experience, and in so doing they were diluting from its universalistic appeal. Yet both the *Sharīʿah* and the *Fiqh* still possessed a much broader applicability than Western secular law. Herein lies the significant role of the *Sharīʿah* as the builder and sustainer of Islamic society in the totality of its earthly existence and in the projection of its promises for eternity. The *Sharīʿah* regulated the essentials of man's relationships to God, neighbor, and self. It was a system of duties that the *Sharīʿah* created, a system which was not only religious and ethical but legal in a non-canonical sense as well. It specifically defined for the faithful what actions are *forbidden* unto them (*ḥarām*), what are *required* of them (*farḍ, wājib*), and what is recommended (*mandūb, mustaḥabb*), or what is tolerated (*mubāḥ, jāʾiz)*, and what is disliked or frowned upon (*makrūh*).

The role of the *Sharīʿah* and *Fiqh* may be likened unto a combination of canonical law and the "law of the land." It not only defines for the faithful the prescriptions for the exercise of religious, ceremonial, and ethical obligations, but governs the private lives of all pious Muslims. In one or the other of its four juridic schools, the *Sharīʿah* regulates certain aspects of the Muslims' semi-public relationships, e.g., marriage, divorce, inheritance. It also compels respect for itself, if not acceptance from the state.

The *Fiqh* administered a scheme of duties but had only partial ties with the real legal systems of Muslim peoples in more recent centuries, with the exception of the Wahhābis of Arabia and the Ibāḍis of ʿUmān (Oman) where it still constitutes the whole law. The changes in the *Sharīʿah's* role in governing the broader aspect of the Muslim's life were due partly to the converts clinging to their inherited usages and partly to the fact that what sufficed for the nascent community in Medina was not sufficient for an empire embracing a heterogeneous populace and permitting whole communities of Jews and Christians to govern themselves without being integrated into the Islamic fold.

As a result of Islamic resurgence in recent times the *Sharīʿah* has become the law of faith and land in Iran, Libya, Sudan, some of the Gulf states, and is becoming the law of the land as well as of the faith in Pakistan.

ʿĀdāt

Peoples conquered by the Islamic polity were willing to apply a veneer of Islamic phraseology to conceptions of their own religions. The Muslims themselves, particularly the new converts, conversely allowed themselves to be influenced by local customs or *ʿādāt* of the conquered peoples. *ʿĀdāt* consisted of a variety of local usages having the sanctity of law; such usages not only differed from place to place, sometimes radically, but often obscured, if they did not contradict, the *Sharīʿah.*

ʿĀdāt as a form of "local law" crystallized into a legally applicable corpus in lands ruled by the Ottoman Turks. It developed two systems of legal procedure, one administering ordinances of the *Sharīʿah* with emphasis on private and family affairs and pronouncing decrees on purely personal religious questions, e.g., details of ritual law, law of oaths and vows, and the other sustaining the working courts of the land by administering codes based on local custom and the decrees of local rulers.

The canon laws of Islam, like the institution of the caliphate, served as a binding force in the organization and management of the affairs of Islamic society. There were in addition other forces at work cementing the ties of the community. These relate to concepts and practices engulfing a much broader and more intimate side of the Islamic community, namely, family bonds and common observances that permeated the whole social and economic life of the community.

The Family

The family to Islam is the cornerstone and the mainstay of the community, as it had been to the Arabs before Islam. What Muḥammad did was to take the Arabian conception of the family and fit it into the framework of Islam. Essential ingredients carried over into Islam are those relating to plural marriages, the place of women and children in the persisting patriarchal family, and the rules governing the conclusion of marriage. These would encompass also the preliminary steps like the *mahr,*[10] *khiṭbah,*[11] and *ʿaqd al-nikāḥ,*[12] without which marriage cannot be finalized; there is also the matter of verifying intent, i.e., when the parties declare their consent to marriage and the husband pays the dowry. All such Muslim steps toward marriage are survivals of pre-Islamic practices.

Islam on the other hand did introduce some changes. The *mahr,* for instance, is assigned by the Qurʾān to the wife as a form of surety, which adds the material element to the spiritual bond of marriage and makes of this innovation a more honest and forthright approach. The marriage contract, moreover, possesses no specifically religious character. It may be formalized either in the mosque or in the home of one of the parties according to a defined ritual and a legal procedure. The contract spells out the terms by which marital relations are to be conducted and under what conditions dissolved. It also defines the respective rights and obligations of both sides, delineating the role of tutors, specifying when minors or those adjudged legally incompetent can marry, stipulating the terms of inter-faith marriages, the marriage of slaves, and related matters.

The occasion of marriage is one of great celebration and festivity throughout the Muslim world. It provides one of the great outlets for social intercourse and enjoyment. In a way it serves to emphasize the great significance attached to family life as a force for unity in Islamic society.

Social Institutional Observances

Numerous social practices and ceremonies continuously observed have strengthened the notions of belonging and common identity in Islam. The birth of a son to the Muslim family, no less than the marriage fetish itself, is a special joyful event. Animal sacrifices are made and the flesh is distributed to the poor; alms are offered and Muslim prayers are whispered into the child's ear. When named, seven days after birth, he usually carries a name by which the Prophet was known—Muḥammad, Maḥmūd, Ḥāmid, Muṣṭafa—or a combination of ʿAbd (servant of) with one of the ninety-nine variants by which God is addressed—al-Qādir, al-Ḥāmid, al-Razzāq. The daughters usually receive the names of the women in the Prophet's family—Khadījah, Fāṭimah, ʿĀʾishah, Zaynab.

The circumcision rite is strictly observed by all Muslims like the marriage ceremonies; it provides an important landmark in the life of the youthful Muslim. If it is performed at age seven, it signifies his passing from the strict care of his mother, to whom the Muslim infant belongs, to a helping relationship with his father; at this date he begins his life as a man or launches his formal study of the Qurʾān at school.[13] The daughter by contrast stays close to the house and there receives what education the social status of the family permits. The great concern of the parents is a properly arranged marriage; and most of their training is dedicated to the cause of turning them to become good housewives and mothers. Modernization has undermined much of this custom. Muslim women today are entering the professions, especially educational and medical, in increasing numbers.

Memorization of the Qurʾān used to be at the core of the Islamic educational program. When completed, the youth became a *ḥāfiz*[14] and with it he acquired considerable prestige in society. After memorizing the Qurʾān, he began the formal study of such related subjects as the exegesis of the Qurʾān (*tafsīr*), the Traditions (*Ḥadīth*), law (*Fiqh*), grammar (*naḥw*), lexicography (*lughah*), rhetoric (*bayān*), and literature (*adab*). With the diminishing role of Qurʾānic schools in the educational systems of Muslim countries during the last century, increasing numbers of Muslim students have been studying in Western schools. Here they enroll in broader secular courses pertaining to the sciences and the humanities; indeed, the role of the traditional Islamic curriculum outside of specialized religious schools and educational curricula of the Islamic states—Iran, Arabia, and Sudan—has been increasingly circumscribed in recent years.

Teaching in the past usually took place either in the courtyard of the mosque or in the master's house. Students formed a *ḥalaqah* (circle) around the master who devised a curriculum as he thought best and stressed memorization of passages from the Qur᾿ān and commentaries as well as the master's own writings. Assiduous and attentive listeners received his authorization (*ijāzah*) to repeat his lessons in another city. In this manner the works of distinguished masters were disseminated throughout the Muslim world. Thus do we have a scholarly tradition serving to provide Islamic society with a unifying intellectual response.

Regular institutions were founded and maintained by the caliphs for the purpose of promoting the "religious sciences," such as the *Dār al-Ḥadīth* (House of Traditions) and *Dār al-ʿIlm* (House of Knowledge) of the early ʿAbbāsids. The al-Azhar of Cairo evolved from the *Dār al-ʿIlm* prototype; it was founded by the Fāṭimid caliphs of Egypt at the beginning of their reign in 969 A.D. The al-Azhar, oldest living university in the world, is emulated by two other institutions, the Zaytūnah of Tunis and the Qarawīyīn of Fez in Morocco.

These schools were later supplemented in the eleventh and twelfth centuries by *madrasahs,* which really amounted to seminaries for the study of the practice of religion and the propagation of the orthodox Sunni doctrine. Examples of these *madrasahs,* teaching according to the Shāfiʿi rite,[15] are the Nizāmīyah of Baghdad and the Nūrīyah of Damascus, founded and named after Nizām al-Mulk and Nūr-al-Dīn Zangi respectively. Ṣalāḥ al-Dīn (Saladin) also founded *madrasahs.* Later the Mamlūk Sultan Rukn-al-Dīn Baybars created a *madrasah* pattern which included all four rites within its walls, but with separate quarters.

These *madrasahs* represented a sort of state education and served to popularize a uniform conception of Islamic law, the sinew of the cohering Islamic society. From the eleventh century onward, certain esoteric groups such as Ikhwān al-Ṣafā᾿ (Brethren of Purity), Qarmaṭians (Carmathians), and Ismāʿīlīs began to develop their own schools; so did the Ṣūfis. These specialized centers of learning, though interested primarily in preserving their own ways and practices, nevertheless maintained a body of teaching which served to enhance the general and lasting aspects of Muslim culture.[16]

The impact of modernism has induced a marked contrast in many aspects of Islamic life. While the *madrasahs* are still functioning and attracting students, primarily as schools of canon law, the exigencies of the modern age and the new areas of knowledge opened up by great technological discoveries have led to the establishment of ultra modern "houses of knowledge," or universities, in almost all the principal urban centers of the Islamic world supported often by well organized elementary and secondary school systems patterned along European or American models.

Feasts

The pattern of day-to-day living scarcely varied from one end of Islamdom to the other and served no less than other institutional practices to reflect the common imprint of the Islamic way on adherents of the faith. Preoccupation with feast celebrations brought the faithful together on frequent occasions.

While various feasts peculiar to a locality in the Islamic world are celebrated with all the attending fanfare that makes for greater regional and communal identity, there are certain feasts celebrated simultaneously throughout the Muslim world. The *ʿĪd al-Aḍḥa* (Feast of the Sacrifice)[17] commemorates the 10th of dhu 'l-Ḥijjah which marks the end of the pilgrimage. Not only the pilgrims but also Muslim families everywhere sacrifice according to ritual a sheep or camel and in the banquet that ensues the poor are invited to share.

Another popularly observed feast, the *ʿĪd al-Fiṭr* (The Feast of bread-breaking),[18] is celebrated on the first of Shawwāl according to the Muslim calendar and is the occasion for the display of new attire for those who can afford it. Another feast celebrated throughout the Muslim world is the *Mawlid*, the Prophet's birthday, on the 10th of Rabīʿ I, one of the younger feasts, observed officially from the twelfth century and undoubtedly instituted as a result of the fanfare associated with the Christian observance of Jesus' birthday.

Other Muslim feasts that enjoy regional or sectarian observance include the *ʿAshūrā* mostly in Berber lands, with its carnival-like atmosphere while the Shīʿites on that day commemorate the death (680) of Husayn (Hussein), the Prophet's grandson, at Karbalā' (Kerbala), in Iraq with a Passion performance and a *ta'ziyah* (consolation) procession in which it is not unusual for the devotees to cut up their flesh and beat their bodies in a form of self-mortification long abandoned in the Christian world. There are in addition numerous other celebrations localized in nature and mostly carry-overs from ethnical pre-Islamic backgrounds.

Funerary rites are distinctly governed by Islamic religious concepts and are the occasion not only for the pious to gain credit on Judgment Day but to be reminded of one of the most significant transitory movements on their path to the hereafter. The special Islamic ritualistic observances in preparing the dead for burial, the resting position of the body with the head pointing to Mecca, the funeral banquets on various days, the special prayers recited at each stage, alms giving, annual sacrifices and numerous other performances all tend to remind Muslims of their common institutional observances both in pleasure and in sorrow.

The "Public Good"

The purely Arabian pre-Islamic concept of *murū'ah* (manliness) left a strong imprint on Islamic society. Its effect was felt in a different context than originally conceived. Originally *murū'ah* impelled the Arab to defend *'irḍ* (honor). In Islam *murū'ah* compels the defense of *dīn* (faith), with a strong emphasis on morality and the near identification thereof with piety and beneficence. The spread of mysticism and its legitimization in the twelfth century added a new dimension, that of love. While love to the mystics was the love of God, a personal expression of feeling, the stress of love by extension to the group provided Islamic society with one of its strongest media for strengthening the notion of "public good" or "general welfare" (*maṣlaḥah*).

The Calendar

The Muslims have many lesser yet important unifying institutional observances. Their calendar, for instance, is peculiarly their own. It consists of twelve lunar months each alternating between

29 and 30 days in length for a total of 354 days. To compensate for the eleven-day discrepancy, the Muslims follow the old Arabian practice of adding a day to the last month of the year eleven times in a thirty-year period. The months are known by purely Arabo-Islamic terms.[19] The days begin and end at sunset, Friday being the day of rest or congregation; but the night of a day, which ends at dawn, is that which precedes not what follows it. The divisions of the day conform to the astronomical movements of sunrise, apogee, and sunset; they are regulated, however, not by these but by the times of prayer. Persians have their own solar calendar applying to the commencement of Hegira and similar in length to the Gregorian calendar, which is applied by them and the Sunnis. The Muslim calendar, however, remains operative because of religious requirements. The Muslim era commenced in 622, that being year one of the Hegira.

Economic Factors

Economic practices in the heyday of Islamic communal strength and the institutions built thereon reflected a certain commonness among Muslims, namely, preference for agriculture and cattle-raising at home and trade abroad. This is shown also in the type and range of taxation sanctioned by the *Sharīʿah* which appears to stress the products of the soil.

The *sūq,* bazaar or marketplace in the towns and cities of Islam, constituted the hub of social as well as economic activity. The overland trade from the chief Muslim cities in the East—Baghdad, Damascus, Aleppo, Alexandria—which was funneled eastward and westward made for considerable diffusion not only of wares but of usages, ideas, and common institutional practices clearly stamped with an Islamic spirit which foreign travelers could not help but observe in the Muslim trader. Traders in East Asia and sub-Saharan Africa were instrumental in the spread of Islam from the tenth to later centuries of the Christian era.

Muslim merchants formed a very important social class, controlling prices and trade with far-off lands. The tales of Sindbād the sailor, the recordings of Ibn Baṭṭūṭah in his far-flung journeys in the fourteenth century, even the stories consecrated in the

Arabian Nights all mirror the spirit and genre of adventure associated with the Muslim trader.

The articles of manufacture, increasingly diffused throughout the Muslim World and abroad from the late eighth century onward, reflect very clearly the peculiarly Islamic imprint. Materials used, as well as design and execution in vases, tapestry, leather and metal works, textiles, silks, embroideries, fine linens, brocades, all still bear the name of the cities that excelled in their manufacture—Damask (Damascus), Muslin (Mosul), Cordovan (Cordova).

Commercial transactions over vast areas and on a broad scale gave rise to a number of commercial institutions which were clearly adopted by the merchant states of Renaissance Italy and thence disseminated throughout Europe. Among these are practices relating to sale, hiring, warehousing, wages, interest, exchange, banking, and the like. The stress on contractual obligations, the good faith associated therewith, surety guarantees for the debt of a traveling merchant by a creditor, the promissory note and bill of exchange, the contract of deposit or warehousing, the injunctions against usury as forbidden in the Qurʾān,[20] are some specific examples. The lender by not seeking to profit from his loan is registering an act of pious generosity for which Allah will reward him on the Day of Judgment.

Yet in the areas of commerce where the Qurʾān did not prevail, Europe became the beneficiary and the inheritor; we refer chiefly to the banking institutions and commercial practices of Muslim traders as they developed principally in the ninth and tenth centuries.

In conclusion, the institutional observances and practices that caused Islamic society to cohere are not exhaustive. Attitudes of mind conditioned by religious stimuli are most difficult to delineate. There is what may be termed an "Islamic spirit" which gave vent to a pattern of individual and communal behavior that placed a characteristic stamp on the devout member of this society, a society theocratic in structure yet not altogether restrictive.

What we have related are some of the more tangible institutions and related observances at work. But the strong not always distinguishable ethical undertones motivating behavior are not to be dismissed lightly. Morality as ordained by the Qur'ān was a strong binding element in Islamic society. This we have already seen in a number of instances: in the stress on family ties, which is at the foundation of the Islamic community. There is so much emphasis placed on respect for elders that this emphasis has acquired nearly the sanctity of law. The injunctions in the Qur'ān and Traditions prescribing behavior for men and women are universally honored where the faith is practiced. The stress on justice and fidelity in dealings, the sanctity of oath and trust, the honoring of obligations prescribed by the Qur'ān for the faithful, and the general prevalence of an egalitarian sentiment, all have left a distinguishable mark on Muslims in their relationship with each other and with outsiders.

CHAPTER 9

Heterodoxy and Orthodoxy

THE OVERWHELMING MAJORITY of Muslims today subscribe to Islam of the *Sunnah* or Sunni Islam with its faithful adherence to the doctrine evolved in the nascent Medinan period of Islam under the four Orthodox Caliphs. Subscribers to this doctrine are known as orthodox or Sunni Muslims. They constitute over 90 percent of the entire Muslim community today. All Sunnis are considered one sect although juridically they subscribe to one of the four recognized rites (*madhāhib*, sing. *madhhab*): Māliki, Shāfiʿi, Ḥanafi, or Ḥanbali. An adherent may pass from one into the other without ceasing to be known as an orthodox or Sunni Muslim.

Heterodoxy in Islam owes its origin basically to two historical factors. One resulted from political challenges to existing authority, with the disputing parties invariably taking on the sanctity of religious protection and thus giving rise to a multitude of sects. The other resulted from attempts to provide rational bases for the basic tenets of the faith, leading to the proliferation of philosophical schools of approach to theological beliefs. This trend was abetted by efforts to reduce the rather legalistic and somewhat impersonal implements of the faith to a more personal experience, thus encouraging the mystical approach to religion. The one impact they all had in common was to detract from the theological, political, and consequently social unity of Islam.

The first blow to Islamic unity took place twenty-five years after Muḥammad's death; and it was the result of political, not religious, considerations which arose from Muʿāwiyah's desire to wrest the caliphate from ʿAli, Muḥammad's son-in-law, the fourth and last of the Orthodox Caliphs. Muʿāwiyah was then Muslim governor of Damascus, and the son of Abu Sufyān, Muḥammad's chief Meccan opponent, the Umayyad head of the Qurayshite-ruled Meccan commonwealth. Muʿāwiyah was intensely disliked by many Muslims who had suffered strong privations at his hands before the conquest.

In the ensuing first civil war in Islam, ʿAli won the battle (Ṣiffin, 657) but lost the aftermath when through a ruse thought up by Muʿāwiyah he was compelled to submit to arbitration the caliphate, which he legally possessed.

Khārijites

A group of ʿAli's followers, mostly desert Arabs inspired by the democratic free spirit of their environment, objected to ʿAli compromising his caliphate by responding to the appeal for arbitration and broke away from him, insisting that there should have been no appeal save to the Book of Allah. They became known subsequently as *Khawārij* (Khārijites, or those who "exited"). Unhappy about the dissension generated by maneuverings of those who claimed the right to leadership over Muslims by virtue of family connections with the Prophet or the Quraysh, they took the position that the caliph should be selected from the entire Muslim community, not just the Quraysh.

The Khārijites merit special attention for the views they held because they are regarded as the earliest fundamentalists of Islam. They were the first to insist that the words of God in the Qurʾān must be taken literally and should not be subject to interpretation. Faith without commensurate deeds would not lead to salvation in their judgment. What has been decreed will come to pass. God, however, will not manifest Himself physically in the afterlife to the elect, as other Sunnis believed. They insisted that sinners will suffer damnation, and grave sinners eternal fire while other Sunnis held that no one who has believed will be made to suffer eternally. Indeed, the Khārijites eventually developed their own commentaries on the Qur'ān and *Ḥadīth*. Their law derived strictly from both and the exemplary conduct of the Prophet Muḥammad.

Of equal significance are their views concerning the community. In some respects they were elitists, arguing that Islam was targeted specifically for Arabs. They were unkind to non-Arabs joining Islam. The community to them consists of individuals who share their faith in God and His world. There is no appeal in their eyes save to the Word of God as enshrined in the Qur'ān. As fiercely democratic in their outlook as they might have been, the Khārijites still recognized the need for leadership, albeit in their eyes it was only temporary. To them the leader served as God's agent. If he did not fulfill his duties, he was to be overthrown. Their criterion for selecting him is decreed in the Qur'ān (49:13): "the most honorable among you in the sight of God." Their conception of the *imām's* qualification was the same as the one applied in the selection of tribal chiefs before Islam. But loyalty to faith now superseded ties to family and tribe. If the *imām* should falter in his leadership, he was to be removed, by force if necessary.

Jihād for the Khārijites was the fifth not sixth duty mandated by the faith. The responsibility for it rested with the individual not the community. Indeed, Khārijite men and women often fought without the benefit of leadership in the battlefield. They fought for God not for booty. Only weapons would they accept for their share of booty. Women were the equal of men in every respect. So liberal was their attitude towards the sexes that the status of the child was determined by both. They led a life of simplicity and poverty, abstaining from smoking, drinking, singing, or even laughing. So strict were they in the application of justice that non-Khārijite Sunnis said of them: "they could do no injustice." They held firmly to the belief that words without deeds were valueless. Their greatest contribution to the values of Islam lies in their insistence that every Muslim must manifest positive values without being impelled to do so by decree of *imām* or government, and that this manifestation should serve as a guide to all human beings.[1]

While the early Khārijites were intolerant of those who did not share in their beliefs, refusing to have any social intercourse with them, their descendants today, known as Ibāḍites, after their early leader ʿAbdallah ibn Ibāḍ, hold much more moderate views. They can be found still in Oman, East Africa, and parts of Algeria.

Shīʿites

Another party, mostly city Arabs influenced by Persian ideas, clung to ʿAli with worshipful affection insisting that only he and his descendants had the *legitimate* right to be caliphs. They were undoubtedly influenced by the divine-right-monarchy concepts of pre-Islamic Persia and were joined by Persians on a permanent basis after 1500. They called themselves *Shīʿat ʿAli* (The partisans of ʿAli) to be known later as plain "Shīʿah" or "Shīʿites." They are today the largest single sect next to the Sunnis, constituting about 14 percent of the total, and numbering about one hundred million, including all splinter and radical groups.

Shīʿism for all practical purposes is the religion of Iran, modern Persia, and over 50 percent of the Muslims of Iraq are also Shīʿite. During the Umayyad caliphate they, like other religious minorities, particularly the Christian, were tolerated and left primarily to themselves. The early Umayyads put up with them because they were anxious to enlarge their secular powers and expand their dominions. Indeed, the Umayyad caliphs with the exception of ʿUmar II were considered by their adversaries as "irreligious" and "unpious."

This toleration, however, soon disappeared under the ʿAbbāsids when the Shīʿah had helped wrest the caliphate from the Umayyads in 750. One hundred years later in 850 the caliph al-Mutawakkil became particularly harsh with the Shīʿah, destroying their venerated shrines: the tombs of ʿAli at Najaf and his more venerated son Ḥusayn at Karbalāʾ. In the ensuing atmosphere of increasing hostility, the Shīʿah in their bid for survival began to practice dissimulation (*taqīyah*), that is, they outwardly purported to be espousing other than what actually constituted their real beliefs.

Unlike the Sunnis who were loyal to the duly empowered caliph, the Shīʿahs professed loyalty to an *Imām*, leader or guide, who was a direct descendant of ʿAli, on the grounds that ʿAli allegedly had inherited from the Prophet both his spiritual and secular sovereignty, i.e., the power both to interpret and to enforce the canon law. Thus in lieu of the caliph, who was imbued with no spiritual authority by the Sunnis other than to set an example for piety, the Shīʿahs recognized an *Imām* who, until his disappearance, was regarded as an infallible teacher and the only source of religious instruction and guidance. When the twelfth *Imām* mysteriously disappeared the collective body of Shīʿah ulema began to exercise the prerogatives of the office pending his expected return, with their chief, the Ayatollah (divine word of God), now serving as the highest spiritual authority in Shīʿah Islam. He claimed the right to veto decisions of the ruler if, in his opinion, they contradicted the provisions of the canon law of Islam.

The infallibility of the *Imām's* teachings, according to Shīʿah conceptions of divine successorship, comes first from Allah, then from His chosen mouthpiece Muḥammad, then ʿAli, and finally his legitimate descendants. By reason of kinship with Muḥammad through blood and marriage of his daughter Fāṭimah, ʿAli not only sired the Prophet's only grandsons, al-Ḥasan and al-Ḥusayn, but initiated at the same time a "legitimate" line of successorship divinely ordained and guided.

The line from Ḥusayn produced nine of the twelve *Imāms* acknowledged by the main body of the Shīʿahs, commonly known as "Twelvers" (*Ithna ʿAsharīyah*). Their fate, however, was not very pleasant—four died of poison, and most of the others either fell in battle against the caliphs or were executed for sedition. The twelfth, youthful Muḥammad, simply disappeared in 878 in the cave of the great mosque at Sāmarra without leaving any heir. Hence he has become known as the *Muntaẓar* (awaited) *Imām* whose return will usher in the golden era of true Islam shortly before the end of this world. Thus the messianic concept so dear to Christianity finds an equivalent of a sort among the Persians of today, as it had with their spiritual predecessors of yesteryears like the Zoroastrians and related sectarians.

This hidden *Imām*, who is not dead but merely in a stage of occultation, is destined to reappear as the "Mahdi." Some false alarms had been sounded by the famous Muḥammad Aḥmad (1879), Mahdi of the Sudan, and a little earlier by the so-called "Bāb" (lit. "the gateway," that is, to the Mahdi's reappearance) whose movement inside Persia in the 1840s was ruthlessly suppressed but succeeded in flourishing outside the country in such areas as Chicago and Los Angeles under the guise of Bahā'ism.

The Twelvers' variety of Shī'ism was formally and forcibly imposed on a then predominantly Sunni Persia by the early Safawid Shahs in the year 1502. These Shahs subsequently claimed themselves to be descendants of the seventh *Imām*, Mūsa al-Kāẓim, each regarding himself as a place-holder (*locum tenens*) of the hidden *Imām* until such time as he chooses to return. His spokesmen and intermediaries are the *mujtahids*, the interpreters of dogma who have been serving in the capacity of higher theologians.

Ismā'īlis

It is important to note that Shī'ism opened the floodgates for the overwhelming majority of the splinter sects, no less than seventy-three according to tradition, that sprang into being in subsequent centuries. One sect that agrees with the Twelvers is the Ismā'īli or "Seveners"; they honor the line of succession down to the sixth *Imām*, Ja'far al-Ṣādiq (d. 765), then regard his eldest son Ismā'īl (d. 760) as the seventh (whence the appellation "Seveners") and last *Imām*.[2] He too in the eyes of his followers is the Imām-Mahdi who becomes the hidden leader and whose return they await.

Both in their cosmogony and in their religious beliefs generally, the Ismā'īlis reflect a very pronounced influence derived from Greek philosophy in its primitive stage of development. The Pythagorean system with its stress on the number "seven" was consecrated by the Ismā'īlis who have predicated all cosmic and historical developments on the number seven. Neo-Platonism imparted to them the conception of gnostic knowledge through emanation in seven stages: (1) God; (2) the universal mind (*ʿaql*); (3) the universal soul (*nafs*); (4) primeval matter; (5) space; (6) time; (7) the world of earth and man. The Ismāʿīlis acknowledge the prophet-legislator roles of seven prophets[3] who are considered founders; but the position of others, treated as "silent" legislators,[4] seven in between each set of two of the founders, is also respected. Next and parallel but at a lower level come the propagandizers (*ḥujjah*) and simple missionaries (sing. *dāʿī*).[5]

While Sunni Islam, with its emphasis on the fulfillment of the law (*Sharīʿah*) and of duties, was essentially non-proselytic, the non-Sunnis and especially the Ismāʿīlis actively labored to gain followers. They sent missionaries throughout the world of Islam to preach their esoteric (*bāṭini)* doctrine, an activity which had a drastic effect on Islamic society and reflected one of the most pronounced facets of religio-political internecine conflict in Islam.

The esoteric approach to doctrine looks beyond the outward manifestation, insisting that the apparent (*zāhir*) is merely a camouflage of the true inner meaning which is purposely hidden from the non-initiates. Such an interpretation is quite familiar to the land where Gnosticism was first announced to the world. The Sunnis, on the other hand, pay strict attention to the literal pronouncements of the Qurʾān since to them it is the unembellished word of God. But the Ismāʿīlis and other sectarians subscribing to their views argue that one must look beyond the manifestations of expressed words and seek the inner meaning of the verses. This bold proposition is only one step removed from that sore spot of controversy among Muslims which revolved around the classical debate of whether the Qurʾān was or was not created.

Some historians[6] argue that behind this seemingly religious controversy lies a subtle political plot, an attempt by Persians overwhelmed in Islam to undermine Arab hegemony. ʿAbdullāh the son of Maymūn al-Qaddāḥ (d. ca. 874) of Ahwāz (Persia) not only perfected the Ismāʿīli religiopolitical system, but also used his religious doctrine to exploit Arab-Persian enmity in the hope of destroying the caliphate and gaining political hegemony for himself and his descendants. His pattern of scheming gave birth eventually to the Fāṭimid dynasty of Egypt and Tunisia; and one of his disciples, Ḥamdān Qarmaṭ, a peasant of Iraq, gave birth to the movement named after him, the Qarmaṭian.

Qarmaṭians

The Qarmaṭians (Carmathians) appealed to native masses, both artisans and peasants, Persians and Arabs. The movement, bearing a sectarian coloring, appeared to revive the ancient feud between the townsman and the nomad. Admission to this predominantly communistic sect sharing in property and wives was by initiation. The Qarmaṭians made use of an allegorical catechism which derived principally from the Qur'ān but accommodated other creeds, appealing thereby to men of all races and castes. They insisted on tolerance and equality and organized the only well-disciplined guilds of tradesmen and artisans in Islam; indeed, some authorities believe that their concept and organization of the guilds within a fixed ceremonial and ritualistic structure led to the rise of Freemasonry, with its clear reflections of Arabo-Islamic influences, and the Medieval guild system.[7]

But the Qarmaṭians did not preserve their tolerance for long; indeed, shortly after they came into being in the third century of Islam they developed into an exceedingly militant and violent movement, leaving behind trails of blood in Syria and Iraq. They exercised dominant influence for a while not only in these two countries, but in the Arabian peninsula as well. They even raided Mecca in 930 and carried off the Black Stone from the Ka'bah, not to be returned until 951. Ultimately they fell, but their beliefs survived. The Fāṭimids of Egypt with their kindred doctrine fell heir to their domains and communicants. Today they survive in the highlands of Southern Yemen.

Assassins

It is interesting to note here that the dreaded order of the Assassins of Alamūt and Syria, the scourge of many a Crusader or Muslim earmarked for death, were neo-Ismā'īlis. The founder of the order, Ḥasan ibn al-Ṣabbāḥ was a native of Persia who had returned from Egypt as a Fāṭimid missionary. He seized the strategic natural fortress of Alamūt in 1090. Then in his capacity as the grand master (*dāʿi al-duʿāt*: missionary in chief) of the order, he found himself in a strong position to raid all around northern Persia with impunity. His emissaries, after being keyed up with *ḥashīsh*, could execute anyone marked for death anywhere. They cultivated the art of "daggermanship" and were so successful that traces of their success survive even in our Western vocabulary with the term "assassination." This was perhaps their only notable bid for immortality.

The Assassins spread terror everywhere, and for nearly two centuries all efforts to suppress them by force failed. It was only with the advent of the Mongols who attacked and destroyed their strongholds in 1256 on their way to destroy Baghdad that their menace subsided.

Their organization and doctrinal beliefs were modeled on Ismāʿīli antecedents. They purposely minimized religious instruction, attached little significance to the role of the prophets, but actively labored to encourage daringness in the young initiates. At the head of the order was the *Dāʿi al-Kabīr* (grand preacher) followed by the grand priors, each of whom was in charge of a specific territory, and at the bottom of the hierarchy next to the ordinary propagandists stood the *fidāʾi* (self-sacrificer). The *fidāʾi* was ever ready at the command of the chief to execute orders blindly, with visions of an earthly paradise exciting his soul. The gardens in and surrounding the castle at Alamūt were not only filled with beautiful shrubbery but graced beside by the presence of real live black-eyed *hūris* to the delight of the Assassin whose vision of Paradise, as described in the Qur'ān, was made real on earth.

The Mongols' assault on Alamūt dealt the order a mortal blow. But the end came at the hands of the Mamlūk Sultan Baybars who in 1272 destroyed their Syrian strongholds at Maṣyād, where Rāshid al-Din Sinān (d. 1192), the "old man of the mountain" to the Crusaders, resided and whence he had continued the order's policy of spreading terror.[8]

The survivors of the order, whose numbers are not precisely ascertained but are estimated at ten to fourteen million, are known as Khojas or Mawlas. They are located principally in the

Bombay area of India, with a sprinkling of them in northern Syria and Iran as well as Oman and Zanzibar. Their acknowledged titular head is the Agha Khan, whose headquarters are supposed to be in Bombay. But these alleged descendants of the last grand master of Alamūt find Paris and Switzerland more suitable for the exercise of their spiritual leadership. The grandfather of the present Agha, who claimed descent from the *Imāms*, attracted world attention when his devout followers once gave him his weight of some 250 pounds in gold, and on another occasion in diamonds. These fortunes were then allocated for charity.

Druzes

Another Fāṭimid missionary by the name of al-Darazi (d. 1019), appointed by the caliph al-Ḥākim (d. 1021), began to spread the Ismā'ili doctrine in the hamlets and vales of the southern slopes of Lebanon among a conglomeration of indigenous Aramaeans, infiltrating Persians, and Arabs of the desert. The ground had been prepared by the presence there of adherents to the Shī'ah and Ismā'īli doctrines. The preaching of al-Darazi centered on the notion that the intolerant caliph al-Ḥākim, notorious for his persecution of Jews, Christians, and orthodox Muslims, represented the last in a series of incarnations of the one and only God. Other extremist Shī'ah had also been preaching that 'Ali and his descendants were such incarnations. The general tendency of Shī'ah sects was to preach methods of bridging the gap between God and man. This is also the aim of mystics, as it has been throughout human history.

When the master al-Ḥākim died prematurely, victim of a conspiracy headed by the caliph's own sister whose chastity he had questioned, the faithful followers denied that he was dead, arguing that he had gone into a state of temporary occultation whence he will re-emerge when the time comes.

Al-Darazi himself, narrowly escaping with his life, headed north, and in the remote Taym valley at the foot of Mt. Hermon he began to preach the new doctrine named after him, the "Durzi" or "Druze" way. His ministry was cut short and he fell in battle two years later. Many of those who believed in his message preferred to call themselves "*Muwaḥḥidūn*" (unitarians) rather than "Durzis." Indeed, the doctrine formulator of Druzism, Ḥamzah al-Labbād, a Persian like al-Darazi, denounced him. He too, however, was killed, in Cairo, by an infuriated mob incited by orthodox Fāṭimid theologians.

The most important features of Druzism were enunciated in the middle of the eleventh century. It was to be a *bāṭini* (esoteric) religion, since prudence decreed secrecy; thus did an important principle of the religion come into being, namely, that in the "absence" of al-Ḥākim no part of his religion was to be made public. Access to the sacred handbooks was to be limited only to the initiated; these constituted a few of the *ʿUqqāl* (sing. *ʿāqil*: wise, intelligent).

The *ʿUqqāl* are highly selected individuals who must subscribe to a very rigorous ethical code after surviving the ordeals of a protracted period of trial and probation in which they must prove themselves trustworthy and able to keep secret. Following the ceremonial rite of induction, the initiates must conduct themselves with decorum and dignity and abstain from such vices as wine, tobacco, and abusive language. The most pious, called *ajāwīd* (godly), go so far as to abstain from partaking of food even at high levels of entertainment in the fear that it may have been acquired by illegitimate means. Women can also be initiated if they qualify. The Druzes observe strictly monogamous marriages. Their *ʿUqqāl* hold their religious meetings on Thursday evenings in unostentatious secluded places known as *khalwahs,* usually located on hill tops overlooking their villages.[9]

Spreading northward, mostly into the southern mountains of Lebanon, Druzism gained converts among the Arab tribes roaming the area. These tribes supplied them with the families like the Maʿns, Tanūkhs, and Shihābs, who subsequently became their leaders and feudal lords, and whose descendants have not ceased to play determinative roles in the sociopolitical life of southern Syria and Lebanon until the present time.

The Druzes today number under half a million and are concentrated principally in southern Syria, Lebanon, and northern Israel. They are headed by Shaykh al-ʿAql, guided by the *ʿUqqāl,* and followed by the majority of uninitiated Druzes known as *Juhhāl* who do not partake in the religious ceremonies.

The primary function of the *ʿUqqāl* is to apply the laws of the Druze religion and to assist every Thursday in the ceremonies of the faith. They practice their cult in a very simple chamber devoid of all furnishings and ornamentation, and having only a few mats on the floor. The ceremony is conducted in three stages. In the first, all can participate provided they don the proper attire (a white head band encasing a red turban, a free flowing shirt-like garment known as "*shirwāl,*" and a sleeveless coat called "*ghumbāz*"). This session lasts ninety minutes. The second stage is conducted by those who are a bit more advanced in their study of the faith. They have the right to pose questions illuminating principles of Druzism. The third stage is reserved for the *Ajāwīd*, distinguished by special garments, and preoccupying themselves with the role of "revealing truths" (*kashf al-ḥaqāʾiq*). In a period of two and a half hours the *Ajāwīd* concentrate on the six commandments of their faith:

1. Being sincere;
2. Devotion to coreligionists;
3. Expressing horror at paganism;
4. Never having recourse to the devil;
5. Believing in the unity of al-Ḥākim; and
6. With eyes closed, submitting in heart and soul to his will.

A devoted Druze is one who recites the "*Fātiḥah*" faithfully and expresses his total submission to the will of the "Master of Time," that is al-Ḥākim, and his minister Ḥamzah, and is loyal to the Creator. They believe that God descended to earth in the form of a man to impart happiness to those loyal to Him. The sacred texts of the Druze consider al-Ḥākim this incarnation. He becomes man to share in man's mode of life. He is called "al-Ḥākim" (the ruler) because he rules over the entire universe. He is that universal intelligence (*al-ʿAql*) whom God has empowered to write the holy scriptures. He is the first cause—the cause of all causes. He will return on the day of the last judgment to judge all.

When al-Ḥākim disappeared mysteriously February 23, 1021, his followers believed that he had fulfilled his mission and would return only at the end of the world.

Nuṣayris

The Nuṣayris, numbering less than half a million at the present time, inhabit the northwestern corner of Syria, with Latakiya on the Mediterranean forming their great urban capital. Minor enclaves of Nuṣayris are found in the center of Syria, along the Euphrates in Iraq, in Kurdistan, and in Iran. They extend into the Cilician region of southern Turkey. It has been presumed that they take their name from Muḥammad ibn Nuṣayr, a notable of Basra, who in 859 proclaimed himself the gateway (*bāb*) of the tenth *Imām* (ʿAli al-Naqīy) and of his eldest son Muḥammad who disappeared (went into occultation) in 863. Others say he took for *Imām* the eleventh (Ḥasan al-ʿAskari) and his son Muḥammad, who disappeared. Most consider Nuṣayr's successor, Ḥusayn ibn Ḥamdān al-Khaṣībi (d. 957 or 968) as the real founder of the Nuṣayri sect. He hailed from Junbula, a town between Wāsiṭ and Kūfa in Iraq, heartland of the Qarmaṭian and Zanj movements, and was patronized by the great efflorescing dynasty of the Ḥamdānids who made the Aleppo region a center of cultural life in the tenth century.

While a pagan and Christian substratum underlies the Nuṣayri sect, its principal elements today derive from pure south Arabian stock: Kinda, Ḥamdān, Ghassān, Buhra, and Tanūkh. It was one Ḥasan ibn Makhzūn (d. 1240) who imposed on this grouping its ruling families, clans, and ethnical structure. The Nuṣayris settled in Syria in the wake of the exodus of the Crusaders' remnants driven out by the Mamluks of Egypt. They are usually referred to as Alawites and it is from their ranks that the Syrian leadership of today derives.

Their religious beliefs are similar in broad outlines to Ismāʿīli Shīʿism. From the ineffable God according to Nuṣayri cosmogony emanates the spiritual world of heavenly beings, or stars, giving form to the "great luminous world." This is done in seven stages with the aim of leading back to the source the "little luminous world" of fallen beings imprisoned in bodies after reviving them. Brought back to heaven, they form the seven last classes (*ahl al-marātib*). Next comes the "little world of darkness," of extinguished lights—souls that damnation caused to be transformed into bodies of women and animals. Lastly comes the "great world of darkness" wherein dwell all the "adversaries" of the great luminous world. In it are the demons who had undergone numerous metamorphoses in corpses of slain men or slaughtered animals still quivering after death and who are now reduced to inert matter. Just as the fall takes place in seven stages, so does the path to heaven of the chosen or elect lead through seven cycles (*adwār*) or divine emanations.

According to the teachings of Abu 'l-Khaṭṭāb, the common articulator of doctrine for both Ismāʿīlis and Nuṣayris, revelation consists of emanations from the ineffable God, object of adoration, the first being the Name (*ism*), the articulating prophetic voice (*nāṭiq*), the signification (*maʿna*) of divine authority. In the cycle pertaining to Muḥammad (the *Muḥammadīyah*) signification is expressed through five privileged names: Muḥammad, ʿAli, Fāṭim (masculine form of Fāṭima since women are held to have no souls), Ḥasan, and Ḥusayn. ʿAli was thought to surpass them, and was identified by hyperbolism with the signification, whence the origin of the "god ʿAli" notion among the Nuṣayris.

Initiation among the Nuṣayris is accomplished in three stages. The first consists of a solemn pledge in which the word of the initiator fertilizes the soul of the initiate in three seances. The ritual followed is that of the other extremist Shīʿah sects and can be traced back to the Sabeans of Ḥarrān. In it the initiate partakes of the cup of wine in anticipation of Paradise. The process of initiation symbolizes the seven canonical rites of Islam: the five ceremonial obligations plus *jihād* and *walāya* (devotion to the ʿAlids and hatred of their adversaries). The Qurʾān is regarded as an initiation for devotion to ʿAli.

The Nuṣayris observe a number of annual festivals not all Muslim in origin—to wit, Christmas, Epiphany, the feast of St. Barbara, the 17th of March, together with what they term "masses," in addition to the Muslim feasts of Aḍḥa, Fiṭr, ʿAshūrāʾ and even the Persian Nawruz.

Matāwilah

The Shīʿah Twelvers in Lebanon are commonly referred to as Matāwilah (those who profess love for ʿAli) and constitute a powerful element of that country's population. They are concentrated today in the southern outskirts of Beirut and form a dominant element in the population of the two large southern cities of Sidon and Tyre. Once strong in the northern regions around Jubayl (Byblos) and Kisrawān, today they form the majority in the southernmost region of Lebanon and have been the unfortunate victims of war between the Palestinians and Israelis.

Originally they were of Persian stock, having been transplanted into the Lebanon range by Muʿāwiyah in his efforts to weaken the ʿAlids in their challenge to his political authority late in the seventh century. The appelation "Matāwilah" was not applied to them until the eighteenth century. Over half a million strong, they managed to enjoy freedom of faith but not economic equality, nor a commensurate proportion of political privilege (shared until the 1976 civil war by Maronite Christians and elitist Sunni Muslim families of Tripoli and Beirut); hence, their alliance with Palestinian refugees during the Lebanese civil war.

Today they constitute the plurality sect in Lebanon and are represented by both "Amal" and Hizballah, which seeks with Iranian support to create an Islamic republic in South Lebanon.

Zaydis

The sect closest to Sunnism among the Shīʿah is that of the Zaydis. They take their name from Zayd, the grandson of Ḥusayn. First to challenge the caliphate of the Umayyads following his grandfather's martyrdom at Kerbala, he was killed in street-fighting in Kūfa, in 740. His followers continued the struggle, but to no avail. They became a united community only after ʿAlids laid claim to spiritual leadership under the influence of the sect's founder, Ḥasan ibn Zayd (d. 864), who first established a state south of the Caspian Sea. A contemporary, al-Qāsim al-Rassi (d. 860) first laid down the basic elements of their teachings, which betray strong affiliation with rationalist Muʿtazilite theology. Zaydism is anti

Murji'ite in ethic and puritanical in that it rejects Sufism. Indeed, no Sufi orders are permitted in the Zaydi state of Yemen.

Worship among Zaydis parallels other Shī'ah observances with minor departures. Like them, they do not follow an impious leader in prayer, nor do they touch meat of animals not butchered by Muslims. They are against mixed marriages, nor do they allow *mut'ah*. All their wars are regarded as manifestations of *jihād*, thus entitling the participants to the prerogatives thereof. Because Zaydis are not all concentrated in Yemen, they tend to hold diverse views on legal questions which are not considered essential to their sectarian beliefs. Thus we find many Zaydis on the side of Sunnis, and vice versa, in disputes. This, perhaps, is a reason why for all practical purposes they are treated as the fifth Sunni *madhhab*. The basic requirement for leadership among Zaydis is that the *Imām* be of the 'Alid family (*ahl al-bayt*) without regard to successorship through either Ḥasan's or Ḥusayn's line. Qualification is by ability and learning, not by lineal heritage. This would account for the lack of sustained lineal descendants in the imamate.

While it cannot be fully established, the Zaydis today are believed to number between six and eight million.

Shī'ah Extremism

Space does not permit us to treat in detail the numerous offshoots of Shī'ah Islam which have taken to extremist views in ascertaining a separatist identity for themselves. Suffice it to say that the extremists, or "*ghulāh*," not only share the common Shī'ah view that leadership in Islam, both physical and spiritual, must come exclusively from the house of 'Ali, but some of them have gone so far as to place 'Ali before Muḥammad. Indeed, there are 'Ali deifiers among them (*'Ali Ilāhis*), concentrated mostly in Iran and Turkestan in central Asia, who argue that the Archangel Gabriel not only mistook Muḥammad for 'Ali when God commissioned him to deliver the message, but that 'Ali was indeed the incarnation of God. Akin to them in belief are the Qizil-bāsh (red-capped heads)[10] of eastern Anatolia and the Bektashis of Turkey and Albania.

Sunnism

The main body of Islam is known as *Ahl al-Sunnah wa-'l-Ḥadīth*, or followers in the path laid out by the Prophet himself and believers in his *sayings*. The source of primary religious authority to them is the Qur'ān and the *sunnah* (path) and *ḥadīth* (sayings) of the Prophet. *Sunnah* and *ḥadīth* together constitute the *Tradition*.

That this body of semi-sacred text should figure prominently as a source of religious and legal guidance is the logical outcome of Muḥammad's function as God's spokesman. Surely he who was selected to transmit the sacred word of God could not be less inspired in his sayings concerning details of daily life. To establish the hallowedness of such details is important in the eyes of the jurists who often find more need for the Tradition than for the Qur'ān as a source of official guidance to meet the requirements of imparting legality to decisions.

In the first few decades *ḥadīth* was circulated orally, first by the Companions of the Prophet, then by those who heard it from them. This method of transmission opened the gates to a flood of fabrication, and within a few generations the sayings of Muḥammad appeared to transcend all logical bounds.

For more than a century *ḥadīth* passed from mouth to mouth because attempts to write them down had been discouraged. Had the narrators of *ḥadīth* been all pious men, the continuation of oral transmission might have been tolerated. But there were those who wanted to appear pious when they were not at the expense of inventing *ḥadīth* to justify their manner of life or dogmatic views. Invented *ḥadīth* played an important role in the rise of the sects and the justification of their own non-orthodox teachings. With the spread of forged *ḥadīth*, religious opinion tended to become confused.

The Corpus of Tradition

Finally, in the second half of the eighth century encouragement was given to the compilation and verification of a corpus of traditions, and the first surviving result was the *Muwaṭṭa'* of Mālik ibn Anas of Medina. His compilation can not be classified as strictly religious since it is more in the nature of a *corpus juris*; Mālik recorded every tradition that had been used to give effect to a legal decision.

The relation of law to religion in Islam is here clearly illustrated. This law was revealed to Muḥammad as the will of God for the benefit of worshipers. God *is* the sole head and legislator of the community. Muḥammad is His agent, not vicar. "Consequently, to violate the law, or even to neglect the law, is not simply to infringe a rule of social order—it is an act of religious disobedience, a sin, and involves a religious penalty."[11]

The actual work of sorting out the thousands of traditions that sprang into being, eliminating the dubious ones and arranging those verified by a careful system of authentication, was not undertaken until the latter part of the third Islamic century. In the period between 815 and 912 traditions were sifted and reclassified according to their relation to the various aspects of religious life and practice.

During this same period the jurisprudents compiled all six collections which later were canonized by the Sunni Muslims. Leading among them is the *Ṣaḥīḥ* (The Verified) of al-Bukhāri who had spent sixteen years journeying through Muslim lands to collect upward of 600,000 *ḥadīths*; of these he included only 4,000 in his work.[12] Of the other five compendia,[13] only the *Ṣaḥīḥ* of Muslim (817–875)[14] is cited as frequently as Bukhāri's.

Ijmāʿ

When the orthodox community was confronted by a situation wherein neither the Qurʾān nor the acknowledged body of *Ḥadīth* provided adequate guidance, theologians applied the principle of *ijmāʿ* (consensus). *Ijmāʿ* was invoked to support religious observances and was explicitly sanctioned by prevailing canon law. This is as close as Muslims could come to agree on a principle of innovation by universal consent.

Ijmāʿ became a very important principle for the justification of religious beliefs or practices not specifically sanctioned by the

Qur'ān and *ḥadīth*. Much of these antedated the Islamic era, deriving from customs and norms of the Jāhilīyah period. While they were present all along, it was not until after three hundred years of Islam that their presence was detected. By then it was too difficult to uproot them from the lives of men. Since it was not easy to find traditions that would abrogate the practices of pre-Islamic days, the next logical alternative was to acknowledge their legality by means of *ijmā'*.

What is worth noting here is that not all Muslims accepting *ijmā'* as a means of legislation understood it in the same context. In Medina, for instance, *ijmā'* simply meant the consensus of the citizens of Medina, not of the whole Muslim community which was neither solicited nor recognized. Under the 'Abbāsids *ijmā'* was applied much more widely as a means of gaining fealty for the caliphs. It was used also to win legal recognition for the six canonical books as sources of authoritative information on the *sunnah* and *ḥadīth* of Muḥammad.

The more conservative interpreters of religious law in Islam would restrict *ijmā'* to the early teachers of the law, the *fuqahā'*, also known collectively as *mujtahidūn* (sing. *mujtahid*: an official interpreter of the *Sharī'ah*), or to those who are dedicated to the proper interpretation and application of what orthodox Islam sanctions. In terms of time this would confine its development to the earliest period, a period which could not take in the decisions of *mujtahidūn* belonging to a generation not contemporary with Muḥammad. The Shī'ahs pay special deference to the principle of *ijmā'*, and have not ceased to apply it until the present time, even though the exercise of *ijmā'* is restricted to the religious class of ulema and the Ayatollah, who is regarded as the Imām Faqīh, or leading jurisconsult.

Qiyās

The next most widely recognized source of authoritative support of religious beliefs and practices among the orthodox Muslims is that embodied in the principle of *Qiyās* or analogical deduction. *Qiyās* simply is the way a belief or practice gains official credence and support on the grounds that it is similar to a practice or belief clearly embodied in the Qur'ān, *Sunnah*, or *ijmā'*. Before *qiyās* was officially recognized, Muslim interpreters of the *Sharī'ah* had exercised *ra'y*, private opinion, in the teaching of doctrine. Indeed, it was in an attempt to curb the widespread use of *ra'y* in a delicate area of religion that *qiyās* came into being as a more acceptable alternative.

The use of *qiyās*, however, was not free of controversy. Muslim theologians debated earnestly and almost continuously the extent and range of its application. Some argued that *qiyās* should be restricted to the area of "material similarity"; others advocated its use also in the not-so-well defined area of similarity in motive or cause. What enabled the principle of *ra'y* to gain acceptance in limited quarters, although it was merely the product of *ijtihād* was the lack of agreement among the *mujtahidūn*, who preferred the device of individual interpretation. In spite of its obvious shortcoming in purporting to achieve a uniform consensus, *qiyās* was one way of maintaining the progressive development of the community of Islam in conformity with the religious sanctification needed.

But as political upheavals within the community and the assault of the barbarians from without tore away at their political unity, which was mostly nominal by the thirteenth century when the Mongols made their appearance, the great majority of Muslim jurists and theologians were determined to salvage what they could to preserve the uniformity of religious conceptions and beliefs by "closing the gate of *ijtihād*" (*sadd bāb al-ijtihād*). This meant that however erudite a Muslim may be in his knowledge of the *Sharī'ah*, *Sunnah*, and *Ḥadīth*, he could no longer officially function as a *mujtahid*, or an authoritative interpreter of the canon law. Logical formalism set in; no possibility of *bid'ah*, questioning an accepted decision based on *ijmā'*, or "innovation," would be tolerated.

This was a very significant development for Islam and for its capacity to adapt to changing needs and circumstances. In barring *ijtihād*, no new interpretations, regardless of circumstances, could gain support and general acceptance. With the closing of the gate of *ijmāʿ*, the panic-stricken ulema opened wide the gate of the "Dark Ages," or the "Medieval Era," in Islam, an era that stretched over five hundred years. Only in our century has there been a concerted attempt to resurrect *ijtihād* as the means of moving ahead on the path of renewal and progress.

Madhāhib

The *madhāhib* (sing. *madhhab*: juridical-religious rite) were responsible for reducing the *Sunnah* to practical use. Where *ijtihād* may have served to keep Islam abreast of political and social upheavals, the emergence of the accepted juridical-religious rites tended to keep the faithful on the proper path of fulfilling their religious and non-religious obligations as members of one broad socioreligious entity. The actual administration of law was the prerogative of civil and military officials of the caliphs. The *dhimmis*, or protected non-Muslim communities, were subject to their own administrative and judicial procedures, provided they paid the *jizyah* and remained loyal to the caliph.

These laws, predominantly secular in nature, varied from province to province as they had been heavily influenced by local laws; in Syria by Syro-Byzantine laws which the Umayyads did not hesitate early in their caliphate to adapt to their needs as they arose; in lands once dominated by Persia, by relics of the Sasānid laws, which again were not completely wiped out by the Islamic conquest. Even in Jāhilīyah Arabia customary and legal practices managed to survive in Islam where the *Sharīʿah* did not provide specific alternatives.

During the first century and a half of Islam, canon law was applied without reference to what might be termed "secular" matters. When the ʿAbbasids supplanted the Umayyads as caliphs, they proclaimed a return to the pietistic religious devotional life purportedly neglected by their predecessors. The *fuqahāʾ* were encouraged to set forth the principles that might be adopted in the fulfillment of religious obligations quasi-juridical in nature.

Sometime in the course of the third Muslim century, the principles for observing religious obligations jelled into certain categories or classifications. Categorization tended towards one of four *madhāhib*, each bearing the stamp of the norms prevalent in the geographical region where the *madhhab* gained its widest following. It is important to note that these four rites are in agreement on all points vital to Islam as a socioreligious force; all acknowledge the authority of the Qur'ān and *Ḥadīth* as sources of ultimate law for Islam, and all Sunnis who adhere to one of the four "ways," as they must, do not compromise their orthodoxy by switching a *madhhab*.

Ḥanafite

The earliest *madhhab* formed was that of Abu Ḥanīfah (d. 767), known as the "Ḥanafi" rite or juridical school. It reflects the views of the jurists of Iraq much more than do other rites; manifesting considerable toleration in the use of *ra'y*. In many respects it is less rigid in its doctrinal interpretations than the other three *madhāhib*. The laws derived therefrom might be construed "liberal" when compared to those of the fundamentalists. The school is dominant among Turkic peoples in Central Asia, in Turkey, the Arab countries of the Fertile Crescent region, Lower Egypt, and India.

Mālikite

The next school in order of time is that founded by Mālik ibn Anas (d. 795) of Medina. As expected, it reflected strongly the views of the jurists and the practices associated with that city. Mālik was appointed judge in Medina and while serving in this capacity he gathered together his decisions into the corpus called *al-Muwaṭṭa'* (the Levelled Path). Like the jurists of Iraq, those of Medina preferred to depend more on the traditions associated with the Companions of Muḥammad than with the Prophet himself. When it came to conflicting traditions, Mālik and his followers after him simply made an arbitrary choice.

The time factor figured prominently. If for instance the conflict was between a tradition attributed to the Prophet and another to one of his Companions, they chose the Companion's. Two of Abu Ḥanīfa's disciples, Abu Yūsuf and Muḥammad Shaybāni, became responsible for solidifying the views of their master; unlike him, however, they did not decline to serve in judicial posts in Iraq. They shared with their Medinan counterparts, followers of Mālik, the view that it is safer to stay with the traditions that were generally known and less prone to conflict than to accept the irregular ones, however significant they might appear to be. They too attached more importance to the Companions' traditions on the grounds that these could not have existed without knowledge of the Prophet's *ḥadīth* and *sunnah.* They sought harmony, even if it meant resorting to arbitrary choices, and rejected prophetic traditions contradictory to the Qurʾān. They regarded the traditions associated with the Companions' successors as equal in importance to those of the Companions themselves. Adherents of this rite are strong in North Africa, particularly Algeria.

A juridical school, strong in Syria-Palestine, but of very limited range, that of al-Awzāʿi (d. 774) developed an attitude similar to the Iraqi-Medinan, stressing perhaps a little more the Prophet's *sunnah* but still seeking to interpret it in the light of the Companions' traditions. As this school differed little from the other two, it disappeared from the scene very early.

Shāfiʿite

The third important school in time was that founded by al-Shāfiʿi (d. 820), who had been a disciple of Mālik. More than any other jurisprudent he left the most telling impact on the development of Islamic jurisprudence on the basis of the Qurʾān and *Ḥadīth* in his *Risālah.*

While Mālikis and Ḥanafis were prepared to accept as binding the traditions of Companions and their Followers (*al-Tābiʿūn*) if they accorded with the observances prevalent in the community, al-Shāfiʿi would not accept such traditions as legally valid if they did not sustain the Prophet's authority. Al-Shāfiʿi was well versed in his knowledge of the Qurʾān and the *Sunnah.* It was he who defined the components of the *Sharīʿah* as consisting of: (1) Qurʾān, (2) *Sunnah*, (3) *Ijmāʿ*, and (4) *Qiyās* and reduced the use of *ra'y* to secondary importance even though it was at that time the method of decision most popular in the principal cities of Islam. He established furthermore the principle that no tradition directly received from the Prophet himself and properly authenticated could be superseded. Indeed, from his point of reference, an authenticated tradition automatically rendered invalid any tradition attributed to a Companion or Follower (*Tābiʿ*) that conflicted with it. If there was a conflict between two traditions authenticated as the Prophet's, then the one closer to the Qur'ān and the *sunnah* of Muḥammad himself was to be preferred.

It was al-Shāfiʿi who elevated the authority of the *Ḥadīth* to its position of pre-eminence, if indeed he did not give it a higher authority than the Qur'ān itself by making it the authoritative interpretation of Allah's sacred words as enshrined therein. "God had made obedience to the prophet incumbent on all believers, and therefore what he said came from God as the Qur'ān did."[15]

By giving more weight to the authority of the *Ḥadīth*, al-Shāfiʿi strengthened the trend making for rigidity in the adaptability of canonical law. Had his doctrines been strictly observed, Islam would have lost much of its dynamism and its capacity for adjustment to change. Indeed, in the period of "medievalism" in Islam, from the thirteenth until the present century, the influence of this doctrine was very strongly felt.

When al-Shāfiʿi predicated the validity of an act on conformity with *Ḥadīth*, a corpus limited in its development to the exigencies of Muḥammad's Meccan-Medinan world of two decades of preaching, he *ipso facto* circumscribed its applicability to the needs of an expanded Islamic community in an increasingly complex world. To decree that the sanction of the *Sunnah* and the Qur'ān is necessary for the sustenance of progressive measures may be desirable, but by narrowing the means of interpretation the Shāfiʿite paved the way for *bidʿa* (innovation). Where there was a strong determination to pursue measures, even if they did not appear to conform to the letter of the *Ḥadīth*, the blessing of authoritative sanction could be gained by the would-be innovators simply inventing a suitable tradition together with a convincing *isnād* (a verifiable chain of transmission) traceable right to the Prophet himself.

Al-Shāfiʿi may have been a man of strong integrity, but successors yearning for "new things" did not always resist temptation. In this regard the Māliki-Ḥanafi approach was more flexible: simply to take the tradition that best suits a situation, never mind whether it is the Prophet's, a Companion's, or a Follower's. Besides, did not Muḥammad in his capacity as spokesman for himself prove to be quite adaptable to changing circumstances? Indeed, did not even Allah come to his rescue at a moment of crisis or serious confrontation with the proper *āyah*, His brand of "*ḥadīth*"?

This stress on prophetic confirmation of a *ḥadīth* contributed to the widespread fabrication of *isnād* to give validity to a spurious tradition, which made the task of the compilers like Bukhāri, Muslim, Ibn-Māja, and others who sought to sort out hundreds of thousands of *ḥadīth* for the purpose of authentication laborious if not impossible.

When the *Sharīʿah* was being fixed and defined in the third century of the Hijrah, purportedly for all time, the doctrine of al-Shāfiʿi left the strongest imprint thereon. The formula was to identify the *sunnah* with the contents of *ḥadīth* known to be from the Prophet, then to give it the blessed approval of *ijmāʿ* of the *ulema*. The line was henceforth drawn: on the side governed by the *Sharīʿah* was orthodoxy; on the other, heterodoxy maybe, but heresy nevertheless. It was in this century, the third, that the *ulema* finally agreed on the acceptance and interpretation of *ḥadīth*; there was no more room for criticism and emendation. The last word had been spoken. The individual *mujtahid* could apply his personal judgment (*raʾy*) only on questions of detail not already defined but not on substance.

Al-Shāfiʿi, a forceful thinker who had a unique grasp of principles, a clear understanding of the problems, and the singular ability to muster forth persuading arguments, stands above other Muslim jurisprudents in terms of the impact he left on the *Sharīʿah*. The school of jurisprudence founded by him is strong in Lower Egypt, Syria, India, and especially Indonesia.

Ḥanbalite

The fourth school is that associated with Aḥmad ibn-Ḥanbal (d. 855), known as the Ḥanbali. Aḥmad himself did not establish a separate school; this was rather the work of his followers, strong in Iraq and Syria. The resultant *madhhab* was the most conservative of the four. Its strict and rigid views caused its eclipse during the Ottoman conquest in the sixteenth century, the Turks being more favorably disposed to the Ḥanafi rite.

But Ḥanbalism was revived again in the eighteenth century with the rise of Wahhābism in Arabia. The triumph of the house of Saud and its strict espousal of the Ḥanbali doctrine gave Ḥanbalism new vitality and validity, in central Arabia at first, then later among all those who today espouse the return to fundamentalism.

The Ḥanbalis adhere to the literal wordings of the Qurʾān and *Ḥadīth* and are least compromising on matters pertaining to prophetic traditions, with a fanatical insistence on the strict fulfillment of religious duties and responsibilities exactly as defined by the *Sharīʿah*. Being concerned with matters that can be classified under the category of religious or canonical law, they are independent of caliphal and secular authority. Neither sultan nor caliph could interfere with the decisions they made; indeed, it was the duty of the ruler rather to support and enforce such decisions by providing for the appointment of the *qāḍis* (judges).

Owing to the concept that law in the Islamic community is essentially indivisible and the fact that in reality the caliph, sultan, or *amīr* governed the community according to the tenets of the *Sharīʿah*, there did not develop a corpus of genuine secular law until very recent times; nor was there anything that could be termed "secular" legislation. Adjudication of wrongs (*mazālims*) was on an ad hoc basis in judicial sessions. When a question of "constitutionality" or "legality" arose, a summary was submitted to a jurisconsult, called a *mufti* versed in the rules of the *madhhab* of the litigants. The opinion he gave was in the form of a *fatwa* and it might or might not be honored.

Until the rise of Ottoman hegemony in the Muslim world, these *muftis* were men of no definite official status in the community and were independent of the secular side of the administration. In the Ottoman Empire they were graded in an officially recognized and operative hierarchy headed by a chief *mufti* in Istanbul known as *Shaykh al-Islām* (head spokesman of Islam).

It is in these various *fatwas* that we are able to perceive how the *madhāhib* were able to put into force their views and principles. In these we can also detect the impact of doctrinaire interpretations regarding the *Sharīʿah* on local customs, resistances to them, and the extent such local customs have been assimilated in orthodox Islam.

Far from compromising the powerful unifying appeal of the *Sharīʿah*—indeed, far from even lending it flexibility—the *madhāhib* did not detract from the orthodoxy of canonical law ordained by it. Despite the spread of heterodoxy, the spirit of the *Sharīʿah* continued to permeate all facets of the community's social, political, religious, and even literary life. It is "the epitome of the true Islamic spirit, the most decisive expression of Islamic thought, the essential kernel of Islam."[16]

CHAPTER 10

Formalism and Free Expression

THE SIMPLE DOCTRINES of Islam deriving from the injunctions of the Qur'ān, supplemented by the *ḥadīth* and *sunnah* of Muḥammad, formalized in the *Sharī'ah* as a coherent entity and put into practice by one of the four *madhāhib*, would have served the Muslim community's needs well and long if it had remained in the world of Mecca-Medina. But when a small community develops into a world empire, the simple puritanical and coherent doctrines formalized for the original Islamic community could not remain unquestioned or unchallenged.

Outside Influences

The challenge came from the quarter of "free thought" and "free expression," qualities very strongly imbedded in Arabia and dear to the Arab's heart long before the Greeks provided him with the vehicles for systematic expression: logic and reason. Powerful stimuli came also from contact with non-Muslim Arabs and non-Arabs following the first two stages of expansion, 634–642 and 700–732. The Umayyad caliphs were particularly tolerant of non-religious views and of non-Muslim religions as well. Their court at Damascus was worldly and relatively tolerant from the point of view of Islam's religious interests. Being concerned primarily with worldly gain, the Umayyads strove after dominion (*mulk*), made no attempt to propagate Islam, and favored Christians like the renowned al-Akhṭal, the poet, and John of Damascus, the celebrated church father who served also as a high ranking official in the administration of the Arabo-Islamic empire.

In the atmosphere of tolerance and free exchange (680–750) fostered by the Umayyads a general intellectual fermentation began to take place. The lands newly acquired by the quick-minded sons of the desert were impregnated with all sorts of theological and philosophical concepts dating back to man's beginning in time. Even before the impact of Hellenism was felt, following Alexander's conquest of the Middle East, the area was rife with religious and philosophical literature. The dualistic philosophy of Persia penetrated Islam as it had previously permeated the doctrines of Christianity. Logical and metaphysical speculations originating in India and the dialectism of the Christian fathers also left an impact on the molding of Islamic beliefs.

Greek knowledge found its way into Islam partly through the heritage of the Near East, and more directly in the second century of the Hijrah when Greek learning became attractive to Muslim thinkers.

In the early stages, such non-conformist Christian sects as the Jacobites or Monophysites contributed their share of Neo-Platonic speculation and mysticism. The Nestorians have been regarded as the earliest teachers of the Muslims, particularly in the area of medicine. The Muslims were in contact with the center of Zoroastrian and Neo-Platonic learning at Jundi-shāpūr, with the pagan stronghold at Ḥarrān where strong Neo-Pythagorean as well as Neo-Platonic schools thrived, and also with the Jews first in and later out of Arabia. The general Christian debate over doctrine at the time of Islam's emergence appears also to have contributed to Muslim theological and philosophical debates, particularly in the realm of dogmatics.

An early interest in the logical writings of Aristotle was fostered by the translations of the priest-physician Probus of Antioch during the first half of the fifth Christian century, almost a century before the rise of Islam in Arabia. Jacob of Edessa (640–708) had undertaken an extensive translation of Greek theological writings into Syriac, the intermediate step before Arabic. The Syrian thinkers were interested in Pythagorean and Platonic wisdom and in their moralizing collection of aphorisms, also in Aristotle's logic which was directed towards the end of elevating knowledge above faith, a very important point of departure for later Muslim Aristotelians and a great stimulant for Muslim thinkers such as Ibn Rushd (Averroës). That aspect of Platonic philosophy which treats of the soul's consciousness of its own inner essence had not as much significance as the trend towards Aristotelian logic. Thus in Islam were galvanized these two important trends characteristic of Plato and Aristotle.

The early Muslim thinkers took up philosophy where the Greeks left off (as did the great Medieval thinkers of Christiandom continue the dialogue where the Muslims left off). The aim of Muslim thinkers was to reconcile such Platonic concepts as the creation of the world, the substantiality of things spiritual, and the immortality of the soul with the more popular Aristotelian emphasis on reason and the consequent subordination of the spiritual and ethical to the rational process. The stress was on the *virtue of knowing*, which served to buttress the cause of dialectics among Muslim thinkers and to play up the importance of *intelligence* (*ʿaql*) as the next most important "determiner" after God.

As Aristotle's thinking was suited to the Syro-Arab conceptual approach to philosophical thinking, his teachings emerge as a source of reference to them. They were especially interested in his principle: *all that exists, including the soul itself, exists by intelligence.* This formula proved itself to be quite attractive to the Arab mentality which stressed the approach of *knowing things as they really are.* Thus in Aristotle Muslim thinkers found the great guide; to them he became the "first teacher."

Having accepted this *a priori*, Muslim philosophy as it evolved in subsequent centuries merely chose to *continue* in this vein and to enlarge on Aristotle rather than to innovate. It chose the course of eclecticism, seeking *to assimilate* rather than *to generate*, with a conscious striving to adapt the results of Greek thinking to Muslim philosophical conceptions, but with a much greater comprehensiveness than was achieved in early Christian dogmatics, which were similarly influenced by Greek thinking.

Among the earliest to take an active interest in Aristotelian logic were the Muslim grammarians and mathematicians in the eighth and ninth centuries who resided mostly at Basra in Iraq. Basra was also the home of the jurists who developed the principle of *qiyās* as a tool of canonical legislation and who also acquired, on account of it, the title "the people of Logic." Its influence was felt equally in a broader segment of the Muslim doctrinal system.

The Qur'ān, as we observed, was understood to provide *precepts* but not doctrine and the *Ḥadīth*, guidance, but again no doctrine. In the evolution of a Muslim doctrinal system, Christian influences, both Orthodox and Monophysite, mostly in Damascus, left a determining imprint; as did the Gnostic and Nestorian theories in Basra and Baghdad.

Among the first doctrines to come under the attack of logic was that of "freedom of the will," already accepted by the Christians of the east, and through them by the "rationalists" among Muslims. The orthodox theologians who resisted the application of pure logic to matters of doctrine countered with dialectics (*kalām*) to suppress what they termed a "violent innovation."

The "science of reasoning," however, had been accepted as a medium of exposition; the jurisprudent and the theologian began to apply it in their deductions. The result was a form of categorization of methods. The *exoteric* method made use of "free thinking" to scrutinize accepted beliefs for rational truths regarding the fundamental problems of the universe pertaining to the concept of God and the soul, irrespective of whether they conformed or did not conform to established doctrines. The dialectical method, on the other hand, favored the attainment of so-called "truths" in a way compatible with the established beliefs of Islam.

Such categorization was the natural product of the clash between two basic approaches to the same issues. Those who preferred the traditional approach, namely, the orthodox spokesmen, insisted on respecting the way of the *Sunnah* as established by the *Sharī'ah*. They were for the most part descendants of the early

Arab believers. The "rationalists," on the other hand, derived largely from the new converts, descendants mostly of Byzantine and Persian elements steeped in Hellenic and Zoroastrian theological and philosophical traditions.

In the early stages of the clash, the debate may have been looked upon as academic, or an experiment in logic; with the passing of time and the persistence of the debate, the theologians decided to fight the rationalists with their own weapons. They began to employ logic in affirming religious principles and thus took to the path of scholasticism. Europe in the upper Middle Ages became the beneficiary of the Muslim experience; the scholastic thinkers of the Church followed in the steps of their Muslim counterparts and, like them, sought to reconcile religious dogma with the dictates of reason.

Classification of Schools of Thought

The orthodox Muslim writers on the schools of thought in Islam and the sects attempted to classify them into certain recognizable categories. Two renowned authors, Ibn Hazm (d. 1064) of Muslim Spain and al-Shahrastāni (d. 1153) of the Abbāsid east, engaged in the study of sectarian proliferation and thought. Al-Shahrastāni, a principal authority on the sects, had listed seventy-three; and because his predecessors who had dwelt on the subject made unclear differentiations among them, he himself endeavored to distinguish between them on the basis of how they reacted to the principal areas of controversy over religious doctrine.

For a premise in distinguishing between the schools and classifying them, he chose the position each adopted regarding points of contention in doctrinal interpretation, namely, the matter of: (1) predestination and free will; (2) the divine attributes of God; (3) promises and threats, faith and error; and (4) revelation, reason, and the *imāmate* or leadership. On this basis, al-Shahrastāni was able to classify the contenders into the following schools: Qadarites, Ṣifatites, Khārijites, and Shīʿites. He also classified the opposing schools or those who held divergent views. The Qadarites, for instance, stressed the doctrine of free will, while the Jabrites denied it; the Ṣifatites argued for the eternal nature of the attributes of God, while the Muʿtazilites denied they were eternal; the Murjiʾites stressed that human actions must not be subject to human judgment, while their opponents, the Waʿdites, insisted on the condemnation of man in this life, before the Day of Judgment; the Khārijites played down the importance of the role of secular leadership, i.e., the caliphate which they considered merely a human institution, while the Shīʿites went so far as to consider their *imām* as divine.

This categorization of positions on doctrinal views into factions, represented by Muʿtazilites, Jabrites, Ṣifatites, Khārijites, Murjiʾites, and Shīʿites, accounts for the principal schools of thought that have endeavored to interpret Islamic doctrine, often to justify positions which did not always accord with the prevailing orthodox view.

Murjiʾites versus Qadarites

In outlining the range and tenor of doctrinal conflict in Islam, one would have to make mention of two schools which had been influenced by Greco-Christian theologians: the Murjiʾite and Qadarite. The Murjiʾites, or "postponers," acquired their title from the doctrine they preached, namely, that judgment of human actions should be postponed until the Day of Judgment as promised in the Qurʾān. They were less concerned with the question of rule in Islam and were willing to tolerate the Umayyad rulers when the pious looked upon them as usurpers. But in the realm of faith (*īmān*), they clung tenaciously to belief only in the unity of God and in the Prophet Muḥammad and to no other basic concept. They were genuinely convinced that no one who adhered to this position could actually perish even if he should be a sinner. This was quite in contrast with the doctrine of the earliest dissenters, the Khārijites, who insisted that the unrepentant sinner was destined for Hell even if he had professed Islam.

The Qadarites, believers in divine decree, championed "free will"; they opposed the Jabrites (Necessitarians) who denied free will to man and argued that God only had all power to arbitrate.

Among the earliest protagonists of free will was al-Ḥasan al-Baṣri (d. 728), who is also regarded as one of the first systematic theologians as well as mystics of Islam. He stood above others for his orthodox views and personal piety.

The Qadarites insisted that man had power over his own deeds even though the fate of man had been preordained. Their concepts stemmed somewhat from the resignation of the Muslim to his fate in the war on the heathens. Muslims went into battle convinced that God held full power over their destinies and that if death or life were predetermined they were powerless to escape God's will. If they should fall in battle, however, they would be transported directly to Paradise. Hence "Kismet" was the logical outcome of such rationalization.

But in the sophisticated environments of the city where most Muslim thinkers functioned and found themselves in disputation with the Christians, they were confronted with the problem of having to reconcile this philosophy of predestination, that had grown out of necessity and common belief without much intellectual support, with the Qurʾān's specific appeal to man's own self-determination to good, to courage, and to actions that would please God.

The Qadarites' espousal of the doctrine that man is responsible for his actions was eventually held to be a heresy because the preaching and teaching of predestination had gained too strong a hold on Muslims to be displaced. Maʿbad al-Juhani, the earliest teacher of free will, was executed in 699 for his doctrine.[1]

In the period that saw the execution of al-Juhani, Medina was the center of intellectual life. In the city of the Prophet and the pious caliphs, free thought in religion had little chance to assert itself. The primary preoccupation of intellectual striving was the study of the Qurʾān and the collection of *Ḥadīth*.

Muʿtazilite

Though rationalization in an Aristotelian sense had no chance in Medina, it gained a following in Iraq among the students of al-Ḥasan al-Baṣri. One such student, Wāṣil ibn-ʿAṭāʾ (d. 748), seceded (*iʿtazala*) from the councils of his master; and all those who shared his views and followed suit were henceforth known as *Muʿtazilah* or Muʿtazilites. They were par excellence the protagonists of rationalism and the doctrine of free will. Their supporters at one time encompassed leading Muslim thinkers and caliphs, like al-Maʾmūn (d. 833).

With the Muʿtazilites, rationalism reached its peak; theirs was an important breakthrough, for up until Umayyad times the prevailing theological view was that "reason" should not apply to the revelations of God. The barrier to the rational interpretation of Muslim theology was now removed; and what agitated Muslim minds was more than the issue of predestination versus free will. Among the important issues now subjected to rational analysis was the question of whether God's attributes (*ṣifāt*)—all ninety-nine of them—constitute an integral part of His essence, as the theologians had argued, or are qualities independent of His essence and not co-existing with Him, as the Muʿtazilites now had the boldness to proclaim. The Muʿtazilites insisted on God's divine unity, and received for their tenacious view the further appellation by which they became known: *ahl al-tawḥīd wa-'l-ʿadl* (proclaimers of God's unity and justice).

Those who had hitherto argued that the Qurʾān was the uncreated word of God were now disputed by the Muʿtazilites, who insisted that the Qurʾān was created in time. The idea of the uncreated word of God, an important principle of Christian theology—"in the beginning was the word and the word was with God"—was perhaps behind the Muslim Traditionist's insistence on the Qurʾān, the word of God, being by similar reasoning also uncreated. These Muslim theologians could have been influenced by St. John of Damascus (d. ca. 748)

While the Muʿtazilites endeavored to respect this view, they nevertheless went on preaching that the Qurʾān was created and sent down to man. They were persecuted for this type of reasoning and dubbed heretics; it was not until the caliphate of al-Maʾmūn (813–833) that they gained reprieve and official support.

Theirs was the "thinking" class view and they drew the line between *reason* and *revelation*. They asserted the supremacy of reason as distinct from faith and resorted to reason as the deciding factor between good and evil. The creation of the Qur'ān was officially proclaimed by al-Ma'mūn, as were other Mu'tazilite doctrines later. The once persecuted Mu'tazilites were appointed to official posts by the caliph; indeed, he went so far as to sanction an inquisition (*Miḥna*) for the purpose of enforcing their doctrine.

Some of the leading spokesmen of Mu'tazilism included al-'Allāf (d. 841) who taught that God's very essence consists of knowledge. His reference to "creation" as an intermediary between the Eternal Creator and the transient "created" world betrays Platonic influence. He made distinctions between the absolute world of creation and the accidental world of revelation. He also challenged the orthodox theological view of a physical resurrection of the body and considered human actions as natural and moral. Al-Jāhiz (d. 869) insisted that man by the exercise of reason is capable of knowing the Creator and in comprehending the need of a prophetic revelation.

It is interesting to note that the four orthodox rites came into being almost simultaneously with the prevalence of Mu'tazilism, patronized not only by al-Ma'mūn but also by his immediate successors until the caliphate of al-Mutawakkil (842–847). When the renowned *qāḍi* ibn Dā'ūd, who had espoused Mu'tazilism, served as "chief justice" for the empire he used the office to propagate their doctrine.

Their success however was relatively short-lived; the orthodox theologians, and others victimized by the *Miḥna* for having rejected the notion of a theology based on reason, found a vocal leader in Aḥmad ibn-Ḥanbal, a strong traditionalist. Through the support of the conservative caliph al-Mutawakkil they gained ascendancy with the view that the Qur'ān is uncreated. The restoration of orthodoxy followed soon after the official proclamation.

Ash'arism

While Mu'tazilism left a dent on the prevailing orthodox conception of religious tenets and their application, the compromise within the orthodox body in terms of the acceptance of the rational approach to the religion of Islam was also very important for the process of adaptation and readjustment. The Ashʿari movement which legitimized the scholastic interpretation of religious dogma was by far the greatest single force working for such adaptation.

The most articulate spokesman of the anti-Muʿtazilite school was al-Ashʿari (873–935). For forty years he was one of them but chose to break away and revert to orthodoxy. This gave him the extraordinary advantage of having assimilated their views and all they had to teach; he had mastered their logic, philosophy, and science of reasoning and now sought to apply their weapons in support of the orthodox view. His aim as an independent agent was to reconcile their position with that of the Traditionists, known also as Ṣifatites.

Al-Ashʿari's was an open approach; his contemporary the mystic al-Junayd (d. 910) had followed the same method, but only in quiet preaching and secret teaching to a few followers. Thus for the first time the methods of scholastic philosophy were being systematically applied. They reached perfection with the *qāḍi* Abu-Bakr al-Bāqillāni (d. 1012). Scholastic Ashʿarism's greatest following was in the environs of Baghdad. Elsewhere it was suspected and often confounded with Muʿtazilism.

With the advent of the Seljuk Turks in the middle of the tenth century, the Sunni caliph was freed from his subservience to the local Shiʿite dynasty, the Buwayhid, which they destroyed. The Buwayhids actually had favored the Ashʿari system and had endeavored to propagate its teachings following the death of the founder. Although the Seljuks had subscribed to Sunni Islam, less than a century later, the Seljuk ruler Tughril Beg (d. ca. 1053) persecuted the well-known Ashʿarite teacher al-Juwayni[2] (d. 1085) and even exiled him. But Tughril's successor Alp Arslan had a very wise and knowledgeable vizier, Nizām al-Mulk, who not only subscribed to the Ashʿarite view but even founded a theological school named after himself, the renowned Nizāmīyah, for the purpose of perpetuating the Ashʿarite system. Al-Juwayni was then restored to favor.

Far from Baghdad in Andalusia, the noted rationalist ibn Ḥazm fiercely opposed the Ashʿarite view; but then came al-Ghazāli (d. 1111), a teacher and then head of the Nizāmīyah, to establish its orthodoxy and to promote its dicta as the universal creed of Islam.

Gradually Ashʿarism spread from Iraq eastward to Persia and southward to Syria and Egypt during the critical century of the Crusades and the ascendancy of the strong Sunni dynasties: the Kurdish-supported Ayyūbids (1186–1260) and their successors, the Baḥri Mamlūks (1250–1389). It spread westward into North Africa, to be accepted by the fiercely unitarian and Ṣūfi-inclined ibn Tūmart (d. 1130) and his Almohad (*al-Muwaḥḥidūn*) dynasty, which for a while controlled most of the Maghrib and Muslim Spain.

The Ashʿari system of theological reference has continued to exercise predominant influence in Islam. The only rival to cross its path is the Māturīdīyah of al-Māturīdi of Samarqand (d. 944), a contemporary of al-Ashʿari, who belonged to the Ḥanafite *madhhab* and whose stronghold was among Muslim Turks. His creed was an important source of reference for Muslim theology since he attempted to steer a middle course between materialistic teachings on one hand and ideas associated with pure speculative philosophy on the other. His chief complaint against the Muʿtazilah was that their doctrine was too abstract to be understood by the Muslim public. It would seem that he was seeking to make what he approved of their views more palatable to the partisans of the orthodox conception. His was the medial path and his system was built on reconciliation of views and compromise.

Al-Ashʿari sought, for instance, a compromise between the Muʿtazilah views of the attributes of God and those of the Ṣifatites; he admitted the existence of these attributes but did not liken them unto human attributes and conceded their eternity with the Deity. As pertains to God's visibility, al-Ashʿari argued that He can be seen independent of the limitations of human sight. As to the important question of free will, he denied that man had power over his will but affirmed that man did have control over his responsibilities even though they were willed by God.

Al-Ashʿari treated all the important doctrinal points of contention pertaining to God, the Qurʾān, the question of sin, the role of intercession, and other matters, articulated his views thereon, and produced for the first time in Islam a systematic theology. He held firmly to the belief that one can not apply rational knowledge to divine things outside the provision and sanction of the Qur'ān. He argued that one may know God by the application of reason, which was consonant with, if not derived from, the divine revelation as embodied in the Qur'ān.

Everything that exists is due to the will of the Supreme Intelligence, God. One can not account for nature by reference to nature's forces, but rather through the medium of some divine creative act. In this regard, al-Ash'ari showed strong kinship with the Greek Atomist theory as it relates to Greek natural philosophy.

It would appear that al-Ash'ari's supreme effort was directed towards the reconciliation of *Reason* and *Revelation*, and to do so he resorted to *kalām* or "scholasticism." Thus did he turn their own weapons against them, and thus did he defeat the Mu'tazilites.

His doctrine was formalized by a disciple, al-Nasafi (d. 1310), who placed less stress on formalism and more emphasis on the importance of rationalism in establishing religious truth.

From the time of its establishment onward, the Ash'arite system prevailed among Sunni theologians following a strong boost in the twelfth century from al-Ghazāli. From the tenth century to the present, only twice was there a breach in the quiet realm of theological life dominated by the Ash'ari system: once by the Wahhābis of Arabia in the eighteenth century and once by the Bābis of Persia in the nineteenth century.

Ṣūfism

The Ṣūfi way is highly personal, and, as its merits become better understood, is experiencing a revival and expansion outside the main lands of Islam. It has been rightly described as an arduous journey of love in which not everyone who undertakes it may reach the blissful moment. The aim is to unite with the Creator, a part of whom resides within every created being. A major clue is to be found in the Qur'ān where the Lord declares: "We have created every living being and breathed into it its soul." Thus, according to Ṣūfi rationale, a bit of God dwells within each of us and all we need to do is to tune in to it to become united with God, here and now, not in the hereafter as advocated by organized religion.

This the mystic seeks to accomplish by means of what he or she describes as the *ṭarīqah* (the path) that will lead one to becoming one, however fleetingly, with the Creator. Hence, the Ṣūfi seeks union with the Creator by undertaking the arduous journey of disciplining the lower self to permit the transition to the higher self, which is what achieves this union. The Ṣūfi differs from the non-Ṣūfi Muslim in that the former seeks an awareness of the Lord while the soul is still entrapped in its body, whereas the non-Ṣūfi Muslim is content to pursue the path laid out in the holy book of Islam, which, if followed carefully, will bring about the ultimate presence with God following death, resurrection, and the judgment that he or she expects to pass and thus be ushered into the presence of God eternally. It is a bodily presence, rewarded with all that the Qurʾān defines as the rewards of paradise, portrayed again in material terms. The Ṣūfi on the other hand seeks the presence of God in an intense sense of awareness that is highly spiritual and nonmaterial.

The Ṣūfis came under severe criticism by custodians of the *Sharīʿah*, who argued that only through *ʿilm*, or knowledge of the holy text and the exemplary conduct of the Prophet, can a person expect to pass muster on the Day of Judgment and gain direct access to God. This is what some have described as the deductive approach to knowledge of God. The mystics on the other hand pursue an inductive or experimental approach, which to them is the fuel that propels them into the presence of God, here and now.

Some very sophisticated treatises have been written to show where the core of the core of the heart resides, wherein in turn the Lord too resides, on the assumption that God is present in all of us, not simply up in some intangible heaven. Hence the task is to undergo the journey that will lead to that core. Since not all Ṣūfis can pursue an identical journey, theorists have come up with the notion that there are as many paths to God as there are Ṣūfis, each pursuing the path most suited to the workings of his psyche. The journey is therefore both one of ascent and descent, into the inmost of the higher soul to achieve this unity. As defined by them, the journey passes through seven stages, and the accomplishment of each is rewarded with a *ḥāl* or blissful state. Those who succeed will attain the ultimate, namely *fanā*ʾ, or the moment one passes away from physical awareness, and *baqā*ʾ, or the indwelling in the divine, however fleeting that might be.

The path to God is best exemplified in the classical work of Farīd al-Dīn ʿAṭṭār (d. 1229) of Nishapur translated under the title *The Conference of the Birds*, a religious philosophical poem featuring the flight of many birds led by the hoopoe on a lengthy journey over valleys and mountains in search of the ideal representation of God, who dwells in the Tree at the End (*shajarat al-muntaha*). But of the thousands of every kind who set off on the flight, only thirty make it to the Tree at the End, only to discover their own reflection, or God, in themselves. It is an allegory best exemplifying the journey of the Ṣūfi's soul as it passes many a travail before reaching the end of its journey.[3]

The early mystics first cultivated asceticism, denying the body its appetites and urges and spending much time in seclusion, fasting and praying, in order to mortify the flesh and suppress its appetites. Celibacy was heavily stressed, a near requirement at first because marriage and progeny were deemed distractions from that concentration essential to achieving the ultimate quest.[4]

A good example of such self-denial and dedication was that of the famous female mystic Rābiʿah al-ʿAdawīyah (d. 801) of Basra, described by her biographer as "that woman who lost herself in the Divine, that one accepted by men as that second spotless Mary." Her total devotion to God, for which she set the highest example, made her turn away the hand of many a suitor, including the religious and the pious, the rich and the mighty. Somewhat analogous to a Christian nun proclaiming herself married to Jesus, she would say every time, "I am married to God." As proof of her total dedication, and in her own words:

> O my Lord, if I worship Thee from fear of Hell, burn me in Hell; and if I worship Thee from hope of Paradise, ex-

clude me thence; but if I worship Thee for Thine Own sake, then withhold not from me Thine Eternal Beauty.[5]

In the realm of Ṣūfism most Sunni and later some Shīʿah Muslims found a common denominator irrespective of their philosophical and theological views. *Ṣūfism* is the Islamic version of asceticism and mysticism. The whole underlying philosophy of Ṣūfism was to interject a *personal* element in the otherwise impersonal legalistic approach to the fulfillment of religious devotions. The result was the introduction of asceticism into religious practice and of mysticism into religious thought. While it is not considered a distinct sect of Islam, Ṣūfism certainly can be looked upon as a pattern of religious contention which found a lasting place in the body of Islam.

The protagonists of asceticism and mysticism, like all other diverters, traced the development of their movement to Muḥammad, the Qurʾān, and *Ḥadīth*. Muḥammad often withdrew to the cave atop Mt. Ḥirāʾ overlooking Mecca, where he spent days at a time meditating and where he received the first revelation from God. He also had much respect for the Christian ascetics, especially the legendary monk Baḥīra. The Prophet's *Miʿrāj* (night journey) had a mystical flavor to it in that it represented a journey to God. The mystic's yearning to achieve oneness with God and to demonstrate the unity of all being provided much incentive for the formulation of Ṣūfi theories. The ascetic quality exhibited in the life of the Prophet and his pious Companions set an early example. The attention paid in early Islam to the joy of being rewarded by God, and conversely the fear of punishment for disobeying God, gave much encouragement to a life of self-denial, meditation, and concentration on the worship of God. The rightly guided first four caliphs were noted for their simplicity of living and for their pious approach to the affairs of this world out of consideration for the promises of the next. Early Muslims, inspired by their example of austere living, went even further and gave up all concern for the affairs of this world, preferring to live in poverty, in wanderings, and in retirement from the material comforts of this world.

The attitude in the first Islamic century was predominantly ascetic and not so much mystical. It became increasingly mystical in the second century under the influence of Greek, Hindu, and Christian stimuli. The monastic attitude in Christianity was by then well established in the lands where Islam became dominant. The Christian preoccupation with the idea of "purifying the human soul" must have spilled over into Islam where the pious Muslim became inclined in the same direction. This type of mysticism in the early stage of development was more practiced than defined. Its gradual evolution and subsequent movement from speculative mysticism to theosophy was bolstered by the strong impeti it received from the Hellenistic legacy.

By the tenth century, and under the inducements of Indo-Iranian concepts, it became theosophical. The continuous striving of the devout Muslim to identify himself with the cause of all being culminated with the execution of one such devotee, Manṣūr al-Ḥallāj (d. 922), for having audibly proclaimed *ana al-Ḥaqq* (lit. "I am the Truth"). This was his way of identifying himself mystically with the Creator, a pattern of mystical expression familiar to the old Persian Gnostics but baneful to the orthodox Muslims.

Among the earlier Ṣūfis who articulated the path to mystical union with God was Ḥallāj's master, Junayd (d. 910). In his writings Junayd endeavored to show that man's supreme effort in this life is to fulfill his covenant with the Creator as ordained in the Qur'ān; he argued that it is man's duty to return to his primeval state, and to Junayd the mystical path of achieving ecstatic union with God is the only way.

During the early period of its development the spokesmen of mysticism came mostly from the class of orthodox teachers. By the time of Junayd, however, they began to derive from Muslims who were not brought up in the traditional religious disciplines but represented rather the artisan classes of the towns where the Aramaic and Persian ethnic groups were strong. In certain instances the espousal of the Ṣūfi doctrine was a sort of protest against the social and political abuses engendered in the early schisms, i.e., Khārijite, Shī'ite, and the like. They hoped to achieve this type of reform by appealing to the religious consciousness of the Muslim and inculcating him with some sort of spirituality not awakened by the legalistic stress of orthodox doctrine on prescribed acts of devotional expression.

This in turn had its impact on the social structure of the Islamic community. Not only did the Ṣūfis strive hard to make converts among their fellow non-mystics, but they became actively engaged also in missionary-type activities and propagandistic preachings in most of the lands of Islam, particularly in the safer confines of the periphery where the persecuting arm of the orthodox theologian could not reach them. They were suspect to the orthodox teachers from the start. The Shīʿah divines were equally suspicious and outrightly hostile to them.

Ṣūfi concepts and practices drew them further apart from the orthodox doctrine, especially when Ṣūfi leaders began to publicize the underlying philosophy of their mysticism and to gain a larger following. The Ṣūfi appeal and "…strength lay in the satisfaction which it gave to the religious instincts of the people, instincts which were to some extent chilled and starved by the abstract and impersonal teachings of the orthodox and found relief in the more directly personal and emotional religious approach of the Ṣūfis."[6]

Clearly, the growth of Ṣūfism was in reaction to the intellectualism of orthodox Islam and to the legalistic injunctions of the Qurʾān, devoid as they were of the natural and personal impulses for man to contemplate his Creator in the intimacy of his soul and mind.

The three essential ingredients of Ṣūfi philosophy are *light*, *knowledge*, *love*, the means by which a strong direct consciousness of divine presence is experienced. There is no acceptance of the idea of an incarnate God as in Christianity. The Ṣūfi looks upon man as partaking of God's essence, but he does not believe in the savior principle or in any sort of intermediation between man and God. He has a highly unitarian conception of the Deity. What the Ṣūfi aims for is a glimpse of immortality while he is still entrapped by life in this world.

To achieve personal unity with their creator, the Ṣūfis laid out the "path" (*ṭarīqah*) that would lead to gnosis (*maʿrifah*) or mystic knowledge of the Lord. The "path" of ascension to divine union (*tawḥīd*) with God passes through stages known commonly as "stations" or "states"; the last stage is that of *fanā'*, or passing away in God, which is the ultimate desire of a successful mystic. The Ṣūfi at this point ceases to be aware of his physical identity even though he continues to exist as an individual. Ḥallāj expressed the mystic's sentiment most eloquently at the moment *fanā'* is achieved, in his proclamation:

> I am He whom I love, and He whom I love is I.
> We are two spirits dwelling in one body.
> When thou seest me thou seest Him,
> And when thou seest Him, thou seest us both.[7]

It is not surprising that the Ṣūfi attitude should provide a bridge between Islam and Christianity. Ṣūfis and Christians share the conception of God as love; both regard man as having been created in God's own image out of love for man, that man might behold the image of God in himself and attain the desired union with Him. The difference is in ends: the Ṣūfi seeks union with God first in *this* life, while the Christian expects it in the life to come. The Ṣūfi's equivalent of Christian notions of incarnation is *ḥulūl,* the stage of indwelling with God.

As the mystic was seriously convinced of the presence of divine truth in him through his ability to attain direct communion with the Creator, it is little wonder that he should gloat over his alleged superiority to the prophets whose communication with God is looked upon as more formal than personal.

But to believe in the divine presence in you is one matter; to proclaim your identity with the "Truth," which identity is reserved by the highly unitarian orthodox theologians to God and God alone, is to commit the *kabīrah*, or the major unpardonable sin; this is *shirk* of the highest order because the Ṣūfi is associating a partner, in himself, with Him who "hath not partners."

The one salutary byproduct of Ṣūfi theory is the stress on the meeting of the spiritual and physical world in man, placing him thus at the center of the universe.

The Ṣūfis were persecuted as heretics. This led to discretion in public utterances and to the expression of mystic yearning in such metaphors as wine and love. Their language therefore became veiled and allusive, if not secretive; and only those who were apprised of the secrets could grasp the inner meaning of the wealth of Ṣūfi poetic literature that had sprung into being.

Their audacity in certain instances made discretion a matter of prudence. Abu Saʿīd (d. 1049), a Persian Ṣūfi, went so far as to argue that the *Sharīʿah* was unnecessary for those who had reached the end of the "path." Obligations like responding to prayer at the appointed times or performing the pilgrimage were not to supersede the *dhikr*, the ritual litany of the Ṣūfis, argued Abu Saʿīd.

In the fourth and fifth Islamic centuries the Ṣūfis grew in numbers and commensurately in strength. They began to take on peculiarly distinguishing features. In the beginning the *dhikr* (mentioning the name of God often, as enjoined in the Qurʾān), served to concentrate the mind on God. Later, when Ṣūfism became organized, it came to embrace clear liturgical tendencies marked by the recitation of chants and litanies. The orthodox theologians feared, and rightly so, that the Ṣūfi *dhikr* sessions would weaken the significance of the mosque as the place of congregation. They were angered with the Ṣūfis for downgrading the prescriptions of the *Sharīʿah* for attaining religious truth on the ground that knowledge of theology and law does not lead to knowledge of God, as was zealously maintained by the theologians. Not this rational and second-hand knowledge of the ulema but rather the direct personal experience of the devoted Muslim, the *maʿrifah* that culminates in absorption into the Godhead, was posited as the only way to attain religious truth and satisfaction.

While the orthodox view condemned celibacy, as Christian asceticism condemned marriage, the Ṣūfis equivocated on the subject; but the prevalent trend among them by the fifth century of Islam was to refrain from marriage.[8] It was not so much their practice of celibacy that contramanded the orthodox doctrine as it was their increasing veneration of their *shaykhs*, to the point that they made saints out of them. This indeed ran contrary to the grain of the fundamental notion of Islam, namely, that nothing should distract from the uncompromising devotion to God. The decrees of the *corpus sancta*, Qurʾān and *Ḥadīth*, as interpreted by the theologians, regarded the invocation of anyone other than God in supplicatory prayer as tantamount to passing into polytheism.

In popular Islam, however, encompassing the rank and file of Muslims on the fringe of the Islamic heartland, there was much closer contact with the religious practices of Christians; the rank and file Muslims evolved as a consequence a sort of "folk religion" version of Islam, and they were not readily distracted from their non-orthodox approach to God by the thundering threats of orthodox theologians.

A rather extreme departure from the orthodox norm, touching almost on *shirk*, is the strong devotion accorded the *shaykh* or leader in some Ṣūfi orders. An important Muslim authority on the subject regards the posture of the Ṣūfis on this issue as one of the fundamental tenets of their beliefs. The posture is predicated on the theory that knowledge of God can be achieved through the intercession of saints. In this regard they show a strong affinity with concepts deriving from Gnostic and Christian sources. Indeed, the Ṣūfis went so far as to institute a hierarchy of saints topped by the *Quṭb*, pole of the world, assisted by a host of deputies and superintendents on earth.

Acceptance by Orthodoxy

That this type of approach to God should gain ascendancy among rank and file Muslims is due considerably to the excessive dogmatism of the orthodox theologians and their undue stress on pedantry arising from rigid legalism or formalism. The performance of the prescribed acts of worship did little to quench the soul of the Ṣūfi who yearned for a more personal identification with God.

The gains of the Ṣūfis became more explicit in the eleventh century when they won over to their cause some of the ablest thinkers of Islam. Their persistent defiance of the orthodox view culminated in the great compromise which gained for Ṣūfism official recognition and acceptance from their adversaries. The credit belongs to the respected theologian al-Qushayri (d. 1072) who urged his colleagues to acknowledge the Ṣūfi doctrine of mystical communion with God. But the real architect of Ṣūfism's triumph was the celebrated Abu Ḥāmid al-Ghazāli (d. 1111). His impact on orthodox Islam is no less comparable in magnitude than Augustine's and Luther's on traditional Christianity.

Like Augustine six centuries before, al-Ghazāli felt the torments on his soul of the relentless personal search for a satisfying experience of the divine. He had explored the avenues that lay open before him: the speculative, metaphysical, and doctrinaire, but to no avail. He found no religious truth in the philosophies of the day familiar to him. He refused to take the path stretched out before him because the tormented spirit within him was crying out for a type of fulfillment which he could not realize by the traditional method. So he abandoned his professorship at the renowned Niẓāmīyah school of theology at Baghdad and went about his search with great determination to explore more fully the existing theological systems; but again he could find none of the satisfaction he yearned for. Neither Sunnism nor Shīʿism could provide him with the satisfaction he sought. Out of despair he turned at last to the mystical path, and it was through it that he found the personal contentment he had been seeking.

It is indeed to the glory and enhancement of Islam that al-Ghazāli did not stop at his discovery of personal contentment. He chose to announce the results of his discovery to all Muslims and wrote as a consequence his own "Confessions."[9]

In this classical autobiography al-Ghazāli discusses how he found religious truth in the Ṣūfi *dhikr* which materialized when he abandoned all the corruptive influences of the flesh and rid himself of "evil thoughts" and desires. He shared with the Ṣūfis, whose works he had thoroughly imbibed, the basic credo that the path to God can not be intellectually delineated, but lies rather in a mystical experience. Like St. Francis of Assisi, al-Ghazāli abandoned the wealth and prestige of his professional standing, also his wife and family, and set out on extensive wanderings to tell others of his great triumph over himself in attaining closer communion with God.

The beliefs of al-Ghazāli are set forth in his important writings like *The Revivification of the Religious Sciences*, the *Folly of the Philosophers*, and the *Niche of the Lights*.

His services to Ṣūfism and Islam were well summed up by a leading Western authority on Islamic theology[10] who pointed out that al-Ghazāli revolutionized the interpretation of religious dogma resting on the Qurʾān, *Sunnah*, and exegesis so as to bring it into a closer awareness of personal experience. The same can be said of his efforts in making philosophy and theological rationalism more palatable and understandable to the average Muslim. In leading theologians to work less on the scholastic and more on the historical precepts of Islam's development, he made it possible for those who hitherto resisted the ascetic trend now to accept it. In so doing Ṣūfism gained acceptance and respectability in the eyes of its erstwhile opponents. While Ṣūfism did not attain to full orthodoxy, at least it succeeded in making orthodoxy more mystical.[11]

Al-Ghazāli was the great mystic of eastern Islam. His counterpart in western Islam was the Hispano-Arab ibn ʿArabi (d. 1240). Ibn ʿArabi evolved a sort of Logos doctrine which bears strong kinship with the Neo-Platonic school. The "idea" he concerned himself with is that which represents the creative or rational principle behind the universe, the "first intellect." Muḥammad the Prophet to ibn ʿArabi is the first reality because in his opinion he stands for the perfect man. "Every prophet is a Logos whose individual Logoi are united in the idea of Muḥammad, the perfect man is he in whom all the attributes of the macrocosm are reflected. The reality of Muḥammad is the creative principle of the universe, and the perfect man is its cause."[12]

While ibn ʿArabi is difficult to decipher, and his writings are more enigmatical than understandable, his views tend towards the Ṣūfi aim to achieve a more intimate experience of the divine, a part of which is regarded by him to exist in all living beings. Ibn ʿArabi sees the perfect man "as the visible aspect of God in relation to the world," He speaks of Muḥammad "Lord . . . the source of all mysteries, and the cause of all phenomena." In his *waḥdat al-wujūd* (unity of existence), he projects the doctrine "that things pre-exist as ideas in the knowledge of God, whence they emanate and whither they return."[13] The world is merely the outer aspect of God, a mirror reflecting multi facets of His oneness.[14]

In his famous work, *Tarjumān al-Ashwāq* (*Interpretation of Divine Love*), Ibn ʿArabi wrote:

> Within my heart, all forms may find a place,
> The cloisters of the monk, the idol's fane
> A pasture for gazelles, the Sacred House
> Of God, to which all Muslims turn their face:
> The tablets of the Jewish Law, the Word
> of God, revealed unto His Prophet true.
> Love is the faith I hold, and whereso' er
> His camels turn, the one true faith is there.[15]

Ṣūfi Organization and Orders

The Ṣūfi way was becoming acceptable. Many of the ulema who had opposed it for centuries as a deviation from the true practices of orthodox Islam now accepted it, some following the example of al-Ghazāli, the leading member of the ulema class who changed course and took to Ṣūfism. Al-Ghazāli published a gigantic work, *Revivification of the Sciences of Religion*, in which he juxtaposed the formal Sunni Islamic with the Ṣūfi version, thus portraying Ṣūfism as truly Islamic. Henceforth there was a growing conviction that Ṣūfism was a legitimate and acceptable trend in Islam. Not only did the ulema begin to join the Ṣūfis in large numbers, but also the masses, who saw in it a form of redemption and satisfaction not afforded them by the routine religious observances that had done little to enrich their souls during the centuries of the *ummah*'s decline.

It is at this juncture of Islam's history that the Ṣūfi *shaykh*, with his reputation for piety and dedication to God, became a magnet for training those who could not undertake the journey unassisted, as did the earlier mystics. Seeking out a *shaykh* of renown and asking to become a disciple was the primary incentive for organization. It also catapulted the *shaykh* and the order, eventually named after him, into the center of both religious and social life. It is relevant to note that the Ṣūfi orders came to fill an important spiritual vacuum, which occurred after the Mongols destroyed

Baghdad, hitherto seat of the caliphate and spiritual capital of Muslims in 1258, and in the ongoing battles that devastated eastern Islam economically, socially, and culturally.

The Ṣūfis became organized in the twelfth century when they saw the need for hierarchical discipline. There came into being about twelve major orders. The rallying center was usually where a saint resided. To organize was the logical extension of their extreme reverence for and pride in their *shaykhs* whom they often beatified. The need for organization resulted also from the increasing number of novices and disciples who had to have some formal and definable position among the senior devotees. With organization, converts became linked in a widespread number of brotherhoods; and in such organized brotherhoods we have the only type of ecclesiastical organization in Islam.

A member of the brotherhood was known as a *faqīr* (fakir) or *darwīsh* (dervish). Before he would be accepted he had to undergo two years of intensive training as a novice (*murīd*). Following this, he underwent a solemn rite of initiation and received the symbol of investiture, namely a special frock (*khirqah*). Following his formal acceptance into the order, the novice associated himself closely with the *shaykh* until he rose to the status of a leader.

The Ṣūfi fraternities extended over the whole length and breadth of the Muslim empire. Their elaborate code of ascetic moral discipline stressed (in a manner suggestive of the Christian way to salvation) repentance, abstinence, renunciation, poverty, patience, satisfaction, and trust in God.[16]

The diffusion of the *Epistles* of the Brethren of Purity (*Ikhwān al-Ṣafā'*), an encyclopaedic compendium with strong Neo-Platonic impulses that had a material influence on the development of the esoteric Ismā'ili sect, contributed to the crystallization of the orders' organization and philosophy.

The impulse to organize received also a great boost from the monistic and all-encompassing philosophy of ibn 'Arabi. In the mystical interpretation of Islamic doctrine, which ibn 'Arabi claimed was revealed to him as the "Seal of Saints," he set himself up as a rival of the orthodox theologians. His views were particularly appealing to the Muslims in the Persian and Turkish zones of Islam. Under the influence of his views the mystical schools became gradually closed circles of initiates.

It is important to note that the mystical approach to God, even at the zenith of its development, did not gain a large following among the Muslims. Perhaps the aberrations to which it became susceptible from the point of view of the orthodox believers account to some extent for its relatively unpopular appeal. The Ṣūfis, we noted, tended to clothe their expressed yearning for the divine in their writings, particularly in odes and poetry, in terms that the neutral observer found very difficult to comprehend outside their Ṣūfi context. The use of "love" and other rather mundane, if not sensual, terminology to conceal Ṣūfi metaphors was too real not to be taken at face value. He who reads the poems of the famous Persian poet Ḥāfiz finds it difficult to determine from them what is in reference to the divine and what may easily be taken as expressions of worldly love. Love and wine figured prominently as metaphors in the allegedly mystical verses of Ḥāfiz which together with Saʿdi's attained a stylistic perfection foreign to earlier verse. The outstanding poet of the Ṣūfis, Jalal-al-Dīn al-Rūmi (d. 1273), is less prone to such bewildering interpretations. Indeed, in his deeply moving verses lies the acme of mystical expression. In his poetry embodied in the *Mathnawi* (Mesnevi) we discover that al-Rūmi has expressed all that is to be said on mysticism. Jāmi (d. 1492), another Persian mystic poet, wedded romance to his mystical writings.

Among the important *ṭarīqahs* (orders) that were established, mention should be made of the Qādirīyah, named after ʿAbd al-Qādir al-Jīlāni (d. 1166), once a preacher with powerful appeal to his listeners in Baghdad. Al-Jīlāni stressed tolerance, piety, and philanthropy. His followers built for him a *ribāṭ* (monastery) outside of Baghdad and continued in his path. His numerous descendants were responsible for a number of offshoots of the Qādirīyah order, some of which, like the Rifāʿīyah, were not nearly as tolerant as the parent organization. Another, the Badawīyah[17] located primarily in Egypt, acquired notoriety for their orgies centered around the founder's tomb at Tanta in the Nile Delta.

The Ṣūfi movement gained a stronger foothold in the Maghrib on account of its strong political links with the ascendant Mahdi ibn Tūmart (d. 1130) and the Almohad dynasty in the twelfth century. The Almohads from the start were closely affiliated with the Ṣūfi movement. Through this association the Berbers who were not deeply inclined to Islam became more intimately involved with the religion of the Arab conquerors. Ṣūfi Islam attracted the Berber because it tolerated his animistic proclivities. To the Berber convert the *shaykh* was not much unlike his "holy man" who was alleged to possess magical powers.

The strong foothold of Ṣūfism in western Islam enabled it to influence the eastern wing firstly through ibn ʿArabi who hailed from Murcia in Spain and secondly through al-Shādhili (d. 1258) who studied in Fez but settled in Alexandria, Egypt.

Most of al-Shādhili's disciples were artisans who were discouraged from an all-out mystical living. While he favored no organization, a generation after his death witnessed the rise of the Shādhilīyah. The order evolved a ritual that transcended the Qādirīyah's in elaborateness. Its offshoots were more numerous than theirs. The two extremes were represented; one by the ʿĪsawīyah, noted for their swordslashing ritual, and at the opposite end by the Darqāwa of Morocco and western Algeria.

The Turks and Mongols were no less susceptible to Ṣūfi influences, among whom, as with the Berbers, the *ṭarīqahs* developed from a substratum of Shamanism or animism. The oldest order, in which women unveiled participated in the *dhikr*, was the Yesevīya. The next order of consequence came in among the Osmanli Turks of Anatolia under the name of Bektāshi. Some say it was the product of the Yesevīya.

The Bektāshis were much more syncretistic, enjoying connections with esoteric Shīʿism on one side, folk Christianity and Gnosticism on the other. They were much more extreme than other Ṣūfi orders in their discarding the ceremonies enjoined by the *Sharīʿah*. Their rituals betrayed strong analogies with the cultic observances of Christian communities next to whom they lived. The Bektāshis at one time were a powerful order because of their close association with the Ottoman Janissaries up to the time they were suppressed in 1826.

The urban Turks favored the Mevlevi (Mawlawi) order, founded by the mystical Persian poet Jalāl al-Dīn al-Rūmi. The *dhikr* of the Mevlevis revolved around the pirouetting of the initiates which accounts for their being termed the "whirling dervishes." Like the Bektāshis, the Mevlevis suffered loss in strength when the secular modern Turkish republic came into being in the 1920s. They still have a few *tekkes*, however, in some of the larger cities of the Middle East. In recent years these and other orders in Turkey are increasingly reasserting themselves.

Another well-known order is the Naqshbandi, which was first started in Central Asia by al-Bukhāri but managed to work its way westward through India until it found for itself a wide following in western Asia and Egypt. One can see more clearly the mystical appeal to the divine in a prayer of the Naqshbandis recited at the end of the *dhikr:*

> Oh God bless and preserve our Prophet Muḥammad in the beginning. Bless and preserve our Prophet Muḥammad at all time. Bless and preserve our Prophet Muḥammad in the High Heavens till the Day of Judgment. Bless and preserve all the prophets and messengers, the angels and the righteous worshipers of thee from amongst the dwellers of the heavens and earth. May Allah, the Merciful and Exalted be graciously pleased with our Lords, the possessors of high esteem Abu Bakr, ʿUmar, ʿUthmān, ʿAli (the Orthodox Caliphs), their (righteous) predecessors, Thy devotees and Thy followers till the Day of Judgment. Gather us unto Thy mercy, Oh Most Merciful, Oh God, Oh Living, Oh Creator. There is no god but Thee, Oh God, Oh our Lord, Oh Most Forgiving, Oh Most Merciful, O God, Amen.[18]

The literature of the Ṣūfis is rich and revealing of their unselfish mystical search for God. Indeed, Islam's Ṣūfis have left us a most heavily endowed body of devotional literature, enough to evoke the envy of all those who have dedicated themselves to the worship of the one God.[19]

A more lasting impression on the orthodox body of Islam was felt during the seventeenth and eighteenth centuries when a number of outstanding orthodox scholars strove to restate the bases of Islamic theology independent of the set dogmatism and formalism enshrined in the orthodox manuals of religion. These scholars attempted to place more emphasis on the psychological and ethical elements in religion.

The Ṣūfi influence in the Shīʿah world was persistent, albeit circumscribed, from 1500 on after the triumph of the Safavid whose roots were in a Ṣūfi order. Here Ṣūfi doctrine and Shīʿah "orthodoxy" fused in the work of Mulla Ṣaḍra (d. 1640) and Shaykh Aḥmad al-Aḥsāʾi (d. 1826), the systematizer of Ṣaḍra's beliefs into a heterodoxy termed Shaykhīyah. Their chief doctrine stressed the necessity of having an open channel of communication with the "Hidden *Imām*" of the Shīʿah. It is this one concept that gave rise almost immediately to the Bābi movement and its offshoot Bahāʾism.

CHAPTER 11

"Medievalism" and the Dawn of "Renaissance"

THE TRIUMPH OF Ashʿari orthodoxy represented the first significant religious development of any consequence down to present times. Several factors may account for this subsequent dearth of theological agitation. The political dislocations in the body politic resulting from the Crusades, the split of the ʿAbbāsid empire at the seams and the Mongol invasions, the rise of multiple dynasties, and the disappearance of caliphal authority as a force symbolizing spiritual unity, the deterioration of commerce and sources of wealth, the stepped up incursions of Tartar and other Turkic invaders, all contributed to a widespread spirit of uncertainty.

In the atmosphere of mounting social and political insecurity, the doctors of Islamic law and the theologians deemed it essential to the religious survival of Islam that further theological agitation or the application of *ijtihād* to dogma should cease. It was agreed that further efforts to interpret doctrine when coupled with the assault of the rationalists and philosophers on the bastions of the theologians would only serve to widen the areas of disagreement and loosen the bonds of unity essential for the preservation of Islam as a vital religious element in a society confronted with political and social disintegration as well as economic decline.

The "Medieval" Era

And so the Islamic world marked time, as if it had come to a standstill, for the next seven centuries. The only upheavals of any consequence were political: the rise of the Ottoman Turks and the extension of their political control over much of western Asia and northern Africa from the sixteenth century to the twentieth. Being ardent Sunnis, the Turks entrusted the direction of religion and law to the orthodox in a hierarchical structure headed by Shaykh al-Islām, accountable only to the sultan, who preserved for himself the prerogative of final decision.

Political turmoil in Persia enabled a new dynastic family, the Safavid, steeped in Ṣūfi traditions, to come to power at the beginning of the sixteenth century; and with its triumph, the forceful conversion of Iran from Sunni orthodoxy to Shīʿah heterodoxy took place. Still no stimulus for any rethinking or adaptation of religious doctrine was deemed essential. There was no felt need for it, because the Islamic world was still convinced of its superior military prowess, and for good reason. Had not the Muslim Turks beat back the combined forces of Europe in the Crusades? Did not the sons of Osman with their mighty and seemingly invincible armies sweep all before them right to the walls of Vienna? The Islam they experienced appeared to meet their needs. The world of Islam was sufficient unto itself; so was the prevalent credo of the faith.

The turning point came when "infidel" Europe began to assert the superiority of its own arms over the leading Islamic power, the Ottoman. This was brought home to the Arab portions of the Islamic world when Napoleon invaded Egypt in 1798 and gave a visible demonstration of modern know-how. The once confident Muslims, at least of Egypt, now vividly witnessed for themselves the product of the West's material advancement. The West, it would seem, had raced past the Islamic world in the push towards the future. The nineteenth and twentieth centuries with all their revolutionary social, political, and intellectual accomplishments gave the inquiring Muslim much to ponder, much to rethink. The dawn of a new era had arrived.

Muslim intellectuals concerned with the fate of their inherited faith began to apply themselves to the task of adapting this faith to the exigences of a modern world propelled by great scientific and technological achievements. Behind them now trailed the traditional forces of religion. The tenets of the faith as then observed seemed insufficient to bolster a sagging Islamic society in confrontation with a revitalized and materially advancing Western society, a society with sufficient force and dynamism to impose itself as if at will on a prostrate Muslim world. The West moved against the Muslim East with full impunity not only by the power of arms and conquest, but more importantly by the weight of its intellectual stimuli laden with revolutionary ideas.

The fundamental problem now confronting Islam was not how to bring about a "Reformation" in the religion, because the orthodox body was not at war with itself, but how to effect a much needed "Renaissance."

The triumph of scholastic theology and its perseverance had occasioned none of the abuses which brought about the Protestant revolt in Europe. Islam had no clergy to dictate to it. The ulema, theologians and jurisprudents, never attempted to enlarge on the Qur'ānic conception of how the faithful must gain salvation. The Ṣūfis already had pointed a way. Their movement gave those seeking a more flexible experience of religious contentment the means for it. They were careful not to cross swords with the orthodox theologians. Islam consequently achieved a sort of inner harmony and serenity which Christianity in the Europe of the sixteenth century, shaken by the aftermaths of the Reformation and Counter-Reformation, may well have envied.

But the bridge that al-Ghazāli had built between Ṣūfism and orthodoxy did not last. Ṣūfism gradually drifted towards pantheism with the triumph of ibn ʿArabi's assertion that all creation mirrored facets of God while orthodoxy kept moving towards greater transcendence as the ulema stressed God's uniqueness. Ordinary Muslims simply followed a middle path. When we hear of fatalism in Islam, less attention is paid to the fact that it was the result of ignorance and poverty, which became widespread with the deterioration of trade in the Near East from the fifteenth century onward, than it was occasioned by the dictates of theology or belief in predestination.

In the centuries following the prevalence of Ashʿari theology, there was but one abrupt and short-lived fundamentalist reaction, directed largely against the Ṣūfis. It took place in the fourteenth century when the Ḥanbalite ibn Taymīyah (d. 1328) and his disciples attempted to rid orthodoxy of Ṣūfism. When tensions relaxed in the subsequent centuries, a sort of equilibrium was worked out between both sides: the Ṣūfis steered clear of interference in orthodox theology and the orthodox theologians felt freer to join Ṣūfi orders. The participation of theologians had the sobering effect of preventing Ṣūfism from degenerating into outright pantheism, but aberrations were not altogether eliminated.

The Ḥanbali fundamentalists, however, did not give up the hope of reintroducing puritanism; and nearly four and a half centuries later they were in a position to assert once again their puritanical views. By the middle of the eighteenth century it was evident that the orthodox theologians had not succeeded in keeping the Ṣūfi system from eliminating the aberrations which they were accused of harboring. Sunni theology in the meanwhile seemed to be compromised by the theologians giving in more and more to Ṣūfi demands. A general downgrading appeared to be in progress. Reaction was bound to come from the more doctrinaire, and in this instance fundamentalist, theologians.

Wahhābism

The founder of this movement around 1744 was Muḥammad ibn ʿAbd al-Wahhāb (d. 1787) after whom its opponents named it, albeit the adherents themselves use the term *muwaḥḥidūn (*unitarians) instead. They adhere to the Ḥanbali rite as interpreted by ibn Taymīyah. The founder was born at ʿUyaynah in Najd into the Banu Sinān of the tribe of Tamīm. He studied theology at Medina then spent many years in travel, tutoring in Basra and Baghdad for nine years. Next he went to Kurdistan, Hamadhān and was in Isfahan when Nādir Shah reigned over the region, which would explain his sojourn in Qumm, bastion of Shīʿite theology today. Here he studied peripatetic philosophy and Ṣūfism, which he advocated for a short while. It was in Qumm that he was converted to Ḥanbalism, and upon his return to his native town he publicly preached the doctrine outlined in his work, *Kitāb al-Tawḥīd* (Book on Unicity). He and his family were forced to leave ʿUyaynah on account of his "unorthodox" views. He was received at the tiny village of Dirʿīyah by Muḥammad ibn Suʿūd (Saud), its chieftain, who converted to Wahhābism. It is alleged that the two dynamic personalities came to an understanding at this time: ibn Suʿūd would exercise sovereign and ibn ʿAbd al-Wahhāb religious authority over territories won over to their joint leadership. The structure of the alliance that they cemented has remained in force until today.

The doctrine of the Wahhābis excludes all innovation introduced into Islam after its third century of being. It upholds the *Sunnah* and the six canonical books of *Ḥadīth*. It attacks the cult of saint worship centered on shrines and mausoleums and regards such manifestations of worship as deserving of death. Those engaged in it were accused of polytheism, as were those who invoked the name of a prophet, saint or angel in prayer. All valid knowledge derives strictly from the Qurʾān and the *Sunnah*. To deny divine decree (*qadar*) in all acts constituted heresy in their eyes, so does interpretation of the Qurʾān.

The founder of the movement insisted on attendance at public prayer, the payment of *zakāh* on undeclared profits resulting from trade, genuine adherence to the creed, and the avoidance of smoking, intoxicants, and abusive language.

The Wahhābis were not modernists; they were rather traditionalists who attacked innovations such as those of the Ṣūfis, which they treated as heresy. They also attacked the other orthodox rites for compromising with the Ṣūfis and tolerating their "perversions." They were puritans fired with the zeal to purify not only the religion of what they deemed infidelities but also corruption in manners and religious practices in Arabia, which they attributed to laxity in enforcing religious injunctions.

Incited by Wahhābi zeal, the family of Saud not only took to the conquest of Central and Eastern Arabia, but attacked also

Arab settlements in Iraq, destroying the sacred shrine of the Shīʿah at Karbalāʾ (Kerbala) in 1802. They warred on the hereditary Sharīfs of Mecca in the Ḥijāz and succeeded in capturing and "purifying" the sacred city in 1806. Both the Ottoman sultan in Istanbul and Muḥammad ʿAli, governor of Egypt, were challenged by the bold defiance of the Wahhābis and compelled to strike back twice in 1812–13 and 1816–18 breaking momentarily Wahhābi power. The Saudi family's political power was reduced and their erstwhile vassals, the Rashīds, now governed in their place. But a century later the well publicized king ʿAbd al-ʿAzīz ibn Suʿūd succeeded in reconquering Arabia. Both the Sharīfs of Mecca and the Rashīds of Shammar were uprooted altogether and permanently from Arabia. By 1926 he was in control of the Ḥijāz and following the 1934 war with *Imām* Yaḥya of Yemen, the important province of ʿAsīr on the Red Sea coast passed under his control as well. Wahhābism triumphed with the triumph of ʿAbd al-ʿAzīz and his sons have served as monarchs of what was renamed Saudi Arabia ever since.

In 1912 ʿAbd al-ʿAzīz founded agricultural colonies and settled his devotees in them. They referred to themselves as *Ikhwān* (brethren) to stress their placing religious ties over those of family and tribe. The able-bodied were armed, and could be called upon on short notice to participate in a *jihād*. Meanwhile, they devoted themselves to agricultural pursuits. Starting in the province of Qaṣīm, they came to number eventually about seventy, each with between two and ten thousand settlers. Each colony (*ḥijra*) consisted of three strata: bedouin-farmers, missionaries (*muṭawwiʿūn*), and merchants.

The impact of Wahhābism was soon felt outside of Arabia. Their example encouraged all those who were disaffected with the practices of Islam in their societies. Their doctrine soon spread to India in the east and the Niger in west Africa. In both areas they took to the path of militancy, combatting by force those who did not submit to their version of Islamic puritanism. Their stronghanded methods, intolerance, and extremism evoked the resentment and condemnation of the Muslims at large and set the local governing authorities against them. In their zealous attempts to impose their creed, they conducted themselves no differently than did the ill-fated Khārijites, the earliest puritans at the beginning of Islam. As their violent intolerance of those who disagreed with them began to subside, the Wahhābis went about the task of reasserting the unmitigated monotheism of the early Muslims. The drive for greater observance of the monistic principle was at the expense of the partisans of transcendentalism among whom the Ṣūfis now had played an important role.

What is of significance also is the fact that the reassertion of uncompromising monotheism started in Arabia where the orthodox faith was launched nearly twelve centuries earlier. It would seem that Ḥanbali puritanism was in accordance with the inclination of the Arab, particularly when we note that in the post-Ghazāli period the transcendentalists were predominantly non-Arab: Berber, Turk, and Persian. One can not assume from such a deduction that the choice of creed was motivated by preference deriving mostly from ethnic instinct, or that with the rise of Ṣūfism to eminence, the *Mathnawī* of Rūmi had come to replace the Traditions in importance; yet for many Persians and Turks the gains of transcendentalism symbolized to them a sort of revolt of the "nationalities" against the idea of the Arab ascendancy in Islam. Rather, one may attribute this to the inherently divergent conception of how to reach the Deity among the Semitic Arabs and the non-Semitic nationalities. Was it not in the Indo-Aryan world that the notions of transcendentalism were formally articulated—Gnosticism in Persia, Platonism in Greece?

When the needs for reform became more obvious to the enlightened disciples of the *Sharīʿah*, the motivation came from the orthodox reaction against the growing deterioration which seemed to lead to animism (*jinn* worship) and pantheism rather than from pressures by the Western world. The tensions built up in Islam between the orthodox and the Ṣūfis generated the urge for reform.

Challenge to Reform

The call for the reinterpretation of the tenets of Islam was somewhat sporadic but clearly evident in certain parts of the Islamic world. Not all of the impeti can be construed as religious in nature, neither was the approach to reform necessarily novel. Al-Murtaḍa al-Zabīdi (d. 1790), a Yemeni of Indian origin, found al-Ghazāli's theories suitable for his interpretations, and the end result of his efforts was the reassertion of the Ghazāli type of orthodoxy. With the spread of the printing press in the nineteenth century, a great number of medieval theological works were printed and circulated from Egypt and India. The increasing interest of European scholars in Islam, manifest in a variety of their publications on the subject, also served to bring out the contrasts between the earlier and later conceptions of the religion.

The probe went deeper and new issues were interjected. Modern scholarship and its stress on textual criticism brought out the distinctions between the pure Qurʾānic text and the mass of accretions accumulated over a span of several centuries which heavily weighted Islam and precluded a more adaptive view of it. A great deal of opposition to reassessing the tenets of the faith in the light of modern needs resulted from myopic interests. Hosts of spokesmen, ulema, *muftis*, *qāḍis*, custodians of and propagandists for the *Sharīʿah*, stood to lose their sources of gain were they to be exposed for having promoted unduly a vast body of "guiding precepts" that might now be proved irrelevant, if not un-Islamic, from the point of view of the Muslim's needs in a progressing society, a need that could enjoy the circumspection of Islam by the application of pure Qurʾānic sanction.

As the spirit of revivalism soared, enlightened Muslim scholars recognized the need to stress the spirit rather than the letter of the *Sharīʿah*. Christian Europe already had faced this problem a century or so earlier, albeit not without agonizing reappraisals of dogma accompanied often by violence in the Reformation and Counter-Reformation era. The Muslim world did not have to endure what Christian Europe had experienced before, owing to the fact there are no entrenched or vested religious interests wrangling over dogma because there is only one dogma in Islam: there is no god but God, and all sects agree.

Islam throughout the nineteenth and twentieth centuries has been challenged and confronted by Western views of "modernism" and rapid technological advancement in the West. Those willing to make adjustments have found the theocratic spirit permeating all facets of the Muslim's life restrictive. When the Christian West had been similarly confronted by material progress, it responded to the confrontation by distinguishing clearly between "what is Caesar's" and "what is Christ's."

Western-style modernizers in the Muslim world have argued until recently in favor of separating what the West has regarded the *secular* from the *spiritual* as the *sine qua non* of progress. This element has applied itself to the task of reevaluating the fundamental tenets of their religion in the light of modern needs. They are interested in enjoying the fruits of modern science and technology within a legitimate religious framework. They are content to stress the compatibility between spiritual loyalties and a desire for the material offerings of a rapidly advancing world.

Once again the rationalists have asserted themselves in the world of Islam and have set themselves to the task of rethinking their religion on the basis of the premises they inherited with Islam. They find much they can strip it of, namely the deadweight of medieval accretions, without in any way compromising their fundamental religious beliefs.

Their efforts to date have been rather sporadic and lacking in consistency because of the wide range of views regarding modernization prevalent in different parts of the Muslim world. The impetus to reinterpret and reapply Islamic tenets varies from Morocco to Indonesia, depending on the local need responsible for it. That there should be no wide-scale deliberate approach to reform is the logical consequence of the absence of an organized ecclesiastical system to take charge of the situation. In recent times the great theological institution of higher learning, the Azhar of Egypt, has been serving in a self-styled fashion as the ultimate recourse for the doctrinal reinterpretation of orthodox Islam. Because of the Azhar's conservative orthodox views, the modernists have not always been able to look to it for encouragement and support. Indeed, not until very recent years did this bastion of traditional orthodoxy begin to expand its teaching curricula to include the secular sciences. Further liberalization is not likely to take place in the wake of resurgent rarefied "traditionalism."

"Modernism"

The first serious dent on Azhar thinking was made by the modern Egyptian reformer Muḥammad ʿAbduh (d. 1905), whose reforming activities aimed at the purification of Islam from corrupting influences and practices, *not* the revision of established orthodoxy. ʿAbduh felt the change could be achieved with the reform of Islam's higher education, which in his times was heavily governed by theological precepts. Educational reform to ʿAbduh was the *sine qua non* for the reform of Islam. He sought a readjustment of Islamic doctrine to accommodate modern thought. One way to achieve this adjustment, he argued, is to eliminate *bidʿa* (unorthodox innovations). By introducing reform along these lines, ʿAbduh believed he could supply the means for checking the encroachment of Western ideas laden as they were with Christian polemics which he felt were undermining the bases of Islam.

For precedents ʿAbduh looked back to that century of Islam's development which anteceded the formulation of the orthodox doctrine of Islam, that is before the principal juridical rites were established. His antagonists, foremost among them being the Wahhābis, chose to harken to the puritanical doctrine of ibn Taymīyah instead. ʿAbduh by contrast may be considered a modernist. The results of his broad preachings fostered not only a modernist school of thought but also a reformed traditionalist school, the *Salafīyah*, spearheaded by Muḥammad Rashīd Riḍa, a disciple of ʿAbduh.

ʿAbduh's reform measures targeted in the first instance Muslim higher education at the pinnacle of which stood the Azhar. When ʿAbduh began to advocate reform, there had been in existence for some time a secular system of primary and secondary education, but no institution of secular higher learning. ʿAbduh sought the establishment of this type of institution in order to insure the separation of secular and religious education. Then the religious reformists, it was argued, would be able to update the Azhar upon which institution the reform of Islam depended, particularly since the Azhar had long since become the center of Islam and had come to exercise a determining influence on issues affecting religious beliefs.

Beside the establishment of a secular system of education, other tangible reforms included higher salaries for instructors, larger allowances and better care for students, more liberal library holdings, closer exchanges with provincial mosque schools, and the revival of the Arabic language in its pure classical form as the medium of print for the great theological works of medieval Islam.

The printing of classical treatises led to a literary revival that stressed the employment of classical Arabic as the vehicle of expression. Was not Arabic after all the language of the angels, the Qurʾān and Islam! In 1900 ʿAbduh spearheaded a society specifically for the purpose of reviving the Arabic sciences.

The most eloquent testimony of ʿAbduh's religious views is embodied in his classical treatise *Risālat al-Tawhīd* (*The Epistle on the Unity* [*of God*]),[1] which is the principal exposition of his basic theology. In it ʿAbduh stresses the need to purge Islam of its superstitions, to correct the Muslim's conception of the articles of his faith, and to eliminate the errors that had crept into Islam on account of the misinterpretation of its texts. He insisted that the exegesis of the Qurʾān should be simplified and modernized.

Early in his life ʿAbduh was enthusiastic about pure philosophy, but later on he reached the conclusion that it was not in the best interest of Islam. Yet he still made use of logic, arguing that the science of reason is not the possession of philosophy. With the use of reason he intended to establish a rational interpretation of Qurʾānic text so as to adapt it to the modern needs of a society anxious to maintain the spiritual ties enjoined by the sacred book.

The exercise of reason in matters of faith ran contrary to the Ḥanbali form of exegesis, which remained faithful to the literal interpretation of the revelations contained in the Qurʾān, tailored as they may have been to the needs of the community's forebears over twelve centuries earlier. They imitated precedents set by ulema who could not believe that the word of Allah might be construed differently, if necessary, to make it conform to the requirements of man and the vicissitude of his motions in time and space.

What is significant and meritorious in ʿAbduh's reassessment of Islam's capacity for adaptation to modern needs was his insistence on the need for *ijtihād*. He argued for the reestablishment of *ijtihād* as a tool for reinterpreting the tenets of the faith, and insisted that it must be made the right of all generations of Muslims to apply these tenets as the circumstances called for it. ʿAbduh preached tolerance of other sects and enjoined that others do the same. He sought to soothe the anxieties of his religiously minded listeners by stating that they need not fear any non-reasonable conflict between science and the precepts of their faith. Applying reason to bring about changes that would conform to the demands of a modernizing society could not be un-Islamic.

ʿAbduh's ideas of reform were evident in his unfinished commentary on the Qurʾān. His modernist views lie mostly in his advocacy of measures which he believed were in conformity with the fundamental precepts of Islam. While he was no innovator or synthesist in the tradition of the great medieval reformer al-Ghazāli, by stressing the need to apply reason to faith he loosened the iron grip of immobility on the religion of Islam after lifting it from its medieval setting, and made possible the reformulating of doctrinal concepts in a modern context.

The legacy of ʿAbduh lies chiefly in the modernist revival which he launched, aiming, as we have seen, at introducing the changes that would make the religion adaptable to a rapidly transforming world. He preached the return to the simplest and most essential forms of the religion. In doing so the ulema were expected to establish a common base for bridging differences among Muslims differing in sectarian loyalties. ʿAbduh countered those casting aspersion on Islam for sanctioning polygamy, easy divorce, even slavery, by arguments showing that such practices are not integral to the faith, but rather accidental and subject to change.

ʿAbduh's concepts and preachings of reform yielded two continuous trends. One trend persisted in a secular vein, abetted by Western notions of modernism, but without attempting to abandon the dogmas of the faith. The other trend was towards evoking the support of the tradition established by the "righteous forefathers" (*al-Salaf al-Ṣāliḥ*).

The secular modernists believed in separating church and state in Islam. They thought it possible to restrict the *Sharīʿah's* provisions to religious practices only. Some went so far as to substitute Western laws for those of Islam that had applied hitherto to government. An extreme example of this can be seen in Turkey, where under Ataturk Western laws replaced Islamic law in an all-out effort of secularizing society and modernizing it without regard to theological sanction. For a while under Nasser Egypt appeared headed in a similar direction. This pattern of modernization is predicated on the assumption that Islamic *Sharīʿah* enactments are not compatible with modern legal needs, an assumption which the "fundamentalists" in recent years have been laboring to eradicate by word and deed.

The *Salafīyah* have upheld the faith and example of the Orthodox Caliphs and the Companions of Muḥammad without endorsing the rejection of the canon law, as have the secularists. Together with the modernists they have rejected the authority of accretions held valid by medieval authors. In common with the modernists they have placed their trust in the Qurʾān and *Sunnah* as a valid source of guidance in the modern world. But unlike them, the *Salafīyah* rejected Western-type ideas grounded in secular realism and rationalism in providing guidance for the reform of Islamic society. Reform to them must be based on the orthodox teachings of Islam and its traditional precepts of organization.

Reformed "Traditionalism"

Since the reinterpretation of the Qurʾān was essential for the success of both the modernist and *Salafīyah* trends, Muḥammad ʿAbduh's unfinished commentary on the Qurʾān was continued upon his death by one of his disciples and the architect of the *Salafīyah* movement, namely the Syrian Rashīd Riḍā (d. 1935).

Besides serving as editor of the Qurʾān commentary begun by ʿAbduh, Riḍa founded the *Manār (Lighthouse)*, a journal publicizing the *Salafīyah* notions of reform. The *Manār* gained a wide audience and following from Morocco to Indonesia.

Riḍa like ʿAbduh treated the modernists with caution and did not hesitate to condemn the extremist measures directed against

Islam by the followers of Ataturk in Turkey. When pressed, Riḍa's group would resort to a fundamentalist approach to the teachings of orthodox Islam. This much they had in common with the Wahhābis, but without being drawn into the latter's strong sectarian proclivity.

The *Salafīyah* have been dubbed "Neo-Ḥanbalites"; conservative yet favoring the reopening of the gate of *ijtihād* and applying it anew to issues of law and theology. This stems from the fact that Riḍa and his followers harkened back to the puritanical doctrines of ibn Taymīyah and one of his followers, ibn Qayyim al-Jawzīyah (d. 1355).

For a while, before modern Turkish secularists broke with traditional Islam, Riḍa accepted those pan-Islamic ideals preached by the reformer Jamāl al-Dīn al-Afghāni who favored the political revitalization and unification of the Islamic world under the central leadership of the sultan-caliph. But the intensity of his conviction and zeal tended to scare not only modernists, but conservative Muslims as well, many of whom were uncomfortable with his preachings in their very homelands.

The checkered and colorful career of al-Afghāni took him to all parts of the Islamic world. He was born and raised in Persia, but in his preachings he was transported to India (1869) where he was first exposed to Western ideas and ways. Next he journeyed to Istanbul (1870) to address students, but was compelled to leave (1871) by the Shaykh al-Islām who held the ranking position in the Ottoman empire as official spokesman for Islam. He came to Egypt, where for a while he rallied around him many of those who were to lead revolutionary trends later. In 1879 he was expelled by the Khedive on account of his agitations against the British and interference in the internal affairs of Muslim countries. He returned to India then left for Paris where he founded and edited the periodical *Al-ʿUrwa al-Wuthqa* (*The Most Firm Bond*), which was designed to serve as the mouthpiece of a revitalized Islam. Later (1884) he was joined by ʿAbduh when he too was expelled from Egypt because of his ties with the Egyptian nationalists. Al-Afghāni returned to Persia (1889) to become prime minister where he rallied around him a core of revolutionaries and disciples. A year later (1890) he was arrested and taken to Turkey, but he managed to get away, this time traveling to London (1892). He was lured back to Istanbul by the sultan, where he died in 1897.

The strong impact of al-Afghāni on the political destinies of the Islamic countries that felt the fiery eloquence of his nationalistic preachings was evident in the 1881 Egyptian show of force against the British in Egypt, the 1906 revolutionary movement in Persia, and the 1908 Young Turk revolt in Turkey.

The legacy of al-Afghāni as a reformer lies chiefly in his political preachings. He awakened the conscience of his audiences to the need of ideological and political unity in the Islamic world if it were to resist the political and ideological encroachments of the West. This he hoped to achieve through reforming Islam and making it a vital force for unity by adapting it to modern conditions. He advocated force and revolution if need be to bring about Islamic unity. There was no doubt in his mind that Islam had the capacity to make the necessary adjustments. He went so far as to envision a unity between Shīʿah and Sunnis. He was not able, however, to penetrate the conservative shield of the ulema to reach the mass of Muslims. His converts, as a consequence, derived mostly from the "Efendi" class that thrived on the status quo and had no particular interest in seeing it overturned. The success of his preachings was contingent on purging the minds of the masses of foolish notions and superstitions, but the ulema were in his way. Al-Afghāni had confidence in Islam's capacity to survive the "purge" because Islam inspires freedom of religious belief, permitting everyone to reach perfection just short of prophecy. He shared with the modernists the view that reason can serve the ends of religion and that a revised program of education can serve to update the thinking of the ordinary Muslim and train his morals.

In his *Manār* Riḍa continued the trend fostered by al-Afghāni's *ʿUrwa* which aimed at promoting social and economic as well as religious reforms on the premise that Islam is suitable for modern life and exigences. The *Sharīʿah* was held to be sufficient for providing adequate precepts of government to Muslim rulers if encumbrances deemed un-Islamic could be eliminated. Riḍa also believed that tolerance among the various sects of Islam could be achieved. He too advocated the use in schools of common text material in order to insure uniformity of religious education.

The *Salafīyah* through the *Manār* called for the establishment of an Islamic society (*al-Jamʿīyah al-Islāmīyah*) to watch over reform. It was to have its headquarters at Mecca, with branches in all Muslim countries, and enjoy the patronage of the caliph.

The *Salafīyah* opposed secular nationalism in its radical extreme, the nationalism represented by Kemal Ataturk and his new Turkey, which strove consciously to break with its Islamic traditions. The brand of nationalism preached by Muṣṭafa Kāmil of Egypt and his *Liwāʾ* Party in 1908 was equally repugnant to them, for this group was no more interested in religious reform than Kemal of Turkey. The *Manār* on the other hand supported the Wahhābis of Arabia, as militantly traditionalistic as they were, because of their religious puritanism. The *Manār* attacked the Ṣūfis and *bidʿa* as much as the ulema who would substitute human for divine law. The *Manār* sought to simplify Islam by stripping it down to its pure tenets and practices as they were observed in the days of the Prophet and the first four caliphs. It proposed the reduction of the *madhāhib* to one and recommended flexible civil laws, provided they are based on the Qurʾān and the *Sunnah*. The *Salafīyah* like the modernists believed that Muslims should build schools not mosques. They were not satisfied with just preaching; they sponsored missionary activity among Muslims with the establishment of the *Jamʿīyat al-Daʿwa wa-'l-Irshād* (the Society for Propagation and Guidance).

The scope of the *Salafīyah's* work ranged into the political field where again the reformist ideas of Afghāni were more clearly continued. The aim, like Afghāni's, was to evoke a Muslim nationalism that would infuse the Muslim world with sufficient dynamism to withstand, then turn back the colonial assaults of the Western world. Socially, they probed for norms from the folds of Islam that would make available to the devout Muslim the niceties of modern life without jeopardizing the religious requirements of Islamic society.

The intellectual fermentation engendered by the modernists and *Salafīyah* has had a lasting and far-reaching effect not only on religion but also on the genre of Arabic literature in the twentieth century. The range and nature of this influence lies beyond our present study. But it may be noted that much of the literature typified by the Egyptian school of Ṭaha Ḥusayn, Tawfiq al-Ḥakīm, Maḥmūd ʿAbbās al-ʿAqqād, Aḥmad Amīn, and others has been influenced either by the secular modernists or by the *Salafīyah*. The theme and content of their writings often reflect the conviction that modernism is not incompatible with their religion.

The Indian Reformist Movement

In India, reformism dates back to the sixteenth century and to the work of Shaykh Aḥmad Sirhindi (1564–1624) and Shah Waliyullah (1702–1762). Both men laid the groundwork for nineteenth century Islamic revivalism in the subcontinent. Shah Waliyullah preached when Moghul India was in a state of decline and when Hindu and Sikhs challenged the Muslim minority, burdened as it was with internal disunity and conflicting factionalism in the Sunni-Shīʿite disputes and the ulema-Ṣūfi confrontations over Islamic observances.

Sirhindi focused on the need for Muslims "to purge their lives of un-Islamic practices and to reform popular Ṣūfi practices, which he believed were responsible for much of the syncretisms that had threatened the identity, moral fiber, and survival of Indian Islam in its multiconfessional setting,"[2] hence the need to implement the teachings of the Qurʾān and *Sunnah* as in the days when Islam was best observed.

Having been educated in Mecca, Waliyullah was influenced by the contemporary Wahhābi movement. He was also a member of the Naqshbandi order, which had taken the initiative toward reform. For Waliyullah, religious reform was the *sine qua non* for restoring Moghul political power. In this respect he might be seen as a forerunner of al-Afghāni, who saw in the reform and purification of the faith the platform for united political resistance to colonial encroachment.

Waliyullah is credited with reconciling conflicting schools of thought in Indian Islam resulting from the influence of Ibn Arabi of Murcia, the great mystic philosopher, and Sirhindi's teachings, the former denying all existence outside God (a form of pantheism) and the latter stressing unity of experience. Waliyullah interpreted this apparent conflict as being merely a problem of semantics. With this approach, he reconciled the two conflicting schools and proceeded to urge "Ṣūfi leaders to cleanse their practices of un-Islamic, idolatrous, and antinomian tendencies."[3]

Waliyullah is best remembered for his condemnation of blind imitation (*taqlīd*) and insistence on reviving the process of *ijtihād* to resolve differences among contending Muslim sects and schools of thought, which meant that modern thought could not be excluded from the process.

The challenge of modern ideas to Islam did not elicit a consistent pattern of response. The reaction of the Egyptian thinkers spearheaded by the *Manār* followers is but one of several. Another school of modernizers is the Indo-Pakistani, which is less traditionalistic than the Syro-Egyptian. Like the Arab modernizers they believed Islam could be subjected to rationalism without jeopardy to the authority of the Qur'ān and the *Ḥadīth*. They were to test, however, the validity of traditions which had been accumulated over a protracted period of time outside the requirements of the Qur'ān and *Ḥadīth*. Such accretions, it was believed, tended to load the faith with a body of spurious dogmas and injunctions that contributed little to the enhancement of Islam but prevented it rather from adjusting to the demands of modern life.

In India, and later in Pakistan when the split took place in 1947, enlightened Muslim thinkers led by Sir Sayyid Aḥmad Khān (d. 1898) actively labored to accommodate what was suitable of Western knowledge to their conception of a modernized Islam. Perceiving the role of modern education in the accomplishment of their goal, they founded a system of higher education, today known as ʿAligarh Muslim University. The system introduced Western knowledge into the curriculum on the assumption that Islam is in conformity with science and similar studies.

The social ramifications of a modern approach to the study of man in present-day society were noticeable when educated Muslims began to question some of the social practices rooted in the religious tradition, such as plural marriages, "easy divorces," and slavery. With a new bold and critical view towards the increments of the past in the face of strong opposition from the ulema, these modernists challenged not only their inherited way of life but also the authority on which it rested, which meant the body of religious practices passed on from generation to generation with all its un-Islamic features.

The trend set by Sayyid Aḥmad was continued by another Indian, a Shīʿite Muslim by the name of Sayyid Amīr ʿAli, whose noted work *The Spirit of Islam*[4] embodies an eloquent testimony concerning the powers of Islam to adjust to modern life. Like other reformers he advocated return to the simple unadulterated texts of the Qurʾān and the verified sayings of the Prophet. He condemned on the authority of the Qurʾān what came to be regarded as evil practices: polygamy, divorce, purdah, and the like. In his judgment Islam can eliminate the blight into which it had fallen by breaking the stranglehold of the past and by reopening the gate of *ijtihād*, or independent judgment, and vesting it in the ulema.

Amīr ʿAli went much further in his radical departure from the past by declaring openly that the Qurʾān was the work of the Prophet Muḥammad. In the view of a modern writer, this position is defensible "because the doctrine that the Qurʾān is 'uncreated,' i.e., literally the word of God, was not finally established until the third century of the *hijra*."[5]

The Indo-Pakistani School leaned towards apologetics. Apparently it was more concerned with a defense of Islam than with outlining a feasible program of reform. The Persian poet-philosopher Sir Muḥammad Iqbāl (d. 1938) belonged to this school. Like other Eastern intellectuals he had studied in the West, in England and Germany. He took up law, as did Mahatma Gandhi, to acquire financial self-sufficiency in order to pursue his intellectual interests unencumbered by the need to gain. While his poetry in Persian and Urdu is widely read by scores of dedicated followers who have all but immortalized his name in

Pakistan, it is in his English writings that we must search for his views on the revitalization of Islam.

In 1928 Iqbāl delivered a series of lectures, entitled *Six Lectures on the Reconstruction of Religious Thought in Islam.*[6] "These present the first...thoroughgoing attempt to restate the theology of Islam in modern immantist terms."[7] Like other Muslim modernists, he called on his followers to adopt the principles of vitalization that made Western societies strong and allowed them to leave the once dominant Islamic world far in its trail. Modern science to him was a chief reason. He stressed rather strongly the compatibility of science with Islam. "The knowledge of Nature," he argued, "is the knowledge of God's behavior. In our observation of Nature we are virtually seeking a kind of intimacy with the Absolute Ego; and this is only another form of Worship."[8]

Iqbāl was also deeply inclined to Ṣūfism; perhaps he was enmeshed in what the orthodox ulema would construe as a "hopeless tangle of thought." Evidence of this "hopeless tangle" is often betrayed in his writings, which may help explain the rather elusive character of his views.

The writings of Iqbāl provide an index to diverse currents in the religious, social, and political thinking of Indian Muslims, as each and all could find a source of reliance, if not succor, in his expressed poetic and philosophical views. He approached the problems confronting Islam on such a high plane of philosophical interpretation that the speculator, political agitator, or a young Muslim inclined to Marxism can find what he seeks of comfort in Iqbāl's works.

Iqbāl's approach to Islam rested on the belief that its tenets and sacred texts must be rethought and reinterpreted allegorically. He began from the premise that the Muslims possessed the free will to reinterpret. Such doctrines as pertain, for instance, to immortality have both ethical and biological bases. Hence the Islamic conceptions of heaven and hell may be treated as reflections of a state of mind.

He resorts to Qur'ānic revelations in order to prove that humans possess the freedom to interpret in a creative sense. The Fall of Adam "is an allegorical reflection of man's rise from a primitive state of instructive appetite to the conscious possession of a free self capable of doubt and disobedience," also "the emergence of a finite ego which has the power to choose." He condemns the traditional conception of fatalism as morally degrading, an "invention of men with little grasp of philosophical truth" who have perpetuated it out of self-interest.

The basic supposition of Iqbāl, like those of the Muslim modernists of Egypt and Syria, is that religious reforms can be achieved without the need to sever connections with the social institutions of Islam, in contrast to the strong advocates of a thoroughgoing secularism like the Kemalist Turks who set themselves to the task of achieving it. Again the compelling factor was the need for preserving Islamic solidarity as a counterpoise to the aggressive intents of a materially superior West.

In this regard, reformers concede that the initiative for change must rest with the religious element of Islam. Iqbāl undertakes to project interpretations that could easily be branded heretical by the pious without providing his disciples with concrete methods to achieve the needed transformation. On specifics he is precise, but on fundamentals he withdraws to the comforts of the Ṣūfi realm of retreat.

Radical Departures

The fermentation of thought resulting from probings for a reform of Islam has resulted sometimes in a radical departure from the basic Islamic norm, and has given rise to splinter movements that can be scarcely termed Islamic. Yet they have quoted the Qur'ān to justify their existence; and they have also taken the initiative to reconstitute Islam in a manner suitable for their treatment of the Qur'ān and *Ḥadīth* to provide, as they were convinced it would, the cornerstone of Islam's "modernization."

The problem lies in the fact that these popular movements tended towards the realization more of political and social than religious reforms. Indeed, they are not altogether devoid of nationalist sentiments, the preachings of al-Afghāni being a case in point.

The secular trend has not served to cement the bonds uniting

Muslims because it has encouraged *ethnic nationalism* rather than *communal universalism* among them. The architects of modern Turkey, nominal Muslims that they are, may well have attempted to uproot the concept of universalism altogether from the social life of the nation, had they not encountered resistance from the Turkish folk.

Another radical departure is the policy of modern secular leaders in predominantly Muslim countries ranging from Egypt to Pakistan to Indonesia, a policy which uses the principle of communalism in Islam as a political weapon against imperial encroachments on their lands, as it was used decades ago to confront the physical occupation of their countries and the presence of foreign troops on their soil. Until very recent times, even after independence was gained, young Muslim nationalists, however minimal a role religion played in their personal lives, have not hesitated to marshal the forces of Islam to combat "the foreigner" and show that they will not be influenced by decisions contrary to their likings or political ambitions. These nationalists have been operating on the premise that they can answer the West by brandishing against it the sword of Islam in a modern form of *jihād* as was attempted on the eve of World War I under the appeal of "Pan-Islamism." This is not an effective weapon, as the recent history of Muslim countries attests, because of the predominance of secular nationalism whenever confrontation of the two takes place. Religious solidarity had been weakened; how could it sustain the political arm of Islam? Ayatollah Khomeini pointed a way in Iran with the establishment of the Islamic republic. Through it he expected to rekindle the dynamism of Islam not only to achieve much needed reform, but to demonstrate also how Islamic solidarity might be reinstituted beyond Iranian borders.

The Trend Towards Eclecticism

Numerous societies, movements, and ideologies bearing the stamp of modernism have sprung into being during the past century in response to a variety of urges emanating from Islam. Most of these, like *al-Ikhwān al-Muslimūn* (The Muslim Brethren), have had more of a sociopolitical than a religious orientation and therefore do not concern us in this study. What is relevant can be deduced from a brief account of certain movements that have responded to the call for a modern approach, namely, the Aḥmadīyah of India and the Bābi with its offshoot the Bahā'i of Persia. The former has attempted to preserve an Islamic identity, while the latter has shown every evidence of losing a distinguishing Islamic character and no longer qualifies for a detailed treatment in this study. Both sprung from Islam, yet both have chosen the course of eclecticism and syncreticism in their beliefs and preachings to the point of risking their Islamism for heresy in the eyes of their orthodox coreligionists.

The Aḥmadīyah

The Aḥmadīyah movement was founded by one Mirza Ghulām Aḥmad Qādiyāni (d. 1908) who launched his career with the proclamation that he was divinely charged with the mission to reinterpret Islam in the light of the requirements of the modern age. He moved cautiously and in his doctrinal pronouncements he deviated but little from the posture of the moderate orthodox reformers.

As his followers grew in numbers and his pretensions grew commensurately, he proclaimed himself the "Promised Messiah of the Christians," a prophet and the "Mahdi of Islam," as well as the "return of the Krishna for the Hindus." He was soon branded a "heretic." When his first successor (*khalīfah*) died in 1914, the followers, now dubbed Aḥmadīyah after the founder, split into two groups. The majority elected Aḥmad's son Maḥmūd as their *khalīfah*; but a minority bolted and withdrew to Lahore, now in Pakistan. The majority, or Qādiyāni, stood by the founder's claim to prophethood and continued to recognize Maḥmūd as the *khalīfah*; the minority, or seceders, discarded both and organized themselves into a "society for the propagation of Islam" with a new leader. They then endeavored to become reconciled with orthodox or Sunni Islam, but the ulema have been reluctant to accept them.

Both branches of the Aḥmadīyah launched extensive missionary activities with sub-Sahara Africa becoming the chief target of their syncretistic preachings. Here, as in the East Indies, they encountered rivalry from Christian missions operating in the same areas; yet their ranks were steadily swelled by African converts until they number today over a million followers. Their missionary activities have extended even into England, Germany, and America.

Up to the present time, the movement does not seem to have suffered from its preachings on the fringe of orthodox doctrine. In many instances converts gained to Islam through Aḥmadīyah efforts often are won over to the Sunni doctrine through the subtleties of the orthodox fathers using the Azhar as a lure. Every year several thousand African students are enrolled in the theological and related programs offered by the Azhar. They return to their homelands more deeply imbued with the Sunni doctrines of Islam.

From the point of view of doctrinal interpretation the Aḥmadis depart slightly from the basic orthodox position. What is significant in their interpretation is the notion that prophecy did not end with Muḥammad, hence their justification for Ghulām's role; also their conviction that the Qur'ān is open to "inexhaustible meanings"; and as "each succeeding age discovers fresh properties and new virtues, the same is the case with the Word of God, so that there may be no disparity between God's Work and His Word."[9]

The Aḥmadis are convinced of the Qur'ān's superiority over other non-Muslim sacred texts, which accounts for their zeal to spread it. When the alleged superiority of the Qur'ān is coupled with a non-doctrinaire attitude towards the role of Muḥammad as not having ended, the Aḥmadi arms himself with the motivation to expound his version of Islam's function in the modern age. As long as he does not defile the honor of the Prophet, the Qur'ān, and himself in his preachings, he is at liberty to interpret the tenets of his faith to meet the challenge of any given situation. His belief in continued revelation from God tends to strengthen the Aḥmadi conceptions of Qur'ānic text. His strong mystical orientation abets such an understanding; "the deeper truths of the

Qurʾān are the result of divine assistance; the light of the reason unaided by God is too dim to bring those truths into view."[10]

The Aḥmadīyah claim to modernism lies principally in a liberal interpretation of the Qurʾān, which is translated and disseminated as part of their zeal to spread Islam, in their increasing reliance on reason, and in their willingness to accept modern science. The secret of their success is their willingness to adapt to any given need, even to the point of inconsistency, to gain credence for their doctrine.

At first, "reason" was suspect; Ghulām Aḥmad did not believe that Islam should be championed through rationalism, but rather through the authentication made possible by revelation and divine assistance. The Egyptian reformer Muḥammad ʿAbduh on the other hand advocated the "precedence of reason over the literal meaning of the Divine Law in case of conflict between them."[11] Later on, when Aḥmadi missionaries were confronted by Christian rivals in search of converts, they did not hesitate to resort to reason, arguing that "objections raised against Islam are due either to a lack of serious reflection or because passion is allowed to prevail over reason."[12]

The Aḥmadis' stand on science countenances the important premise that Islam encourages the study and use of science, as proven historically when Muslims in medieval times made basic contributions to the sciences. If the spirit or text of the Qurʾān is used as a measure, there can be no contradiction; indeed, science is more incompatible with Christianity, it is argued, than it is with Islam.

Similarly the Aḥmadis find Ṣūfism perfectly Islamic on the grounds that "the leaders of thought among them [the Ṣūfis], never diverged a hair's breadth from the path chalked out for them by Islam." Furthermore "they have been the true expounders of Islam, and during the decline of the Muslims it is they who held aloft the beacons of true Islamism." In continuing their defense of the Ṣūfis the Aḥmadis argued that "There was never any question of their departing from the Holy Qurān [*sic*] or the traditions of the Holy Prophet." What the orthodox termed as "Ṣūfi aberrations" the Aḥmadis defended by denial, holding that the Ṣūfis "put down all those beliefs or practices that savoured of asceticism, monasticism or esotericism as un-Islamic [*sic*] and wholly foreign to their own convictions."[13]

Bābism and Bahāʾism

Bābism originated not from Sunnism but from Shīʿism. Like the Aḥmadīyah, this earlier movement was also eclectic. In the former centuries we witnessed the rise of equally eclectic and syncretistic movements: the Nuṣayri, Druze, Yazīdi, a number of Shīʿah sects, then later, in the Turkish period of ascendancy, of the Bektāshi order.

The founder of the Bābi sect is Sayyid ʿAli Muḥammad of Shīrāz who had been an adherent of the Shaykhi school of philosophical thought among the Shīʿahs. The sect's name derived from the symbolic name "Bāb" (gateway) by which Sayyid ʿAli called himself in reference to the "gateway" through which divine truth is said to be revealed unto the believers. It was on May 23, 1844 that Sayyid ʿAli, "moved by the Spirit of God," officially proclaimed his mission to the Persians, in the city of Shīrāz where there had gathered together "eighteen spiritually prepared souls, men of religious wisdom to whom it had been given to understand divine realities."[14]

The core of Bābi teachings lies in Sayyid ʿAli's belief that he had been divinely commissioned to warn his listeners of the coming of the "great promised One," "Him-whom-God-shall-manifest,"—the "Latter-Day Revelator," "The Lord of Hosts" promised in the revealed sacred writings of the past, who would establish soon the Kingdom of God on earth.

The Bāb preached a peculiar mixture of liberal religious doctrine reinforced by a heavy dose of Gnosticism which actually yielded little success. His followers were few and scattered throughout Persia. Persian officials, not to mention the Shīʿah fathers, did not take too kindly to Sayyid ʿAli's personal and doctrinal claims. By inciting his listeners the Bāb compelled Persian authorities to arrest him and, following an uprising of his followers, to execute him as a common criminal in 1850.

But the movement established by the Bāb did not die out

as the Persian authorities had hoped. It merely changed form and proceeded to grow and spread, mostly outside Persia. Instrumental in the further spread of the beliefs established by Sayyid ʿAli was a disciple, Bahāʾullāh (d. 1892) who had taken charge of the majority of the Bābis following the split that ensued upon the death of the founder.

Bahāʾullāh continued to elaborate on the doctrine of the Bāb in such radical terms that he and his successors managed to draw it outside the religious fold of Islam. Since then the original doctrine based on Islam has taken on the trappings of a universal religion resting on two sustaining principles: *pacifism* and *humanitarianism.*

Bahāʾism is not considered an Islamic sect. Both Shīʿites and Sunnis have dubbed it a heresy and its followers subject to the law of Apostasy. The movement was driven out of Persia largely because of the intense persecution to which its adherents were subjected.

The core of Bahāʾi teaching lies in the collective writings of the founder, the Bāb, known as *The Bayān* (Expositor) with its stress on awaiting "Him-whom-God-shall-manifest." In the period of "awaiting," the devotees are exhorted to prepare themselves spiritually for meeting Bahāʾullāh. What is significant about Bahāʾullāh's teachings is their source: Torah, Bible, Qurʾān, which makes the movement highly eclectic and imparts to it the basis for a universalistic appeal.

Bahāʾism utilizes a sophisticated approach founded on the premise that man cannot achieve a higher spiritual status if he does not perfect the powers latent in his body and soul; training the body, it is said, provides man the organism to manifest his spiritual side. Education, according to the "world teacher" (Bahāʾullāh), plays an important role in summoning all of mankind to one spiritual world-consciousness.

The Bahāʾi view is that Muḥammad arose at a time when people in Arabia were submerged in ignorance and superstition, and that he changed the situation by calling to the worship of one God and inculcating his followers with high moral standards through a code of laws and ordinances suitable to the spiritual and material needs of his day. The Muslim "church," however, soon departed from the real spirit of Muḥammad's teachings. But

Muḥammad had taken the precaution of preparing his people for the "great latter-day Bahāʾi revelation," as witnessed in the *Ḥadīth*. The time of the spiritual awakening, equated with resurrection, was to be accompanied by signs mentioned also in the Bible, that is when religious faith has decayed and general demoralization set in.

So the early converts to Bahāʾism accepted the new calling with the understanding that the Bāb is the promised Mahdi and Bahāʾullāh the Christ (spirit), as both seem faithfully to have met the prophesied condition and time of appearance.

The Bahāʾis evolved a liberal cult conforming to the essential ingredients of other faiths—temple worship, fasting, prayer, good deeds to supplement creed and dogma, separation of state and church, and the unification of mankind through common institutions acceptable to all, such as what Bahāʾullāh represents, based not on separation of church and state but on the union of religion and state.

The Bahāʾi modernist outlook stems from the conception that peace is desirable and can be achieved in the federation of all small and large nations and the establishment of a universal governing body supervised by one system of adjudication. Bahāʾism teaches cooperation in all affairs, between capital and labor, East and West. Cooperation materially and spiritually will make of various peoples one harmonious world-family.

There is no conflict between the divine and the natural; there exists rather, it is stated, scientific harmony between the two and perfect accord throughout the whole of creation. Indeed, natural science in the view of the Bahāʾis "teaches man how to live properly upon a human plane." Man can discover and utilize the laws of nature; but the laws of God are revealed unto man only through His mediators: Christ, Muḥammad, the other prophets, and Bahāʾullāh.

The near-avid interest in modern thinking by the Bahāʾis bespeaks their respect for it as an aid to religious fulfillment. "This general and widespread spirit of modern thought," they argue, "has been as a plough which has prepared the religious ground of the world to receive the spiritual seeds of universal religious ideals."[15] Bahā'is regard themselves as being in perfect harmony with modern trends on the grounds that "the modernists of all religions are teaching many of the same principles as held by the followers of the Bahā'i Cause."[16] Conflicts in the past between science and theology are attributed to "imaginations and superstitions" which religions had accumulated over the centuries to make them unacceptable to science. Since these are held to be outside the realm of the actual teachings of the great prophets like Jesus and Muḥammad, dispensing with such unhealthy accretions in no way compromises the basic teachings of these religions. And by eliminating them there would remain no area of conflict between theology and science.

What makes the Bahā'is modernists in their outlook is the conviction that their doctrine and teachings are free from the superstitions of the past and are compatible with modern science.

The Role of Extra-Sharīʿah Legislation

Radical movements typified by the Aḥmadis and Bahā'is are symptomatic of the impact of modern thinking on traditional beliefs and organizational concepts in Islam. In recent times they have not appeared as widespread as modernists had expected. The trend rather has been to tailor *Sharīʿah* provisions to the needs of present day Muslim societies.

Under the impact of Westernization, Ottoman rulers attempted in the nineteenth century to supplement and or replace *Sharīʿah* decrees in the area of civil and criminal law. This trend continued in the twentieth century, particularly in Muslim lands under European tutelage. In recent years the tendency has been to reverse this trend and give *Sharīʿah* legislation primacy over non-*Sharīʿah* derived laws. Countries like Saudi Arabia and Libya have pointed a way. In Iran following the Khomeini revolution the *Sharīʿah* has become the only source of legislation.

Those who have held more liberal views of the *Sharīʿah* were Muslim humanists seeking reforms in keeping with the modern spirit and the spirit of Islam as well. The resulting reforms until the recent decade appeared to betray careful considerations, stemming from the search and utilization of precedents in the *Sharīʿah* but without encroaching on the spirit and intrinsic philosophy underlying it. There is no outright innovation, but the trend towards an eclectic system of legislating for modern needs within the more broadly interpreted tenets of the canon law is clearly in evidence.

Muslim heads of state and legislators today may seem to be resorting to a form of *ijtihād*, justified by the argument that it is their prerogative to override a traditional canonical principle if the interests of the modern public demand it. Invariably they resort to the argument that they are not innovating outrightly but simply choosing from the opinions of accepted, albeit rival, jurists. They have circumvented *Ijmāʿ* with the argument that it can not be established how encompassing public consensus really was when resorted to in the past. They have also drawn a line between the *compulsive* and *permissive* nature of canonical decrees on the grounds that by exploiting the permissiveness of a decree they are committing an act of conscience which they are willing to risk should they be called upon to account for it on the Day of Judgment. One of their stronger arguments, however, is that a divine ordinance can not be binding for all time when the condition and circumstance of its promulgation have changed.

What has encouraged the trend towards extra-*Sharīʿah* legislation in recent times is the insistence of the innovators that even in the earlier centuries caliphs and local rulers did not hesitate to make use of customary law (*ʿādāt*) and set aside the *Sharīʿah* where specific issues not fully treated therein were involved; these related often to the areas of commerce and crime.

In the nineteenth century under the political impact of the West, the Ottoman Porte began to give in to demands for formal legislation outside the purview of *Sharīʿah* specification. A good example is the introduction in the early 1800s of commercial and penal codes reflecting Western prototypes; a civil code along the lines established by the Code Napoleon was promulgated in Egypt in the 1870s.

At the turn of the century, also in Egypt, secular courts besides those decreed by the *Sharīʿah* were established; and in more recent times these courts have nearly taken over adjudication of issues formally reserved to the *Sharīʿah* courts, namely those related to personal matters and family affairs. Even courts of appeal, unheard of in the earlier Islamic periods ruled by the *Sharīʿah*, have been introduced. New court procedures designed to bypass the *Sharīʿah* have operated alongside the traditional with the aim of eventually supplanting the latter altogether.

Modern legislation has even invaded the privacy of family relationships which formally were understood to belong strictly to the domain of the *Sharīʿah*. The Law of Family Rights, promulgated by the Ottomans in 1917, is largely in force still in Lebanon; while in Syria and Jordan it has been replaced by even more progressive codes.

The trend in Arab countries towards more secular codes during the era of Western tutelage has been reversed in recent times. Only in the Fertile Crescent countries, dominated largely by secular ideologies, do we witness the dominance of non-*Sharīʿah* laws. The choice of courts for purposes of litigation was left at first to litigants. In Turkey, the whole legal system is based on secular premises. Elsewhere, the aim of secular enactments often has been the amelioration of decrees derived from the *Sharīʿah*, particularly in the areas of family affairs and women's rights with the view of extending privileges not experienced previously.

Laws passed in recent years in most Arab countries have raised the marriage age to eighteen for a boy, seventeen for a girl; in earlier times child marriages had been very common. Marriage contracts specify often the terms that the wife can dictate beforehand and have enforced afterwards. In Iraq such innovations have been slower to come, owing to Shīʿah-Sunni differences over these matters. In Saudi Arabia and other countries that have proclaimed the *Sharīʿah* the law of the land—Sudan, Libya, Qatar, and the United Arab Emirates—only those decrees deriving strictly from the *Sharīʿah* are valid.

The same type of mitigation is evidenced also in testamentary bequests; the aim is to broaden the base so as to enable the testator to bequeath property to other than legitimate heirs.

Mortmain (*waqf*) was hitherto under strictly *Sharīʿah* procedures. The system was highly abused; land set aside for philanthropic purposes was often taken out of cultivation and in recent times converted to private use. What was to be a pious benefaction had become a private benefaction. Reform of the *waqf* system started with Muḥammad ʿAli in Egypt when in the opening decades of the nineteenth century he confiscated all of the land. The system survived as an independent operation until 1924 when the ministry overseeing it was placed under the control of parliament. There were further modifications in 1946 which permitted *Sharīʿah* courts to pass on all proposed *waqfs*; but with the 1952 revolution private *waqf* was abolished altogether. Syria in 1949 prohibited the creation of family *waqfs* and sought to liquidate those in existence. Lebanon in recent decades followed suit. Similar patterns were pursued in Tunisia and Algeria.

Such are samples of the type of change that has been stimulated by increasing contacts with the West. Self criticism among the educated is becoming rapidly more evident in Muslim lands. This new generation, educated for the most part in Western institutions and sciences, is convinced of the necessity of adaptation to modern needs. A good number of them are prepared to push through the barriers to social readjustment erected by traditional *Sharīʿah* decrees, not all of which can be shown to enjoy the full sanctity of Qurʾānic approval. And with the power of ulema on the increase in many Muslim lands, it is a matter of time before such decrees will come under heavy scrutiny.

The Society of Muslim Brethren (*al-Ikhwān al-Muslimūn*) came into being in 1928 for the express purpose of applying the tenets of Islam to the needs of a modern industrial society. For them and other Muslim purists, the *Sharīʿah* was to provide the wherewithal for erecting a modern society rooted in its Islamic past as best exemplified by the first Islamic state, which the Prophet Muḥammad started. The society survived until 1954 when President Nasser of Egypt suppressed it but did not extirpate it from Egyptian life. Today it is expressing a renewal and is operating more openly in Egypt and Jordan. Its members have been accused by the Baʿth-led Syrian government of fostering sedition against its rule on sectarian and ideological grounds.

The Society represents an attempt to revive through revolution if necessary early Islam's precepts of social governance and political stewardship. The movement generated by its activities is imbued with strong religious zeal and a determination matched only by militant nationalism. Their opponents reject the assertions that they can meet the challenges confronting the modern Muslim states with revived traditionalism. Moreover, the Society's opposition to purely secular governments on the grounds that Western-style democracy and its institutions are irreconcilable with Islam's precepts of government has gained support but is far from acceptable to the majority of Muslims. It remains for skeptics to be convinced that progress is realizable only through reviving the theocracy of early Islam.

Moderates believe that the route to progress lies in the application of those decrees of the *Sharīʿah* that would comport more with the spirit than with the letter of the Qurʾān. In the heyday of its accomplishments Islam demonstrated a remarkable capacity to absorb a variety of seemingly incompatible philosophies and contradictory religious conceptions. The same spirit of moderation can have today, as it had in yesteryears, a role to play. There are persistent trends in that direction, albeit lately the voice of the "fundamentalists" appears to be louder. Indeed, even those liberal forces which had once given direction to Islam as it attained glorious heights can still serve the same ends today in the view of progressive modernists. The two forces, one making for "puritanism" and the other for "innovation" can complement each other today as they had in the past development of Islam into a universal ideology. Some concerned Muslims have argued the need today for the reassertion of that catholic tendency in Islam that allowed it to make adjustments when called for. They see roles for both "fundamentalists" and modernists in the continuing spiritual uplifting of Muslims in comfortable surroundings. Through the interplay of views, compromises can be reached and methods can be agreed upon, as had happened in early Islamic history, when it resulted in such principles of legislation and instruments of progress as *Ijmāʿ* and *Qiyās*.

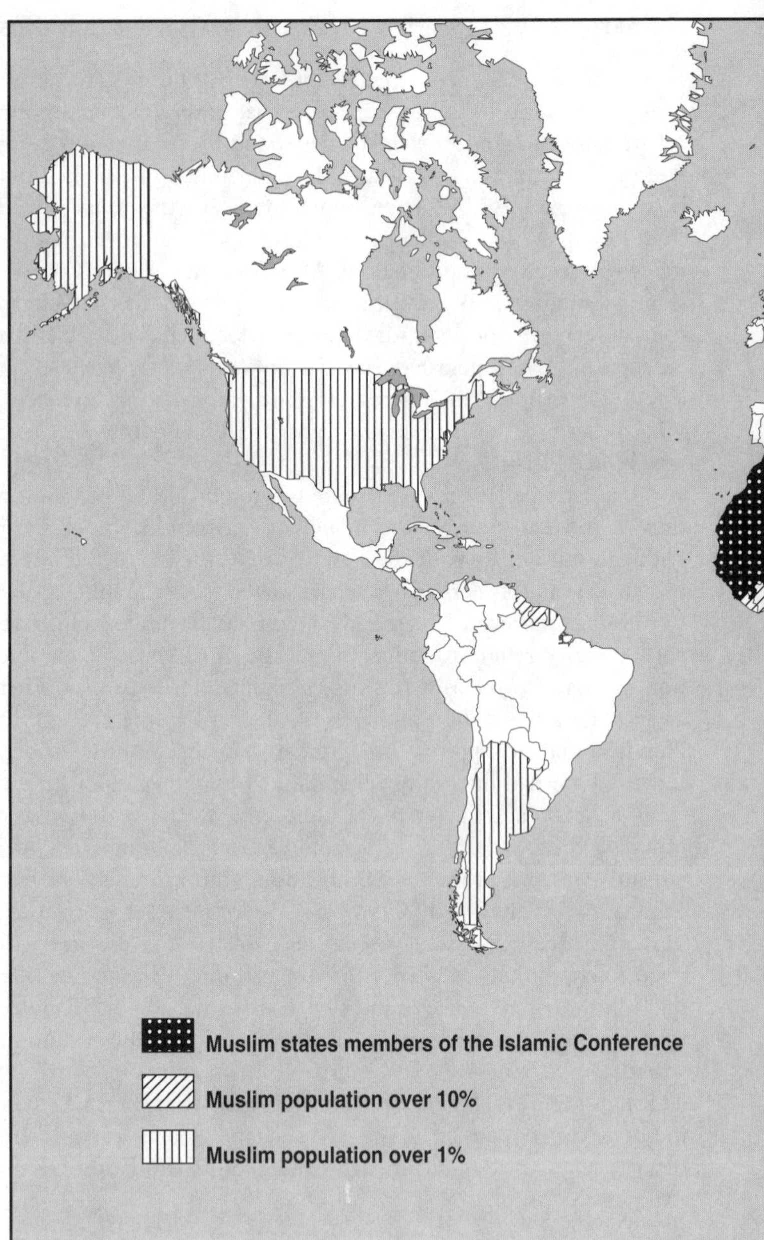
Muslim states members of the Islamic Conference
Muslim population over 10%
Muslim population over 1%

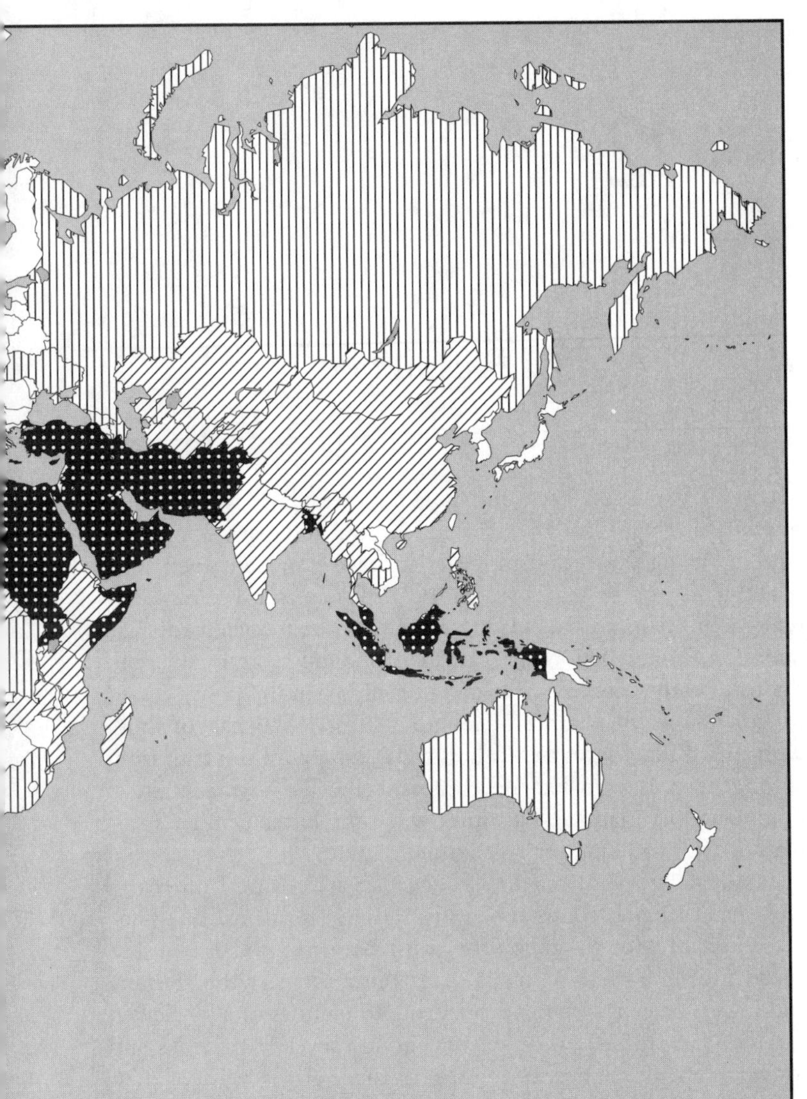

World Muslims Today

CHAPTER 12

Islamic Resilience

MEDIEVAL ARRESTATIONS and sporadic attempts at revitalization notwithstanding, Islam's capacity for survival and expansion in the face of strong detractions appears to have gone on unencumbered. This may be attributed to the resilience and dynamism latent in the religion and readily activated when warranted. The same forces of attraction that gained a large following for Islam in the first century continued to attract even when the polity ceased to function as an adjunct of religion. Nearly one half of those who regard themselves as Muslims today came into the faith from among peoples who had never been subjected to the political domination of Islam, and at times when the luster of Islam's imperial power had long ceased to shine.

Neither the sword nor the work of an ecclesiastical order can account for Islam's continuous gains in new following. The phenomenon of growth, therefore, must be attributed in the last analysis to its powers of appeal and ability to meet the spiritual and material needs of peoples adhering to cultures totally alien to the founders, the desert Arabians, but at a level of religious and sociopolitical development familiar to them at the time of their conversion. Continued growth can be explained also in terms of Islam's willingness to tolerate views and practices stemming from alien cultural norms brought into Islam by the converts which a more rigid system of religion would not countenance. Flexibility at this, the crucial stage, of conversion is an important factor contributing to Islam's success. What would ordinarily be deemed heretical at the instance of conversion inevitably drifts or is lured towards orthodoxy. The spread of Islam into Southeast Asia and sub-Saharan Africa presents a vivid example of its dynamism while its ability to survive in areas once dominated by communism is a testimony to its remarkable resilience.

The conversion of native inhabitants in Java, Sumatra, the Celebes, Burma, Malaya, Thailand, Indo-China, China, and the Philippines was the product largely of persuasion, the work of Arab mariners and merchants from the twelfth to the sixteenth centuries. Much of the success resulted usually from the initial conversion of a local reigning prince who was followed into the faith by his subjects. In most instances such conversions were the result of individual initiative and not of any large-scale deliberate missionary activities as pursued by various Christian missionary societies, often competing in the same areas. Success is also the result of lack of immediate insistence on the full Islamization of the convert.

Islam in Southeastern Asia

Malaysia

The Islamic peoples of the Malay archipelago are the largest in the world. In Malaysia itself they constitute over 50 percent of the population or 18,000,000, which consists also of substantial Chinese and Indian communities. Prior to the arrival of Islam, the Malays were followers of animism and Hinduism, some of which still underlies Malay culture and language. The influence of *ʿādāt* was visible in both traditional Malay society and politics, specifically in the *ʿādāt Perpateh* and the *ʿādāt Temengong* political systems. Neither is considered either non-Islamic or un-Islamic as evinced in the sociopolitical practices in these two systems as pertains to inheritance, succession, divorce, and family law.[1] In the feudal setting, Malays *ʿādāt* norms continued to be observed with Islam being complementary. Magic, superstitions, spirit-worship, taboos, resort to the power of shamans and medicine men (*pawang* and *bomoh*), *jin* and Iblis (equated with evil spirits) pervaded the daily life of most Malays, especially in the rural areas.

In the British colonial era prior to independence, the first formal education for children, especially in the rural areas, was religious, beginning in the mosque and carried through the primary level with stress on memorization of the Qurʾān. British-style education targeted the aristocracy and stressed secularism. Both contributed to the passivity of the Islamic factor in the life of Malays. Still, when compared to the attitude of the Dutch and Portuguese in their Asian colonies, British schools and educational policy in the colonial period might have downgraded the role of Islam but were more sympathetic to Malayan efforts.

The genesis of the Islamic reformist movement was the result of the teachings of al-Afghāni, Muḥammad ʿAbduh, and Rashīd Riḍa, whose message called for better equipping the Muslim for the modern world by seeking renewed strength from within. But the reformist message in four decades of activism did not succeed in broadening or even opening up new vistas to the ethnic-oriented culture of the Malays.[2]

Islam did not gain official recognition as the religion of the state until after independence in 1957 and the establishment of the Federation of Malaya with each state's hereditary sovereign or sultan being the head of Islam as well. Islam is so closely identified with the Malay culture that *masuk melayu* (lit. "to become Malay") is the designation for becoming a Muslim.[3]

Prior to acquiring independence, a number of factors combined to check the growth of Islamic influence, religiously and politically. Foremost was Malay ethnic nationalism coupled with opposition from the ruling establishment—sultans, conservative ulema, and colonialists. Factors militating against a pan-Malayan Islamic state was the pluralism of Malayan society. Another factor militating against establishing a clear Islamic identity, here as in Indonesia and elsewhere, is the ambivalence of the Malay, torn between their ethnicity and their religion. Both are rooted in the people's psyche with the two being closely intertwined and inseparable, hence the ambiguity towards both. Yet Islam is still a significant and integral factor in Malay culture as reflected in their world view, in their literature, and oral traditions. They adhere to the fundamental obligations of the faith, observe its ceremonial requirements and in their constitution recognize that a major prerequisite to be a Malay is being a Muslim; without the faith, one ceases to be a Malay.

Realizing the integral nature of Islam to Malay identity, and to secure legitimacy in the eyes of the Muslim masses, the United Malay National Organization (UMNO) decided to include Islam as one of its chief objectives after it became a nationalistic organization in 1946. It established a department of religious affairs and education and installed some of the prominent Muslim leaders in the party's executive council. But, when Malaya gained independence in 1957,* Islam was not granted a prominent role in the governance of the state. Nation-building took precedence over Islamization. As independence was being negotiated and a draft constitution prepared, the British saw to it that the drafting committee of five members headed by Lord Reis did not include a single Muslim.[4]

The National Council for Islamic Affairs, created in 1968, has served as a federal advisory council for religious affairs. The activist *dakwah* (*daʿwah*) missionary movements, targeting students and middle-class Muslims, has been put under strict control since 1979. Tunku Abdul Rahman, Malaya's long term leader, hailed as the father of Malaya's independence, served as Prime Minister for fifteen years before becoming first Secretary-General of the Islamic Conference. As secretary he revealed his secular views when he vehemently spoke out against Ayatollah Khomeini, questioning his qualifications to be a religious leader.[5] This was to please no doubt his Saudi hosts who had been viciously attacked by the Ayatollah and to make known at the same time that he did not have confidence in Islam to solve the problems of the state with its multiethnic and religious groupings. As he put it in 1962,

---

*Federation of Malaya (1948–1956), partially independent. Federation of Malaya (1957–1962) fully independent. Malaysia (1963–present), comprising Malaya, Singapore, Sarawak, and Sabah. In 1965 Singapore left the union. *Ed. Note.*

"I would like to make it clear that this country is not an Islamic State as it is generally understood; we merely provide that Islam shall be the official religion of the State."[6]

The picture becomes clearer in the 1970s and 1980s: in keeping with UMNO's original aims more deference was paid to Islamic principles but without being pressed by the Islamic Party of Malaya (PAS) to abandon its Malayan substratum. Islamic activism represented by *dakwah* activities is now rooted in the political and social life of the country. Islamic reassertion is another ongoing phenomenon. Islam seems to have at last submerged other identities in Malaysia. The UMNO-led government has also contributed to the same end. The government's Islamization policies have become catalysts to the assertion of the faith at the state level with sultans in charge of managing Islam.[7]

Economic turmoil in the late 1990s resulting from the severe depreciation of its currency led to significant popular demonstrations and lashing out by the Malay prime minister Mohamed Mahathir, against an international Jewish conspiracy and accusing George Soros, the financier responsible for the currency turmoil, of seeking to destabilize an Islamic state. The popular deputy prime minister, Dr. Anwar Ibrahim, a devout Muslim described as "a charismatic mix of modernity and Muslim activism, a contrast to the secular and cultural Islam of the United Malay National Organization and the fundamentalism of the Islamic Party of Malaysia," was accused of corruption. He was tried and jailed on unproven charges for having challenged the prime minister, which only intensified the activities of Islamists and the pressure against the unpopular prime minister.

SINGAPORE

In Singapore only 17 percent of its three million inhabitants are Muslim. It is an island republic of 5,444 square kilometers constituting at one time part of the Muslim State of Johore, whose sultan the British pressured into ceding them the island in 1819, effectively in 1824. At that time Singapore's small population was entirely Malay Muslim. The British opened the island to largely non-Muslim immigrants from India and China, which accounts for Muslims becoming a minority today. In 1963

Singapore joined the Federation of Malaya as the fourteenth state but opted for full independence as a separate republic in August, 1965.

Being a minority did not preclude Muslims from being active in the exercise of their faith. They have erected over one-hundred and fifty mosques since the first, that of Molaka built in 1820. The biggest and the real national monuments in Singapore today are the Sultan Mosque and the Chulia Mosque. The Majlis al-ʿUlama has built a series of modern new Islamic centers around the island. There is complete free movement of Islamic literature in English, Malay, and Tamil. Over 1,500 Singapore Muslims perform the pilgrimage to Mecca annually. Muslim personal laws are enforced by *Sharīʿah* courts since their establishment in 1958. Ten years later the Ulema Council was established to supervise mosques, *awqaf,* Islamic schools, and Muslim cemeteries. It supervises the *Sharīʿah* courts and collects *zakāh.* Islamic education is taught in ninety schools as well as an option in government-sponsored schools. Most *imāms* are trained abroad.

Muslims lag behind the rest of the population in university graduation, the professions, and higher services, where their numbers are well below the average. The government usually has one minister from their ranks in the cabinet. Economically, they are among the poorest and only a few of the youth succeed in gaining employment. There is no open persecution nor much effort to help them advance. In 1982 there were only ten Muslims in the parliament out of a total of sixty-nine members. King Faisal of Saudi Arabia provided assistance to the Muslim Missionary Society, established in 1932, to erect a large Islamic Center, which also runs a medical clinic and a legal center enabling at the same time some 6,000 students to learn Arabic in an expanded Islamic education effort. The Muslim Convert Society is the main *daʿwah* organization; it has managed to gain some 8,000 converts within a few years.[8]

Indonesia

In Indonesia Muslims number around 180,000,000 or 87 percent of the population of some one thousand inhabited islands. In spite of Islam being the overwhelmingly majority religion, the leaders of this largest Islamic entity in Asia have at no time since independence in 1954 opted to erect the land into an Islamic state. Sukarno, its first president, and his successor Suharto preferred the idea of a secular state guided by the Javanese-influenced philosophy that made paramount "the belief in one God" with tolerance of and equal treatment for all other religions. The Ministry for Religious Affairs has directorates with responsibility for Muslim, Protestant, Catholic, and Bali Hindus. The strategic location of the Indonesian islands, at the crossroads between the Indian Ocean and the China seas, accounts for the divergent ideologies affecting Islam here.

In the thirteenth century Marco Polo described a few small Muslim states in northern Sumatra, which evolved into a number of significant sultanates. European impact was felt from the sixteenth century on and the establishment of the colonial system under Dutch, British, and Spanish impeti in this region, not to mention the more embedded Indian influence spanning a thousand years. The relatively late start of Islamization accounts for the divergence of influences on Indonesian societies.

Arab Muslim traders with Chinese ports during the first centuries of Islam alighted in the archepelago but made no attempt to gain converts. When the attempt was made from the fifteenth century on, Islamic power was concentrated in Ottoman not Arab hands. A new generation of trading ports sprung up along the coasts; new cities evolved and prospered on maritime commerce; new egalitarian societies developed with the sultanate being the dominant political form: Malaka in the fifteenth century, Aceh and Banten in the sixteenth, Makasar in the seventeenth. They eventually linked up by incorporating the agrarian areas in between.

Islam failed to gain the Indo-Chinese peninsula after repeated attempts in Siam and Cambodia, but it succeeded in uniting the myriad islands of the Malay Archipelago and in becoming the new common religion, with Malay the language, though written in the Arabic script. Spreading east to the Moluccas and Sulu islands, it strengthened the notion of a shared destiny and contributed to the delimitation of the area known henceforth as "Indonesia."[9]

Indonesian Islam evolved from a blend of animistic and pantheistic concepts of very old vintage. Qurʾān, *fiqh*, and *Sunnah* do not permeate Islamic observances even though Islam has penetrated every facet of life and cultural norm. This is evident in Indonesian laws, rules of conduct, ethical conceptions, and esthetic ideals. Islam, nevertheless, has made these societies that constitute Indonesia today an important base for political and social action in the development of the country.[10]

It is more appropriate to speak not of one but of numerous Muslim communities in Indonesia. As one scholar put it, "Responses to Islam include adherence to a fundamentalist scripturalism, the elaboration of complex syncretic theosophies, the absorption of Islamic elements into primal religions, the eclecticism of intellectuals, and combinations of all of these."[11]

The interplay of Islam with indigenous customs and norms resulted in a curious dichotomy; and while their observation of cultic rites may not be entirely orthodox, the faithfulness of carrying out religious obligations attest the power of Islam's grip over the lives of Indonesians. In view of the heterogeneity of Indonesian cultural and social structures, Islam to the Indonesian becomes a unifying and durable cultural ideal, the realization of which gives him social status and prestige. It is the element of prestige associated with adherence to Islam, here as elsewhere in Africa and America, that accounts for its success in Indonesia.

Islam in the whole region is not simply a religion but rather a mark of cultural identity. However, having arrived late on the scene, Islam was not able to erase old memories of the past, particularly the Indo-Javanese, nor to win the struggle against them. But Islam historically succeeded, here as elsewhere, in integrating a large part of the preexisting elements. This accounts for the survival in Islam of the *ʿādāt* (customs) of the past, as evidenced particularly in Java with its 95 million people where the deep-rooted ambiguity of Islam has been classified by Clifford Geertz as a contrast between *santri* and *abangan*.[12] The former denotes the "orthodox" Muslim deriving from urban areas and largely of merchant families; the latter, village dwellers who have colored Islam with preexisting pagan rituals. They are less confirmed in their beliefs, retaining much from the old Indianized kingdoms that continued to serve as a base of their structured social pyramid topped by *priyayi* (lit. "younger brothers") aristocracy who are responsible for administrative tasks.

The ambiance of Indonesian society is reflected in the membership of its Parliament. The parties holding most seats since the 1980s do not project an Islamic image, being rather a coalition of functional groups. The moral basis of the state is spelled out in the Pancasila (Five Principles), which is incorporated in the preamble of its constitution: belief in one God; a just and civilized humanity; unity of Indonesia; democracy led by the wisdom of unanimity arising from deliberation among representatives of the people, and social justice for all Indonesians.[13]

Religious devotion is not uniformly observed, albeit it is high. *Ṣalāh* and the *Jumʿah* congregational prayer are strictly observed in all regions, as is the month of fast (Ramaḍān) and the pilgrimage to Mecca by those who can afford it. The Wahhābi-style reform movement launched in Central Sumatra in 1803 by ulema after performing the pilgrimage to Mecca provoked the Dutch and enabled them to suppress Indonesian uprisings in the wars of 1826–1830 and the Aceh War of 1873–1910. This would not have been possible had not those who insisted on a more strict application of the *Sharīʿah* divided the Muslim community.

In 1912 the literalists founded the Muḥammadīyah, directly inspired by the Salafiyah advocates in Egypt. It established its own network of schools, teachers' colleges, hospitals, and orphanages "by which it both met social needs and spread the reformist message," remaining since then the most prominent private educational and social welfare institution in the country."[14] Sarekat Islam (Islamic Federation) was founded the same year for the purpose of improving conditions for Muslim traders. Its goals were primarily political.

In 1926 the more significant Nahdat al-Ulema (Revival of the Ulema) was founded. It represented an attempt by Muslim traditionalists to counter the increasing influence of the reformist movement whose advocates had preached the rejection of the four *madhāhib* (rites) of the Sunnis and direct recourse by every *mujtahid* to the Qurʾān and *Sunnah*. The ulema saw in this an attempt to bypass their role. In countering the Dutch, the Japanese, who occupied the country during World War II, endorsed an Islamic policy that served to gain popular support and forward their own policies. They claimed to be the liberators of Islam. They relied on Islamic teachers and the network of Islamic schools as instruments of mass indoctrination. They cultivated also Muslim leaders and tacitly encouraged Muslim aspirations for an eventual Islamic state of Indonesia.[15] In 1943 they erected a single organization, the Consultative Council of Indonesian Muslims, out of the existing ones in order to give them the central authority required; it served also to give the Muslims a unity and national stature that they did not have previously.[16]

After the war, debate was launched over the role of Islam in an independent Indonesia. Those who opposed it argued that it would upset the balance between Muslims and other elements. Those who supported the idea argued in favor of endowing the state with a moral base, such as advocated by Islam.[17] The debate terminated with Sukarno in 1945 proclaiming the Five Principles, a compromise whereby Indonesia was to be neither an Islamic nor a secular state. Both Muslims and Christians were skeptical about the formula and Muslims eventually were disillusioned with the structure of the new state. In 1948 a civil war broke out with the Islamic leader proclaiming himself "Imām of the *Dār al-Islām*" to combat the secular authority in charge of the republic, which was dubbed an evil entity in league with the enemy, the Dutch. A similar uprising was launched in 1952, lasting until 1965 in South Sulawisi. In 1953 an Islamic entity was proclaimed in Aceh. Rebellions took place due to the state not being made into an Islamic entity where Muslims could better fulfill their duties to God within the context of the *Sharīʿah*.

In the Sukarno era the Masyumi Party, the voice of the reformist Muslims, became the vehicle for translating principles into laws. The Nahdat al-Ulema Party obstinately opposed it because of Sukarno's increasingly radical nationalism coupled with his pro-Western leanings. The Masyumi would have nothing to do with his government. Moderate as it might have been, the

Masyumi at the same time opposed the Dār al-Islām rebellions. It lost ground, however, in the first general elections of 1955, with the Nahdat al-Ulema increasing their seats from eight to forty-five compared to fifty-seven for Masyumi, which had proclaimed itself the Muslim Party of Indonesia. The Nahdat cooperated with Sukarno's increasing eccentricities, gaining more popularity while the Masyumi backslided because of its lack of flexibility.

With Suharto, the Five Principles were to become more firmly established and Islam to serve as the full expression of ideas—religious, cultural, and social—but not of a political ideology. The Masyumi saw in this policy the triumph of man-made laws over the divine revelations underlying Islam. Anger spilled over and affected the Christians since government policies were interpreted as serving to Christianize Indonesia, especially in view of the rapid growth of Christian numbers in Java where conversions were held responsible for an increase to 11.6 percent by 1971. For the first time in a generation there were serious violent outbreaks against them in South Sulawisi and West Java. In 1998 violence against Christians led to the burning of a number of their churches plus loss of life. Still, in the 1971 elections, all Muslim parties combined mustered only ninety-four out of three hundred and fifty seats.

The government felt strong enough in 1973 to pass some controversial laws, one being a new marriage law to transcend the complex and divergent legal systems dealing with family matters inherited from pre-colonial times. The aim was to introduce order and consistency in the system of laws relating to marriage to ensure that there would be no legal impediments to mixed marriages in Indonesia. They legalized civil marriage and improved the legal status of women by regulating laws governing divorce, polygamy, and forced marriages. Only anger ensued; Parliament was stormed by Muslim youth; the Ministry of Religion and Muslim leaders were incredulous over not having been consulted. The idea that applications to divorce or to contract a polygamous marriage should be made to a civil court was seen as an affront. It flouted Islamic law by granting a Muslim woman the right to opt out of a marriage in order to marry a non-Muslim. The government capitulated in the end. The final version of the bill as approved retained some of the elements of the original but in some respects enhanced and formalized the public position of Islamic law in Indonesia.[18]

The significant implication, other than accommodating the Muslims' position, is that, for the first time, a marriage law for Muslims has been codified by the state ensuring a measure of consistency in Islamic court decisions that recourse to teachings of the Prophet and decisions of the ulema could not. Muslim activists were not content with a government that appeared to them more pro-Christian and pro-West than pro-Islam and *Sharīʿah*, since a higher proportion of positions in the army command and senior government positions went to Christians than demography justified.

Indonesian Muslims remained divided on how to accommodate a government that refuses to erect the country into an Islamic state, with the moderates among them willing to accept the principle of deconfessionalization of Indonesian politics and democratization of Indonesian society. Extremists, on the other hand, opted for nothing less than erecting the country into an Islamic state. They are emboldened by the heightened awareness of Muslims outside Indonesia and the increasing activism among them. A more strict observance of Islamic injunctions, as pertaining to performing obligations and observing dietary laws, is in evidence. In the elections of 1992 religion was a critical factor. President Suharto and his wife decided to perform the pilgrimage that year. When Bacharuddin Jusuf Habibie, the current head of state, served as Minister of Science and Technology, he formed a new organization, the Indonesian Islamic Intellectuals Association, to promote Islam in Indonesian society. Abdurrahman Wahid, head of the large national Nahdat al-Ulema established a political organization called Forum for Democracy. The process of accommodation and confrontation has not yet run its course.

Following massive unrest, demonstrations and riots by students leading to numerous deaths, Habibie replaced Suharto in charge of government in 1997 in spite of his close ties to his unpopular predecessor.

Yet in spite of all the prevailing unrest the visibility of Islam has increased, as demonstrated by the building of new mosques everywhere and the increase of Muhammadan societies. Both help steer the countryside towards Islamic orthodoxy. In the meantime, toleration of non-Muslim communities has decreased.

As Islam takes firmer hold and the youth demand a greater share of the resources of the state, one can expect an intensification of efforts to strip the Suharto family of the huge wealth illicitly reaped through monopolization of basic economic institutions. Pressures have increased on Dr. Habibie, and he may confront the opposition led by a daughter of former leader Sukarno. This may or may not bode well for Islamists, given the secular trend the opposition represents. Nevertheless, such popular leaders as Amien Rais may yet prove themselves as principal players in the movement to bridge the Islamic and the secular trends, and perhaps win a more pronounced role for Islam in the affairs of state. Unfortunately, intolerance seems to have set in as the impoverishment of the Muslim population grows, which explains the activities of extremists against their more prosperous Christian and Chinese neighbors, in the form of looting, burning, and in some cases, killing, especially in the countryside. The behavior of Indonesian troops and the intervention of the Australian army in East Timor has further eroded Habibie's position. Of note is the fact that the underlying element concerning the struggle for Timorese independence is the discrepancy in religious adherence. East Timor has a significant Catholic population, which is an influential factor in the political struggle that degenerated into all-out violence in 1999.

THAILAND

It is difficult to assess the numerical strength of Muslims in Buddhist Thailand today in view of the government's policy to minimize the role of Muslims in Thai society. It is alleged that in 1982 there were about six million Muslims, four million of whom were Malay. If correct, their numbers would have constituted 12 percent of the inhabitants in lieu of the 4 percent figure released by the government. They are scattered over the whole of the land, with heavy concentrations in the south, bordering on Malaya, the capital area of Bangkok, and in the north around Chiang Rai where their mosques can be seen.

At one time there were small states south in the isthmus, where the largely Malay inhabitants had converted to Islam in the fifteenth century. With the conquest of the peninsula by the Thais beginning in the fourteenth century, which culminated with the incorporation of all these statelets in 1767, the power of the Muslims was circumscribed. At first they were allowed to administer their own affairs under their own sultans but in 1902 Muslim administrators were deposed and Muslim lands lost their autonomy, passing under the direct administration of Bangkok.

In 1832 the Thais conquered the Muslim state of Pattani on the Malay peninsula and the British recognized this conquest in 1909. In 1789 four thousand Pattani Muslims were uprooted and taken to Bangkok, accounting for the existence of over one million in the capital today. Other Muslims in central Thailand are also descendants of Muslim prisoners who mixed with local converts. Those in the northeast and north are descendants of Chams who were brought from Cambodia when it was conquered by Thailand. Also in the north, there are many Muslim descendants of immigrants from Yunnan in China.

According to available statistics, there were 5,250,000 Muslims in Thailand in 1976, constituting half the population of the south. Overall they worship in some 2,500 mosques, only 2,078 of which were registered under the Royal Act of 1947 relating to mosques.[19] There are very few qualified *imāms* to guide the Muslims but the Qurʾān is available in the Thai language, one version by Hajji Ibrahim Qureshi, another by Shaykh al-Islam Hajji Ismail. Copies of Malay translations are imported from Malaysia. There are copies of the Qurʾān in Arabic, but Islamic literature in Thai is meager.

Several thousand Thais perform the pilgrimage annually. Islamic laws pertaining to the family are enforced in the southern provinces that have two *qāḍis* appointed by the government for each of these provinces and a State Committee for Islamic Affairs for all of Thailand headed by the Shaykh al-Islam, who is appointed by the state.

There are about four hundred Islamic schools (*pondoks*), but Islam is not taught in them. The government established its own Islamic education institutions (*ponoh*) and an Islamic College in an attempt to control Islamic education. Not many Muslims reach the higher level, and no more than a few hundred graduate from college. There were no more than thirty engineers and forty physicians in the late 1980s. Most Muslim Thais are farmers, fishermen, and traders.

In 1976 there were fourteen Muslim deputies in parliament and two deputy ministers in the government. There are many local Muslim organizations but no overall one to unite them. The Thai Welfare Association, the Young Muslim Association of Thailand, and the Thai Muslim Student Association are the most important.

Muslim Thais are under pressure to assimilate, forced to take Thai names to dilute their identity. The government seeks to replace Muslim with Thai schools and to destroy the influence of the Malay language among them. Islamic feasts are ignored. Between 1973 and 1975 some five hundred Muslims were killed in the south.[20] To counter Thai pressures, Muslims in the southern region formed the Pattani Liberation Front in 1968 and the Pattani United Liberation Organization afterwards with the aim of achieving independence for the four southernmost provinces by armed guerrilla struggle.[21]

CAMBODIA

The country traces its origins to the Kingdom of Champa of the Middle Ages and its affinities culturally with the then Hindu states of Java and Malacca. When these regions adopted Islam, the Chams, who had been persecuted and subjugated by the invading Vietnamese, embraced Islam en masse.[22] Large numbers of them emigrated to Cambodia where they found protection and refuge. This accounts for the Cham origin of a great number of Muslim Cambodians today.

If numbers can be ascertained, the Muslims of Cambodia in 1974, before the onslaught of the Khmer Rouge, would have numbered over half a million, with only 20,000 being of Javanese origin, whose ancestors are said to have emigrated to Cambodia in the thirteenth century. All adhere to the Shāfiʿi rite. They lived in fourteen of its seventeen provinces with the highest concentration in Kampong Cham (ca. 300,000), where they constituted about 36 percent of the population. The Chams speak their own language and the Javanese, Cambodian. In 1974 they had about 185 mosques with 59 in Kampong Cham province and nine in the capital of Phnom Penh. Following the onslaught of the Khmer

Rouge, the Muslim population was reduced to about 335,000.

Muslims of Cambodia live in compact villages, with a few in the cities where they engage in trade and industry. The spiritual center is in Chruoy Changvar, near Phnom Penh, where many of the top Muslim officials, and the supreme chief also live.

Most Cambodian Muslims are farmers; others are fishermen, butchers, and boat-builders. The majority of the Muslims of Javanese origin live in Chruoy Changvar. All have been members of the Islamic Association with headquarters in Phnom Penh. Historically, they maintained good relations with the king; he favored them and appointed their supreme chief, who was considered a member of the royal court.

Before the Khmer Rouge disruption, the Muslim community of Cambodia was well organized. Each village was governed by a *hakam* and assisted by a *kalik* (*qāḍi*). The *imām* led the prayers, the *ketip* (*kātib*) taught Qurʾān, and the *bilāl*[23] called to prayer. The *hakam* was elected by the community. Each village had an Islamic school. Students advanced in learning were sent to Malaysia, Saudi Arabia, and Egypt for further training.

Severe disruption of Islamic communal life occurred for the Muslims when the Khmer Rouge took over the country in 1974. Thousands of citizens, Muslim and non-Muslim alike, were massacred, their women violated, and many forced to flee the country. Malaysia took in 25,000; others emigrated to Thailand, Saudi Arabia, France, and the United States. Many of their leaders, *imāms* like Tabib Ahmad and Tuan Syahed Ali, were killed, as was the chief *qādi*, Serong Yusof, in four years of brutal persecution. Since then, the Islamic Development Bank has provided much needed relief for the Muslims with no objection from the government.[24]

VIETNAM

Muslims in Vietnam derive from the same ethnic origin as those of Cambodia: the Cham. There were about 55,000 of them in 1982. The non-Cham Muslims, a third of the total, are converts in the land. Before the Communist takeover in 1975, they lived in little groups: 20,000 Chams in the provinces of Ninh-Thuan and Binh-Tuan, in a multitude of small villages with Cham Hindus (50,000 in Vietnam) as neighbors; about 25,000 Chams of Cochin-china in the Mekong Delta; and about 9,000

Muslims of Saigon (Ho Chi Minh City) of different origins. There is a small community with a mosque in Hanoi. After 1975, some 1750 Muslims emigrated to Yemen and settled in Taʿizz. Many more requested to leave for Malaya. The Cham Muslims were not subjected to persecution, but they could scarcely carry on an Islamic way of life with their schools and mosques closed.

Their cultic practices were in sharp contrast to those of their Hindu neighbors. Because of their protracted isolation from the mainstream of Islam, their conception of Islamic theology was tenuous; their religious spokesmen, for instance, ignore Arabic, language of the Qurʾān, and read the sacred book without comprehending the text. Their vision of Allah and Muḥammad in the scheme of their faith is blurred. They invoke ʿAli, whom they consider the "Son of God," in their prayers. Their very incomplete knowledge of Islam until recent times resulted from little official Islamic indoctrination and from the syncretistic and pantheistic influences of the religious climate in the Far East. This is evident, for example, in their mosques, which are less Islamic than Oriental in their decor. The *mihrab* bears such imprints as dragons, flowers, bamboo shoots, and other Chinese designs. Ramaḍān is observed for three days, and only by their religious spokesmen. The break of the fast is followed by a banquet served in the mosque itself, with the food being prepared and supplied usually by their Cham Hindu neighbors in nearby villages with whom they maintain good relations.

PHILIPPINES

In 1982 the Muslims of the Philippines approximated six and a quarter million out of a total population of 54 million, but the government chose to acknowledge only 2,200,000. They are a majority in thirteen provinces, which were to serve as the basis of a Bangsa Moro Autonomous State, according to an agreement of December, 1976. Muslims are concentrated mainly in Mindanao, the Sulu Islands, Basilan, Zamboanga del Sur, Zamboanga del Norte, North Catabato, Maguindanao, Sultan Kudarat, South Cotrabato, Lanao Sur, Lanao Norte, Davao Sur, and Palawan. Lands inhabited by Muslims are 45 percent of the total.

There are about three thousand mosques in the country, especially in the south. The Qurʾān has been translated into Maranao, the most common language among Filipino Muslims. There exists a Philippines Muslim University in Marawi City with an Institute of Islamic Studies. There is, however, no Muslim literature in the local languages, but Arabic is cultivated by the educated. The university, with some six thousand students, teaches Islam and trains ulema, as does the Muslim College in Jolo with some three thousand students.

The inhabitants of the Archipelago are divided by language and traditions, and sometimes by their observances of Islamic tenets and practices. They adhere to the Shāfiʿi rite. Most Muslims are farmers and fishermen. The rate of illiteracy among them is high, disease and infant mortality widespread, and unemployment much higher than the national average. University graduates did not exceed fifteen thousand in the early 1980s. Their most active organizations are the Muslim Association of the Philippines in Manila, Ansar al-Islam in Marawi City, the Converts to Islam Society in Manila, and the Sulu Islamic Foundation in Jolo. In 1983 an Islamic Dawah Council of the Philippines was organized for the purpose of bringing all Muslim organizations under one umbrella.[25]

Islam reached the islands in the fourteenth century and had already left its stamp on the socio-economic and political system in the south when the Spaniards made their appearance two centuries later. Muslim sultanates in the south were sufficiently organized to stave off Spanish conquest and Christianization. It took centuries of combat before they succumbed to the conquerors. Following independence in 1946 Muslims studied in northern schools and participated in the government, which also encouraged Christians to migrate to Muslim territories in the south.

In the sixteenth century the islands of the Philippines were in an advanced stage of Islamization when King Philip of Spain (after whom the islands were later named) gave orders to his admirals "to conquer the lands and convert the people (to Catholicism)." It is against such a background that the "Moros" or Muslims of the Philippines had to battle to preserve their existence. Spain, however, could never conquer the south, which became part of a united independent Muslim state of the Sulus, and was compelled to recognize its independence. In 1896 President McKinley acquired the islands from Spain with the intention of Christianizing and civilizing the inhabitants. Sulu resisted and did not succumb to the Americans until 1914, after a long and heroic struggle. On March 11, 1915 its sultan was forced to abdicate but was still recognized as head of the Muslim community.

The sultanate was recognized again in April of 1940, and Bangsa Moro was incorporated in the Philippines. After independence from the United States, the indigenous populations of the northern islands, which had been forcibly converted to Catholicism by Spain, now pursued the same policy vis-à-vis the Muslims, as did the United States after 1915 when it opened up Muslim lands for Christian immigration from the north. The flow reached alarming proportions after 1939, with the Catholic Church behind much of the brutal de-Islamization and Christianization policies pursued in the south, as it had been behind the Inquisition in Spain that had claimed many Muslim victims centuries earlier. This is what induced Muslims to take up arms to defend themselves and preserve their identity.

Muslims suffered great hardship in the 1970s, when the Philippine army worked to crush their resistance and destroy their villages, compelling many to seek refuge in Sabah (Malaysia). Their fate, and that of Islam generally, has been tied ever since to the internal struggles of the islands. Muslims here, as elsewhere, have had to fight to preserve their identity and assert themselves. They are represented officially by the Moro National Liberation Front, and so recognized by the Islamic Conference, headquartered in Saudi Arabia, and the central government of the Philippines. Not until the late 1970s were they able to "implement" the tentative agreement reached with the government in order to institutionalize Moro's position among the Muslims.

Obstacles to achieving and maintaining a solid front in this struggle are attributed to a number of factors: language barriers, "differences in territorial identifications, economic activities, social and political structures, art forms, and hierarchies of values."[26] Divisions among clans and status played a negative role until the Islamic resurgence began to focus on Muslim consciousness in ways that transcended traditional identification. Migration, however, reinforced exacerbated relations between Muslims and Christians, at a time when the central government had failed in their efforts to ameliorate the lot of Filipinos generally.

The government used harsh policies either to lure the Muslims into launching military undertakings against their own interests, as when they tried to undo the Malaysian rule in Sabah in 1968, or when they staged a massacre in 1971 of some seventy old men, women, and children in Manili, a barrier in North Cotabato. The massacre convinced Muslims that collusion existed between Christian politicians, settlers, and some commanding officers of the Philippine constabulary in Cotabato and Lanao.[27] This led Muslim leaders to close ranks and pledge themselves to uphold the rights of their community by whatever means possible, including force if necessary.

The massacre also had international ramifications. Colonel Muʿammar Qadhdhāfi of Libya began a program of aid for Muslim refugees and their religious activities, followed by military and diplomatic support. But Christian assaults continued. Deluged by natural and political misfortunes, President Marcos proclaimed martial law in 1972. It was abused in Muslim territories where discontent attributed to economic and political causes escalated into widespread violence. When the government undertook to collect arms, the Muslims made it clear they would not surrender theirs, having already been convinced of collusion between Christian adversaries and government forces.

In 1973 fighting spread through Cotabato, Zamboanga, Basilan, Sulu, and Tawi. It is at this stage that the Moro Liberation National Front was able to rally under the banner of Islam those hitherto divided by language and other barriers. Libya and Malaysia provided the funds for weapons and refuge. They sought recognition and support from the Conference of Muslim Foreign Ministers at their meeting in Kuala Lumpur in 1974 on grounds that the Moros of the Philippines were engaged in a war of national liberation. The Conference did not recognize the call for independence. They promised aid, called for reconciliation with the central authorities of the Philippines, and appealed to "peace-loving states and religions and international authorities" to use their good offices to ensure the safety and liberty of Philippine Muslims.[28]

In 1976 the government held talks with Qadhdhāfi and agreed to sign a preliminary agreement acknowledging most of the MNLF's demands: autonomy for the Muslims in the thirteen provinces, Muslim courts, a legislative assembly, executive council, and an administrative system. In addition, they were to have representation in the central government, security forces, control over education, finance, and their economic system with a right to a "reasonable percentage" from the revenue of mines and minerals. The central government retained control over foreign affairs and defense.

These concessions did not last long, for in 1980 the government declared the agreement (never truly implemented) void. The MNLF was stymied in its efforts to gain recognition within the government structure of the Philippines. Reflecting the sentiments of the Muslims generally, the MNLF now undertook to work for separatism. Ideologically it called for asserting a Muslim identity and advocated radicalism to achieve its ends. Foreign support, in the meantime, was dwindling since MNLF's aims did not comport with the pan-Islamic perceptions of its erstwhile supporters.

Even after Corazon Aquino replaced Marcos, Muslim demands and interests were not given the priority they sought. The fact that they were not in agreement among themselves as to avenues to pursue to such ends impacted negatively their cause. In the struggle for recognition, however, their Muslim identity was reinforced. They were more assertive of their rights, but the political framework for realizing them was not to be achieved just yet.

Other Asian Countries

There are strong Muslim communities in a number of countries on the fringe of the Indian subcontinent and East Asia, in Japan, Korea, Taiwan, Hong Kong, Myanmar (former Burma), and Sri Lanka.

In the case of **Korea** we have a good example of a nascent Islamic community that owes its origins to the 1950s and the Korean War in which Turkish Muslim troops participated. They brought an *imām* with them, set up a place of prayer and many Koreans, who had established contacts with the Turks, were impressed enough with their Islamic lifestyle that they converted to Islam.

When the Turkish contingent left, the first Korean converts launched their own efforts to propagate the faith and expand the Islamic community. They were encouraged by the support they received from the Muslim countries. In 1963 they numbered about a thousand; in 1971 three thousand. The Korea Muslim Federation was created under the leadership of Hajji Sabri Su Jung-Kil.

In 1966 the Federation was reorganized and the Korea Islamic Foundation (equivalent to *awqāf* in Muslim countries) was established. The following year the Korea Muslim Students Association was founded. The Foundation oversees regular religious and social functions and provides Islamic education to the youth. It also undertakes to establish Islamic institutions. Within ten years young Muslim Koreans were acquiring an Islamic education in a number of Islamic countries, ranging from Indonesia to Morocco.

The government of Korea under President Park Chung Hay donated five thousand square meters of land in the city of Seoul for the building of a mosque and an Islamic community center. Construction was completed in 1976, the cost being met partly by local Muslims and the rest by the donations of coreligionists from the Muslim heartland. The complex includes the mosque proper, conference rooms, office space, an Arabic language institute, the office of the Korea Islamic Foundation, and other offices. Another mosque was opened in Pusan in 1980. In that year the entire village of Sang Yong near Kwangju converted to Islam, which induced the new converts to build a third mosque in 1981. The Korea Islamic University was launched in 1980 and completed within ten years.

The building of mosques and institutions allowed the community to increase in size from 4,000 in May of 1976 to 22,000 six years later. Male conversion to Islam was averaging two and a half times that of females. Most Muslims are young, and through marriage are expected to increase the community. Its dynamism is reflected in the triennial master plans of growth. With the first plan (1974–1976) the Federation launched an Islamic propagation program through the mass media; started its own publications, intensified Muslim students' activities, increased the use of Arabic, established a scholarship foundation, arranged student exchanges with Muslim countries, founded a Muslim Institute, and completed a translation of the Qur'ān in Korean. The second plan (1977–1982) established Muslim communities around the three mosques, launched the Islamic university, built an Islamic library, a Muslim orphanage, and medical facilities. The third plan, launched after 1982, aimed at building mosques in all areas of Muslim concentration in Korea.

We have in Korea an excellent example of a dynamic community at work without encountering local resistance or encumbrances. It seems to be well accepted by the Korean population at large and well treated by the government, which does not differentiate between Muslims and other Koreans.[29]

Starting from nothing forty years earlier, the Muslims of Korea are well on their way to exhibiting the powers of Islam at work when not forcibly resisted. The Korean establishment no doubt sees the benefits it stands to reap with the rest of the Islamic world through its tolerance and support of Islamic efforts at home.

Islam in **Japan** owes its existence to the beginnings of the twentieth century. Muslim Tartars escaping Russian expansionism first introduced it. One Abdul-Rashid Ibrahim, who arrived in Japan in 1909, is credited with gaining the first converts. Their numbers increased as more Tartars arrived. The first mosque was established in 1935 in Kobe, followed in 1938 by another in Tokyo. Some ten associations have served to bind together the community scattered over Tokyo, Kyoto, Kobe, Naruta, Tokoshima, Sendai, Nagoya, and Kamizawa. In 1982 Muslims numbered some 30,000; half of whom were native Japanese, and the rest of different origins. With complete freedom of religion in Japan, the number of Muslims is expected to reach 100,000.

The Muslims of **Taiwan** number about 80,000. All belong to the Ḥanafi rite. They had five mosques in 1982. There are no Islamic studies in the public schools. They are treated equally with the rest of the Taiwanese and are represented in the National Assembly and the Yuan (legislative body). Most belong to independent professions and some serve in government and the armed forces. They are united in a Chinese Muslim Organization.

Islam reached Taiwan in 1661 during the Ming Dynasty, when a Chinese army landed on the island and freed it from Dutch rule. Among the soldiers were many Muslims from Fukien Province. They grew in numbers in the centuries to follow. Muslims were persecuted after the Japanese captured the island in 1895. This state of affairs lasted until the end of World War II. With the triumph of communism on the mainland, Chinese Nationalists emigrated to Taiwan and a new wave of Chinese Muslims arrived with them from all parts of China, including even Eastern Turkestan. Many occupied high posts in the Nationalist army and government, including General Ma Ching-Chiang.[30]

Survival in China

Available statistics do not reflect the numerical strength of Muslims in China. Authorities insist that a genuine tally will point to over sixty million. The survival of the Muslim community in China in the face of overwhelming odds is an index of the religion's capacity to face up to an ideology that favors the destruction of organized religion. With the relaxation of official attitudes following the death of Mao Zedong, opportunities of surviving have improved for most religions in China.

To speak of continuing dynamism here would be to belabor the issue; but to deduce through a brief perusal of Islam's development in China the qualities that enabled it to withstand the organized powers of this Communist state should help us gain some appreciation of Islam's capacity for survival, a tribute to its powers of resilience.

Recent Chinese scholarship points to official Chinese contacts with Muslims as early as the seventh century when an envoy of the Caliph ʿUthmān presented tributes to the imperial court as a prelude to the establishment of friendly relations with China. This occurred in 651, second year of Yonghui of the T'ang Dynasty, held subsequently as the date for Islam's arrival in China.[31] Shortly thereafter Arab and Persian Muslim merchants began to arrive by sea and by land to settle and trade in Ch'angan (Xian) and in coastal cities like Canton (Guangzhou), and Hangchow (Hangzhou). The extent of contacts can be judged by the fact that Chinese annals record thirty-seven formal missions from Muslim rulers to China by the launch of the ninth century. Indeed, in the middle of the eighth century the famous Chinese scholar Du Huan was taken captive by Muslims during an expedition westward (in 751) and lived among Arab Muslims for twelve years, returning in 762 to record the earliest Chinese account of Islam in his now lost *Recollections*.

While some Muslims settled early in Chinese port cities, others offered their services as mercenaries to the T'ang in quelling uprisings. They stayed on as formal residents. Chen Yuan states in his *Records of Chinese Islam* that during the Yuan Dynasty, the Huihui (Muslims) of Central Asia had become numerous and influential, with more than one hundred of them listed in the *Records of Clans*.[32] It appears that Yuan rulers, in an effort to create a counterforce to the scholar-gentry class, gave official posts to foreigners. There were many Muslims among them who served as governors of provinces or in central administration posts. They occupied leading positions in the intellectual life of China as well, excelling in literature, medicine, astronomy, and in military sciences. By the time of the early Ming Dynasty they had become deeply influenced by Han culture.

Yet accounts still show that the Huihui's perception of Islam was colored by Confucian and Buddhist beliefs. The call to prayer from the top of minarets was interpreted by their non-Muslim neighbors as an invocation of the name of Buddha. At the end of the Ming Dynasty, Wang Dai-yu wrote *The Islamic 'Great Learning'* on the model of Confucian books. And during the reign of Yongzheng, Liu Zhi wrote *The Islamic Philosophy of Human Nature and Reason* with a taint of Confucianism of the Sung Dynasty.[33]

By the thirteenth century Arab, Persian, and Central Asian Muslims had settled over the whole country. On account of their mingling with Hans, Uighurs, and Mongols, they came to be treated as a nationality of their own: the Hui. Judging by the incomplete knowledge Chinese scholars had about Islam and Muḥammad, some have concluded that Islam was strong primarily among foreign elements, principally traders. There was no discernible missionary activity carried out by Muslim elements. Eventually, Chinese Islam emerged as a blend of both Islamic and Chinese civilizations.

The Qurʾān played a significant role in the instruction of the Hui, chiefly in childhood, at the hand of *akhunds* in mosques. Stress was on memorization, in Arabic, with *akhunds* interpreting the meaning for the learners. The tradition continued until the 1920s.

The tradition of educating *akhunds* for mosque service began with Hu Pu-zhao (1522–1597). The system employed was to provide systematic teaching and lectures on the content of the Qurʾān. The text itself was not yet printed. Students simply copied what scholars recited, mostly from memory. Chinese Muslims attached great importance to the recitation of the Qurʾān and cherished the relics upon which the words were engraved, be they bones or parchment, particularly in the Sinkiang (Xinjiang) area.

The first engraving and printing of the Qurʾān was done under the auspices of the Ching Dynasty ca. 1862, sponsored by Du Wen-xiu of Yunan. Passages pertaining to prayer were compiled into selections to be used on different religious occasions. These selections made it possible for readers to learn the Qurʾān in Arabic.

For centuries no full fledged translation of the Qurʾān was attempted on grounds the true meaning might be lost and an improper rendering of it would be blasphemous. It was not until the latter half of the eighteenth century that a systematic translation was undertaken, and of select passages at that, mostly for practical purposes. Attempts at a complete translation began in the second decade of this century by Li Tieh-zheng, published in Peking (Beijing) (1927) as *Kelan* (The Qurʾān), done from a Japanese version abetted by Rodwell's English version. Several other full translations followed soon thereafter. The first full Chinese version done by a Muslim, to which also a commentary was attached, appeared in 1932, at Peking, the work of the *akhund* Wang Wen-qing. Other translations in this vein appeared in 1943 and 1946. But the *Koran in Standard Chinese Translation with Commentary* was published in 1958 based on an English version checked by a number of Chinese *imāms* with the Arabic text.[34]

Yet, while interest in formal Qur'ānic learning, and by inference in Islam, was mounting, the Nationalist government of China began to follow a policy of minority assimilation but without a concomitant anti-religious campaign. Clashes complicated by USSR involvements in Mongolia, Manchuria, and Sinkiang resulted from Nationalists' attempts to strengthen their control over these provinces. The war with Japan brought on a lenient policy towards minorities; and in February of 1939, upon the petition of the Chinese Islamic National Salvation Federation, the study of Islamic culture was formally inducted into the curriculum of Chinese universities.

The Chinese Muslims have clung to peculiarly Muslim customs: marriage, burial rites, the dietary laws, religious celebrations, circumcision, adoption of Qur'ānic names, and they have even maintained Muslim dress like turbans; they still use Arabic and Persian expressions, and they tend to prefer military to civil posts.

Communism finds in religion a repugnant competitor for loyalties. The Marxist-Leninists have argued that religion is a distorted and fallacious expression of natural sociological forces. Religious beliefs, attendant rites and organizations are not considered permanent institutions; they came into being in response to certain historical conditions and will vanish when they are removed. When people find themselves helpless in a class society where "exploitation" prevails, belief in miracles and the blissful life after death provides them with a consoling diversion. So if socialism can eliminate the material conditions favoring religion, religion itself will automatically disappear.

Yet how do we account for the constitutional guarantees in China for religious freedom? The Communist Party is convinced that with proper scientifically rationalized theories they can point out to the masses the fallacy of religious conceptions and allow religion thereby to die a slow natural death. The object is to avoid modern-style martyrdoms upon which organized religion had built in the past. With the elimination of class oppression and vestiges thereof, religion should disappear. So the Chinese Communist rulers have tacitly endorsed freedom of religious belief while actually seeking the negation of this freedom.[35]

The Communists have been discreet in their treatment of Islam because of political considerations; but their attitude towards this and other similar religions is unequivocal. Islam to the Communists is a device to consolidate the "feudalistic divine right state" established by the Arabs in the first century and a half of its existence. Islam demands blind obedience, they say, and incites in its followers enmity towards other religions. Islam, it is further argued, has allowed itself to become the tool of imperialist nations, like Turkey, England, and France in the nineteenth century. Pan-Islamism endorsed in the past by the "Imperialists" is a reactionary philosophy.

The policies of the official government in power, at first the non-Communist then the Communist, have not succeeded in daunting the spirit of the Chinese Muslims in recent times. These Muslims have had a solid territorial base in the northwest and have succeeded in the past in exercising considerable autonomous political influence. The Muslim uprisings here and in Yunnan Province during the nineteenth century reflect a strong spirit of independence which the Communists respect. The consensus is that the Muslims in China, under the guise of a nationality rather than a religious minority, have received better treatment than some other religious groups.

Tolerance of Islam has its international significance for the Chinese Communists who, until the dissolution of the Soviet Union, were in competition with the Russians to win over powerful Islamic states like Indonesia and the Arab countries. If they are not lenient at home, they could hardly expect support from their national's coreligionists where China entertains political ambitions in Southeast Asia, the Middle East, and Africa.

When the land was being communized, the Muslims were singled out for special treatment in the Agrarian Reform Law of 1953. Land owned by mosques and *imāms* was to be retained with the consent of the Muslim community residing there. *Imāms* were to have the right to engage in production of the land as a form of livelihood "if they have no other means of making a living and are able and willing to engage in agricultural work."[36]

While allowing Muslims certain freedoms, Communist authorities launched campaigns with the aid of Muslim cadres to de-Islamize them. Respected well-trained Muslim cadres were used in order to give the appearance that the initiative for the "unification," then the "transformation" was a spontaneous movement. Such organizations as the China Islamic Association and the China Hui (Chinese Muslims) Cultural Association were formed to carry out the Communist plan for control of the religious, social, economic, and political activities of the Muslims, and of all other minority group activities. Not only are these organizations instruments of the Communists in "re-educating" the Muslims, but they also serve to further their foreign policy objectives. The China Islamic Association, for instance, played a determining role in securing diplomatic recognition for the Chinese Communist government from the United Arab Republic, Syria, and Yemen.

The Association has served its benefactor well by acting as an agency for contact with Muslims abroad, sponsoring cultural missions, and translating Communist writings into Arabic, particularly Mao Zedong's (Tse-Tung's) works.[37]

The China Islamic Association, the Communist front organization, was to promote love of the fatherland, assist the People's Government to implement its religious policy, and take part in the campaign to safeguard world peace. Muḥammad and the Qur'ān are called in to further the cause; as the chairman of the Association proclaimed:

> Sage Mohammed once said to a Moslem: 'If you love your Fatherland fervently, it is just like being faithful to your religion. . . . For the sake of our Fatherland and for the sake of our religion we certainly will stand on the same battle front

with peoples of all other races in the country fighting to protect the People's Fatherland.'[38]

The Qur'ān was to be treated in the same light as other literature enlisted in the service of Marxism: the parts that could be used would be taught, the rest would be ignored. If need be, the Communist Party and government were ready to extend a benevolent hand and provide leadership to "patriotic" and "law-abiding" Muslims.[39]

The Chinese Communists have their own subtle ways "to nibble away" at the institutions of Islam. In 1952 they published a translation of the Qur'ān in Chinese in order to make it possible for the "ordinary Hui People...to deeply understand the Koran..." and "basing themselves on the religious teaching of the Koran, to unite, mutually help each other, promote culture, develop production and render service to the people."[40]

The Communists have adapted the substance of the Qur'ān to their own schemes, and particularly to verify the "truth" of Marxism. For example dialectical materialism asserts that the "state of being determines ideas" or that truth is discovered and verified only through practice. They claim to find justification for this point in the Qur'ānic text: "...Allah brought you forth from the wombs of your mothers knowing nothing."[41] The underlying assumption here is that knowledge comes from the outside world, and that "correct knowledge and knowledge that agrees with subjective facts come from actual practice."[42] The point of justification is the Qur'ānic verse: "Most of them follow naught but conjecture. Assuredly conjecture can by no means take the place of truth."[43]

To promote labor, the Qur'ān is cited as not providing for rest periods before or after the hour of congregation on Friday. The Qur'ān, it is further argued, speaks negatively of individualism and egoism and enjoins unity and cooperation. It frowns on prejudicial views and identifies those who dissent with the idol-worshipers. The love preached by Islam is for all good people. "As to those who are hostile to the people, although they may be intimate friends and close relatives, we must sever all connections with them and bring them to censure and justice."[44] If communism can be identified with Allah's will and the work of the authorities with the mission of Muḥammad, then the verse of the Qur'ān they cite can apply to their schemes:

> Thou wilt not find folk who believe in Allah and the Last Day loving those who oppose Allah and His messenger, even though they be their fathers or their sons or their brethren or their clan.[45]

Their aim is the peaceful reform of the Muslims by convincing them that what they believed in is wrong, the result of their misinterpretation of the Qur'ān.

The Muslim Classics Institute was established in 1955 by the Communist regime to train *imāms* who have the "exalted qualities of fervent love for their Fatherland and fervent love for Socialism and can handle well the Arabic language, understand the principles of the Moslem faith . . ."[46] It is not an ordinary cadre they seek but a well-indoctrinated religious leader whose position would make his new interpretations of Islam authoritative and acceptable to the Muslim masses.

There is a deliberate curtailing of religious instruction in Islamic middle and primary schools, and in certain of the larger cities there is no instruction at all. It is permitted only in mosques. There is a lot of indoctrination, on the other hand, in the area of materialism. In the mosques it is not unusual to see devout Muslims absorbed in the study of social structure theories, Communist principles of economics, and the doctrines of Mao Zedong.[47] There are subtle attempts to break down the fasting rites, dietary laws, and other institutional observances of Islam.

But the Muslims have been resisting, sometimes by passive methods—where they are few in numbers—and often by violent methods—where they are numerically strong. Independent-minded Muslims like the Pingliang in Kansu and the Kazakhs in Sinkiang resent the state's efforts to "reform" them. In 1952 an agrarian reform was carried out in Pingliang, and land belonging to a mosque was confiscated. The Muslims revolted and the rebellion became widespread with the Communists being compelled to move troops in to quell it. There was destruction of communication lines; public granaries were ransacked, and a number of areas in Kansu came under the control of the rebels. The Communists decided to pacify them through a "comforting delegation" sent for that purpose. Frequent rebellions followed by Communist pacification and appeasement have characterized this region for a long time.

Muhammad Rizq Bekin is an exiled Muslim activist from Eastern Turkistan (Sinkiang) who presides over the Eastern Turkistan Foundation, a non-profit organization promoting the cause of the twenty-six million Muslims in the province. He accused Beijing of embarking on a campaign to exploit the natural resources by assimilating the inhabitants with the much larger Chinese population. This is done by massive colonization of what is known as the Sinkiang Uigur Autonomous Region of the People's Republic of China. Although Islam made its appearance here in 86 AH, Muslims are not allowed to build mosques or schools, to travel to Mecca, or maintain their own religion and culture. Scholarships for university study go to Chinese students since their language is the qualifying one.

The region is rich in natural resources including oil, minerals, and agricultural land, but the inhabitants are among the poorest. Bekin called this the "human rights century" and pleaded with Muslims of Arabia to pressure China economically into guaranteeing their rights. The World Muslim League started to provide assistance in the form of literature and books since the Chinese authorities do not allow teachers and preachers to be sent there.

Over two hundred uprisings are said to have taken place, with more Chinese Hans brought in each time. In 1993 their numbers exceeded five and a half million, twenty six times the number in 1949. In one bloody incident in a town near Kashgar in 1990 over one thousand were killed when the authorities used tanks and aircraft to prevent the building of a mosque in the area. Large numbers have fled to Turkey, including Bekin. The government provided them with homes, land, and money, and they are treated as brothers, not refugees. Bekin himself came as a boy, joined the army, and attained the rank of general before retiring.[48]

Islam in the Former Soviet Union

Muslims first reached Central Asia in the seventh century through conquest. In the eighth century they acquired a foothold with the Umayyad expansions. Islam became so well rooted that in the subsequent centuries Bukhara and Samarkand and other cities of this region evolved into important centers of intellectual activity.

One of the earliest examples of mass conversion was that of the Bulgars residing along the Volga, where their Khanate developed the first Islamic state and eventually led to the Islamization of what later became Kazan. The influx of Turkic peoples expanded the Islamic community. Within half a century Arabic was displacing Runic as the script of these Turkic peoples. In 922 their king, Almush, embraced Islam and in 986 they even attempted to convert Prince Vladimir of Kiev to Islam. In 1236 they were overrun by the Tartar armies of Batu Khan and his Golden Horde. Batu established his capital at al-Sara (Sarai) on the Volga. Eventually, Islam became the religion of these Tartars. Uzbek, Batu's great grandson, completed the conversion of his people to Islam. In the fourteenth century Ibn Battūtah, the great Muslim traveller from Morocco, noted that the new converts lived in Muslim communities, spoke Turkish, and adhered to the Ḥanafite rite of Islam. Sultan Uzbek ruled the largest Muslim state along the Volga.[49]

Timur Lang overran the Golden Horde's state and devastated their region in 1395, thus enabling Muscovy to emerge and eventually take over the rest of the area. The remnants of the Golden Horde were reconstituted into four Khanates: Kazan, Astrakhan, Siberia, and Crimea. Kazan was the most advanced in arts and crafts, from whose experiences Europe benefited. Ivan IV earned his title "the Terrible" following his successful rebellion against the Golden Horde khanate in 1552, completing its conquest in 1557. He massacred its peoples, devastated the land, destroyed the khanate's great centers, and forcibly converted survivors to Orthodox Christianity; those who did not convert were expelled.

In 1783 Catherine II invaded the Crimea, seat of the Ottoman-backed Giray Khanate with its capital at Bağçe Saray. In a single battle at Karasu Bazaar, nearly thirty thousand Muslims were killed. About three hundred thousand Crimean Muslims were compelled to flee. The remaining khanates were subjected in due course: Kazakhstan and Daghestan shortly after the fall of the Crimea, Ferghana in 1783, Khiva in 1786, and Bokhara in 1850. In 1920 Ferghana and Khiva were incorporated into the newly established Bolshevik state. The czarist conquest completed the subjugation of the Turkic Muslim tribes of Suvar, or Sabir, east of the Urals and the Azeris, Daghestanis, and other elements in Transcaucasia.

It took czarist Russia three centuries to complete the conquest of western Turkestan, home of the great Muslim Turkic khanates. There were fifteen major rebellions against the ruling czars, all ending in suppression. Yet, Islam still made progress right up to 1917. Even when Muslim modernists sought to make the necessary adjustments, local authorities proved to be a stumbling block. When the Bolshevik Revolution took place in 1917 a number of localities declared their independence, and Lenin at first recognized them. He withdrew recognition when the Revolution's triumph was assured.

During the rule of Catherine the Great, survivors of the former khanates were allowed at last to openly practice their Islam. They gradually recovered and were able to restore their sense of community, and build mosques and schools. By 1897 there were some 1,555 mosques and 6,220 Muslim schools.[50]

Afghanistan and Persia were also stripped of states under their dominion. Thus did the centers of Islamic civilization in central Asia pass under the control of imperial powers. Kazan was once the center of a university attended by over seven thousand students. It enjoyed a Muslim press printing over 2.5 million copies of two hundred and fifty Islamic works by 1902, a library frequented by 20,000 readers. Mosques were built at the ratio of one for every one hundred and fifty worshippers.

The 1917 October Revolution induced Muslims to rebel and seek independence in such areas as Bashkiri, Khiva, and Ferghana under the leadership of strong local Muslim leaders. Most of them lost their lives under Stalin, who rejected the idea of a binational Muslim-Russian Federation within the USSR. To weaken the Muslim states, the Soviets divided the Muslim community into some forty-two entities along dialectical Turkic lines and terminated the teaching of Arabic language and Arabic script. War was declared on Islam, its beliefs, culture, and legacies.

Between 1897 and 1939 the Muslim population suffered drastic reductions through the killings that followed the suppression of their rebellions. Artificial famines in 1921 reduced the number of Kazakh and Kirghiz Muslims by a million or more, with another million dying in 1929 from hunger due to Communist confiscation of their herds. This was followed by Russian colonizers who took over the land of those who had died.

The Soviet government created fifteen republics of which six were Turkic. There were ten Muslim entities within the Russian republic.[51] Four more Muslim nationalities were scattered over three autonomous regions, two in Russia[52] and one in Georgia.[53] Five of the six republics are in Central Asia[54] and one in the Caucasus.[55] These divisions were created for administrative purposes. Russian was the official language in all the republics and national languages were kept alive to maintain the folkloric character of the Muslim entities or, as Moscow put it, to preserve the cultural heritage of the nationalities.[56]

The Muslim population of the former Soviet Union is put at some sixty-five million. Administratively, Islam was subject to an official statute drawn up in accordance with Article 124 of the USSR's constitution. Religiously, they were governed under four directorates, each presided over by a *mufti* elected by an assembly of the believers: (1) the Sunnis of European Russia and Siberia (Oufa in Bashkiria, its seat); (2) Northern Caucasus and Daghestan (Bujnaksh in Daghestan, its seat); (3) Sunnis and Shīʿites of Transcaucasia (Baku in Azerbaidjan, its seat), and (4) Central Asia and Kazakhstan (Tashkent in Uzbekistan, its seat). The overall head is the grand mufti of Russia.

Tolerance was the purported aim, but in reality it was to control and frustrate any attempt at organized living among Muslims. It was also designed to circumscribe and reduce religious identity in countering state policies unpleasant to Muslims. The pilgrimage was not encouraged because Moscow preferred to be the *qibla* of Islam. All other prerequisites of the faith were allowed to be observed.

Nevertheless the Muslim identity of these states survived under the Communist governments following the revolution. But the process of subversion aimed at organized religion generally has not escaped them. The Soviets launched a deliberate policy of Russification, and in places like Kazakhstan the process of denomadization and collectivization radically transformed the economic traditions of the Kazakhs and with them, their whole manner of existence. Russians settling in Muslim territories were a major factor in the ethnical disintegration of Muslim tribes. The more Slavs settled here, the more Russian cadres could be depended on to perform the task of breaking down nationality and institutionalized religion in schools, administrative posts, centers of cultural activities, and the like.

Only in areas where Muslims are densely settled and heavily outnumber non-Muslims do Islamic religious practices and institutions survive.[57] This is particularly evident in Uzbekistan where Islam is a strong religious and cultural force, ardent and rich in a long past to which the Uzbeks cling fanatically. To be sure, the indirect technique of persuasion was at work here as elsewhere in the Communist world, but secular atheistic groups sponsored by the Communists could not achieve their goals. When called for early in the 1920s, Stalin and Lenin affirmed to the Muslims of Turkestan that "your beliefs and customs, your national and cultural institutions are henceforth free and inviolable." The Bolsheviks were then fighting for survival.

Resistance reduced tolerance in the later twenties on account of the war on feudalism and the radical social transformation preached by the Communists. Pan-Turanism, espoused by the mullas, brought on persecution. Communist authorities nevertheless labored to stress the common points of Islam and Marxism: "The Qur'ān is plainly in accord with the program of the Communist Party which can and should be construed as conforming with Islam."

World War II and the desperate struggle for survival against the invaders brought the state and religious institutions into closer rapport; a *modus vivendi* was worked out between state and church that has remained in force.

The secularization and modernization of the USSR did not portend the destruction of Islam here anymore than was the case of Kemalist Turkey in the twenties.

The important institution of *waqf* was entrusted to the supervision of the state, but with the religious associations having a voice in the selection of the civil personnel directing it. In many cases these Muslim associations received priority for construction material and other scarce items.[58]

Notwithstanding the vicissitudes of its existence in the Soviet Union, Islam managed to conserve all that which had been rigorously indispensable to its existence. To be sure, its political, economic, and social life was arrested; but as an expression of individual faith, Islam was allowed to persist.

Islam did lose some of its followers to communism in the face of strong social and moral pressure but it continued to survive in spite of all subtle and open Communist manipulations to rationalize it out of existence. Again Islam was able to hold its own and manifest strong powers of resilience through which it staved off complete subversion, here as in China.

After 1964 anti-Muslim propaganda aimed at being "scientific" and the struggle against Islam was to be carried out on an ideological level. Those deemed "honest" were spared the brunt of Communist assaults, but not those adjudged fanatics by Soviet leaders.[59] In the 1970s fifty-four theoretical seminars were held for more than two thousand educators specializing in anti-Islamic activity. Close to a thousand students were then enlisted to spread atheistic beliefs in clubs organized to that effect. The media were enlisted to decry Islam as harmful for industrial discipline and as an enemy of growth and progress. In the Khrushchev era, measures to circumscribe Islam and its observances proved much harsher, with Islamic institutions becoming the special targets.

Kettani mentioned that before 1917 there were 26,000 mosques, religious functionaries numbered 45,000, Islamic schools in the thousands with enough *awqaf* (pious endowments) to finance them, all of which were confiscated by the government. By the mid 1980s there were no more than 450 mosques in the whole Soviet Union. Tashkent, with some 1.5 million Muslims, had only twelve mosques. Functionaries numbered less than 8,000 in 1982; only two *madrasahs* (religious schools) survived, unable to handle more than twenty-five of the four hundred candidates applying to study. Only thirty Muslims were allowed to perform the pilgrimage to Mecca each year. The Qur᾽ān was printed six times since 1917 but with no commentary in any of the languages spoken.[60]

That the Soviets respected Islam's potential as a revolutionary force outside its borders with implications for Muslim elements within them is attested by their military involvement in neighboring Afghanistan, coming on the heel of the successful militant Islamic revolution in next door Iran. Perhaps this involvement was to serve as a visible warning to potential anti-Marxists among the Muslims of the Soviet Union. It might have also reflected fear of a possible Islamic fundamentalist style rebellion in the Central Asian provinces where Turkic Muslims are heavily concentrated.

The situation improved somewhat after Khrushchev. Islam could be practiced more openly, but with restraint. Prayers were not forbidden and Islamic festivals could be celebrated. The state undertook to pay the Islamic organization for the *waqfs* they had confiscated. Muslim leadership conducted itself wisely and Soviet authorities recognized it as a civil entity. The growing recognition of Islam around the world as a dynamic force coupled with the heroic resistance of Muslim groups, as in Afghanistan, to pro-Communist rule sharpened awareness of Muslim youth and inflated their pride of belonging to the Islamic community. Moreover, economically the Muslim areas have the greatest impact today on the Russian economy as they did before the dissolution of the USSR. They are sufficient in foodstuffs, suffer little shortages, and provide most of the cotton, 75 percent of the electricity, over 50 percent of the oil, and much of the basic minerals—zinc, lead, etc.

Strange as it may seem, Soviet emphasis on implementation of the socialist system had a positive effect in eliminating ethnic rivalries from formerly feuding Turkic Muslim tribes. It led to standardization of their ways of life and deemphasis of differences characteristic of a nomadic existence. The Communist regime "put an end to rivalries and national antagonisms." It has also "suppressed the cultural particularism of religious and ethnic minorities and has brought into being a national consciousness in ecopolitical and social fields."[61]

It is an irony of fate that with the hardships and suffering endured by the other liberated republics, the Muslim ones are in a position to be a positive factor following their independence in the recovery of the others. They can now interact from a position of freedom and potential strength. But first, they must make necessary internal adjustments to cement government and society, a necessity that has proven difficult to achieve in predominantly Shīʿite Tajikistan where the old guard refuses to give in to mounting Islamic resistance aiming at establishing an Islamic state with encouragement from Iran and Afghanistan. In the current struggle inter-tribal harmony is breaking down and civil strife is hindering the development of this potentially prosperous state, given its rich oil deposits.

Nevertheless, Muslim leaders led by the ulema of the liberated republics are seriously contemplating instituting one Islamic republic to embrace them all. Rich Muslim states such as Saudi Arabia have undertaken a policy of strengthening their Islam and millions of Qurʾāns have been distributed. Other aid in joint commercial ventures have been launched by Turkey. Planes fly directly now from Turkey to the capitals of the Turkic republics in efforts to draw them into closer working relations with the Islamic heartland. The Chechens, who had remained unwittingly in the Russian Federation since the breakup of the Soviet Union, have battled fiercely for independence under a leadership brandishing Islam as a rallying force.

CHAPTER 13

Islamic Dynamism

Islam in Africa

The remarkable spread of Islam in sub-Saharan Africa is a testimony to the faith's dynamism. Of the forty-five countries that belong to the Organization of Islamic Conference, twenty-three are located in Africa. In America, Islam is spreading at a rapid rate among African-Americans. In 1982 African Islam had a population of 192,400,000. Only in Uganda, Benin, and Gabon do Muslims number less than 50 percent.

The diffusion of Islam in Africa can be attributed to three different factors: conquest by colonial powers and incorporation into larger units wherein they found themselves a minority; movement through conversion of non-Muslim populations to Islam; and Muslim emigration to low Muslim-density areas.[1]

The growth of Islam in this region is remarkable. After having served for thirteen centuries as the overwhelming religion of Arab North Africa, the spread of Islam into the south, and in areas where Christian missionary activity has been strong, is evidence of its dynamism. From Somalia in the east to Mauritania in the west, Muslims range from nearly 50 percent (Nigeria) to 99 percent (Mauritania). In the rest of the continent south of the sub-continent they exceed 40 percent of total, with most of this gain occurring in this century.

Muslims adhere either to the Māliki (in West, North, and Equatorial Africa) or Shāfiʿi (East and South Africa) rite. Large numbers in Algeria, Tunisia, Libya, and Egypt, as well as South Africans of Indian origin follow the Hanafi rite.

Here, as in Asia under colonial rule, the lot of Muslims was not always favorable. Most wars of resistance to colonial encroachment in Africa were inspired by Islam and led by Muslims. The army and the church were employed to pacify and control them. Their children could not compete with those who graduated from mission schools. Thus, where they constituted a minority or not an overwhelming majority, they were handicapped, marginalized, and impoverished. This is particularly evident in East Africa where Muslims were targeted by Christianizing missionaries.

In 1982 Muslim minorities totalled 114,200,000; 93 percent lived in eight countries: Nigeria, Ethiopia, Tanzania, Kenya, Mozambique, Ghana, Ivory Coast, and the Congo Republic (Zaire). Their numbers exceeded ten million in three: Nigeria, Ethiopia, and Tanzania.

The propensity for survival and growth attests the dynamism of the faith in Africa south of the Sahara. Why has Islam been able to manifest such propensity for growth? One might view this in the context of how Islam confronted traditional religion. In Africa religion is based primarily on kinship, with the ritual commencing at family level then rising through the clan and tribe, not unlike pre-Islamic Arabian tribal tradition. Islam in Africa cut across family, clan and tribe and made religious adherence the unit for intertribal relations. In the second instance, traditional Islam, like Arabian religion before Islamization, had an oral base with mediation by indigenous practitioners, who make use of sacred places and objects and depend on magic. Islam, on the other hand, has a written scripture, a prescribed ritual, a historical tradition, and an intertribal clerical class. Thirdly, traditional religion appeals to nature and varies in degree of god-consciousness from monolatry to polytheism. Islam, however, is monotheistic, and, while not rejecting a spirit world, it has a philosophical and theological tradition that gives it considerable systemization.[2]

Since Islam's appeal varies from one tribal tradition to another, one cannot speak of uniformity in its spread and acceptance. It is the strength or weakness of the tradition of the tribe that conditions its response to Islam.

When the Arab Muslim penetrated Africa in the earlier centuries, he was seeking to traffic with precious minerals and ivory, not to proselytize. The caravan trade from Cairo and the nomads of Upper Egypt extended their reaches to Chad and Kufra in the eleventh century. By the end of the twelfth, a Muslim kingdom had been established at Kanem. Other traders reached the Great Lakes and the Congo in east and east central Africa. But in the western extremity the Berbers and Zanātis rallied to the Arab conquerors, and soon the Sanhājas became the most vigorous agents of the new faith in its spread southward. Until the eleventh century the traffic north and south centered on the caravan trade. After penetrating Mauritania, these Muslim traders established themselves in the adjacent regions as far south as Ghana.

The credit for Islam's penetration south of the Sahara may be attributed to the Almoravids *(al-Murābiṭūn)* who in the eleventh century were its principal promulgators. Islam in this region thrived on the fluctuating fortunes of warring local societies. The steadfastness of the Muslim in conflicting situations proved a major source of appeal to the natives.

A new cycle of conversion was generated at the start of the thirteenth century through the aegis of the Mandingas, founders of the Mali Empire. It began with the conversion of a sovereign and his entourage. When a century and a half later the Songhay replaced them, Islam remained the religion of the bourgeois and lettered class who had formed a coherent element in the principal cities like Djenne and Timbuktu. The Songhay relit the torch of Islam on the Niger.

At the end of the fifteenth century the brilliant Askia dynasty was established by Sarakole chiefs. When Mamadou (Muḥammad) Touré went on a pilgrimage to Mecca the security of the important commercial route running through Muslim lands was assured, and with it the eastern and western currents of Islam running south into Africa converged. Mamadou came back from the pilgrimage with an investiture from the nominal caliph, a relic of the ʿAbbāsid line then located in Cairo, and he proceeded to model the organization of his kingdom along Islamic precedents. Islam was now firmly implanted in central Africa.

After seven centuries of effort Islam gained a solid position in the cities and won over important ethnical elements, but it was not yet firmly established among the masses. The concerted drive mounted by influential chieftains, vigorous nomadic groups, and the militant zeal of the Ṣūfi brethren like the Tījānīyah and Qādirīyah were not only reminiscent of the old Murābiṭ spirit but, when coupled with the Berber fervor, the drive was bound to keep Islam on the move.

Refreshed by Qādirīyah incentive, pastoral Muslims of the north penetrated from the west into the sedentary strongholds and often imposed themselves by the force of their arms on the peasantry, as in Hausa, a land already Islamized. They founded new kingdoms in what is today Nigeria, and their imperial sway lasted till the beginnings of the nineteenth century. A wandering Shaykh of Mecca, Muḥammad ʿUthmān Amīrghāni boosted the influence of Arabian Muslims in his extensive voyages; indeed, an order was established, named al-Amīrghānīyah after him, which played a significant part in furthering Islam. Parallel to the Amīrghānīyah drive, the predominantly Berber Tījānīyah penetrated as far as Hausa. These orders were responsible for imparting their characteristics to African Islam.[3]

The colonial onslaught on Africa, especially in the second half of the nineteenth century, caused considerable radical modification of the conditions abetting the spread of Islam. Paradoxically, both French and British colonial expansion tended to encourage the expansion of Islam.

Stepped up economic activity, the security of travel and communication, the development of cities, the free effulgence of Islamic culture in public places were the natural outcome of the peace imposed domestically in French and British dominated territories. These and similar factors played an important role in the propagation of Islam. The proselytism of merchants was now replaced by the proselytism of the soldier, and manifested itself in a variety of efficacious forms.

Often the native's identification with Islam was unconscious; he adopted the veneer of Muslim observances, customs, names, and the like because to him it was an entrée for identifying himself with prosperous commercial communities. A significant attraction for the convert was the opportunity to link himself with a prestigious group and enjoy the hospitality and solidarity of Islam, two precious advantages placed immediately at the disposition of the neophyte.

Interestingly enough during this later period of conversion to Islam, the process was not the work of Muslim traders astride the traditional caravan routes or in control of interior markets; the agents of Islam were now more varied, numerous, and powerful, situated in the port regions of the western coast. There were Shīʿahs from Lebanon, Sunnis from Syria, Aḥmadīyah, and Ismāʿīlis from India-Pakistan, many of whom were liberated repatriated slaves who had adopted Islam earlier and sought to preserve it following emancipation in order to avoid the reprisals of their former milieus.[4]

In Nigeria, for example, the British enlisted the support of the Muslim chieftains; and in cooperation with the latter, the Islamic way gained more following. The law of the *Sharīʿah* was increasingly applied to the land and became more widespread. The rigid adherence of the Fulānis to the laws of Islam experienced no parallel, with the exception perhaps of Wahhābi Arabia.[5]

The French administration contributed to the strengthening of Islam in West Africa by organizing the pilgrimage to Mecca, building mosques down to the village level, and depending on the aristocratic Muslim minorities in the towns and villages among whom they found competent administrators.[6] Often by design the French administration favored the Muslim expansion because to the administrators Islam was "a known quantity"; moreover, a generation of experience in administering Algeria where French rulers became familiar with Arab-Muslim bureaucratic practices provided an easy outlet for carrying out the same procedures in black Africa. This entailed, for instance, in the

Senegal, substituting Qurʾānic for African customary laws which hitherto had served merely as an adjunct of faith to the Muslim, not to the African community at large.

Favoritism extended to Muslim chieftains fostered a sort of pro-Islam snobbism. Non-Muslim chieftains assigned administrative positions found it important for the exercise of authority to give an Islamic base to their authority; such a religious base was regarded as indispensable to a society where command was looked upon as sacred in essence.

Notwithstanding certain negative reactions to its increasing presence in African societies, Islam in some parts of Africa wrought only superficial changes while in other parts it made deep inroads on indigenous cultures. Some say Islam made more progress in the seventy-five years of French dominion than in the nine previous centuries.[7]

A peculiar role of African Islam is the political. This was evident even in pre-colonial rule, in the shaping of distinctively Muslim political institutions. It could be seen also in the close ties established by Black Muslim states with their Arab counterparts north of the Sahara, particularly in the 1950s and 1960s when the struggle for independence intensified. It gained additional strength in the 1970s when revenues from oil enabled Arab states to assist these states in their economic development and to undercut their ties with Israel, with whom the Muslim Arab states were warring. Thus, in Chad, Ethiopia, and other states where Islam is not the majority religion, we have witnessed its politicization for the purpose of achieving a rightful status and a share of national power.

In countries where Islam is the predominant religion, it plays a significant role in politics at all levels, perhaps owing more to the influence of social rather than religious factors. Ṣūfi brotherhoods like the Khatmīyah and Anṣār in the Sudan, as well as powerful surviving elements of the Hausa-Fulani Islamic emirates of northern Nigeria all managed to hold on to power during colonial rule on the basis of the authority acquired through appeal to Islam a century earlier. Where distinct Islamic institutions had not developed (Guinea, Niger, Mali) Islam was not able to enjoy a commensurate political role. A contributing factor to Islam's reduced role is the westernized secularized outlook of leaders boasting of good Muslim connections yet educated in European institutions (leaders like Sekou Touré of Guinea and Modibo Keita of Mali). They preferred to rest their power on a secular party organization instead of a politicized Islam.

While in nineteenth century West Africa Islam made gains as a result of "holy wars," in Senegal and northern Nigeria, in this century it has exhibited a much less combative attitude. Converts were attracted by a relaxed approach to the prescribed ceremonial obligations of the faith. Children might not pray regularly but they usually attend Qur'ānic schools.

Black Muslims of Africa have not ceased to maintain important educational ties with Arab Africa. Thousands have converged on al-Azhar University to perfect their knowledge of Islam. The role of the Marabus, or religious leaders and leaders of powerful *ṭarīqas* or Ṣūfi brotherhoods is no less conspicuous in shaping the Islamism of their followers and disciples. Tījānīyah, Qādirīyah, and Murīdīyah all managed to strengthen their religious, political and economic authority in the process, most conspicuously in a country like Senegal (over 80 percent Muslim)[8]

Reasons for Gain

How can we explain the reasons for Islam's substantial gains deep in the heart of Africa? How do we account, moreover, for the gains acquired under the benevolent eyes of dominant "Christian" nations and in the face of an intensive rivalry for converts staged by Protestant and Catholic missions?

One good reason is the fact that Islam is free of the onus of identification with the "White Devils" who extended their political dominance over the blacks while Christianity is not. Secondly, while Christian blacks felt restrained because of religious identification with the white man from rising against him, the Muslim black experienced no such restraint; he readily joined demonstrations and outbursts directed against the white overlord. Islam gave vent to black nationalism and gained favor in the eyes of nationalists when Christianity could not.

Of greater relevance for explaining the reason is the fact that Islam represents to the indigenous inhabitant a cultural force; by identifying himself with it, the African is lifting his morale, enhancing his social standing, and acquiring a new dimension of intellectual growth.[9]

Islam is strongly entrenched in Africa today. If it were at all looked upon as a measure of defense against the West, the growth of the religion in recent times suggests that the establishment of even the most cordial ties with European nations will hardly detract from Islam's continuing spread in the African continent. The advantages it enjoys in its growth stem from its minimum demands and maximum promises to the convert; also from its remarkable capacity first to absorb, then ultimately to purify and integrate norms of cultural response quite alien to the orthodox tenets of Islam.

Islam in Africa is capable of countenancing the "sacred" and the "sacrilegious," the spiritual and the secular, the political and the religious, and a variety of what may appear as non-spiritual criteria. An African may be regarded as a Muslim even if he has only a superficial knowledge of the faith and despite the fact that he may have brought into his laconic Muslim beliefs from his previous animistic affiliations a variety of local observances and usages.

To be sure, many pagan and superstitious practices survive in the Islam of sub-Saharan Africa. Many are the African Muslims who have not abandoned all their animistic beliefs and practices. There are certain African groups, particularly in Senegal among whom the men subscribe to Islam while the wives continue their animistic practices.[10]

It is interesting to observe that the animism of Berber and black in Africa comprises certain traits to which Islam can adjust here more readily than elsewhere, like Southeast Asia. In the black-African milieu, religion and society are looked upon as one and the same; so it is in the orthodox conception of Islam. In black cosmogony the world is in the process of continual creation and man is in harmony with his world of creation. Islamic theology conceives of this in similar tones: the world is the creation of God; man is also the creation of God; God's creation is perfect, so must man and the world be perfect. Departures from this norm in African animism and in Islam are due to the evil deeds of man. Both in black and Muslim interpretations, the community combines the religious and social functions and strives to enforce submission to the Deity so it will reflect the divine order in all of its terrestrial facets.

At a time when the African seemed to collapse under the burden of modern civilization and the social and religious system of animistic traditions, Islam comes to his rescue with an offer to reinstate himself within a new framework not entirely alien to him in its broad confines. An established propensity for the symbolic, the esoteric, and the mystic renders him receptive to the Ṣūfi way. He is intrigued by the Ṣūfi path and is often lured into embracing Islam by it. He finds a certain compatibility between the animistic priestly and Muslim Ṣūfistic practices. Ṣūfism indeed has remained one of the great magnets for Islam in Africa.

Islam defines for the African in precise terms the concept of the divine which had become more or less confused in his thinking. He looked upon God as creator, but he also regarded Him as the chief of a pantheon consisting of secondary deities. Islam could not tolerate such a conception; so the neophyte is taught strict monotheism, and not to associate partners with the Deity. He learns to appreciate a simpler and more forthright religion than he had previously experienced. In Islam he is an *equal* associate among those who do not attribute status levels even to their God.

The adherence of blacks to Islam poses no special difficulty. The case of conversion is abetted by the reduction of the ritualistic formalities to a minimum; this is indeed one of the chief factors in Islam's rapid penetration of black Africa. There is no need for a preliminary study of doctrine; all the convert needs is to have some knowledge of the fundamental principles of Islam and to accept them. By solemnly pronouncing the *shahādah* before witnesses, he is formally introduced into Islam. Before long he is fully acquainted with the traditional largess of Muslim institutions. The Muslim community at large takes care of the matter of integrating the neophyte socially and inculcating him with the right amount of knowledge concerning dogma and ritual. He enjoys the privileges that result from his adherence to the global society of Islam and all its attending benefits.

Islam has the added advantage over Christianity today of being propagated by non-Westerners. At a time of strong nationalistic anti-West outbursts, this is a distinct advantage. Islam, if it chooses, can play on the emotions of agitated Africans and black racists. It is not a strange antipathetic system of beliefs to the African because Asians and Africans who profess and preach Islam play down differences of color, language, and ethnical affiliation. Asians and Africans seem to control Islam which appears to blacks as a typically Afro-Asian form of social and religious life. "In proclaiming himself a Muslim many a youth is not adhering to a religion (witness how many prefer the European way of life, aside from maintaining a certain façade), he is giving proof of his Africanism. He is asserting a dynamic sense of independence. There is today a vulgar infatuation for Islam."[11]

The prospect of being treated as an equal is a real incentive for the black to adopt Islam. Indeed, the Islamic stress on equality has been a powerful inducement for the popularization of Islam in Africa. Welcomed as an equal into the Islamic community, the neophyte delights in a newly acquired sentiment of social elevation. He finds himself suddenly in a milieu that does not discriminate between African or Asian, black or white. The convert's whole moral attitude is radically transformed in Islam. Equality is manifested both in the family and in the community. Wherever he goes the Black Muslim can expect equal treatment in the society of Islam; nowhere will he find himself without interlocutors or guarantors among fellow Muslims regardless of their ethnic and tribal backgrounds. He ceases to be alone; this is a godsend and welcome reprieve for an African who is usually made to feel out of his own element when deprived of the warmth of social belonging.

Race and color are not material to his Islamism. There is no feeling of inferiority; self-dignity and pride are accentuated through the stress on equality and brotherhood among all African Muslims. By adhering to Islam the African is not asked to abandon his strong national feelings, nor is he expected to undergo revolutionary social changes; family and social ties are strengthened not weakened, and loyalty to his people is not diminished.[12] There is the additional factor of common antipathy towards the West in both the Islamic and African predisposition.

An important factor in the popular appeal of Islam is its non-demanding attitude towards the convert: (1) no pressure to convert, (2) limiting Islamic education to the study of the Qur'ān and Arabic, (3) reduction of the role of women to household chores, and (4) no insistence on full conformity or uniformity since it is a rule of Islam to permit monotheists to safeguard their customs and laws within the circle of Islamic government.[13]

Islam can present itself as a unitarian force to the African while Christianity projects the image of a divided and disconcerting ideal. The African is confronted with the Catholic version on the one hand and the numerous Protestant versions of Christianity on the other, much too complex for him to comprehend, let alone digest, the doctrinal points of Christianity. The paradox lies in the fact that Muslims do not project any more a uniform image of Islam than the Christians do of Christianity, yet the appeal of Islam remains stronger.

There are not only the orthodox Sunni Muslims, but also the Berber Khārijites who have a strong foothold in the former "French Sudan" where their impact is felt even in the architecture of the area. In recent years the Shīʿites of south Lebanon have been entrenched on the western, Ismāʿīlis from India and Pakistan on the eastern coast where they control much of the commercial traffic.

The Aḥmadīyah have specialized in missionary activities in Ghana, Dahomey, the Upper-Volta, and especially Nigeria. Differences between the various sects however seem to escape the African, and the total missionary effort adds up to increasing converts for Islam and fewer for Christianity. The reason for this is that at the critical initial stage of conversion Islam tolerates indigenous concepts brought in by the neophyte more than Christianity, provided these concepts do not negate the basic dogma of Islam: There is no god whatsoever but God.

The African proclivity for the mystical way is abetted by the Muslim Ṣūfis, which would explain why the two principal orders of Tījānīyah and Qādirīyah have been successful in the propagation of Islam in Africa. Here the grounds have been adequately prepared by animism, which has succeeded in preserving an attachment to a transforming society.

Islam in a broader context seems to lend itself to a civilization that favors an admixture of the temporal and the supernatural.

The simple practical ritual offered the African by Islam is attractive to him; and he responds readily because in it he sees a manifestation of the universality of Islam. He is pleased moreover by the fact that Islam allows him to preserve under an Islamic guise the magical-medicinal objects of his former animistic ritual. Besides, mystical communication with God and its attending fetish touches a sensitive familiar chord in the African's heart. All the Ṣūfis insist on is the profession of divine unity and leaves to the African his pantheistic inclinations. Islam does not insist on the full performance of the ritualistic observances defined by orthodoxy. If he chooses, the African may pray three instead of five times a day, and he may simplify the ritual if it suits him better.

It is noteworthy to observe that some of the dynamic reformist movements of the Muslim world had strong beginnings in African Islam commencing with the last century. We might view them as activist and militant in their approach. Among them we might list the Mahdīyah of the Sudan, led by Muḥammad Aḥmad (1848–1885), Muḥammad ʿAli al-Sanūsi (1787–1859) in Equatorial Africa and Libya who was a disciple of Aḥmad ibn Idrīs, a disciple of the Wahhābis, and preacher of reform among Ṣūfis, and ʿUthmān Dan Fodio (1754–1817) in Nigeria.

Their aim was to purify the way the faith was practiced among Ṣūfi orders and greater cooperation among Muslims to roll back those who aggressed upon the Muslim *umma*. "Ṣūfism was not suppressed but redefined, emphasizing a spirituality that incorporated a militant activism with its willingness to fight and die to establish Islamically oriented states and societies."[14]

Islam in America

Islam's presence in America is attributed to two factors: immigration from Muslim lands and conversion of both whites and blacks to Islam. The rapid growth of both is largely a recent phenomenon. They manifest another aspect of Islamic growth dynamism, due partly to unfavorable political and economic conditions of their native environments. One might attribute it also to the increasing awareness of Islam's role in world affairs and the influence achieved by the Muslim world in international political and economic developments.

The kernel of the Muslim community in America derives from immigration for whites and conversion for blacks. They have come from Arab countries (including many displaced Palestinians after the series of Arab-Israeli wars commencing in 1948), from Albania, India and Pakistan, Iran, Turkey, Malaysia, Philippines, Vietnam, Cambodia, and other countries where Muslims have been a minority under pressure. Since World War II, many had come to study, only to stay on due (as in the case of refugees) to turmoil at home, and eventually to join the professions, such as education, medicine, engineering, law, and research-oriented industry. They have even excelled in politics, especially in Central and South America where they have reached top positions, i.e. President Menem of Argentina today, a Muslim of Syrian origin.

The number of Muslims in the Americas presently is subject to speculation. All told, in North and South, estimates vary from a few million to eight million. They represent most of the known sects: Shīʿite, Druze, Ismāʿīli and other offshoots. Given the rapid rate of growth and the projection that by the end of the century Islam will become the second largest faith in the United States, one has to presume that its numbers among whites and blacks in North America must exceed the five million mark. In Central and South America, Muslims total over two million, with Argentina and Brazil each having approximately half a million. They are a mixed lot, having to confront a mode of living heavily grounded in materialism and challenging Christian and secular ideals that do not always comport with the injunctions and requirements of their faith.

The story of Islam in America antedates the European conquest of the continent. Some say that Andalusian Muslims visited the American continent long before Columbus, as reported by al-Sharīf al-Idrīsi in the twelfth century. Others claim that adventurers from the Muslim kingdoms of West Africa had visited the Caribbean. Furthermore, it is alleged that the Portuguese and Spanish discoverers were led by Andalusian Muslim mariners who were familiar with the high seas. Some of the discoverers were said to be Moriscos (Spanish Muslims who pretended to be Christians). Andalusian Muslim immigrants of Rabat and Salé in Morocco led the fight against Spanish and Portuguese navies in the Caribbean.

The present Muslim communities in America date back to Columbus. The earliest Muslim would have had to be a navigator on Christopher Columbus' voyage of discovery. Thousands of the Moriscos arrived in America in the sixteenth century with the Spanish and Portuguese colonial armies. Once in the new world, they openly declared their Islam, and even tried to convert the West Indians. But the Catholic Inquisition made short work of them, burning them at the stake for "apostasy." Among the Moriscos was Rodrigo de Lope, Columbus' colleague, and Estevanico de Azemor, the Spanish general who conquered Arizona. There was also Don Estavan the Moor, who was with Coronado in the 1540s seeking the elusive gold cities of New Mexico.

The next group of Muslims to reach America came from Africa as part of the slave trade, starting in the seventeenth century. They tried to keep their faith, often by armed struggle, but that of Makdendal in 1758 ended with his being burned at the stake. The third group to reach the Americas came from Asia starting around 1830. The British and Dutch had replaced slavery by forced emigration from India and Java for "indentured labor." Unlike the Africans, they were not compelled to give up their faith. Then, by the end of the nineteenth century, emigration from the Syrian region began, and still goes on.

Ethnically, American Muslims derive mainly from Asia and Africa. Among the blacks first to arrive bearing Muslim names, were those enslaved. It is reported that 1717 represents the first year when Muslim names like Omar ibn Said, Prince Omar, Ben Ali, etc., are recorded in slave documents.[15] In the judgment of the late Ismail al-Faruqi, slavery did not allow Muslims to perpetuate their religion or culture, as they were forced to adopt the faith of their masters, as well as their names.[16] What Muslim faith they brought with them was quickly absorbed in their new Christian milieu and disappeared. Indeed, in the whole record of enslaved Muslims, those brought to South America were able to establish in Brazil a state of their own in 1830, only to be destroyed after four years in a sea of blood.[17] The fate of these indentured African Muslims after being brought to America and deprived of their dignity and religion has been vividly described by Alex Haley who, in his book *Roots*, traces his origin to the Muslims of Gambia.

Some with Muslim names turned up in Philadelphia in the early eighteenth century. The first Arab Muslim immigrant was Hadj Ali (Hijoly) who was brought from Syria in 1855 to oversee the introduction of camel breeding in Arizona. The earliest Muslim immigrants were in a distinct minority and most were lost to Islam because of marriage and integration in a Christian environment. After World War I, the emigrants included Muslim Tartars from Kazan, Polish Muslims, and Muslims from Yugoslavia and Albania. Muslim immigration after World War II increased, especially from India, Pakistan, Iran, Turkey, and Egypt. It is estimated that these immigrants came from sixty countries, with the Arab community representing the largest among the non-blacks.

The earliest immigrants, mostly from the Syrian region, were individuals who were seeking to better their economic lot. They were unskilled, uneducated, and hampered by language and the work environment. So they struggled in factories, in mines, and as peddlers. Those who arrived in the inter-world war period were relatives and acquaintances of the earlier immigrants. After World War II, immigration resulted from massive displacements in Asia, the Middle East, the Indian subcontinent, Eastern Europe, and the Soviet Union. Nearly all came from rural environments, the uneducated and lower classes of society in keeping with the tradition of former immigrants. While there are centers of concentrations in the New York-New Jersey area, Detroit, Los Angeles and Chicago, the bulk of Muslims are dispersed with enclaves in nearly all main cities and rural areas of the United States.

The presence of Muslims is felt primarily in the larger urban centers, primarily in Detroit, Chicago, Los Angeles, and New York, where their main institutions are located. The earliest mosques were built by Syrian immigrants in Cedar Rapids, Iowa, in 1911 followed by one in Detroit in 1919. In 1912 these early immigrants also formed the first Islamic association, in Detroit. The number of mosques cum institutes has increased to some six hundred. The most recent one in New York rivals the largest structure anywhere. Most are Sunni but with increasing numbers of Shīʿite establishments due to Iranian Islamic groups and other Shīʿite immigrants.

The mosque/institute in Washington D.C. was built after World War II to service the Muslim diplomatic missions. Since then it has broadened its activities to serve as the principal interpreter for Islam in the United States and to coordinate the work of all institutes and Islamic learning activities. There are two Islamic colleges in the Chicago area, day schools and several hundred weekend schools, women's organizations, youth groups, and professional civic organizations.[18]

Several printing presses, book distribution centers, and national and regional denominational magazines have come into being to guide the youth and converts in the exercise of their Islamic beliefs and practices. There are also, in the main areas of concentration, radio and television programs on a regular basis. Funding for initiating such programs or the building of mosques and institutes has come partly from Islamic states (Saudi Arabia, Gulf States, Iran, and Libya) and partly from local subscription among Muslims.

Muslims in the United States are increasing at an annual average rate of 10 percent, through immigration and conversion. The cause of rapid growth in the recent decades has been attributed partly to change in American immigration laws and partly to the demands of the labor market. Unstable conditions in Muslim lands, especially in the Middle East, where the civil war in Lebanon coupled with the ongoing confrontation with Israel has induced many to emigrate. Besides those who came as refugees, there are increasing numbers of professionals (some six thousand Muslim doctors alone). They are also conspicuous in the fields of engineering and scientific research. They constitute a "brain drain" to their homelands and a contribution to the American scientific community. The impact can be seen in the transformation of Islamic values.

Growing awareness of Islam in America has been, to a large extent, the result of American involvement, in peace and war, in Middle Eastern affairs. Muslims in America have had to speak up and defend activities of fellow Muslims when and where possible, given the hostility of the media.[19] Muslim perception of Islam in America is one that accords with the American milieu in which it finds itself. Coordination among the Muslims is conducted by some fourteen Islamic organizations ranging from professional to student and youth groups.[20] In 1952 the Federation of Islamic Associations was formed for the purpose of promoting organization among Muslims in America.

Student groups on campuses have expanded rapidly since first organized on the Urbana campus of the University of Illinois on January 1, 1963. In 1983 they boasted of three hundred and ten student chapters with more than 45,000 members.[21] Financed heavily by the Islamic World Conference (based in Arabia), the aim of such organizations is to encourage conversion to Islam through *daʿwah*. Their activities include the distribution of Islamic publications, training Muslims to get the message across, providing teachers and lecturers, and the like. They have dedicated themselves to the task of explaining Islam with the view of gaining converts. Much of their activity is directed from their headquarters outside Indianapolis. They are more active in intermarriages, which also serves to bring in more converts.

Non-Muslim Americans have been introduced to the teachings of Islam, its culture and heritage mostly through educational and informational institutes and civic organizations, which have contributed to a better understanding and appreciation of the faith.[22] With support from the Saudi Arabian government, the Muslim World League caters to Muslim communities in the West. The League assists Islamic Centers with youth camps and summer schools; provides teachers and *imāms* for these centers; develops prison ministries; makes available fellowships and grants for Muslim university professors; and contributes to the production of television and radio programs, as well as to the establishment of newspapers and journals.[23]

There are other sectarian, missionary organizations. The Ahmadīyah Movement had pioneered in the 1920s missionary activities to gain converts to Islam by establishing a mission in Chicago. Members are now trained in the Missionary Training College in Pakistan. In a seven-year study program they are prepared to contextualize their perception of Islam in a world religious context with recourse to apologetics, mass media, and methods used by Christian evangelists.

Shīʿites have their own organization, the Islamic Societies of Georgia and Virginia, first established by Yasin al-Jibouri. The former grew rapidly through proselytization following its establishment in 1973 and by distributing literature to blacks and whites sent from Iran through its World Organization for Islamic Services via Bilal Muslims Missions of Tanzania, Kenya, and Pakistan. By 1977 it was estimated some 55,700 copies of publications of all sorts had been mailed out free of charge, mostly to African-Americans who could not afford to buy them.[24]

The International Institute of Islamic Thought, located also in Virginia, was established in 1981 "to promote and serve research in Islamic Studies" and to stimulate Islamic scholars to "think out the problems of thought and life pertinent to Muslims in the modern world" as well as to "articulate the relevance of Islam to these problems."[25] The Institute promotes publication of college texts focusing on the Muslim perspective of academic discipline; conducts seminars, workshops, and conventions, and supports on a limited scale work of Muslim scholars. The latest undertaking is "Tawhid Cybernetics," or the creation of a "computerized data bank, assembling all human knowledge in a form suitable for the introduction of purpose in artificial intelligence." When completed it will amount to an electronic "majlis al-shūra" or "a supranational, supracultural ulama capable of providing solutions to problems faced by Muslims."[26]

Muslims in **Canada** are perhaps the best organized in the Americas. The Council of Muslim Communities of Canada (established in 1977) encompasses some forty Islamic associations and mosques from every province servicing over half a million Muslims. They have clearly defined their aims as follows: project an Islamic way of life in accordance with the prescription of Qur᾽ān and *Sunnah*; strengthen fraternal ties among Muslim communities and individuals; promote mutual appreciation and friendly relations with non-Muslims; stimulate Islamic thinking and action; and, coordinate activities of member communities with the rest of the Muslim world.[27]

The fact that, socially, Muslims have become integrated in their communities across the country is a plus in their ability to make the adjustment of exercising their faith in sometimes not very receptive milieus. Such hostility is particularly conspicuous in times of crises, especially in recent years, as militant groups target Western countries deemed inimical to Islamic interests, and as Muslim groups and individuals organize into political action committees to counter the negative and adverse propaganda levelled against them at home and abroad by pro-Israel factions. Others, like the Pakistan committee, seek to encourage members to get involved in local politics.

"Bilalian" Islam

Until recently this group of Muslim converts had been referred to as "Black Muslims," a designation of their choice. The new choice of "Bilalian" is to honor the first Black Muslim, Bilal, the Prophet Muḥammad's first muezzin and one of his earliest converts. From the very inception of this community, its leaders manifested the social dynamism characteristic of Islam in its nascent stage. At first it was the social message of Islam that attracted them. In recent years greater attention has been devoted to rectifying the religious practices so as to achieve a greater alignment with the orthodox teachings of the faith.

The Black Muslims of America have reawakened to the Islamic origin of their peoples prior to enslavement and Christianization. But that speaks for a distinct minority. The bulk of Africans were not Muslim when they arrived on American shores. It was not until the turn of the century that they began to become conscious of Islamic roots, which galvanized in the establishment of the first Islamic association in 1913 to give social cohesion to the "returnees to Islam."

The movement among American blacks was established by the American Muslim Mission, one of the best organized and articulate spokesmen for Islam. It incorporated the tradition left by the Moorish Science Temple, founded in Newark in 1913 by Noble Drew Ali, and the International Negro Improvement Movement of Marcus Garvey. Ali gave a separate identity to the American blacks whom he termed "Asiatic" and "Moorish," inculcating them with a sense of confidence and pride in the Islam he understood. He was the first to make a separation: Islam the religion of blacks, Christianity the religion of whites. Garvey was more interested in improving the black man's social lot, advocating even the "back to Africa movement."[28]

Elijah Muhammad's preachings were a product of these two movements although he claimed to have received inspiration from one Fard Muhammad.[29] Since prophethood requires a conduit to the Divine being, Elijah made use of this to recruit followers and supporters, as his teachings seem to reflect.[30] His Nation of Islam was organized hierarchically and strongly centralized. The *imām* on both the local and national level provided the authority for holding the community together and guiding it. This strong leadership rested on a number of factors: (1) charismatic and centralized leadership commanding loyalty and obedience; (2) an organized security arm (Fruit of Islam) composed of militant former servicemen charged with protecting the community, mosques, and other institutions, headed by Elijah's own son-in-law, Raymond Sharif; (3) business organizations comprising a number of enterprises—bank, fishing company, and a chain of restaurants; (4) educational institutions (universities of Islam),[31] which run a highly disciplined system of education, and (5) a national network of temples (including the West Indies), well organized under the direction of their ministers who control membership and functions.[32]

While at first they did not consciously attempt to identify themselves outrightly with any Islamic sect, their leaders nevertheless considered the community an integral part of the main body of Islam, stating "we here in America who are under the Divine Leadership of the Honorable Elijah Muhammad, are an integral part of the vast World of Islam that stretches from the China Seas to the sunny shores of Africa."[33]

Until the mid-1950s there was considerable friction between regular and Black Muslims. The former accused the latter of unorthodox Islamic beliefs. There were elements among Black Muslims themselves who disputed the views of Elijah Muhammad concerning race and state. For, under the guise of an Islam little understood at first by most blacks, their leader preached a doctrine of black supremacy and deprecation of whites for having oppressed blacks. Indeed, he insisted that Allah is black and Islam is the religion of blacks. His preachings appeared to undermine the very premise of universalism in Islam. Elijah Muhammad was seen as the new prophet of Islam, while orthodox Muslims could recognize as prophet none besides Muḥammad, the founder of the faith. Moreover, their conception of God bordered on that of an incarnate being to whom a believer can immediately relate, not a spirit, transcendent and beyond physical identification.

They also tended to downplay the importance of ceremonial obligations in the disciplining of the believer. *Ṣalāh* (ritual prayer) was not established; *zakāh* (formal tax) was not enjoined upon the adherents, and the *ḥājj* (pilgrimage to Mecca) was not promoted. Yet they insisted that God is near, heaven and hell merely two states of existence. The resurrection taught in Islam was seen as a device perpetuated by Christianity to put off social justice for blacks in this life and make them wait for the promises of the hereafter.

Those, however, who had a closer understanding of Elijah Muhammad's conception of his mission, saw clearly in it the means for achieving social and political equality and the realization of human and legal rights guaranteed all Americans in the constitution. Islam becomes an important vehicle for imparting dignity and pride of belonging to a black community despairing of the promises of Christianity. The appeal to Allah would guarantee what appeal to Jehovah could not: social justice in the black man's lifetime.

While it is difficult to ascertain the numbers of Black Muslims in America today, a fair estimate would put them at over three million. Famous black athletes with obvious Muslim names have served as magnets to attract converts, as have preachings among black prisoners who have become so transformed while incarcerated that jailers wished they had more of them. Growth has been rapid in the past two decades. Many convert in the belief that "Islam is the religion of the black man." Muslim leaders around the world have lent support to this movement with men like Qadhdhāfi making substantial financial grants to help promote their educational institutions and the building of mosques all in the hope that they will observe the true Islam and "the racism in their heart can be wiped out."

The first move toward rectitude is attributed to Malcolm X, who like Elijah, was the son of a Baptist preacher. After performing the pilgrimage to Mecca in 1964, he returned convinced that his leader's preachings did not comport with the true form of Islam. After having once endorsed the idea of a separate identity and a separate existence for the black man within the "Nation of Islam" under its own flag and distinguishing symbols, he announced a change of heart. In a letter from Mecca he declared that "whites as well as non-whites who accept true Islam become a changed people." He added further that "I have eaten from the same plate with people whose eyes were the bluest of blue, whose hair was the blondest of blond, and whose skin was the whitest of white—all the way from Cairo to Jedda and even in the Holy City of Mecca itself and I felt the same sincerity in the words and deeds of these 'white' Muslims that I felt among the African Muslims of Nigeria, Sudan, and Ghana."[34]

Under the banner of Islam, the blacks of America today, like the downtrodden of Mecca in the days of the Prophet Muḥammad, have begun to realize a measure of human dignity long denied them. They are exhibiting the moral qualities associated with practicing believers: abstinence from smoking and drinking, fidelity, modesty, honesty, and above all else, discipline and solidarity with fellow Muslims. There is a growing realization that true Islam rejects racism on grounds that people of all colors and races who accept the Qur᾿ān and teachings of Muḥammad the Prophet look upon each other as brothers and sisters.

That Islam has provided Black Muslims with the motivation Christianity apparently could not is evident in the serious transformations it brought into their personal and social lives. The Black Muslim has become thrifty and industrious; he is taught to depend on himself not on others; to become active in agricultural and manufacturing pursuits, and to lead an exacting regimented life. The Muslims observe the dietary laws of Islam and avoid contacts with whites as much as possible. Strict discipline is observed at home; the respective functions of man and wife in the family are clearly defined. The children are taught the essentials of the faith at home. The male Muslim must engage in gainful work; if he undertakes a small business enterprise, he is assured the patronage and support of fellow Muslims.

Prior to the changes introduced by Wārith, Elijah's son and successor, the center of socioreligious life was the temple and the temple restaurant where many meals were taken in common. While regular Islam insists on one congregational prayer a week, the Black Muslims have conducted up to three such prayer sessions per week.

Discipline among Muslim women is strongly manifest. They are schooled in the need and art of homemaking and taught to take back seats to their husbands, never to talk to strangers, nor wear make-up and fancy dress.

Formal training centers are open for young women known as the MGT (Muslim Girls Training). The Muslims have their own schools, including the University of Islam in Chicago, where they learn Arabic, among other subjects, their supposed native tongue before slavery. Religious and secular subjects are taught with emphasis on Islam, their religion, and the history of the black man, their ancestor.

With the death of Elijah Muhammad in 1975 his rehabilitated son Wārith al-Dīn (lit. "inheritor of the faith") succeeded him. When Wārith had been expelled from the movement, he kept close contact with mainstream Muslim leaders and did not hesitate to voice differences with his father over how Islam was preached among the blacks. Wārith worked systematically to transform the Nation of Islam into a mainstream Muslim community.[35]

Following the death of his father, Wārith toured Saudi Arabia and the Gulf states at the invitation of King Khaled and received in return substantial financial aid to abet the process of transforming Elijah's perception of Islam into the mainstream observances of the faith, namely Islamic orthodoxy. He lectured to Muslim groups in the Arab world and performed the pilgrimage to Mecca. Soon thereafter, in 1976, he declared that his father was not a prophet as he had styled himself, and acknowledged the non-racial basis of Islam, admitting henceforth whites into his community. In 1978 the Gulf States and Saudi Arabia named Wārith al-Dīn Muhammad the head of the main body of Black Muslims, "sole consultant and trustee for the recommendation and distribution of funds to all Muslim organizations engaged in the propagation of the faith in the U.S."[36]

Black Islam was renamed "World Community of Al-Islam in the West" and the followers, "Bilalians," after the Prophet Muḥammad's companion and first muezzin in Islam. The main publication, *Muḥammad Speaks* was renamed *Bilalian News*. The journal broadened its reports to encompass the Muslim world generally and to identify with the rest of the world of Islam. To reinforce the new image of Black Muslims as an integral part of mainstream Islamic orthodoxy a number of changes were introduced. Temples were renamed mosques; ministers, *imāms*, and Islamic injunctions strictly observed.

In 1980 another change took place when the name of the organization became The American Muslim Mission, and its principal publication, *The American Muslim Journal*. Preaching of racial hatred (likening the white man unto the devil) has ceased. Strict discipline was somewhat relaxed with the disbanding of the principal enforcing agency, the Fruit of Islam. In 1985 Wārith decentralized the structure of the community, reduced the authority of the National Council of Imāms, and delegated most of the responsibilities to the local *imāms*. More importantly, local mosques were instructed to become integrated with the broader Muslim community.[37]

Those who did not adhere to Wārith's changes rallied around Minister Louis Farakhan who insisted on following the strict path of Elijah Muhammad by retaining the old name, the teachings and form of organization, including the Fruit of Islam, as instituted by Elijah himself. He adheres to the former hard line separating black from white.

As to the remarkable impact of Islam on the blacks in America one can only judge it in terms of the transformation and deep changes wrought by it on both the individual and his society generally. In the words of Louis Lomax, "Black Muslims were a catharsis for us, purging our innards of the bile brought on by slavery and segregation."[38]

True to form, Islam has strengthened its grip on the believer. It has wrought deep changes, permanent changes, on both the individual and his society, and by extension of black society generally. The validity of Islam among the blacks of America has been reinforced by the acceptance of the main body of Islam throughout the world. In recognizing the universality of Islam, Wārith and his followers have righted the keel of the Islamic ship in America. They have been accepted by official Muslim organizations in America when a decade or so ago there was no traffic between them. At present they have ties and friendly relations with the Federation of Islamic Associations in the United States and Canada. More and more Black Muslims visit the Muslim world at large and many study in Islamic universities throughout the world, notably at the Azhar where Elijah Muhammad had sent his sons to learn Islamic doctrine and acquire an Islamic education. Such graduates have had an effective role in the move towards orthodoxy. They have been abetted indirectly by admonitions of Black Muslims who were not of Elijah Muhammad's persuasion, including the sect that refers to itself as "Hanafis" and number in its ranks leading athletes who had converted to Islam.

This new generation, product of formal Islamic training, is beginning to take charge and to reflect in their teachings the tolerance, solidarity, and charity enjoined by Islamic orthodoxy. Fortunately for them, the concentration earlier on sociopolitical ends had spared the movement the possibility of misinterpretation as concerns Qur'ānic teachings and instructions. It remained thus free of theological disputations and subscribed to no doctrinaire stand from which it could not easily retreat. Having accepted Islam *prima facie,* the Muslim movement was spared the course of eclecticism pursued by Bahā'is and Qādiyāni Aḥmadis in America.

Islam in Europe

There has been a marked increase of Islam's presence in Europe today where Muslim numbers approximate twenty million. They constitute two broad categories: those who were the product of Ottoman Muslim domination in Eastern Europe for half a millennium, and those who came largely as immigrants or workers into Western Europe.

Labor shortage in the 1960s induced large-scale migration of Muslims from Morocco and Turkey to Western Europe. While many came to earn money and return home, many others decided to stay. At present these two nationalities alone account for 1.2 million Moroccan and 2.5 million Turkish settlers, as follows: half a million Berber and Arabic-speaking Moroccan Muslims in France, 160,000 in the Netherlands, around 150,000 in Belgium, and 80,000 in Spain. Turks in Germany exceed two million, followed by the Netherlands at 200,000 and France, also around 200,000. The process goes on with the reunification of families and a third generation already well settled in Europe.[39]

In Western Europe Islam is manifesting itself as an urban phenomenon. Muslims are concentrating in towns and cities and developing their own institutions, lifestyles, and culture. Belgium, for example, has nearly 350,000 Muslims, and Islam has become the largest minority religion in that country. Concurrent with this demographic growth there has been a proliferation of mosques and prayer halls, with some 240 places of worship. According to some scholars, "Europe is more than ever before becoming a space where Islamic, Christian, Jewish and secular traditions come together to fight, support, and fertilize each other."[40] Tensions are unavoidable, as western societies ponder the question whether in a democracy and pluralistic society a western European country is willing to concede place and space to accommodate ethnic and cultural pluralism.[41]

In southeastern Europe it has become painfully too obvious that Muslims are not to be accorded an autonomous or independent status short of a bloody struggle. The policy of ethnic cleansing waged by the Serbs and Croats first in Bosnia and now by the Serbs in their own province of Kosovo with the aim of ridding the area of Muslims proves that the European capacity for tolerance has its extreme limitations.

Ottoman domination served to attract converts for Islam through a variety of inducements, not the least of which is opportunism. Bosnia provides a good example of this. Many a Bosnian convert to Islam served in high office in the Ottoman empire, as did some Croats and a multitude of Serbs who were recruited by the authorities through the *devşirme* and who formed the backbone of the ministries and elite guard of the sultans. Greek sailors who converted to Islam rose to the position of high command of the fleet, as in the case of the famous Kheireddin Barbarosa, who was responsible for the conquest of North Africa for the Ottomans in the sixteenth century.

The second category is the result of vast immigration of Muslims into Western Europe, especially after World War II, in search of economic betterment. Many among them were former colonials of Great Britain and France; in addition, vast numbers of Turks and Balkan Muslims came to Germany as guest workers.

Muslims, however, were in Europe much earlier than that. Arab conquests led to Muslim domination of the Iberian peninsula and southern France off and on from 711 until 1492 when finally ousted in the ongoing Christian crusades waged against Muslims from the twelfth to the fifteenth centuries. Their legacy to Spain served to raise it to the status of a world power for a century or two. Muslim legacy to Spain reached magnificent proportions in learning, architecture, and both cultural and scientific contributions. Muslim Spain served as a magnet for scholars and traders from Northern and Western Europe. Yet the Crusades and their aftermath managed to reduce the number of Muslims in Spain to a few thousand, who survived only by keeping their faith secret and who are known historically as Moriscos.

Sicily, at one time in the ninth century, was also a Muslim

state, as was Crete. The latter survived for a century or so, the former was undone by the Normans in 1246 due to papal pressures on the Holy Roman Emperor.

Islam had been spreading in Eastern Europe even before the Ottoman conquests. There was an active and prosperous community in Hungary from the tenth to the thirteenth century when it was destroyed by Catholic fanaticism. Conversions in this part of Europe were the work largely of Ṣūfi orders that led to the Bogomile heresy within the Christian churches of Bosnia, Albania, and Bulgaria. When pressures mounted against the Bogomiles, they sought help from Ottoman Muslims in 1463. After their lands were incorporated into the Ottoman Empire, they all adopted Islam within a century. Today the Bosniacs (South Slav Muslims), Koretesh (Macedonian Muslims), Albanians and Pomaks (Bulgarian Muslims) are descendants of these first Muslims. Their numbers were enhanced by immigrants from both the Ottoman Empire and the Crimean Khanate.

Albania is theoretically the only country in Europe with a Muslim majority. Due to immense pressures from the Communist government, more Albanians ended up living outside than inside the country. Muslims constitute over 70 percent of Albania's population of three and a half million. Before communism, these descendants of the ancient Illyrians adhered to the Hanafi rite with the Bektashi Ṣūfi order exercising much influence over them. They were guided by a Council of Ulema chaired by a Grand Mufti, which managed mosques, religious schools and education, as it had been under the Ottoman Empire.

When the Ottomans retreated under Austrian pressure from Croatia, Slovenia, and Serbia late in the seventeenth century, the Muslim populations were quickly expelled, except for those of present-day Bosnia-Herzegovina. Muslims of Herzegovina were persecuted by the Austrian regime in the nineteenth century as well as by the states of Serbia and Montenegro during World War II. They lost up to 200,000 victims to the partisans, who were mostly Serbs. They had targeted Bosnian Muslims for being sympathetic to the Germans, in whose armies some served during the war. In one of the worst bloodbaths of history, the Serbs undertook in recent years to end the Muslim presence, even in the independent state of Bosnia-Herzegovina with the tacit blessing of France and Britain who have strong anti-Muslim sentiments in their own backyards and the indifference of other European states who do not look forward to an independent Islamic entity so close to Western Europe.

In 1982 Yugoslavia had the largest concentration of Muslims in Europe with five million or 22 percent of the total population. In 1973 Tito's government recognized the Bosnian Muslims as a nationality with its own separate status within the Yugoslav state, which the Serbs had dominated after absorbing Croatia, Slovenia, then large chunks of newly formed Albania. In 1982 Muslims were a majority in Kossovo at 85.6 percent and in Bosnia-Herzegovina at 51.6 percent. Muslims in Macedonia constituted 31.4 percent of the total inhabitants and numbered half a million. In Montenegro they made up 25.7 percent of the population.

The Muslims of former Yugoslavia were the most cohesively organized in all of Europe. They adhered to the Ḥanafi rite and were managed by the Muslim Religious Union with its four superiorates at Sarajevo for Bosnia-Herzegovina, Skopje for Macedonia, Pristina for Kossovo, and Titograd for Montenegro. Mosques and Islamic communities existed throughout the former federation. Some great libraries containing irreplaceable Islamic works, manuscripts and documents were set afire in the bombardment of Sarajevo in 1992 by the Serbs who were bent on eliminating all vestiges of Islam by targeting not only innocent civilians—women, old men, and children—but also mosques and other Islamic monuments.

Before the latest civil war, Bosnia-Herzegovina had up to two thousand mosques with more under construction. Its organized religious community elected a Reis-Ul-Ulema (Grand Mufti) with his seat at Sarajevo. An Islamic faculty was established at the university level, with origins that go back to Gazi Husrewbeg, the founder in 1536.

As for their origins, the most numerous are Bosniacs (some two and a half million in 1981) who share with the Serbo-Croatians racial and language traditions. Then come the Albanians, who reside in the Kossovo segment of former Yugoslavia and number close to two million today. Muslims of Turkish stock constitute some 150,000 and reside mostly in Macedonia. The Gypsy Muslims number about 100,000 and are among the poorest of all Muslims. There are small coteries of Croatian, Circassian, and other Muslims surviving the absorption drive of Christian Croats and Serbs and numbering no more than several thousands.

Yugoslav Muslims before the disintegration had established and maintained good ties with the Islamic heartland, especially when the charismatic Tito broke with Moscow and allied himself with Nasser of Egypt, Nehru of India, and Sukarno of Indonesia to establish the Third World Bloc of non-aligned nations. The tragic aftermath of the breakup and the cruel war launched by Serbs and Croats to extirpate the rest of Muslims from former Yugoslavia will stand them at low tide with the Muslim world for some time to come.

It is to the disgrace of the world in general and Muslim states in particular for all to stand by and witness for a number of years the genocide of Muslims of Bosnia. Shedding tears and pretending helplessness could not make up for their shameful inaction and withholding the aid they needed to defend themselves. The consequence of Muslim states' relative inaction are bound to be felt with unhappy results for the rest of the world. Muslim governments have set themselves up as targets for the extremist "fundamentalist" parties who can now with certainty point the finger of blame for inaction at their leaders. One million embittered Muslim refugees can generate a movement of vengeance already contemplated by extremists, targeting especially France and Britain for their providing an umbrella under United Nations' guise for the Serbs to roll up Bosnian territory and massacre the innocent.

Yet, in spite of the tragic fate confronting the Muslims of Bosnia-Herzegovina today, Islam is not about to be eradicated from the rest of Europe. Indeed, Muslims have exhibited a remarkable capability for resilience and dynamic adjustments enabling them to survive and increase in numbers. They are organized and have their own mosques and institutes for promoting Islamic education and training *imāms*.

The two million Muslim Turks in Bulgaria were under severe pressure from the Communist state to give up their identities and become Bulgarized. In 1850 a third of the population of what is today Bulgaria were Pomaks or Bulgarian-speaking Muslims. Continuous pressure and a policy of expulsion had reduced their numbers drastically. Not until the breakup of the Communist Eastern bloc and the elimination of extremist rulers have such pressures relaxed. Some seventy thousand Muslims in Roumania were treated relatively well given the ties established by its former dictator with Muslim and Arab states. With its few thousand adherents, Islam in Hungary is a "recognized religion."[42]

In Western Europe the centers of Muslim concentrations are Great Britain, France, and Germany, each with a Muslim population of three million or more. Muslim immigrants to France are of colonial origin. In 1900 there were only one thousand Muslims, rising to six thousand in 1912. Algerian immigration was encouraged after World War I due to the heavy losses the country sustained. So, in 1924 the Muslim population reached 120,000. After World War II, in 1950, it reached 240,000. The greatest immigration came after independence was granted to the colonies, in 1962. The figure has reached almost three million. Yet Muslims of France are not well rooted. About two million are of North African origin, the other third from Black Africa, Iran, and the Arab world. Only about 650,000 have French citizenship. Those of French ethnic origin number around 75,000. They are not well organized and are concentrated in Paris, Marseilles, and Lyons. They occupy mostly menial jobs and are suffering today from strong anti-Islamic sentiments (rooted in the legacy of the Crusades) instigated by rightest parties led lately by Le Pen.

Until 1968 one could detect no organization among Muslims, who were content to practice their Islam in private, although a mosque was built in Paris in 1930, but was not under Muslim control. As they became rooted in the country, Muslims have undertaken to build mosques and Qurʾānic schools. Only the Jāmiʿ Mosque of Paris can accommodate a Muslim Community Center, the rest (some four hundred and fifty) being mostly makeshift. Until recently there was no national overseeing organization and no schools for Muslim children and for training *imāms*. Only the indigenous French Muslims had the proper organizations to serve their needs. French authorities discriminate against them and do not accord them the treatment received by other religious groups. Yet in spite of such hostile attitude towards Islam, the religion has managed to gain over one hundred thousand converts from Catholic Christianity, including the famous ocean explorer, the late Jacques Cousteau.

In the United Kingdom, the growth of the Muslim community parallels the French experience: immigrants derived from former colonies. The earliest such immigrants came from Aden (Yemen) who established themselves in Cardiff where they built a mosque in 1870. They were followed at the end of the century by immigrants from India, who settled close to London. They built the Shah Jehan Mosque at Woking. In the early half of this century Muslims arrived from Cyprus, Egypt, and Iraq. At the outbreak of World War II they numbered altogether some 50,000.

After the war, and by 1950, their numbers had doubled. New peaks were achieved in the 1960s with heavy influx from India, Pakistan, and Bangladesh. The British government clamped down in the 1970s and the flow slowed to a trickle. In 1982 the Muslims of Britain numbered 1,250,000 and today 1,500,000. In 1982 about 700,000 had acquired British citizenship. Only several thousand are of British or West Indies origin; the majority are of the Ḥanafi rite; the rest are Shāfiʿi, Jaʿfaris, or Ismāʿilis. They enjoy a better status than in France or Germany. Among them can be found professionals, physicians, engineers, small business proprietors, and white collar workers. The majority, however, are factory workers or small business employees.

About 40 percent of all Muslims live in the greater London area. Their numbers are increasing due to higher birth rates but their political influence remains limited. About one hundred local organizations are in the London region, fifty in Lancashire, forty in Yorkshire, and thirty in the Midlands. There are three in Scotland, two in Wales, and one in Belfast.

British Muslims are organizing on an increasing scale. The Union of Muslim Organizations was formed in 1970 to oversee some two hundred Muslim organizations. Its efficacy has been restricted by the low level of inter-institutional relationships. The Islamic Foundation of Leicester (established in 1968) specializes in publishing Islamic literature in English. The Muslim Womens' Association (organized in 1962) caters to their own needs and problems. The Muslim Educational Trust (1966) dedicates its efforts to the education of Muslim children. It has won permission from the British government to teach Islam to Muslim children in public schools. Since there is no separation of state and church in Britain, the recognized religions receive support, but not Islam, since it is not recognized, which has proven to be a handicap; marriages by rabbis and priests are recognized, but not by an *imām*. Other discriminatory acts are manifest, especially on the racial level, a shared condition of Muslims in the West European countries.[43]

Germany was not historically a major colonial power, hence it had no former colonial Muslims to contend with as had France and Britain. Historically, Prussia and the Ottoman Empire had friendly ties and were linked in World War I. After the war, many prisoners freed by the French preferred to settle in Germany, mostly in Berlin. Immigrants from Iran and Afghanistan expanded this nucleus of Muslim settlers. There were scarcely more than a few thousand Muslims before the Second World War. In 1951 they were about 20,000. Only after 1966 did their numbers increase rapidly with the influx of guest workers from Muslim countries, predominantly from Turkey. In 1971 the number reached 1,150,000, of which 900,000 were Turks. Today Turkish Muslims alone account for over two million. Those from Yugoslavia and Albania were second highest with 150,000 in 1971 and rising, due to the influx of refugees from Bosnia, to half a million. Children of Muslims born in Germany are entitled to the rights of German citizenship and full integration in German society.

Muslims of Germany belong mostly to the Ḥanafi rite, relatively fewer to the Shāfiʿi or Māliki, and some around Hamburg to the Jaʿfari. Geographically they are spread all over the country, with the highest concentrations in Westphalia and Bayern. There are some 50,000 Muslim students from foreign countries attending German universities at any one time.

The bulk of Muslims are blue-collar workers; several thousand are professionals. Some have their own enterprises. They are hard working, law abiding, and productive. Turkish Muslims in Germany have contributed some five billion marks to the German social security system, receiving only three billion in service from it.

The aroused anger of the German public over increased taxes and higher cost of living coupled with rising unemployment in the key industrial sectors has provided fuel for the rightest neo-Nazi movement that has chosen to target not just these illegal refugees, but the Turkish Muslims as well, as evinced in the fire bombing of Turkish Muslim families. Politically, they enjoy no influence and can only rely on the good will of the authorities and the verbal sympathy of the government in times of such crises.

Organizational efforts have intensified in recent years. There were no local Islamic organizations before World War I. The first mosque, at Schwatzingen near Stuttgart, built by a German nobleman in the eighteenth century was reconverted in 1977 from a museum to a place of worship. The mosque built at Potsdam in 1720 was rebuilt in 1926 and acquired by the Qādiyānis after World War II. Impressive mosques were built subsequently in key German cities. There are some six hundred mosques altogether, the bulk being makeshift. Cologne has forty-two catering to more than a hundred thousand Muslims. There are about forty-five Qur'ānic schools and only one full-time Muslim primary school. There are no regional organizations. The large Islamic center has been managed by a closed organization without defined territorial jurisdiction.

While the rights of Muslims are respected, they are not recognized in Germany as a religious community because most of them are foreigners. This is bound to change as the community becomes more rooted in German soil and German converts increase.

CHAPTER 14

Islam in Transition

THE FORTUNES OF Islam vacillate from one part of the world to another. Under Communist rule, Islam demonstrated remarkable resilience for survival and growth. In Southeast Asia its development hinged on survival, integration, and growth potential. In Africa and America it is a story of dynamic growth and expansion. In the Indo-Pakistani subcontinent and along its fringes, Islam is largely in the state of flux seeking to lay the foundations of the state or, as in India, to counter adversity. In Turkey and Iraq, Islam is poised to play a greater role as an integral force in state and society.

India

Taken together, the Muslim population of the Indian subcontinent would constitute the largest group in the world. In India they number over eighty five out of a population of some eight hundred million. Pakistan and Bangladesh enhance the numbers by close to another two hundred million

Islam came to the subcontinent in 711 with the Arab conquest of Sind province (Pakistan). Traders quickly followed, establishing colonies as far south as Kerala. In the eleventh century parts of northern India were added to the Muslim Ghaznawid state based in today's Afghanistan. The Muslim Ghurids inherited the Ghaznawid state in India: Punjab, Uttar Pradesh, and later, Bihar, Bengal, and Assam. In 1206 the Turkish commander Aybak became independent, thus creating the first Muslim state of India, with the capital at Lahore. When the capital was moved to Delhi, the Delhi Sultanate was created, lasting until the Muslim Moghuls, led by the Emperor Humayun conquered it in 1555. The brilliant Moghul Empire ruled over the whole of the subcontinent until displaced by the British in 1858.

When under assault from outsiders—Portuguese, French, and British—if Muslim rulers were unable to defend the state, it was the Muslim citizenry who took up the task. In the 1820s the Mujahidin fighters were organized under Sayyid Ahmad Shahīd to expel the British intruders. The Sepoy uprising of 1857–1858 and the siege of Lucknow culminated in failure, and for the next half century Indian Muslims could only brood and decry the anti-Islamic policies of the British Raj.

In 1906 the Muslim League was established for the purpose of protecting Muslim rights and countering Hindu domination abetted by the British, who could control such a vast land only by implementing a policy of divide and rule. But Hindus and Muslims struck a common cause and cooperated in the Indian Congress to oust the British. In the 1930s the poet Iqbāl proposed the establishment of a Muslim state, but the Muslims of India did not favor the idea at that time. Mahatma Gandhi led with pacific non-resistance means the well-publicized mass demonstrations to gain independence. But underlying his efforts was the Hindu aspiration for national independence "despite his sincere personal commitment to harmonious inter-community relations."[1]

Fear of potential Hindu domination and revenge induced the Muslims to seek their own state. Ali Jinnah and Jawaharlal Nehru could not agree on the nature of a unitary state and Gandhi could not reconcile the nationalist aims of both. In 1946 Hindu extremists launched a chain of violence against Muslims inflicting great losses in life and property. Partition appeared the only solution and Lord Louis Mountbatten, the last British viceroy of India, transferred power to Jinnah on August 14, 1947 as the first president of the newly created Pakistan (Land of the Pure, i.e. Muslims).

Massive emigrations ensued, most coming from areas in the Ganges valley where Muslims were in a minority. Kashmir, a Muslim majority entity passed under India's control, albeit fierce outbreaks characterized the transfer by its Hindu governor and the Muslims of Kashmir have not ceased their resistance to Hindu dominance since then. Other bloody outbreaks took place also between Muslims and Hindus in Punjab and Bengal, which only accelerated emigration to Pakistan and what became later Bangladesh.

Many of the cultivated Muslim elite chose not to emigrate. Those who did under pressure of persecution reduced considerably the size of Muslim entities. Punjab and Bengal were partitioned even though the majority were Muslim. With its twenty million Muslims, Hyderabad in the Deccan chose to be independent as per the guidelines provided by Mountbatten, but India invaded and incorporated it in 1948. Jammu and Kashmir were also incorporated against the will of their inhabitants.

In 1941 Muslims still constituted 24 percent of the inhabitants of the subcontinent. After partition they were reduced to 9 percent; today they are about 12 percent of India and their percentage is still growing in spite of adverse conditions. They are a heterogeneous lot, marked historically by the stamp of invaders, whether Arabs from the west, Turkic tribesmen from Central Asia, or Afghan and Persians in subsequent centuries from the northwest. Yet the majority derived from the soil of India itself—natives who converted over the centuries in order to escape the Brahmanical caste system that made of them untouchables in the Hindu social hierarchy.

Today the Ganges valley is still the home of some forty million Muslims, or 52 percent of the lot (1981 census figures). In the former Princely State of Jammu and Kahsmir, 64.2 percent of the population is Muslim. In some areas of Kashmir they are between 90 and 95 percent of the inhabitants. In the north their cultural languages are Urdu and Bengali; in the south, Tamil. The southern Muslims derived largely from South Arabian stock and their center of influence is the state of Kerala. Despite minor cultural differences, Indian Muslims have maintained a strong sense of community and attachment to Islam. This was manifested early in this century when every adverse situation affecting the Western world of Islam existed, due to colonial encroachments. Indian Muslim leaders expressed outrage against France and Britain for subjugating Muslim North Africa and sympathy with their fellow Muslims of the Ottoman Empire whose sultan caliph they considered their spiritual leader.

Islamic legacy in India is evident today in the great monuments built by Delhi and Moghul sultans in Delhi and Agra and elsewhere. Local notables spoke Urdu up until independence. Under the British Raj an intense competition developed between Hindu and Muslim civil servants due to the British favoring the Hindus in the bureaucracy. Following independence, Muslim administrators, engineers, and entrepreneurs left en masse for Pakistan, creating a vacuum in the areas they left behind.

The majority of Muslims (72 percent) live in rural areas and pursue primarily farming. In the cities, a good many engage in handicrafts. They are artisans, craftsmen, and menials. Their involvement in trade and commerce is at a lower level; very few occupy leading positions in industry and business in the economic sector. When India was first created, its president, Abu 'l-Qalam Āzād was Muslim, as was the minister of education and a number of justices. Muslims occupied a good many seats in the newly constituted parliament. Their great centers of learning in Hyderabad and Aligarh, seat of the Indian Islamic reform movement, attracted scholars from around the Muslim world. Today, they still maintain an edge in sports and cultural activities but the majority of Muslims remain segregated in all walks of life.

Regarding the sectarian affiliation of Muslims in India, about 90 percent are Hanafis, with about four million Shāfiʿi in the south. Shīʿites of the Jaʿfari rite are concentrated in the northwestern states, mostly in Lucknow of Uttar Pradesh. There are also Ismāʿīlis of the Bohra branch, mostly in Bombay and the Gujerat area. They all get along well today in spite of localized intrasectarian feuds in the past.

By and large, Indian Islam is neither well understood nor allowed to play a positive role in Islamic affairs outside the subcontinent owing to the feud with Pakistan which, as an independent entity, is seen as more integral to the Western world of Islam. India managed to counter this by espousing issues, such as Palestine, to gain favor with Arab Muslims states confronting this problem. The other reason for Indian Islam's lack of attention is fragmentation. India is replete with minority situations and problems due to protection under the country's constitution.[2]

In India, as in other countries discussed, Muslims have organized and broadened the base of activities, as exemplified in the Rābitat al-ʿĀlam al-Islāmi (World Muslim Congress), and the Organization of the Islamic Conference. At present the Jamaat-e-Islami and the Tablighi Jamaat, both centered in Delhi, are active movements; one is attempting to cement ties with the principal Muslim communities; the Tabligh seeks to enhance worship by concentrating mainly on the spiritual welfare of Muslims. They have received aid from other Muslim countries, like Qadhdhāfi's Libya and Ayatollah Khomeini's Iran, especially following intensification of clashes between Hindu and Muslim groups. Both are caught up at present in extremist activities, best expressed lately in the destruction of the historic mosque, Babri Masjid, by Hindu fanatics that led to widespread bloodshed and devastation in the reaction of Muslims that ensued.

Violent episodes have increased the awareness and concern of Muslims outside India over the lot of their co-religionists. They are paying increasingly more attention to such movements and events inside India, especially as Indian Muslims become more visible. They perform the *ḥajj* in numbers exceeding 25,000 annually.

Basic Islamic education is received in the *makātib* and *madāris*, primary and secondary schools. Jamaat-e-Islami has prepared sixty textbooks in various subjects for use in these schools. But these cover only a quarter of their needs. The situation is somewhat remedied by publications under the auspices of Islamic councils on the local state level. India has one of the largest collection of mosques and mausoleums, some on the world heritage list (like the Taj Mahal at Agra), more than any other Islamic country, reflecting the illustrious heritage of Islam in India over the centuries. Indeed, the revival of Islamic texts in Arabic was conducted early in this century by such publishers as the Osmania University Press at Hyderabad, Deccan.

Urdu is the first Muslim tongue in India, as it is in Pakistan. Arabic and Persian have left strong influences on both the script and language. It is the mother tongue of some 65 percent of all Indian Muslims, the others being Bengali, Gujerati, Kashmiri, Tamil, and Malayalam.

Modern Indian nationalism and the emergence of the fanatic aspect of Hindu fundamentalism has tended to galvanize and sharpen differences with Muslims. This has been manifest in the intercommunal riots since 1971 that have only intensified in the last year or so with Hindu extremists seeking to sublimate Islam and its culture. Existing in separate communities, they are bound only by the pan-Islamic organizations within India. This has exposed them to greater persecution by Hindu majorities. The dichotomy of *Dār al-Islām* versus the *Dār al-Ḥarb* (abode of peace versus abode of war) seems to have taken on a special character inside India. Muslim minorities continue to fear assimilation, especially since they have been reluctant to emigrate following their disillusionment with the breakup of Pakistan into separate Pakistani and Bangladeshi republics. They fear also the possible sublimation of *Sharīʿah* personal laws in face of demands by Hindu extremists for one civil code for the whole country.[3] They are not encouraged by the current political system that seems to exclude them from playing any effective role in government.

Following independence in 1947, the governments, both federal and state, have embarked on deliberate policies to deny the Islamic character to institutions that have played key roles historically in enhancing Indian life and civilization, symbolized not only in the great architectural monuments, but in the cultural life generally—from music to dress to cuisine. Islamic education received a blow at both the lower and higher levels with efforts to secularize its curricula or to force Muslims to enroll in Hinduized institutions where the religious beliefs and mythology of the Hindus are freely introduced in textbooks. The aim is to indoctrinate Muslim youth with the religion of the majority.[4]

Bias is experienced also by Muslim entrepreneurs who are not able to obtain loans or permits as freely as their Hindu counterparts. Whenever they achieve visible prosperity, their properties are looted and destroyed in communal riots. Remittances from Indian Muslim workers in the rich Gulf states have increased the comfortable life of local Muslims in acquiring property, educating youth, renovating mosques, and operating Muslim institutions.

Socially, Muslims are better off as a community since egalitarianism marks all aspects of their intercommunal relations, something absent in the Hindu caste system. Their women enjoy more rights than Hindu women and more Muslim girls avail themselves of educational opportunities. Hindus counter by claiming Islam subjugates women and by treating Muslims lower than their lowest caste. When Bohras and Qādiyāni Ahmadi communities came under attack at one time or another, both received strong support from the Muslim *umma* albeit neither sect is considered more than a fringe operation of Islam. Any interference by the secular state was interpreted as endangering the "neutrality" vis-à-vis minority religious groups enjoined by post-Independence ruling governments.

The more Islamic groups came under attack, the greater the effort to unite them, an undertaking currently by the All-India Majlis-e-Mashwarat (Consultative Council). The first all-India Muslim convention was held in Aligarh in 1953. The Jabalpur riots of 1961 led to the disparate Islamic organization to create the Consultative Council to speak for all of them. Muslims of India are moving toward greater cohesiveness and organization in order to strengthen themselves in such areas as education and welfare in anticipation of playing a role commensurate with their numbers and achievements in India's political life.

Pakistan

When Pakistan was established as a country wherein Muslims were to enjoy their faith without being impeded, its founder, Ali Jinnah, was thinking of a land for Muslims, not a Muslim state. This has remained the country's problem ever since—how to reconcile modern Western style institutions with the *Sharīʿah* of

Islam. For two decades provisions of the *Sharīʿah* were restricted to providing prescriptions for the acceptable personal life of citizens. Series of coups and counter coups from Suhrawardi's rule up to 1957 constituted largely a play for power by various groups, secularists and non-secularists.

Islam came into play only when the Jamāʿati Islam of Mawlāna Mawdūdi broke with the Muslim League's modernist elitist approach to state organization and insisted on keeping the Indian Islamic *umma* together. He was against a nationalist entity because, to him, it was un-Islamic, which explains why he opposed the idea of a Pakistan independent of India. When the state was nevertheless created, he worked toward molding Pakistan in the Islamic image.[5]

Mawdūdi was the intellectual product of the reformist Salafi movement of Egypt. He strove to reverse the secularist trend and to achieve greater Islamization. His perception of Islam is the standard one of the reformed traditionalists, namely that the Qurʾān can be interpreted only against a background of Muslim ideology, that Western philosophy has no place in it, and that no synthesis could be effected because religion is the soul and the guiding spirit behind it. Islam, as he rightly put it, is more than a religion; it is, rather, a complete code of life: a political system, an economic system, and a practical religion because it is complete. Guided by such perceptions, Mawlāna Mawdūdi insisted that to translate these into practice required the entire program of life and not merely a fragment of it.[6]

The policy of accelerating the Islamization of institutions has characterized the politics of Pakistan since 1977. In Pakistan today, as in neighboring Afghanistan and Iran, Islam has emerged as the force to reconcile. Indeed, in 1998 the decision was at last taken to make the Islamic Sharīʿah the recourse of all legislation in Pakistan.

Secularism had been proposed by Jinnah as an option for reconciling Hindus and Muslims, the latter constituting 86 percent of the new state. Mawdūdi's option lost out and he was imprisoned in 1948. The principal traditionalists and neo-fundamentalist leaders were also imprisoned in 1953 for stirring up riots. In

October, 1954, Iskandar Mirza, then Home Secretary, proclaimed that religion and "politics could and should be separated."[7]

In the 1956 Constitution, however, Pakistan was declared an "Islamic Republic." Ayyub Khan, who was in charge in 1962, failed to drop "Islamic" from the name. A secular state in line with Ataturk's Turkey failed to gain support. Islamic and modernist groups were now taking the initiative. But neither the ulema nor the Society of Ulema made any specific proposals for an alternative ideology other than to demand a constitution in tune with the *Sharīʿah*. The ulema would have guided the state as their counterparts later in Iran managed to achieve. Another project by the Jamāʿat-i-Islāmi, whose membership derived largely from the urban lower class, was resisted by Muslim secularists.

The 1973 Constitution reaffirmed the right of Muslims to live in accordance with stipulations of the *Sharīʿah*, permitted religious instruction for Muslims and the right to develop their religious institutions and to promote the Islamic code of conduct. No law of the land could contradict the Qurʾān or *Sunnah*. A ministry of religious affairs proposed by Mawdūdi was rejected. The ulema could not serve as the body to ensure that laws enacted comported with provisions of the *Sharīʿah*. Failing to gain a place for themselves in the state organs, the religious groups transformed themselves into political parties. The modernists were the main beneficiaries of the constitutional debate. The Islamic tradition was not taken as a system of law having precedence but rather as a set of general principles. Emphasis was placed on the right of citizens in a modern state rather than on the Muslim community at large.[8] It did, however, restrict polygamy and protect women's rights.

The religious parties did not give up. They managed to press the government enough to keep up the Islamic debate. In 1963 Ayyub Khan was compelled to announce constitutional amendments to strengthen the state's Islamic nature. In 1974 Prime Minister Bhutto declared the Ahmadīyah a non-Muslim entity, followed by legislation banning drinking alcohol and gambling. In 1977 he was pressured into promising to make the *Sharīʿah* the law of the land. Martial law was declared and Bhutto was arrested in July, 1977.

General Zia-ul-Haq, the martial law administrator, who was shortly to become president, had been supported by the religious parties, and he promised more concessions. He declared that the *Sharīʿah* had supremacy over the law of the land. Ordinances were enacted to recognize *Sharīʿah* jurisdiction over some matters of criminal law, punishment for fornication, theft, and the consumption of intoxicants; canon law concerning *zakāh* and *ʿushr* were reinstated, as were measures to curb usury and establish interest-free banking. Institutions were created to promote Islamization, a High Court and Supreme Court structure to abrogate laws adjudged un-Islamic. All this was in line with what Mawdūdi had demanded thirty years earlier. In the summer of 1980 a Majlisi Shūra (Consultative Council) was created to supervise the implementation of the *Sharīʿah.*

With the election of Benazir Bhutto and her replacement with Nawaz Sharif, the role of Islam was not diminished. It remains an insoluble part of the land to which it provided the excuse for its coming into being in the first place. Islam's legitimization derives from a series of compromises between a modernist elite and various religious groups. Islam provided the ideology for its establishment, but the ulema, its custodians, are still not in control.

Myanmar (Burma)

Islam entered Myanmar (Burma) by a number of routes. Arab Muslim traders settled on the Arakan coast in the first century of Islam. In later centuries, Islam spread due to the efforts of Indian and Malay traders. Then came refugees from Yunnan (China), who settled during the nineteenth century in the northern parts of the country.

Sultan Nāsir al-Dīn Maḥmūd Shah (1442–1459) of Muslim Bengal helped King Sulaymān Naramithla establish a Muslim state in Arakan with the capital at Myohaung. It extended as far south as Moulmein during the rule of Sultan Salīm Shah Razagri (1593–1612). Buddhist Burma conquered the Muslim state in 1784. The British wrested it from them between 1824 and 1826. With independence, Arakan was incorporated within Myanmar.

In 1969 Arakan had a population of 1,847,000. By 1982 there were about 2.6 million, of whom about 1,460,000 were Muslims (56 percent of the total). Another 2.1 million lived in other parts of Burma, bringing the total to over 3,600,000, or 10 percent of the total inhabitants of the country today.[9] Burmese Muslims insist their numbers are double the official figures given out by the government. Twenty percent of Tennasserim Division is said to be Muslim. They are a majority in a number of cities outside the Arakan region, the most significant being Moulmein.

Muslims of Burma are of two ethnic origins: Indo-Pakistani (concentrated mainly in large cities) and indigenous Burmese. They worship in more than five thousand mosques; in the large cities can be found several mosques of ancient vintage. Qur'āns exist in the Burmese language, but not much in Islamic literature. Before 1962 about five hundred performed the pilgrimage annually. There are enough Muslim schools to handle about 60 percent of young Muslims. Islam, however, is not taught in public schools. There are many university graduates but they do not occupy a commensurate number of positions in the government, armed forces, or the professions.

Before the military took over in 1962 and socialized the country, Muslims were well integrated with their fellow countrymen. They occupied top positions in the army and government; they had four ministers at one time or another and two judges in the High Court. While the majority of Muslims were farmers, many others were rich traders. They had established a free Muslim hospital as early as the 1930s and a Muslim Central Fund Trust. Their Muslim organizations today include the Jamiat Ulema-e-Islam, the All-Burmese Muslim Organization, and the Islamic Religious Affairs Council.

The brunt of persecution was felt by the Arakanese who were subject to four major expulsions since 1942. A wave of hatred followed in the wake of British departure that year and Muslims were massacred on a large scale. Two hundred thousand fled to neighboring Bangladesh, Pakistan, and Saudi Arabia. Pogroms ensued in the wake of failed attempts by Arakan Muslims to establish their own republic before the Japanese arrived, and again in 1958, 1962 and 1974. In "Operation Dragon King" the military government in 1978 denied Rohingya Muslims national identity cards, offering them instead the status of "foreigners." An orgy of Muslim killings in May, 1978, led to the death of thousands and the forcible fleeing of 16,000 into neighboring Bangladesh. Altogether, 71,000 were evicted that year. By August, 1978, 313,000 had become refugees; most of them were eventually repatriated under pressure of Muslim countries and aroused world indignation. But home again meant they had to face deprivation, misery, and inhuman treatment. Pressure continued and in the early 1980s thousands more from other parts of Burma were forced to emigrate to Thailand and Bangladesh.

The 1980s represented a dark episode for Burmese generally and Muslims particularly, especially when the military staged their coups and took control of the reins of government. The community was persecuted, Muslim businesses nationalized, their lands seized, their schools de-Islamized, and forbidden to perform the *hajj*. Their ties with the outside world were further reduced. They could not publish Qur'āns without permission of the government nor obtain permits to import them. The oppressive rule of the military regime has abated somewhat in the face of international indignation, but the Muslims still endure handicaps out of proportion to the rest of the citizens.

Sri Lanka

Islam reached Sri Lanka in the seventh century, again with Arab traders from south Arabia. Well received from the start by the ruler, they established a trading community that continued to thrive. With the fall of the ʿAbbāsid caliphate of Baghdad in 1258, many Muslims emigrated to Sri Lanka and ties with Muslims of South India were strengthened.

From South Arabia they received the Shāfiʿi rite and from South India their language, Tamil. By the sixteenth century they were concentrated along the southwest coast with their principal centers located at Colombo, Beruwala, and Galle.[10]

When the Portuguese landed in Colombo in 1502, they proceeded to break the political power of the Muslims and to destroy their prosperity, following this up with terror and expulsion. Most were expelled by 1526, and the rest by 1626. They scattered to the islands of Kandy and Sitawaka. Others relocated in the interior towns and along the northern (Purralam) and eastern coasts (Kalmunai) to engage largely in agricultural pursuits. Men joined the Sinhalese army to combat the Portuguese. Others prospered in the Sinhalese Kandyan Kingdom as traders under the tolerance of its ruler.

The Dutch replaced the Portuguese in 1658 but continued their policies of suppression against the Muslims, expelling them from Galle and Matara (in 1659) and Colombo (in 1670). They were not allowed to buy land and were reduced to the status of indentured labor. It was not until the British rescinded these rules in 1832 that the Muslims could enjoy reprieve.

When the Dutch took over Indonesia, Javanese refugees, prisoners, soldiers, exiles, and others were brought to what was then Ceylon, where they eventually formed their own Malay community. Shortly before the British conquest in 1796, the Dutch introduced Islamic personal laws, which the British retained. They treated the Muslims reasonably well during their period of colonial rule. By 1937 they had promulgated a system of "domestic relations" courts, presided over by Muslim *qāḍis*, and organized the *awqāf* under the aegis of Muslim overseers.

In 1901 there were 248,000 Muslims. In 1972 Ceylon became the Republic of Sri Lanka, and the Muslim population numbered approximately 1,168,000, having grown to over 20 percent of the total population of the country. They are concentrated in four areas, with the highest being in the agricultural east coast. Almost all Malays live in Colombo.

Sri Lanka has about 2000 mosques, with 63 in Colombo alone. Large mosques are governed by boards of trustees and some 1500 mosques are administered by a Waqf Board headed by a commissioner appointed by the government. Qurʾān is taught in all mosques, but Islamic literature texts are in short supply with restrictions limiting their import. Muslim personal laws remain in force and a few hundred Sri Lankan Muslims manage to perform the *hajj* every year.

There are no independent Muslim schools; like all others, they have been nationalized. The Ministry of Education does have a Muslim School section that oversees 200 primary and secondary schools. Besides the official curriculum, these schools teach also Arabic and Islamic subjects. The Zahir College, established in Colombo in 1892, is still operating as an independent institution with both primary and secondary schools and some 2000 male students only. The government sponsors a Muslim Ladies' College and a Training College for teachers in the Eastern Province with over 500 students.

There are six *imām* schools, five for boys and one for girls, located in Amparai District, Galle, Colombo, Puttalam, and Kandy. Muslims constitute less than 4 percent of Sri Lanka university students. Indeed, they graduate the lowest percentage of students (under 100 a year) in Sri Lanka. At present, Muslims are poorer than the rest of the population. About 90 percent are farmers and laborers, 9 percent traders, and 1 percent government employees.[11]

There is usually one Muslim minister or two in the government. The mayor of Colombo has traditionally been Muslim. Muslims also have had 21 representatives out of the 151 constituencies in the country, which is double their national percentage. They are completely integrated and loyal to the state. Occasional outbreaks against them notwithstanding, Muslims have been generally well treated.

They have a number of important organizations: the Muslim League, the Ceylon Moors League, the Islamic Socialist Front, the Jamaat-e-Islami, the All-Ceylon Council of Ulema, the Muslim Youth League, the All-Ceylon Muslim Educational Conference, and the University Muslim Majlis. There is, however, no overall supervisory structure.[12]

Afghanistan

In Afghanistan we have the example *par excellence*, not merely of resilience but of resistance to forces hostile to Islamic entities, best exemplified in the ultimate triumph of the Afghan resistance against the Soviet-sponsored leadership in the country. Not only did they roll back the forces of materialist communism, but in the tragic aftermath there was still hope that an Islamic entity would emerge once the feuding Muslim rival parties settled their differences. Today, Islam is the determining force in reordering the government and state and in providing the guiding principles for both. The Islamist movement began in 1960 to counter the attractiveness of Communism to students and the increasingly secular direction of the state.[13]

The majority of Afghan Muslims adhere to the Sunni rite. Afghan Shīʿah belong to the Jaʿfari rite. There is a small Ismāʿīli minority and a few thousand Hindus and Sikhs, as well as a few hundred Jews. The idea of nation-state is a recent one in Afghan political thinking. Historically, it is the immediate community, tribal or agrarian, not the so called "state," that has commanded the allegiance of the Afghans. Religion provides the peasant's life with its intellectual base, values, and codes of behavior. It does not provide a common social base because tribal and agrarian affiliations are determining factors in the Islam observed by each.

This diversity accounts for the different forms of religious expression. There is the intellectual, the head of a Ṣūfi brotherhood, the *ʿālim*, the *sayyid* (descendant of the Prophet), and the village mullah, each with his own perception in projecting an image of Islam. There are differences among Ṣūfi brotherhoods themselves. As one authority put it, "in Afghanistan it would be very difficult to identify an 'official' Islam as opposed to an unorthodox Islam."[14]

Traditionally the tribal structure has been the base of Afghan commitment and resistance to unpopular government at the center. In not providing a single system of norms, ulema as leaders of Islam could not override the exigencies of the popular form of the faith where *ʿādāt* are more important than *qānūn* (law promoted by the state). Representatives of the faith exist independent of the tribal structure, which means they are not empowered to exercise any determinative influence over it.

Geographically, Afghanistan is at the crossroads between India, Iran, and Central Asia. Most currents leading to rebellion in eastern Afghanistan came from neighboring India. Afghans played a role historically in the Moghul dynasties of India, and Persian, the language of Afghans, figured prominently in the court of Delhi. Religious reform movements in India and Afghanistan had a common aim: return to the *Sharī'ah* and the Qur'ān. Increasing emphasis on *ijtihād* as the vehicle for reconciling puritanical Islam with the modern world is a byproduct of Indian reformist modernist trends. The majority of Afghan thinkers and reformers, from the Mujaddidis to Shah Waliyullah to Mawdūdi to the recent Afghan resistance, view the idea of the secular state as alien to Islam and should be resisted in the same manner in which the British had been resisted. The powerful Naqshbandi mystical orders and leaders resisted reformism early in the nineteenth century, abetted by their religious, military, and political influence. In the present, as in the past, resistance, whether to the British or to the Soviets, could not occur without tribal leadership. This explains why there has always been a connection between tribal structure and religious movement. Charismatic leadership carried over from tribal role models.

The *umma* concept is of paramount interest to Afghans, a theme that is accentuated in times of unrest by ulema and mullahs. Not until the beginning of this century did pan-Islam emerge as a political doctrine, and largely to combat the domination of European colonialism over Muslim lands. The first to think in pan-Islamic terms were Afghan rulers seeking to consolidate the nascent state. The history of modern Afghanistan reflects a number of occasions when ulema and rulers would cooperate and other times when the ulema aligned themselves against the policy of the state for making pacts with infidels.

The pan-Islamic trend was most pronounced in the period from the Balkan war of 1911 to the end of the Ottoman caliphate in 1924. During this time the call to defend the Muslim world came from the Indian Muslims and was taken up by the Afghan ulema as well as the modernist movement of young Afghans who were influenced by Mahmūd Tarzi, a disciple of al-Afghāni. The caliphal movement, founded in India in 1919 by brothers Muḥammad 'Ali and Shawkat 'Ali with Abu' l-Qalam Āzād, also a Naqshbandi, at its head, sought to gain recognition for the Ottoman caliph as head of all Muslims. They preached *hijra* for those who wanted to escape foreign domination. The movement ended with the abolition of the Ottoman caliphate, leaving scores of Muslim expatriates in its trail.

The various revivalist movements in this part of the world came to naught for a number of reasons: (1) too much attachment to Ṣūfism, which held less appeal to the young as to their elders; (2) lack of political organization among them, and (3) the necessity to reconcile themselves with modernist movements. "The Islamist movement was born in the modernized sectors of society, and developed from a political critique of the popular movements which preceded it."[15]

The Islamist movement of Afghanistan owes much of its impetus to the Muslim Brethren of Egypt. Its leaders were largely independent of the ulema, although they shared many aims in common, such as how to recast Afghan society in a modernist Islamic mold. Some of these leaders had graduated from the Azhar University in Cairo (dubbed "professors") and became active in the resistance movement led by Rabbani, Niyazi, and Tawana. The movement was called Jamʿiyyati Islami (Islamic Society). They introduced works by Sayyid Qutb and Mawdūdi in translation. Some members maintained contacts with the Brethren movement before and after it had been circumscribed by Nasser of Egypt.

Students, or Taliban (seminarians), inspired by the "professors" took to demonstrations between 1965 and 1972, causing much turmoil on the campus at Kabul. The Muslim Youth group was to become the most militant of the movement Shabnāme-yi Jihād (holy war tract). They demonstrated against Zionism, American policies in Vietnam, and the privileged classes. They opposed the king, his cousin Daoud, Pashtun nationalism, and foreign influence in Afghanistan, whether from the USSR or USA. The student youth movement was hostile to mullahs and ulema because of their conservatism. The ulema of the three eastern provinces were literalists, radical anti-traditionalists, and anti-British imperialists.

The Taliban established a council (*shūra*) to coordinate activities of their movement. They drew up a constitution in 1972 and elected a leader (*amīr*), first Gholam Niyazi and later Rabbani, a deputy (Sayyaf), a secretary (Gulbeddin Hekmatyar) who also supervised the military wing, and a person in charge of cultural affairs (Tawana); ulema and peasants were also represented. Gulbeddin was the only survivor of the *Shūra* after 1975. Student movement leaders sought to displace the ulema in their preaching of religion and politics in mosques throughout the country. The ulema were comparatively few and pro-government, indeed those of Kabul were paid by the government. They sought to introduce reforms by rationalizing sanctions of the religion, i.e., ablution as a hygienic, not merely ceremonial act.

In Kabul the Muslim Youth (dubbed *ikhwān* by their enemies) were aggressive and in the forefront of demonstrations. The young Shīʿite (*Qizilbash* in particular) were politicized by such religious leaders as Wa'ez in Kabul and Muhseni in Kandahar, setting up their own secret Islamist organizations apart from the Sunnis.

The coup, led by Muḥammad Daoud, on July 17, 1973, with support from secularists and Communists was opposed to Islamist ideology. Its success led to the arrest of militant Islamists. Niyazi and Rabbani failed to persuade Daoud to break with the Communists. Islamists divided into two factions: Jamʿiyati Islami and Hizbi Islami. The younger members wanted immediate uprising; the others wanted to win control of the army first and lay the ground for a counter-revolution. The radicals, led by Hekmatyar, won out. Pakistan's army trained them when they regrouped at Peshawar. Disturbed by the nationalist aim of the Pashtun movement, Bhutto sought through the Islamists to counter Daoud. But in the sporadic fighting that erupted against government forces in the next five years, the rebels lost. Hundreds disappeared or were killed and dozens of ulema were summarily executed. Professor Niyazi was murdered in prison, as was Mawlawi Fayzani. Two hundred militants including Nasratyar were executed in June 1979.[16]

The Khalq (People's), a self-styled Marxist Party, came to power in April 1978, and sought quickly to monopolize power by subordinating all forces to a one party, their, rule. Hafizullah Amin, a dominant figure of the new regime, sought to establish a one-class society and friendship with the Soviets. Islam would be respected only if it did not interfere with the instruments of rule. Nur Muḥammad Taraki, the other strong man of the regime, warned against mixing politics and religion. "We respect our mullahs," he declared, "but they should not dabble in politics."[17]

Angered Islamist factions soon closed ranks and galvanized under two leaders. The moderate and Persian-speaking elements followed the leadership of Gulbuddin Hekmatyar, while the radicals gravitated to Borhanuddin Rabbani.[18] Ṣūfi brotherhoods in the West and the Persian-speaking Islamists, largely ethnic Tajiks, were pro-Rabbani; the radical students, especially the Pashtun, pro-Hekmatyar. The latter's faction anathematized its opponents, thus giving the Islamic revolution the pride of place in resisting communism and the Soviets in a way reminiscent of Iran's revolution, while Rabbani sought to conciliate Muslim factions of whatever political coloring. The split hastened the repression visited upon both by Daoud and opened the way for the Communist takeover, which ousted Daoud before long.

Following the Soviet invasion to shore up the sagging fortunes of their ruling puppet, Islamic resistance factions united in a common cause to undo the invasion and unseat the Marxist government. In ten years of sustained effort, with financial and material support from Saudis, the Gulf states, Iran, and military aid from the United States, they succeeded at last in ousting both in 1991.

That, however, did not end the struggle. A coalition agreed on Hekmatyar to head the government of what is construed today as an Islamic state, but factional rivals, or Saudi-backed versus Iranian-backed Islamic factions, have carried on a devastating battle, punctured by periodical cease-fires, to dictate not only which brand of Islam to promote, but also the sharing of power in the structure of the proposed government. In the meantime Kabul, the capital, was virtually laid to waste through aimless rocket bombardment by those who had been party to its being saved from Communist control.

Another issue central to the factional rivalry and fighting is the question whether the Shīʿite Iranian revolutionary brand of Islam or the Sunni Wahhābi Saudi version of it will serve as the determiner of the state's Islamic nature. A complicating factor is the fact that Afghani Islamism resembles neither because it was the Ṣūfi Naqshbandi role that first gave rise to the resistance movements. Wahhābism has been the mortal enemy of Ṣūfism from the days of its inception in Arabia.

The Taliban forces have succeeded in overrunning all but the northwest corner of Afghanistan, the center of the Shīʿite faction. After repeated military attempts to win the rest, the Taliban in 1999 agreed to a formula for a coalition of Muslim factions, including the Shīʿite, to govern the country. But a few days later they were fighting again in the Ghorband Valley, north of Kabul, and the U.N. was attempting to mediate a cease fire and adherence to the agreement both sides had concluded in March of 1999.

Shīʿah and Sunni in Iraq

The Gulf War of 1991 focused world attention on the sectarian composition of Iraq, with special attention being devoted to the alleged mistreatment of Shīʿah and Kurds, whom President George Bush called on to rise against his country's enemy, Saddam Hussein. When they were suppressed, he used this as a pretext for further military moves against Baghdad. This policy has been continued more intensely by the Clinton administration.

The Kurds, like Saddam's followers, are Sunni Muslim: indeed, Saddam fancied himself a latter-day countercrusader like Saladdin who, nine centuries earlier, had come from the same town, Takrit. Ethnically, however, the Kurds constitute a disparate and separate entity than their Arab compatriots in Iraq. So, in assessing the confusing demographic and sectarian picture in Iraq, one must have recourse to the realities of Iraqi politics—domestic, regional, and international—as the key factors, not the religious differences.

The Shīʿah are the majority and are located mostly in the south where the holiest shrines of Shīʿism, Iranian and Iraqi, are located, at Najaf and Kerbala. It is here that the exiled Ayatollah Khomeini spent nearly fifteen years preaching, teaching, and preparing for an Islamic displacement of the secularist rule of the unpopular Shah and his hated American supporters who were blamed, among other things, for creating the dreaded state-run terrorist machine known as SAVAK (counter intelligence cum security organ of the regime).

Nearly eleven out of twenty million, or 51 percent of Iraqis are Shīʿah, 20 percent Sunni Kurd in the north, some 6 percent are Nestorian and Jacobite Christian, and approximately 24 percent are Sunnis. When Khomeini gained power in neighboring Iran, he started implementing his plans for a world-wide Islamic revolution, beginning where it logically made sense, in next-door Iraq, with its Shīʿah majority and the hated infidelic regime of President Saddam Hussein as head of the Baʿth socialist nationalist pan-Arab party, which stressed secular institutions and the separation of religion and state.

The consequences are well known—an eight-year war launched by Iraq and fought by the Ayatollah as a *jihād* against the "infidel" Saddam with immense damage to both countries. Iraq emerged relatively intact while Iran endured greater hardships. In the subsequent war following the invasion and annexation of Kuwait (whose independence the Iraqis never recognized since they saw it as an arbitrary creation of British colonialism in the early 1920s to keep Iraq from having easy access to the waterways of the Persian Gulf), the Shīʿah of Iraq saw an opportunity to implement what one of their ayatollahs called for when first appointed head of the future Islamic republic of Iraq, namely creating their own separate Islamic republic with encouragement from Iran.

The Islamic political opposition in Iraq, up to and after the Persian Gulf War has been attributed to the continuation of the policy of exporting the Iranian brand of Islamic separatism and revolution. Ayatollah Khomeini was blamed for campaigning to turn the Shīʿah of Iraq against the Sunni-dominated government, and for giving the war that ensued a religious coloring, indeed a holy war against "the 'atheists,' 'pagans,' and 'followers' of the Omayyads."[19]

While sectarianism plays its role in the mistrust between Shīʿah and Sunnis in Iraq, the majority of Iraqi Islamic activists have been Shīʿah. The pious continue to labor for the modernization and creation of a governing institution loyal to the teachings and spirit of Islam. The founder and leader of the movement is Sayyid Muḥammad Baqir al-Sadr. What he sought primarily was a government by the pious, not a Shīʿite one. He expected leaders to call to the good and to protest against evil as expressed in the Qurʾān.[20]

Iraqi Islamists were tolerated because they were considered a part of a larger Islamic movement that had been growing since the end of World War II, and because its leaders had not been militant. Acts of sabotage were attributed to Iran's agents and were quickly shut off. Only those Shīʿite leaders who called for establishing an Islamic republic of Iraq in the southern districts (where their numbers are strong) found themselves quickly out of the country. The bulk of the Shīʿah have made concessions to Sunni beliefs with the aim of promoting sectarian cooperation, especially during the war. What they seek is a government that takes cognizance of their numbers, loyalty to the state, and willingness to be a greater part of the governing apparatus.

The ulema had resisted a declining status and continued to insist on their moral obligation to ensure that government actions meet Islamic requirements. They received a great boost on the eve of the Gulf War when Saddam Hussein appealed to Muslims throughout the world to support his efforts "against a coalition of infidels and shameful collaborators who sold their principles for dollars." He did indeed muster broad support from the ulema and Islamic factions, especially in Arab North Africa, Yemen, and Jordan, while his detractors could count only on local support—ulema in Syria and Saudi Arabia—to counter his moves. And on the eve of the launching of the war, the secular banner of Iraq was embroidered with the Islamic battle cry "God is Great" in order to rally more Islamic sentiment. Being an observing Muslim, like most of his Sunni followers, Saddam's demonstration of loyalty to the faith was accelerated by the war. Since the end of the war, Islam's role in society and politics has received greater emphasis, and that is in a state once conceived as secular, socialist, democratic, and pan-Arab nationalist in character.

Reassertion of Islam in Turkey

Modern Turkey was resurrected from the ashes of the Ottoman Empire after World War I with a leadership guided by secular, liberal, and modernist principles. Mustafa Kemal, the founder of modern Turkey, made a radical break with the past in an attempt to block out the rich heritage of the Ottoman Islamic Empire in the belief that his new state would find a niche among European powers. Thus, Turkey, with a Muslim population today of over 90 percent (55 million total) found itself suddenly isolated from the Islamic world and branded a renegade state by Muslim purists. Abolishing the caliphate, placing restrictions on the observances of the faith, introducing secular marriage procedures, and neglecting Islamic places of devotion and worship all served to reinforce a deliberate policy of downplaying religion in the life of the state when under the Ottoman, the last Islamic empire, it was central. As one authority put it, Turkey had become a state "legitimized primarily on non-religious, social and political grounds."[21]

The Ottoman state had started westernizing in the second half of the nineteenth century to the resentment of the Muslim heartland, the Arab provinces, of the empire. Coupled with the encroachments of the West on Ottoman Muslim territories in North Africa and the Levant, the policy was blamed for weakening instead of strengthening the caliphal role as defender of Islamic interests. After independence, Kemalists were chided for abolishing the caliphate, symbol (however nominal) of Islamic spiritual unity; for suppressing religious education; outlawing the brotherhoods; closing down their establishments and mausoleums; rejecting the Arabic script in which the Qur'ān was first expressed for a Latin version, and substituting Western for Islamic attire. "The expeditious secularization imposed on the country by Mustafa Kemal and his entourage created a shock wave through the country which has not yet died out."[22]

The religious problem remained alive during the subsequent period with the majority of Turks now resenting the delegitimization of Islam in their public life. In 1950 the Democratic Party gained power by campaigning on the platform of making amends, which they did, and Islam once again became visible in Turkish life. The teaching of Islam in primary schools became practically compulsory. Religious establishments began to flourish once more: new mosques were constructed, old ones refurbished, and the muezzin's voice rang out in clear, properly intoned Arabic in the call to prayer. The movement to restore and reinforce Islam gained momentum. Sufi orders like the Nakshbandis and Tijanis assumed leadership in the "re-Islamization" of Turkey.

The Democrats under Prime Minister Menderes were not about to allow secular principles to be totally undermined. Menderes ordered mass arrests, targeting at first the Tijani order. Kemal Pilavoğlu, their leader, was sentenced to ten years at hard labor. Necip Fazil, poet and editor-in-chief of *Büyük Doğu* (Great East), a leading Islamic periodical, was likewise incarcerated. In July, 1953, the Democrats passed a bill to "protect the freedom of conscience," but clearly aimed at suppressing Muslim extremists. Such measures were designed to use Islamic education to diffuse republican reform principles and did not prove convincing as increased desertions from the Democratic Party proved. A further blow was dealt by the electorate during the following elections. Leaders of the party found it prudent henceforth to play up to Islamic loyalties and allow the ulema and other religious leaders a freer hand.

It is important to note at this point that creating a "Yeni Turk" (new Turk) to serve the secular state did not have much appeal outside the main urban centers. The overwhelming majority of Turks, being rural, adhered all along to the Islamic way of life. Even the Republican Party endeavored after the 1965 legislative elections to play down their anti-clerical past by first championing religious freedom, then proclaiming publicly the relevance of Islam for Turkish society. Such moves merely reflected the impact of rising Islamic sentiment in the country.

In January 1970 Islamists founded under Necmettin Erbakan the National Order Party, later renamed the National Salvation Party, to promote Islamic rather than Eastern or Western interests. Erbakan criticized Kemalist reforms and demanded that Turks return to ancestral traditions. He blamed many "forces of evil" working against Turkey: "Zionism, Freemasonry, and Papists," whom he accused of seeking to lure Turkey falsely into the Western camp. Only Islam, he argued, could shield the country from succumbing to unhealthy Western values. He called for rapprochement with the Islamic world by, among other measures, instituting a "Common Market for Muslim Countries," in which Turkey would play a leading role by virtue of its technological advantage.

In the coalition government formed after 1974 with Erbakan's party gaining 48 seats in parliament, and he playing a role in it, Islamic education expanded: 143 schools for training *imāms* and other religious leaders with 36,000 students and 1,564 teachers in 1973 to 320 such schools, 111,741 students, and a teaching staff of 3,852 in 1977. A vast program of revising textbooks to support the fundamentalist Islamic tendency was launched by the Ministry of Education. The revised texts in history and literature extolled the notion of Islamic fraternity, gloried in the Ottoman Islamic Empire, and emphasized the importance of religious life and the relevance of Islam to current Turkish civilization and culture. Scholars began to relearn Ottoman, the Arabic script, the abolition of which had cut them off from a rich past, and to launch a scholarly production reflecting pride in Ottoman Islamic legacy.

From the late 1970s on, Kemalist secularism came under severe pressure; Ṣūfi brotherhoods were firmly established, religious schools continued to expand, and thousands of new mosques were sprouting up everywhere. Numerous pro-traditional Islam groups were attacking Republican reforms and demanding the re-Islamization of Turkish institutions.[23] Nearly all political parties were speaking positively of Islam and its role.

The coup of 1980, led by Kenaan Evren, represented a step back and one for reaffirming secularism. Erbakan was arrested, Islamist groups became secretive, and civil servants obliged to display less Islamic symbols in public (no scarf over the head for women, no thin beard along the jaw-line for men). But this was to prove a momentary halt at best.

When Özal replaced Evren the pendulum began to swing more firmly in the Islamic direction, especially since he began to lay the grounds for Turkish economic prosperity in the framework of cooperation with Muslim states, especially the rich Arabian ones whose leaders went to Turkey to invest and enjoy the amenities of its natural endowments. He also undertook to cultivate solid ties with the newly freed Turkic Islamic countries of former Soviet Central Asia. The Organization of Islamic Conferences even made the former Yildiz Palace of Sultan Abdülhamit the headquarters for its worldwide cultural activities.

The success experienced by Islamists after the mid-1980s has enabled the Islamist elite to relate better to their secularist counterparts and not to interact as polar opposites, in the interest (for the time being) of presenting Turkey as a country where the two ideologies can co-exist within "the institutional framework of a pluralist democracy and/or civil society."[24] The current debate is to lend force to such a perception of modern Turkey during what appears to be another stage of transition. The question remains, however, whether the back-to-Islam trend will prove feasible when the secular constitution of Turkey has empowered the military to safeguard the Kemalist secularist reforms.

The military exercised their power once again to oust Erbakan from the premiership and abolish his party, only to see it reconstituted in the 1999 national elections as the Virtue (Fazilet) Party. Until then the Islamists had constituted the largest group in the 550-seat assemly, with 144 deputies and another 90 from other dissenting parties. Ecevit and his minority Virtue Party barely survived in the April 18, 1999 elections, but it remains to be seen whether he will obtain adequate support to constitute a new government.

The Ṣūfi orders are still at the backbone of the Islamist movement in Turkey. They have a large recruitment base, a centralized organization, and funds to support their programs. They are not prepared to participate in a discourse over abstract notions of "pluralist democracy" when they have a clear notion of how their society should be redefined. Nor can much credibility be attached to the term "pluralistic" when the Kurdish rebellion movement is fighting to gain equal acceptance. Islamists operate on the premise that their venerable Islamic traditions had received a momentary jolt under enforced Kemalism and can be reestablished in the future. They have much encouragement and support from Islamic activist groups everywhere. Political scientists can posit all the arguments and rationale for justifying a pluralist society based on cooperating ideologies, which, in principle are diametrically opposed to each other. However, that will not alter the course that Islamists have outlined for Turkish society in steering back to the Islamic way, with which the bulk of Turks, mostly of the Eski (Old) variety are more comfortable.

This trend is visible everywhere—in the prudent display of attire in public, in the attendance to overflow in mosques, to observing the requirements of the Islamic faith with increasing vigor, and with the disaffection over the international politics of their government. In the Persian Gulf War against Saddam Hussein, the government allied itself with the United States-led coalition to bring down Saddam in the face of great disapproval from a large segment of the population. Radical groups resorted to violence against the government's avowed policy that hid behind the claim they were abiding by United Nations resolutions. No mention was made publicly of the large monetary rewards (from the United States, Saudi Arabia, and Kuwait) that induced some government leaders to endorse such a stance.

Catering to the West when Turks are being killed in Germany, abused and treated with contempt in other parts of Europe for adhering to their Islamic ways, and the fact that until today Europe has refused to grant its request to become an integral member of its Common Market, has only served to reinforce Islamist convictions that Turkey belongs not to Europe but to the Muslim world.

Indeed the triumph of the nationalists in the 1999 elections portends a trend away from integration with Europe and toward a greater identification with the Turkic republics of Central Asia who share a common Islamic faith and aspirations for the future.

Turkey's undertaking to contain the violent movements, such as the Kurdish separatist, and accusations of violation of human rights have provided additional fodder to a Europe once mindful of Turco-Islamic dominance in its own backyard, to keep the Turks at bay. Such humiliating treatment has laid the groundwork for creating a new atmosphere and a back-to-fellow Muslims movement. It is bound to strengthen the Islamic alternative, it being the one most likely to revive the identity that once gave the Islamic state, in the heyday of Ottoman achievements, its place in the sun.

"Islamization" of Sudan's Politics

Sudan is an example of a state that had vacillated in the past between activist Islam with the Mahdi and his Khalīfah in the late nineteenth century to secular socialism in the mid-twentieth. Today it seems to have embarked solidly on an Islamic course bordering on the extreme and militant. The chief architect of this new course is the brilliant ideologue and basically moderate Islamist, Ḥasan al-Turābi.[25]

While the Islamic movement elsewhere tended to bypass the democratic process, its main concern in Sudan, until a decade and a half ago, was how to undo dictatorships, including Numeiri's. Numeiri set the present course of Islam in Sudan with support from Turābi, head of the Muslim Brethren of Sudan, when on September 8, 1983, he declared Sudan an Islamic republic and officially proclaimed the *Sharīʿah* the law of the land. His focus was on law and the judiciary. He "used Islam to be on top of the Islamic movement at home and to direct the course of revivalism" and legitimate his own role at a time when Iran had just turned Islamic, Sadat was assassinated by Muslim extremists and the like.[26]

The 1965 charter stressed democracy and individual liberty as basic values. The Ikhwān of Sudan were an offshoot of their Egyptian counterpart, and from 1977 onward were behind Numeiri's policy of Islamizing the non-Muslim south. Islamic issues and perspectives were in the forefront of Sudanese politics in the 1980s. The parties based on Ṣūfi orders like the Khatmīya constituted a powerful rival of the Ikhwān for influence. ʿUthmān al-Mirghāni, its leader, sought to check the further erosion of Ṣūfi political influence by cooperating with the heads of other orders to create a committee for common action: the Islamic Revival Committee.

Not willing to share power with any rival, Numeiri undertook a policy of containment against them. He executed Mahmūd Tāha, leader of the Republican Brothers, "for apostasy" in January 1985, when an assortment of Muslim groups—the Ansār, Muslim Brotherhood, and local Ṣūfi leaders—branded Tāha's religious teachings and interpretation of Islam as heresy. He cracked down on the Muslim Brethren (Ikhwān) in March 1985, accusing them of exploiting religion to undermine national unity and seeking to create another Iran-style republic.

With the fall of Numeiri's dictatorship, a coalition of parties led by the Khatmīya sought to project the Umma Party as pluralist and centrist. Ḥasan al-Turābi had already forged his own alliance under the guise of the Islamic National Front and became the principal opposition leader. As concerns Turābi's own ideas, one might label them as reformed and modernized traditionalism. Islamic renewal (*tajdīd*) to him requires a radical rethinking of Islam's needs in present-day terms. *Fiqh*, the classical vehicle for evolving law can be applied to reevaluate freely the *Sharīʿah*. *Fiqh*, he argued, "was pushed by circumstances to neglect two basic principles of Islamic jurisprudence—the role of the state and the role of the public in the formulation of Islamic law."[27]

The new *fiqh* should concentrate on social rather than individual issues "which may mean that a whole new beginning must be made to build a new legal edifice on the foundation principles of Islam."[28] He emphasized the role the public, not the ulema alone, should play in this process of renewal. In his view, all that affects the status of the Islamic community should be subject to discussion. The Prophet's prototype of a model state may be an ideal standard but not in the forms of religious expression it has taken; a new model may need to be constructed on the basis of this ideal.

Like other advocates of renewal, Turābi stressed the need to revert to the pure teachings of the faith. He advocated no one approach or methodology to bring about *tajdīd* other than to state that it should be based on *tawhīd*, which "demands that the artificial barriers dividing law and morality should be pulled down." He argued furthermore for a balance between elitism and the full and free participation of the masses in the promotion of religion, a balance between reason and revelation, and between faithfulness to the Islamic heritage and the creative expression of religion.[29] For him, renewal is a continuous and ongoing exercise.

The course of politics in Sudan in the last ten years suggests a radical move towards activist Islam. Several Islamic extremist organizations operate freely out of Khartoum. They are anti-U.S., anti-Israel, militant, and prepared to engage in acts of violence to make a statement. Islamic Jihād for the Liberation of Palestine calls for a holy war against Israel and resistance to its ally, the United States, because, as one spokesman put it, "the Islamic world is very angry." A leader of Hamas, the militant Islamic group based in the Gaza strip, asserts the right to combat the "Zionist colonization in Palestine." Working out of Sudan is logical since advocates of such resistance insist that "the question of Palestine concerns not only the Palestinians; it concerns all Muslims." Sudanese leaders have shown nothing but contempt for secular regimes in Egypt, Saudi Arabia, Kuwait, Algeria, and Tunisia, which "they perceive as selling out the interest of their own citizens to serve distant masters in the West."[30]

Hasan al-Turābi, who was educated in France, denied that Sudan is a sponsor of violence (re the five men arrested bearing Sudanese passports who were implicated in the 1992 World Trade Center bombing in New York). His retort was "America wants to target somebody with its shotgun, as a cowboy, and Islam itself is very popular to target." The targeting of Islam as the next enemy, now that communism is out of the line of fire, is a growing theme among Muslims, even those in Saudi Arabia.[31]

There are sympathetic Islamic fundamentalist groups outside Sudan that have channeled millions of dollars to the National Islamic Front. Mujāhidīn fighters of Afghanistan made Sudan a transit place when their own governments in Egypt, Tunisia, and Algeria denied them entry on account of their violent opposition to governments in place and the strong militant Islamic movements they support. Much of this has been going on since General Umar Hasan Ahmad Bashīr assumed the reins of government in Sudan. Khartoum has provided a refuge for other groups like Hezbollah, the Lebanon-based militant group combatting

Israeli occupation of south Lebanon with assistance from Iran.

Sudan is accused of facilitating the travel of extremists by issuing diplomatic passports to their leaders, like Rashīd Ghannūshi, leader of the outlawed Al-Nahda Islamic movement of Tunisia, and Shaykh ʿUmar ʿAbd al-Raḥmān, who had abetted U.S. policy interests by recruiting mujāhidīn fighters for Afghanistan, and who was convicted on rather inconclusive evidence of authorizing the bombing of the World Trade Center and endorsing plans to blow up the United Nations building in New York. Mubārak, upset by Shaykh Umar's stance against his rule, urged the U.S. to extradite him, while Turābi voiced the possible Islamic reaction when he stated that Shaykh Umar's incarceration "will spark a world-wide reaction, a 'revival of Islam.'"

The rise of such militant activities in Egypt is blamed by Mubārak on both Iran and Sudan and on Shaykh Umar's strong following inside Egypt. The Afghan Islamic Mujāhidīn had been forced out of their base in Pakistan because of U.S. pressures, which backfired when these militants (from Egypt, Tunisia, Libya, Algeria, Morocco, Afghanistan, Pakistan, and Iran) found their way not only into Sudan but the United States as well. They are hardened Islamists who have vowed to continue the Islamic struggle against unpopular governments in their countries of origin, as well as against Western nations working against Islamic interests. They have access to financial support, especially from Iran and from the Saudi multimillionaire Usama bin Laden, whom the U.S. considers as number one enemy for championing worldwide Islamic resistance to U.S. anti-Arab and anti-Islamic policies.

Swing of the Pendulum in Algeria

There is a marked tendency today for the swing of the pendulum from left to right, from secular socialism to Islamic communalism, as evident in the current trend in Turkey. We have also noted in the case of Iraq how pressures leading up to the Gulf War of 1991 and the need to have the support of the broader Islamic community led to a greater emphasis on Islamic solidarity and the employment of Islamic battle slogans to arouse a predominantly Muslim population to action. The eruption of violent responses in Egypt to an unpopular regime on the part of Islamic groups reflects another surge of Islamic sentiment.

The most dramatic example of the pendulum's swing is Algeria, a country that when it had gained its independence from France in a pool of blood, chose secular socialism to chart its future course and relied on the Soviet Union for assistance and development. Ahmed Ben Bella, a hero of the Algerian revolution, later put under arrest for fifteen years then exiled by his successors, emerged from exile in Switzerland to lead in the resurgence of Islamic demands for change.

One hundred and thirty years of French colonial rule, coupled with political absorption of the country and followed by three decades of secularizing dictatorial regimes, did not succeed in preventing the resurgence of Islam. One important reason is the persistent Islamic dominance in Algerian rural and tribal society. Resistance to French rule from the outstart was based on the Islamic identity. Indeed, the main organ of publication from the late nineteenth century to the present was the newspaper *Islam*, which called upon the French to respect the peoples' Islamic identity and rights. Algerians had refused to give up Islamic personal law governing individuals and the family to acquire French citizenship.

The beginnings of Islamic organization can be traced to 1931 when Hamid Ben Badis established the Ulema Association. He, like contemporaries Ṭāhir Ben ʿĀshūr of Tunisia and ʿAllāl al-Fāsi in Morocco introduced the ideas of the Egyptian *Salafīyah* movement.[32] The slogan "Algeria is our fatherland; Arabic is our language; Islam is our religion" did not sit well with the French. Nor did the Islam of the ulema, grounded in Māliki rite traditions, which was both urbanized and urbanizing, sit well with folk Islam as represented by the Marabouts and grounded in Ṣūfi practices.

After independence, the ulema movement led in the restoration and application of authentic Islam as the means for eliminating vestiges of colonial rule. The association al-Qiyam (Values) published *Muslim Humanism*, a review for expressing its ethical and religious program. When Boumedienne became president, he dissolved the association (September 22, 1966). Its adherents had sought to enforce a strict Islamic moral code for the whole of Algeria. Obligations of the faith were more closely observed and mosques were being filled to capacity after 1976 by the young, who were seeking an option for fulfillment in the Islamic lifestyle.

The modernist secularist Boumedienne envisioned a different structure for Algeria, so he kept Islamic movements well under control, limiting extremists and preventing open demonstrations. He also sought to deflect the impact by making some superficial concessions, but without noticeable success.

In 1985 hundreds of underground Islamic movement members were tried and incarcerated. The government's firm stand against Islamic groups proved it was willing to exercise the political will to contain them at any price. The government had the support of women groups and the army, as well as the socialist modernist hierarchy, who were all determined to keep the *Sharīʿah* at bay. Popular Islamic pressures, however, did not recede, and President Chadli Benjedid, Boumedienne's successor, finally was compelled to make concessions by permitting the ulema in government pay to speak up openly.

This did not, however, quiet the public, which was frustrated over deteriorating economic conditions and the lack of fulfillment under successive socialist regimes governing Algeria until today. Conditions have worsened and the better social and economic life promised by socialism is not projected for the near future; hence the call for an Islamic solution. Erstwhile die-hard socialists like Ben Bella now see in Islam that energizing force and they deprecate a leadership that sees solutions primarily in terms of Western models and values "conceived according to a rationalist philosophy which is fundamentally alien to us (Muslims)."[33] They call for a policy of scientific and technological development best suited for promoting the well-being of Islamic societies. Islamists insist on an education that reinforces Islamic identity and does not induce the youth to leave for Europe (France) in search of a better life. They also call for turning away from ideologies that "belittle our faith."

Spokesmen for an Algerian Islamic state preach a renewal

based on Islam to combat the festering problems of unemployment, lack of economic well-being, and social inequalities stemming from vestiges of colonial rule. All call for a return to the principle of the *shūra* and to the ways of the *Sharī'ah* to provide the blueprint for a new, more responsive system of government. But, as the facts in the last two years have demonstrated, there is no willingness on the part of the present government to permit any deviation from current policies. When Muslim groups sought to avail themselves of the democratic process and the ballot in the 1992 elections to bring about a change of government, the results that would have given them control of parliament and government were set aside. Western observers and writers tacitly endorsed violation of the democratic procedures they hold sacred for themselves, but not for others if they do not turn out favorable to Western interests. Such is the perception of Neo-Orientalist writers, who are unmindful of how Muslims, already skeptical of Western notions of democracy, might become all the more convinced that only a democracy grounded in Islamic teachings is best suited for their societies.

With the government blatantly setting aside the results of an election heavily favoring Islamist groups, and with the West finding justification for their action, the path to violent action was laid out. Bullets have now substituted for ballots, here as in Egypt. Government officials, ministers, the military, and police are presently under attack; many have been killed; a former leader was assassinated by militant Muslim groups, and violence against government officials has spread to the countryside. Thousands have been arrested and confined to prison camps. Scores of the Islamic Salvation Front's adherents were executed for their militant rising against a government that has denied them the fruits of victory gained by democratic procedures in 1992. But with martyrdom awaiting those battling unpopular infidelic governments, violence is not likely to be curbed in the immediate future. There is now evidence that the present leadership is willing to reach accommodation with Islamists. The results are not yet clear. Indeed, prospects of a long-range solution were dimmed during the April 1999 general elections when six candidates withdrew from the race in protest of the military favoring Bouteflika, an early fighter for Algerian independence, who now gained the presidency unopposed. It remains to be seen whether he will integrate Islamists in his government.

Islamist Gains in Tunisia

In both Tunisia and Morocco the consequences of the Islamic revolution in Iran are still to be felt. For a while, under Bourguiba, Muslim modernists believed they could have a Western-style democracy by integrating Islamic principles in government operations within a secular democratic structure. Bourguiba undertook to "reform" Islamic institutions by pursuing a program of gradualism and consulting with liberal Zaytūna ulema. *Habus (waqf)* were taken over by the government, who now sought to provide the services intended by them: social services, schools, and public works. *Sharīʿah* courts were abolished in 1956 and replaced by state-sponsored courts. The Islamic system of education was incorporated into the state system and the Zaytūna, Tunisia's equivalent of the Azhar, reduced to the Faculty of Theology of the University of Tunis. Codes were introduced that changed personal status.

The dominant themes in the discourse of the following two decades were progress, modernization, and development. But again, there were more promises than vehicles for delivery. One quarter of the young (averaging twenty-five years of age) found themselves with no futures, as jobs were almost nonexistent for them. Bread riots erupted when the International Monetary Fund mindlessly insisted that Tunisia eliminate subsidies of basic foodstuffs as a condition for rescheduling its loans. Trade unions were up in arms. Mzali's government accomplished little from 1980 to 1986 and was dismissed. The Islamist publication *al-Maʿrifah* was banned in 1979 following criticism of Saudi Arabia with respect to the Grand Mosque episode in Mecca. A number of Islamists were arrested the following year after the Gafsa incident.

It was a desperate disillusioned body of educated youth finding themselves helplessly without opportunities for development and economic betterment, unable even to sustain the basics of life, which enabled the growth of the Islamic Tendency as an alternative to failed government efforts. This is not novel for Tunisia since the role of Islam in the country's political life is partly rooted in inherited traditions and partly in the active role it played in seeking liberation from France by providing the cultural, moral, and ideological symbols needed to formulate resistance.[34] The Ḥarakat al-Ittijāh al-Islāmi (Islamic Tendency Movement) only gathered momentum thereafter, especially when Bourguiba's successor, Zine el-Abedine Ali, relaxed somewhat the stringent laws of his predecessor and freed rather than execute leaders of the Tendency who had been accused of inciting to rebellion as agents of Iran.

Islamic Tendency is a movement of the educated youth living mostly in the cities. Averaging between twenty-five and thirty years in age, they resemble their counterparts in Egypt. "Class affiliation is not as important for the rise of Muslim "integralists" as an incongruity between high aspirations and the decrease in economic and political opportunities.[35]

The movement was led by Rashīd Ghannūshi (before his exile) and ʿAbd al-Fattāh Muru. Ghannūshi, like Ḥasan al-Banna, founder of the Ikhwān of Egypt, started his career as a school teacher who attracted students from the secondary through university level. His movement gained a nationwide reputation when it received recognition as a national political party in 1981. When they resorted to acts of violence to enforce the fast of Ramaḍān and following their attack on the bar in a Club Med, the government cracked down in 1981, arrested seventy-six leading militants, and sentenced them to prison. The movement was banned from participating in elections and leaders imprisoned, but they were released in 1984. Ghannūshi's book *Westernization and the Inevitable Dictatorship*, calls not for an Islamic state but for democracy and political pluralism. Arabic journals dedicated to the theme of reform and implementation of Islamic observances or the return to pure Islam had been allowed to be published in the early 1980s.

The Islamic integralist ideology of the movement calls for activism. Not damning the new "Jāhiliyāh" but working for re-Islamization of the community, it is a new *daʿwah* calling for implementation of Qurʾān and *Sharīʿah*. Their ideology resembles that of the Ikhwān of Egypt and reflects the intellectual inspiration of Mawdūdi and Sayyid Qutb, executed ideologue of the Muslim Brethren. They have forged alliances with others, like the Islamic Progressive Movement, but have not succeeded in infiltrating key organizations, like the military, that would have ensured them some success at attempting an Islamic revolution as in Iran. Indeed, they have been accused by the recent government of being in collusion with Iran, which provided the pretext for a general suppression and Ghannūshi's last ditch attempt in his al-Nahḍa (the Rising) to gain ascendancy. He was fortunate that the death sentence passed upon him in a desperate attempt to curb the tendency among the youth was not carried out.

CHAPTER 15

Current Trends

MANIFEST TRENDS in the Muslim world today reveal proof of an increasingly militant attitude on the part of elements and factions determined to assert the primacy of Islamic fundamentals in every area of state and communal life. Governments are called upon to make the *Sharīʿah* the law of the land, to conduct policy in the light of Islamic interests, and to apply Islam in day-to-day life. In Saudi Arabia, the *Sharīʿah* is the only law of the land; in Libya and Pakistan, it is becoming more and more the exclusive source of basic legislation; in Egypt, militant Muslim elements dissatisfied with the regime's liberal policies are pressuring successfully for making the *Sharīʿah* the source of exclusive legislation, and laws are being rewritten to conform with the provisions of Islam's constitution.

Islamic militancy has taken on a violent coloring in a number of areas in the Islamic world. The war of secession in the Philippines, conducted unremittingly for four decades by determined Muslim factions on Mindanao compelled the regimes, first of Marcos and then of Aquino, to negotiate with them (not without pressure from Libya and Saudi Arabia upon whom the islands depend increasingly for direct and indirect economic aid). When, in the name of Marxism, the Khalq Party of Afghanistan undertook certain policies defying Islamic teachings, religious interests, social orientation, and bearing a distinct irreligious marking, the rebellion that ensued forced a direct military intervention by the Soviet Union which engendered a continuous resistance until victory in the name of Islam was achieved. Even in South Africa, a quarter of a million "Cape Muslims" battled often in head-on clashes with the former apartheid regime in order to assert their Islamism in the face of discrimination from both whites and "coloured" Christians.

This brand of militancy can be characterized as a struggle between minority Islamic factions and dominant non-Islamic systems. It may not accurately reflect the intense internal struggles (within such predominantly Muslim states as Turkey, Tunisia, Syria, and Iraq) led by those who favor the reassertion of the rule of Islam in the face of strong secularist counter trends. Nor does it show the extent to which rulers in Muslim lands are prepared to use Islam as a tool for mustering popular Muslim support to enforce policies that may not always comport with Islam's best interest exemplified once by Numeiri's Sudan, Hasan II's Morocco, and Zia ul-Haq's Pakistan). In each of these countries the commitment to Islam as an ideology capable of countering that of left-leaning secularists is stronger than to an Islam calling for the realization of the social justice inherent to it. Skeptics see in superficial appeals in the name of Islam a misuse of religion; and the pious (in such countries as Egypt), while not disapproving, look with askance upon the aims of the established leadership.

What this might portend is illustrated dramatically in the events leading to the end of monarchic rule in Islamic Iran in what has been described as a genuinely spontaneous popular upheaval against a classical example of despotic rule, instigated by the highest ranking "cleric" of Shīʿah Islam, and by the assassination of Sadat in Egypt.

The Challenge of the Islamic Revolution in Iran

The establishment of the Islamic republic guided by a defined Islamic constitution in Iran may or may not set the pattern for other Muslim countries dissatisfied with their respective political orders. That the ulema should take the initiative in fostering such radical changes is not unprecedented. There were a number of instances in the recent history of Iran when the ulema there directly challenged temporal authority. But never had it taken the form given it by Ayatollah Khomeini.

While some believe that this might exacerbate differences between Sunni and Shīʿite ulema, many others believe that this could, in fact, open a new avenue for bridging differences. They share, for example, attitudes towards social injustice, the impact of Zionism and Western material influences on the Muslim world, and the need to strengthen Islamic traditional values to counter such negative influences. Khomeini's followers described their revolution as an *Islamic*, not *Shīʿite* revolution. The Ayatollah even sanctioned the leadership of a Sunni over Shīʿites in prayer as proof of sectarian harmony.

One of the Sunni ulemas' main concern is the role of their Shīʿite counterparts in the government of Iran's Islamic state. They feel the Iranian political system sanctioned by Khomeini and maintained by his successors involves the *fuqahāʾ* directly in government when they would prefer that the government's accountability should be to the people with the *fuqahāʾ* serving mainly to ensure that enactments do not contradict the provisions of the *Sharīʿah*.

Turmoil and violence accompanied the launching of the new republic in 1979, followed by war with Iraq. In the factional struggles which ensued one could detect four foci of political power: (1) the presidency, which under Bani Sadr's brief tenure sought to appeal to the intelligentsia, and rejected the concept of the *vilāyat-e faqīh* (rule by Islamic legalists); (2) the Majlis (assembly), dominated by the Islamic Party and basing its power on appeal to ulema and bazaar elements and favoring the *vilāyat-e faqīh*; (3) street elements reflecting the sentiments of students, the unemployed, and partisans of the revolution, and (4) *Imām* Khomeini, articulator and symbol of the Islamic state who did not identify himself with any of the above groupings.

The storming of the American embassy and subsequent holding of Americans hostage for 444 days enabled the Ayatollah to hold a referendum endorsing the establishment of an Islamic republic, which quickly was implemented with the *Sharīʿah* as the constitution. This, in spite of the fact that most Iranian leaders wanted the revolution to resolve all secondary issues and evolve a post-revolutionary consensus in order to build its political system, which they hoped would serve as a model for Muslims everywhere.[1]

As concerns the potential international repercussion of the Islamic revolution in Iran, extremists believe it could have a negative impact for Western interests as long as these are tied more closely to those whom Muslims regard as their enemies. The world has become more mindful of Islam's role as a political movement. Trust in dictatorial regimes by such powers is expected to diminish, particularly as the Muslim masses demand more of a voice in decisions affecting their well-being.

The lesson of Iran is not lost upon other Muslim countries, which have had a dramatic illustration of how masses might be mobilized in societies that fail to allow for institutionalized change. Action through mass mobilization lends added importance to the sociopolitical role of Islam because, "in the Muslim world, Islam is the only key to the hearts and minds of the people, albeit the impact of material amenities brought on by modern technological achievements cannot be ruled out as a concomitant of faith."[2]

For this example to be emulated successfully, discontented Muslim masses in other countries must count on the leadership of a charismatic personality matching the Ayatollah's in appeal. He personified the activism that Muslims who are unhappy with their political and social lots are prepared to espouse. He labored for justice anchored not in man-made but in divinely ordained law: the *Sharīʿah*; it alone being permanent; it alone conforming to the will of God; and it alone capable of providing necessary legislation governing all facets of the Muslim's commitments to God and fellow man, embracing what we term both temporal and spiritual matters. This is interpreted to extend to international relations as well.

Some scholars attach less importance to any potential concrete impact from Khomeini's example than to its "role as spark and lightning rod for Muslim passion."[3] National and international repercussions resulted from the mosque takeover in Mecca by religious zealots trained in the religion faculties in Mecca and Medina and in intensified Muslim activism in countries ranging from Libya to the Philippines aimed at asserting the primacy of Islamic values in their respective societies. Violence spearheaded by militant Iranian pilgrims during the Ḥājj resulted in over 400 casualties in Mecca.

Khomeini's success in Iran has inspired would-be emulators as exemplified in the Muslim Youth Movement of Malaysia and in the emboldenment of Shīʿite elements throughout the Gulf states seeking to assert the fundamentalism preached by the Ayatollah. Islamic elements in Egypt have taken to the path of violence against their government and non-Muslim Christian minorities, including foreign tourists, whom they had tolerated in the past. Leaders who have identified more with the West than with what is conceived to be Islamic interests have come under fire in Egypt (exemplified in the assassination of President Sadat), Sudan, Senegal, and elsewhere. Secular regimes leaning towards socialism have likewise experienced the pressures of Muslim activists. Hitherto, Tunis was looked upon by Westerners as a model of modern secular liberal progressivism, but recently many young Tunisians have been flocking to centers wherein a greater appreciation of traditional Islamic values can be learned.

The impact of Turkish activists, pressing their country to come to terms with Islam, can be measured by the fact that Turkey has joined the Islamic Conference Organization, and by large numbers of hitherto secularist Turks turning to Islam as a path to the fulfillment of national interests, socially, economically, and even politically. Yet in spite of their gains in local and national elections the Islamist Salvation Party and its leader Erbakan were not allowed to hold the rein of rule for long.

Political Implications of Islamic Activism

Khomeini's revolution has clearly set a precedent for wedding revolutionary idealism to traditional Shīʿite Islamic values. It has also provided a concrete example of how to overcome sentiments of defeat, frustration, and shame engendered by feelings of betrayal fueled by leaderships more self-serving than willing to fight for the greater interests of Muslims who harbor deep resentment and mistrust for both American and British intentions towards them. This is somewhat mitigated by the leadership of both countries and by most of Europe to stop the policy of ethnic cleansing launched by the Serb leader Slobodan Milosovich against the Muslims, first of Bosnia and recently of Kosovo.

What was once regarded as an Arab cause takes on an Islamic coloring and becomes a sacred cause with the Ayatollah's endorsement of the Palestinian struggle against Israel. It is no longer Arab but Muslim rights that have to be recognized. But then the struggle was already taking on more and more of a religious character ever since the 1967 war with Israel and the Israeli conquest of the holy Islamic shrines in Jerusalem, followed two years later by the attempted burning of the Aqsa mosque, the third holiest in the whole of Islam. Islamic annual conferences since then have repeatedly proclaimed the sacred duty of Muslims to liberate Jerusalem from Zionist control.

Jerusalem has served ever since as a potent weapon in rallying the support of Muslims in non-Arab countries from Sub-Saharan Africa to Southeast Asia. In 1970 Qadhdhāfi chided his Muslim neighbors, Turkey and Iran as well, for having any traffic with Israel. In his visits to Malaysia and Indonesia later that same year King Fayṣal of Saudi Arabia declared that the unresolved Palestinian problem was the problem of all Muslims everywhere. He often vowed not to die before he worshipped in the Aqsa mosque after its reacquisition by Muslim Arabs. His vow was not fulfilled.

Organized Arab states failed in their repeated attempts, but the Palestine Liberation Organization, reinforced by powerful Islamic support from the Ayatollah, has resorted more frequently in recent years to the use of Islamic symbols and slogans in conjuring support for its cause. This is by no means novel to the Palestinian struggle. As head of the Supreme Islamic Council of Jerusalem, Mufti al-Ḥājj Amīn al-Ḥusayni led all resistance to Jewish incursions during the British mandate over Palestine in the 1920s. Palestinian fighting units are named after the sites of famous Muslim victories historically: Qādisīya, Ḥittīn, ʿAyn Jālūt (Goliath Spring). Arafat, himself a Ḥusayni, emphasized the Islamic nature of the struggle during a pilgrimage to Mecca in 1978 where he called for a *jihād* (holy war) against Israel.[4]

A consistent supporter of the Palestine cause from its very inception has been the Muslim Brethren movement. In 1948 its members fought valiantly in the trenches of Gaza and spearheaded support for the movement to topple the regime of King Farouk for its alleged betrayal of the cause. Even after being suppressed, its leaders did not cease their activities against leaderships believed to have betrayed both the Arab and Islamic causes by failing to rally behind forces seeking to regain Muslim rights in Palestine. Indeed, Qadhdhāfi's coup against King Idries of Libya was motivated by similar considerations and he remains committed to the Palestinian struggle as much on Islamic religious as on political grounds. "Palestine came to symbolize an alternate Libyan identity; away from the United States and Britain, back to the Arab and Muslim fold. Israel represents all that is anti-Arab and anti-Islamic."[5]

The Ayatollahs have embraced not only the cause of Arafat, head of the Palestine Liberation Organization, but that of dissidents inside Iraq who have accused the Baʿth government of Saddam Hussein of infidelity to Islamic principles, a main factor in the war that ensued between Iraq and Iran. The Muslim Brethren have been accused by the Baʿthi regime in Syria of similar attempts to topple what zealots construe as a secular regime led by Shīʿite ʿAlawites, a heterodox minority, unmindful of the greater interests of the country and its Sunnite majority. In Jordan and Tunis, they are actively recruiting among the youth, particularly students both at the secondary and college levels. Won over to the cause, this element tends to be suspicious of leadership in their country and to look up to activists such as Qadhdhāfi. The so-called "Rightists" in Turkey, who once took to the street and violence, are strongly influenced by Islamic convictions; their action is as much directed against the liberal secularists, branded "Leftists" and Communists, as it is against the laïcism that has been a cornerstone of modern Turkey's ideology since the Kemalist revolution. In 1980 it took a military takeover of the Turkish government to muster sufficient force to curb their activities and campaign of terror.

The Islamic Anti-Israel Resistance Movements

With the failure of the Palestine Liberation Organization to regain a portion of the land for Palestinians after years of frustrating struggles, the Islamic factions surfaced to carry on what they deem a sacred undertaking, a holy war, to regain not only a portion but the whole of Palestine, which, in their eyes, is not an Arab but rather a *Muslim* land and therefore a mandate from God not to alienate any portion of it. The stalling of the so-called "peace process" after a decade of planned failure, has only served to reinforce their convictions. The fact that in the meantime the world of Islam has become more radically Islamic in its approach to international and regional politics has served to reinforce the militant Islamic resolve.

The two groups engaged in a direct struggle against Israel today are Hamas and Hezbollah. Hamas (an acronym for Islamic Resistance Movement) in its covenant of August 18, 1988 called for an uncompromising Jihād against Israel. The movement is an offshoot of the Ikhwān movement of Egypt with headquarters in the Gaza strip from the time before the Israeli occupation. Hamas surfaced with the Intifada, which it has supported and encouraged true to its motto "Allah is the goal, the Prophet is the model, the Qur'ān is the constitution, Jihād is the path, and death for the sake of Allah is the loftiest of all wishes."[6] It has been actively undertaking to challenge Israeli occupation and has attracted adverse attention by avowed determination to sabotage any peace arrangement with Israel by West Bank Palestinians.[7]

The expulsion by Israel of four hundred so-called Hamas activists without ascertaining that all were what Israel claimed they were only served to focus attention on the growing challenge posed by Islamic militants who, since 1988, have targeted, not only Israel but Algeria, Egypt, Tunisia, and Jordan, and even the PLO for its moderate stand.

The other movement dedicated to combatting Israelis is Hezbollah (Party of God), a militant branch of Shī'ite Islam in Lebanon with strong support financially and militarily from Iran. The main aim of Hezbollah is to liberate south Lebanon from Israeli occupation and to erect, if possible, an Iranian-style Islamic republic. Amal, the principal organ of the Lebanese Shīʿah, has stayed apart from Hezbollah's methods of armed struggle; it had won its own for recognition and a greater role in Lebanon's government under the Ṭaif agreement that ended the fifteen-year civil war in Lebanon. The Hezbollah are unflinching in their determination to carry on the war with Israel; indeed their members won notoriety with the bombing of the marine barracks outside Beirut and of the U.S. embassy in Beirut following Israel's invasion of Lebanon, as well as with the rush to martyrdom by young people as they blew themselves up in the process of inflicting casualties on Israeli troops in the south. As with Hamas, Hezbollah's task is single-minded: to force the Israelis out of occupied territories. They have constantly harassed them and their surrogate Lebanese force, the South Lebanon Army, and have unleashed bombardments on north Israeli settlements in efforts to block the stalled peace process involving moderate Palestinian West Bank leaders.

Reinforcing Moroccan Islam

Belief that political leaders should assume a leading role in the activism presently afoot in the Islamic world is not limited to Libya and Algeria. For some time in neighboring Morocco, King Hasan II, whose family claims descent from Faṭima, the Prophet's daughter, has been carefully cultivating the ulema and powerful religious factions in that country as a counterpoise politically to the liberals, left-leaning political factions, and labor. Co-option of Islam as an instrument for self-legitimization only increases vulnerability to an Islamic protest movement reinforced by class dissatisfaction against the established political order and its elites.[8]

The Islamic League (*al-Rābiṭah al-Islāmīyah)* rose in recent years as an umbrella for Islamic associations that had been stressing the return to Islamic orthodoxy. It has pursued discreet if not secret techniques in an attempt to replace the mystical brotherhoods that had been rendered ineffectual in exercising religiopolitical influence. They are basically four in number: (1) *al-Daʿwah* (propagators of the message [of Islam]), essentially nonpolitical and desiring mainly to make Islam known; its leadership is provided mostly by

Pakistanis; (2) a group supported by Saudi Arabia and encompassing associations guided by Abu Bakr al-Jazāʾiri, a professor at Mecca's theological university, and Taqī al-Hilāli, a former member of the Tijānīya who turned against Ṣūfism and Ṣūfi orders and lives in Morocco as a "reforming extremist"; (3) a group comprising literary and university personnel influenced by the writings of the Muslim Brethren (more by al-Banna's than Sayyid Quṭb's and al-Kawākibi's views); and (4) those who have dubbed themselves the "modern Salafis," or those laboring to adapt Islamic orthodoxy to modern Morocco.[9]

These groupings represent some twenty Islamic societies and are basically urban in concentration. They have decried the moral, political and economic degeneration in Morocco and have vowed to pursue an activist policy, peacefully and democratically to wrest control of government in order to bring the course of Morocco in line with Islamic morality. Reformed Ṣūfis have taken the initiative, often through their *zāwiyas*, in forsaking the life of meditation and prayer for that of active training of young Muslim cadres with the aim of purifying their habits and inculcating them with fundamental Islamic morality. To some, this assumption of an active role in society is only one step removed from political involvement, however much the orders disclaim political motives. In the past, ulema and Ṣūfi heads passed on what might be construed political matters, precisely because fundamental Islam makes no separation between various aspects of a Muslim's conduct. Moreover, the ulema have been integrated into the public life, particularly as concerns the overseeing of religious endowments, often as functionaries with political authority. The league of ulema has not failed to speak up on matters affecting its authority, albeit to others this might appear to encroach upon the temporal realm.

Of interest to observers is the role of the Istiqlāl Party of Morocco in the Salafi movement, anchoring as it has been, its political discourses in Islamic legitimacy. The discourses of the party have been impregnated with Islamic slogans fashioned by its leader, ʿAlāl al-Fāsi, and carried on after his death by his successors, most recently by Muḥammad Ghallāb. The three constants underlying such pronouncements are: (1) traditionalism, aiming at what al-Fāsi termed the return to "pure Islam"; (2) egalitarianism, deriving from the actual provisions of the *Sharī*ʿ*ah* and purporting to provide social assurance for all the poor by guaranteeing them their minimum vital requirements; and where the *zakah* does not suffice, by an implementary tax or supplementary levies; and (3) defining an autonomous area in the field of religiopolitics.

Underpinning these constants in Ghallāb's thinking are four principles: (1) democracy, which he treats as basic to Islam, arguing that Muslims were the first to state that the *umma* is the source of authority; (2) that sovereignty is the property of no one but the *umma*; that the Prophet himself never claimed title to sovereignty, absolving himself from all but the charge of providing guidance for the Islamic community; (3) the Islamic notion of "*bay*ʿ*ah*" (the swearing of allegiance to the ruler) which the Istiqlāl conceives as a form of popular referendum rendering advice by a broader based segment of the population to the ruler, and (4) the *shura*, or counseling by an elite noted for his Islamic piety and dedication and who are most knowledgeable in the mechanics of Islamic legislation and its relevance both to state and faith.

But the Istiqlāl is not the only political faction in Morocco eyeing religion as an element of strategy. The so-called "left" has become the target of Islamic societies who have ranged them alongside the "materialists." The socialists have been attacked by their organ, *al-Muḥarrir* (*The Liberator*) for not identifying themselves with the socialism inherent to Islam. The socialists have struck back with arguments that the Islamists dwell on Islamic social justice in order to conceal the revolutionary character of the faith, with which they can identify more readily.

The middle party, consisting of the ulema, are referred to as "integrationists" who seek legitimization for societal motivation, political and religious, through the application of Islamic norms. Their aim is one of centralization of authority and the creation of an Islamic common denominator for all aspects of social endeavors, extending also into the realm of economics and education. The centralization sought might be symbolic, but it represents to activists the single most potent rallying factor in a society torn between conflicting ideological trends.

Countering Islamic Militancy in Egypt

The upward trend in Islamic activism from one end of the Islamic world to the other has not been without opposition. Countries most active in suppressing this movement and its militant manifestations have been those committed to stronger secular courses. Syria for some time has been actively curbing the activities of those who have been indiscriminately called "Muslim Brethren" while Sunni activists without Brethren connections have vocally opposed the secularist Baʿthi regime both on denominational and anti-secularist grounds. Violence against the regime and its proponents led at one time to stern counter measures and to strained relations with neighboring Jordan whose government was accused by Damascus of abetting Muslim Brethren activities in Syria.

In Egypt the relationship between Muslim societies (*al-Jamāʿāt al-Islāmīyah*) and their government under Sadat and Mubārak has culminated in massive arrests of leaders who oppose government policies. This came after a protracted period of deterioration. As noted earlier, Egypt was the home of the first organized activist movement, the Muslim Brotherhood, back in the 1920s. It has remained since then a principal source of Islamic writings of all sorts encouraging greater Islamic commitment. Social and political pressures generated by such writings and their authors have led to recognition of a formal role for Islam not only in the constitution of Egypt but in education and social laws. While Nasser was less prone to acknowledge the role of Islam in ordering the new Egyptian society he aspired to create, Sadat on coming to power labeled himself "the believer-president"; and in the exercise of political power he called on religion and its custodians as a means for its legitimization.[10]

Sadat's national and international policies soon lost him the confidence not only of the neo-fundamentalists (if we may so call the activists) but of secular and nationalist leaders as well. While Sadat encouraged the role of the capitalist entrepreneur, thus indirectly abetting the trend toward widening the gulf between the haves and have nots, opposition factions including the Islamic fundamentalists have preached an Islamic socioeconomic doctrine that calls for a society of owners and workers collaborating.[11] Whereas Sadat took the initiative to oust the Soviets and make peace with Israel outside the context of broader Arab-Islamic policy interests, the Islamic opposition have strongly protested this policy—not out of any consideration for the Soviets, whose Marxism they have violently condemned, but out of resentment for dealings with the country conceived by them and other Arabs as their number one enemy.

Frustration and defeat have contributed to the strong opposition mustered recently by the Islamic activists. While social and technological answers might explain some of the weaknesses of Egypt, the fundamentalists attribute failure to the lack of religiousness and impiety. The Jews, they argue, won the wars against Egypt because they invoked their faith. Arabs lost them because, in their eyes, they had abandoned God, so God abandoned them. The return to God, and thereby Islamic piety, is the *sine qua non* of success in the future.

Advocates of this position first expressed their approval in the last years of Nasser, when he began to call on religion to play an important role in society. This call was buttressed by a foreign imperative: to demonstrate to the Soviets that Islam can provide an alternative socialism to the Marxism they urged on him. To this end Nasser tolerated open writings on the subject by affiliates of the Muslim Brethren movement.

Convinced that if by invoking the moral and physical strength of Judaism Israel could march from triumph to triumph, then it stands to reason that Arabs must call upon the same norms of their own faith if they are to experience similar success. Indeed, the 1973 October war was launched during the sacred month of Ramaḍān (time of the ritual fast) and on the day of Yom Kippur, holy days for both Muslims and Jews. The Egyptian code name for the crossing of the Suez Canal was "Badr," scene of Islam's first military victory in 624. The deep religious connotations of such symbols could not have been lost upon troops composed largely of that element in Egyptian society which is more tenacious in its commitment to Islam.

Islamic fervor intensified after the initial victories of the 1973 war. The regime of President Sadat found it politic to encourage such fervor in support of its own aims. Indeed, Sadat even succeeded in obtaining a religious *fatwa* from the Shaykh of al-Azhar declaring the peace arrangement with Israel as legal in Islamic law.

With the growing power of the Islamic world following the great influx of wealth owing to oil revenues and the dedication of large portions of such resources to the furtherance of Islamic well-being, Muslims became convinced that this is a sign from God who is looking with benevolence upon a people returning to His ways. Islamic organizations came into being everywhere, all of which were dedicated to renewal and propagation of religious commitment. Islamic societies in Egypt and elsewhere reached into the universities with notable success after 1977. Fired up by a renewed zeal, these groups, often led by intellectuals as well as segments of the ulema, tended to become less tolerant of shortcomings in society and its manifest leadership. Violence led to sectarian skirmishes and, finally, the excuse Sadat sought to curb their activities and imprison their leaders. By forcing them out of universities and into the countryside, Sadat had unwittingly contributed to their spreading views prevalent among urbanites that could only lead to sedition in his eyes. Arrests were made allegedly to prevent threats to national unity. Arab enemies of Egypt and the Soviet Union were accused of abetting the activities of the Islamic societies against President Sadat's policies. Some observers allege that had the leadership of these societies confined their preachings to university circles, they might have been tolerated. But to spill over into the streets with publications directing harsh accusations against the government was their unforgivable sin. Their secretiveness and clandestine ways served to arouse suspicion and led to their forcible disbandment by government authorities. Their newspaper *al-Daʿwah* (*The Message*) was shut down. Interestingly enough, some of the government informants were allegedly associates of the Muslim Brethren.[12]

That Sadat feared the potential threat of the Islamic societies to his rule is indicated in the range of measures legally taken to curb their activities. Their mosques, numbered in the thousands, and hitherto part of the group run by the public sector, were closed or incorporated into the government's ministry of religious endowments. Their leading *imāms*, extremely effective with the public in recent times as critics of the government's policies at home and abroad, were among those arrested. His assassination was thus portended.

Mubārak has followed in his predecessor's footsteps by suppressing any attempt to allow the growth of an opposition Islamic party for Islamists to have free access to the democratic process that would give them a voice in affairs of state. The reason for that was the growing strength of the opposition Islamic movement, with their spokesmen in Egypt, as in Algeria, gaining rapidly at the polls in local elections. Mubārak sought to head off a repeat of the Algerian experience but was oblivious to the possibility that his approach might lead to an Iranian scenario.[13] It has intensified acts of violence, directed against Egypt's main source of outside income—tourism—with devastating results (60 percent drop in one year) with the aim of bringing down Mubārak and his government. Arrests, tortures, and execution of Muslim Islamists, terrorist and non-terrorist alike, have only emboldened and encouraged further resistance and violence. Islamists have targeted Mubārak and threatened him with the fate of his predecessor, hence his diligent efforts to lay his hands on Shaykh ʿUmar ʿAbd al-Rahmān, the main moving force behind the surging Islamic resistance to his regime.

The lesson from Iran is that Western-style institutions, when unable to deliver, are subject to discard. The revolution of Ayatollah Khomeini set the pattern for rejection of such institutions. The swing of the pendulum from the liberal secular to the Islamic option, particularly evident in Turkey and North Africa, has been gathering momentum ever since Iran reconstituted itself as an Islamic state.

The 1979 sacred mosque takeover in Mecca by Muslim extremists and opponents of the house of Saud seems to point to growing disaffection with the conduct if not the displayed morality of Saudi Arabia's leadership. The swift and harsh manner with which the rebel extremists were dealt with gives proof of an unwillingness to tolerate departure from the established norm. And in the dispatch of summary justice the government-supported ulema in Saudi Arabia, as in Egypt, endorsed the harsh counter measures of reigning authorities. Saudi Arabia's hosting half a million infidel soldiers to wage war on a fellow Arab Muslim state in the Gulf War has alienated Muslims at home and abroad. This might have fueled the present trend by the new millionaires of the Gulf emirates and Saudi Arabia to help bankroll Islamic movements and leaders like Turabi in Sudan out of conviction and/or resentment of the policies of pro-Western Arab governments.

Fundamentalism and Secularism

What is understood by "fundamentalism" belies the intended meaning of the term. It is not a prescription for literal reading and application of Islam's sacred text if the comparison is to the Christian approach to the Bible. Nor is it a formula for violence to force change in Islamic behavior or to combat the enemies of Islam. What authors seek by it, for want of a better term, is an activism aiming at rejuvenation, renewal, or integration of pure Islamic teaching with institutions governing Islamic societies.

Modernists, on the other hand, start from the premises of Islam, then seek those adjustments that would make it compatible with the dynamics of a modern world, which relies on science and technology to bring about change in society, presumably to ensure a better life for participants.

Modernists in the Muslim world, particularly those educated in Western educational establishments, see in Islamic activism and militancy a setback in time and progress. Distrust stems from a traditionally held norm among the exponents of progress everywhere that looking back into time for the wherewithal of guidance represents a backward step on the ladder of achievement.

But the record of achievement to date seems to belie this notion. Saudi Arabia and the United Arab Emirates, both seriously mindful of the traditional values of orthodox Islam, have set examples in the application of all that is construed an instrument of progress by modern standards in building ultra modern societies.

The most recent fruits of technological achievements are constantly applied in the upgrading of the quality of life. Contrary to what secularists have alleged in deprecating the motivating values of fundamentalist regimes, the latter have demonstrated from Islamic history and its great civilizational achievements that the glorious contributions of medieval Islam to civilization in the arts and sciences have been the result of Islam's approval and encouragement. Indeed, all those who still harken after knowledge often quote a tradition of the Prophet Muḥammad himself, which states: "seek knowledge even in (far away) China."

The knowledge enjoined by Islam is that which contributes to the well-being of the believer, both in a spiritual and physical context, provided there is no violation of the Muslim's commitment to God and solidarity with fellow man. Thus, it is not knowledge, not even secularly induced technological know how, that the purists oppose; rather, it is knowledge void of any ethical content that they suspect and reject. It is the wholesale borrowing of Western secular and materialist values that the traditionalists frown upon. They prefer selective borrowing, and only of that which is compatible with Islam. They reject the affectatious emulation of Western ways in dress and conduct at the expense of Islamic values, which they deem more relevant (since they are truer) to their inherited traditions.

Yet this aspect of rejection is not always reflected in the sociopolitical conduct of rulers of Muslim states. Islamic nationalism has not by any means become the motivating ideology of those states whose constitutional base may or may not openly be anchored in the provisions of the *Sharīʿah*. Indeed, the mosque takeover in Mecca was seen as a form of protest against the alleged un-Islamic ways of the ruling elite in Saudi Arabia. In the Arabian (Persian) Gulf, such states as the United Arab Emirates are systematically commissioning studies of Islamic jurisprudence, particularly the Māliki rite, in order to bring the conduct and organization of law in line with its provisions. This policy is pursued in spite of a full commitment to modernization in all realms of societal endeavors, with education serving as the spearhead.

Those governments outside the Arab world sharing in a commitment to Islam and modernization share equally in the concern over prospects of successfully reconciling the exigencies of a world given to scientific and technological guidance with those decreed by an Islamic ideology that might not always accept the ramifications of such guidance.

Most modernists ready to chance both are willing to stress the universals of Islam and show how they do not depart radically from those of Christianity and Judaism, which Westerners consider to lie at the foundation of their progress. Politically, they are realistic enough to realize that resurgent Islam can not and will not provide the basis of political unification of the Muslim world already characterized by racial and ethnic diversity. Political, social, and economic disparity is too prevalent to be overlooked, or subordinated to the interests of the greater imperative of a renaissance calling for one Islamic government for all. The *Sharīʿah* will remain at the basis of rule, but the instruments of rule are likely to reflect the coloring of each particular Islamic society: Malaysian, Indonesian, Chinese, African, Iranian, Arab, etc. Moreover, attitudes will continue to reflect the range of conservatism or liberalism characterizing the school of jurisprudence upon which development will be based. And since many have more than one school represented in their midst, it will be some time before a consensus will emerge.

One authority who spent decades in Asia notes on the basis of study and experience that a successful renaissance of Islam must ensure that (1) law and government will conform to the word and spirit of Islamic legislation; (2) internal development will reflect grass-roots aspirations, and leadership mirror the desire for independence from foreign influence and control; (3) political and social justice will be within the framework of Islamic legislation (or an "Islamic Socialism") as called for in the *Sharīʿah*; (4) there will be no entangling commitments to superpower blocs of nations; (5) there can be a regional common market and a pooling of resources to withstand the onslaught of more developed economies of the world; and (6) internal resources, both natural and human, will be relied upon for development.[14]

Such preconditions for a blueprint guaranteeing a functional Islamic revitalization are not to be regarded in the realm of dream or unattainability as skeptics are so often heard to declare. The demonstrated material wealth and resources of the Muslim world, foremost among them being oil, can and have provided the means for economic and technological development. Ten of the thirteen OPEC countries are Muslim. Numerous projects have been launched under the auspices of organizations established by Saudi Arabia, Kuwait, and the United Arab Emirates to assist in the economic, agricultural, and educational development of less fortunate Islamic countries in Asia and Africa.

It had been long assumed that modern economics and the Islamic notion thereof would not add up to progress and development. Detractors often cited the Islamic prohibition against interest as the major deterrent in that it made impossible the full play of finance capitalism, a *sine qua non* for monetary flow and investment, without which industry could not develop and thrive. The recent record clearly belies the assertion. The oil producing states have managed to parlay surplus revenue into billions of dollars by investment in interest-earning accounts around the world. Islamic banks observing the spirit of the interdiction on interest taking choose to regard earnings as returns on investment. The proliferation of "Islamic banks" proves that Muslims can compete with financial giants around the world and their investments can not only yield profits, but also the funds that are generously expended in the promotion of developmental projects in the Muslim world at large.

A key institution in the promotion of such activity is the Islamic Development Bank, established in 1974 with an approved capital outlay of two and a half billion dollars. The bank is the direct outcome of the efforts of the Organization of the Islamic Conference in which Saudi Arabia is playing increasingly a dominant role, with the aim of headquartering it in Ṭāʾif. By 1981 the bank had made 189 loans totaling over five billion dollars. Much of the funds went towards deferring the cost of technical improvements and for products to be used to enhance agriculture, fuel supplies, and trade among Muslim countries.

Reinvigoration of Islamic Morality and Intellect

Islamic activism is fueled today by the urgent desire of the purists to reestablish the primacy of Islamic ethics and morality in all the endeavors of Islamic communities throughout the world. The main target of their activities have been the youth, and student groups in particular. It is not, therefore, coincidental that the most vigorous exponents of Islamic education and, by extension, humanism are to be found on college and university campuses both in the Muslim world and abroad.

Summoning the faithful to goodness and the avoidance of what is objectionable in the sight of God is the underlying philosophy of the current trend. Recasting the present day Muslim into that image envisioned by earlier Muslim purists, namely "the ideal man," conceived by the Ṣūfis as "the vicegerent of God," is the major aim of modern Muslim fundamentalists. "Take on the characteristics of God . . . this is our whole philosophy of education, our sole standard!" declared the late ʿAli Sharīʿati in one of his lectures.[15]

The striving after perfection necessitates in the eyes of modern Muslim educators and humanists a careful study of the Qurʾān and the message contained therein. Through it a more intimate knowledge of God and His timeless message for setting straight morals and conduct can be derived. Knowledge of the personality of the Prophet Muḥammad, the ideal man to the purists, can enhance the undertakings of modern Muslim youth in emulating his ways and mirroring his values through which the morality of Islamic society today can be reinforced.

The duty of the intellectual in the eyes of modern preachers of Islamic reform "is to recognize and know Islam as a school of thought that gives life to man, individual, and society; and that it is entrusted with the mission of the future guidance of mankind. He should regard this duty as an individual and personal one, and whatever be his field of study, he should cast a fresh glance at the religion of Islam and its great personages…For Islam has so many different dimensions and varying aspects that everyone can discover a fresh and exact vantage point for viewing it within his field of study."[16]

The return to the basics of Islam for inspiration and guidance is synonymous with a return to the Qur'ān. Much emphasis has been placed lately on this course. Special conferences are being held specifically to study the Qur'ān from every aspect of human educational endeavor, the scientific to the metaphysical, with the deep-seated conviction that this holy text, this cornerstone of Islam's edifice and its mainstay can indeed provide the guidance necessary for shaping the Muslim's future life in a modern world.

Since the Qur'ān is the ultimate source of jurisdiction in effecting a change of course today, it becomes necessary for Islamic ideologues to study carefully its contents for the legislative base it provides in steering an acceptable course. Moreover, any unification of policy and methods that can be accepted by Muslim societies everywhere must have the sanctity of the Qur'ān's approval. Modern jurists are convinced that the Qur'ān deliberately took no firm stand on the type of education a Muslim must permanently subscribe to in order to allow him the flexibility of adapting to the needs of time and place, and more importantly, not to cut off research and debate by means of which the quality of enlightenment through knowledge is enhanced.

For such reasons Muslims historically engaged in every category of science and field of learning without religious constraints. For as the great Muslim thinker al-Rāzi put it: intelligence precedes legislation. Mind ascertains the existence and unicity of God, before the unfoldment of His will in the form of divine legislation through the truths embodied in His word, the Qur'ān, can take place.

Thus modern fundamentalists will not rule out the role of the intellect in arriving at prescriptions for behavior in a modern society that can comport with the will and laws of God. Renewal in Islam for them is by opening the gates to every new form of knowledge that conforms with the teachings and spirit of true Islam.[17]

But the emphasis on knowledge does not derive exclusively from the Qur'ān. The Prophet Muḥammad himself urged believers to seek knowledge and investigate the truths of creation and the world as well as life itself, according to prophetic traditions ascribed to him. Some of these read: seek knowledge from birth to death; he who is not knowledgeable or learned does not belong to my people; he who strives after knowledge is striving after God; whoever follows a path to knowledge, God will facilitate his path to paradise. The Prophet's Companions encouraged learning and humility so that the deeds of believers would rest in knowledge not in ignorance. ʿAli is alleged to have declared that knowledge is more preferable than the accumulation of wealth. The caliph ʿUmar urged Muslims to be humble in both acquiring and dispensing knowledge.

Modern Muslim thinkers like Mawlana Mawdūdi, ʿAli Sharīʿati, and Sayyid Quṭub have argued in their writings that intelligence refers to human intellectual capacity before the revelations of God were enshrined in the Qurʾān to show how thinking in pagan Arabia was captive to fables woven by ignorance and falsehood. Islam liberated the Arab's mind through the teachings of the Qurʾān by stressing the principle popularized by Descartes (d. 1650): "I think therefore I am," which is already enshrined in the Qurʾān: "And in the earth are portents for those whose faith is sure, and (also) in yourselves. Can ye then not see?"[18]

Muslim thinkers like Amir Ali and Muḥammad Iqbal called for the primacy of mind over literalism. They and successive like-minded thinkers point to the role of Islam in the medieval era of Europe in bringing about an intellectual awakening based on the assertion of the principle and insist that it is perfectly consistent with Islam's basic teachings to utilize the mind in making the changes necessary for adaptation to the needs of modern living.[19]

Other thinkers like ʿAli Sharīʿati insist on stating how the Qurʾān not only provides justification for learning but points the way also to areas of expansion of learning: "I extracted from the Qurʾān a whole series of new topics and themes relating to history, sociology and the human sciences. A philosophical theory and scheme of sociology and history opened themselves up before me, and when I later checked them against history and sociology, I found them to be fully correct."[20]

What is significant to the process of Islamic dynamism today is the conclusion which thinkers like Sharīʿati arrive at in reinforcing the conviction that Islamic learning can provide the best means for reasserting the ideal enjoined by faith for a progressive, cohering, and adaptive society. In Sharīʿati's own words,

> From this we deduce the following conclusion: Islam is the first school of social thought that recognizes the masses as the basis, the fundamental and conscious factor in determining history and society—not the elect as Nietzsche thought, not the aristocracy and nobility as Plato claimed, not great personalities as Carlyle and Emerson believed, not those of pure blood as Alexis Carrel imagined, not the priests or the intellectuals, but the masses.[21]

The process of learning and adaptation evolves from the mainsprings of society's structure. Islam's view thereof reposes in the notion that social development and change are contingent on personality, tradition, accident, and the human constituency (*al-nās*). Each society, in its view, has a fixed basis, a particular character, and a path laid out by its governing norms. It submits to definite laws, like living organisms. So all transformation or change ensue from a fixed tradition and immutable laws upon which that society had been first constructed. The human factor is considered vital to any change. The Qurʾān clearly alludes to it in a number of verses: "Theirs is that which they earned, and yours is that which ye earn. And ye will not be asked of what they used to do." (2:134); "Verily God does not change the state of a people until they change the state of their own selves." (13:11) Such verses serve as the criteria for individual and social responsibility in Islam. The individual's own responsibility is clearly delineated in such verse as "Every soul is accountable for what it has earned" (74:38) wherein accountability is directly to the Creator for deeds committed by individuals, singularly or collectively.

Islamic Humanism

Fundamentalists today insist on the return to the humanism taught by the Qurʾān and exemplified in the life of the Prophet

Muḥammad whose entire career was directed at constructing a society under the banner of Islam dedicated to the benefit of humanity and the elevation of the spirit of man. In this context Islam's conception of "humanism" might be construed as stressing those values anchored in the faith's fundamental principles that govern human interaction. This contrasts somewhat with the classical Western understanding of humanism, defined by Webster as a movement that, since the fifteenth and sixteenth centuries, has aspired to restore the universally human values of classical antiquity as opposed to the debased scholasticism of the late Middle Ages. In a more recent context, humanism might be construed as a movement "purporting to advocate the universally human as against utilitarian science, religious dogma, uncontrolled passion (e.g., Romanticism), political strivings, etc."[22] Through the return to the moral refinement of character enjoined by the teachings of basic Islam, present day reformers hope to wean away a generation of Muslims who have looked to the West for an ethic suitable to the process of reordering human relations. As one Muslim critic put it, "Life for Westerners is machine-made. It has lost spirit and warmth. . . . The social life that results shows no evidence of the glory of the spirit of man. . . . The inventions and discoveries made to ease life and advance civilization fail to ease man's disillusion and disquiet of mind."[23]

The underlying premise of Islamic humanism is common to all that treats human relations in terms of reciprocation by individuals of serenity and affection in the spirit of mutual tolerance and understanding. It presupposes an atmosphere of well-being and fraternization, of flexibility and sufferance, and the elevation of conscience of the collective body to the level of calling for the well-being of the individual as the cornerstone of the well-being of society.

Faith in the individual's ability to rise to the task reposes in Qurʾānic dicta, namely "Thou art truly of noble creation," and "Thou hast in the messenger of God (Muḥammad) a good example." The expansion and success of Islam in its early centuries is attributed to the faithful manner in which the adherents carried out the injunctions of the Qurʾān and the admonitions of the Prophet. Subsequent decline is attributed to the abandonment of those principles that insist on a life dedicated to combatting error, injustice and tyranny. It is attributed also to the lack of humanism in relationships between those in authority and the commonalty. This, in contravention of the Qur᾽ānic ordinance, "Preach the way of your Lord with wisdom and fair exhortation, and debate with them over that which is better;" and of another, "Be humble with thine followers, and should they resist say, 'I am innocent of what they do.'"

The Prophet Muḥammad is thus held to have set forth in his personal relationships with his followers the model example for Islamic humanism. His relations were built on affection, love, and tolerance. Philosophically speaking, such are the ingredients of true humanism in the eyes of modern Muslim preachers.[24] To them they repose in the basic injunction of Islam that stresses preaching good and abstaining from evil. They evoke the example of the Prophet who not merely admonished his followers each to undertake changing "with his own hands" the wrong he encounters, but did it himself on numerous occasions. This is the true *jihād* enjoined upon Muslims individually and collectively. This is in keeping with God's address to Muḥammad in the Qur᾽ān: "We have sent thee only as [an act] of mercy to mankind (literally, *the worlds*)," that is to "call to the good and refrain from that which is objectionable [in the sight of God]."

Islamic humanism rests on both the fear of God and love. Believers see in God the ever-watchful eye who guides what they do and what they say to ensure truthfulness. The truthful individual does not seek fault in others but avoids that which causes fault. He abides the Prophet's saying, "Do not do in privacy what you wish not people to witness in open."

Islam pays special attention to humanistic training; it prescribes in detail both spiritual and social programs aiming at providing proper guidance in the quest for moral and spiritual uplifting. This again is in keeping with the Qur᾽ānic dictum, "That there should rise from thy midst a nation calling to the good, enjoining that which is commendable and avoiding that which is objectionable, for they are the successful ones." God guides this nation so it can guide people to God in the spirit of mutual love.

Love becomes a special ingredient of Islamic humanism, the cementing force of the brotherhood constructed on faith in and dedication to the fulfillment of the will of God. It is in keeping also with the saying of the Prophet, "Verily none of you believe unless he wills for his brother what he wills for himself."

The Islamic concept of love is based on love of God, love of the Prophet, and love of the believers in God. The Prophet specified that his love was for those who draw near to each other in his name, reciprocate on his account, and champion justice for his sake. He stressed that God called upon him to serve as His prophet so He could effect the refinement of moral character through him.

The refinement of moral character becomes today a principal goal of fundamentalist reformers. The moral uplifting of society is predicated on the perfection of the individual's own morals. Ethical conduct is rooted in the conduct of a righteous community, in keeping with God's command: "Lo! Allah enjoineth justice and kindness, and giving to kinsfolk, and forbideth lewdness and abomination and wickedness."[25] The Prophet called upon the faithful to be exemplars of ethical conduct. Placing God uppermost in daily acts, praying, fasting, tithing, and performing the pilgrimage are the pillars of Islam. These acts reinforce the moral, upright life, and the very ingredients stressed today by Muslim reformers in their call to moral regeneration in the world of Islam.

The limitations on conduct defined by Islam's *Sharī'ah* are seen as a protective device for the Islamic community and a warning to those who would depart from the provisions of the law. Faith and commitment are indivisible. The Prophet is quoted saying in this regard: "He who has no loyalty has no faith and he who lacks fidelity lacks religion." The Lord is cited saying: "Verily those dearest to Me and nearest to Me in dwelling on the Day of Resurrection are the finest in character."

Women and the Family

The image Westerners have been conditioned to have of Muslim women is one of repressed human beings, second class citizens in their Islamic milieu. This is an unfortunate distortion of their true status. Because the topic has attracted much attention and publicity, we shall dedicate some space to outlining how we could rectify our perceptions. We might have recourse (1) to Western observers, and (2) to Muslim authors. The latter tend to describe the roles, responsibilities, and privileges of women as delineated by Islam in its ideal form, while the former simply describe what they see in actual practice or what Muslim women relate through personal interviews, which may not always conform to the Islamic ideal given the great variety of experiences of Muslim women throughout the Islamic world.

Nearly half a billion Muslim women inhabit countries all around the world. Some are comfortable with their traditional Islamic roles as homemakers and educators of the youth in Islamic ways. Others, who are highly modernized and "liberated" have opted for Western dress and modes of behavior, as well as careers that do not hinge on marital status. Indeed, the latter would be indistinguishable from their Western counterparts were attention not called to their being Muslim. The vast majority, on the other hand, live and interact with others as they have for centuries. A group in between is hesitant about seeking to find some medial position: to conform with the prerequisites of Islamic practices but have the freedom of movement to assert themselves as best they might in order to serve their ambitions and needs in society at large.

Differences cannot be ignored; a village woman of rural Afghanistan is very different from a well-educated Palestinian who is socially and politically active in the struggle to assert her Palestinian identity, or of a Muslim woman in America who has become almost indistinguishable from others in the American milieu, with the exception of new converts to Islam, who pride themselves in exhibiting the head cover that somehow has become the symbol of proper display. Arab women led in what we call "liberation" movements, as exemplified by Huda Shaʿrāwi of Egypt and others who even founded publications early this century for the purpose of promoting the role of women in the family as the medium for imparting Islamic values but within a modern context.

Cultural and geographical differences notwithstanding, there is still that invisible link that provides a common thread for Muslim women everywhere. Muslim authors insist that Islam is "less restrictive than Christianity." As one Muslim woman put it, "All too often, we evaluate Muslim women by religion and not (by) their culture, while evaluating Christian women by their cultural values and not by their religion."[26]

An early candid assessment of the Muslim woman's status in the so called male-female dynamics within a modern Muslim society was done by the Moroccan author Fatima Mernissi, who is convinced that sexual inequality was characteristic of both Muslim and Christian societies. In her *Beyond the Veil*[27] she undertook to achieve a better understanding of the sexual dynamics of the Muslim world and to explore the male-female relation as an entity within the Muslim system. She postulates that the relation of the Muslim woman to Islam and the change in the relation of the sexes is one of the most explosive threats confronting Islamic society in the twentieth century. Domination of Muslim lands by "infidel" powers, she argues, has led to the freeing of Muslim women to take part in the struggle for independence and to become involved with men in the production process. Indeed, as worker and soldier, the Muslim woman demands the rights reserved hitherto to her male counterpart. Hence the assault on the social bastions that have erected such barriers.[28]

That Muslim women are shouldering greater responsibilities in the reordering of their milieu, socially, economically, politically and even militarily is a process that has been underway for some time and has nothing to do with "liberation." It is rather the exigencies of transforming circumstances that necessitated it. Given the expanded public role of women and the control they still maintain over domestic matters as mistresses of the household and conditioners of religious behavior among the young, their powers necessarily expanded eventually into the male domain.[29]

Those who fear that the Islamic resurgence currently underway would restrict the role of women in society ignore the realities of recent history: the hero(ine) of the Algerian war of independence was the woman Jamīlah. Her counterparts among

Palestinians and Iranians have engaged in equally heroic struggles on behalf of family and community. Arab Muslim women never shunned an opportunity to assert themselves within and outside the family and have always played an active role in any form of military struggle, bearing up well under adverse circumstances.[30] They are visible and active. The Palestinian Intifada called upon women to coordinate critical activities when Israelis placed the West Bank in a virtual state of siege.

In the Islamic Republic of Iran they engage in every activity from performing in the Tehran Symphony Orchestra to providing logistics to sensitive government operations, not to mention the military. In Saudi Arabia, as in other Muslim countries, women are very active in education and medicine. They have their own societies around the Arabian peninsula and in banking, they have their own accounts and investments.

The Qur'ān recognizes women as equal to men in religiosity. Transformation of status historically is attributed to change in social circumstances and conditions, not to legislated differentiation. The veil and *purdah* were historical accretions and not mandated by the Islamic *Sharīʿah*, which only called upon women to be modest in public and conceal their charms from all but their own men. Pre-Islamic Arabia had no such observances; it was acquired from contacts with Persian and Byzantine societies, which secluded their women out of deference and honor, not abject treatment, a recognition Muslims saw fit to apply also to their own women. The Qur'ān enjoins modest display for a society whose goal was to achieve piety and avoid temptation and distraction. If abuses occurred, they can not be blamed on Islam.

What is clear is that one cannot generalize on the status or outlook of women in Islam given the great variation of experiences and disposition among them. One can only surmise that the impact of current trends in the Islamic world will invariably lead to more change and adjustment in the Muslim woman's outlook and perception of what her role should be. This could prove difficult as women in Arabia, professors and doctors, were reprimanded and dismissed from their professional positions when, during the Gulf War, they demanded to drive their own automobiles as their Kuwaiti counterparts were doing in Arabia while awaiting return to their country. This is more the exception than the prevailing rule since Arabia is still governed by Wahhābi-imposed restrictions.

Of equal interest to the Western observer is what role women play in the family generally. Because much emphasis is placed on ethical conduct in the Islamic notion of humanism, the role of the family, and particularly of women therein, resumes its paramount importance in the eyes of activists and "fundamentalists" today.

In its basic teachings Islam encourages marriage, children, and parental involvement in their rearing, as it enjoins upon children respect and care for parents in their old age. Islam cements family ties from birth until death. It makes of a cohering family the cornerstone of society, and places a heavy burden on parents in training the young to become upright Muslims and to abide by all that which the Qur'ān and the *Sharī'ah* command. The Qur'ān clearly states, "Is he who founded his building upon duty to Allah and His good pleasure better; or he who founded his building on the brink of a crumbling, overhanging precipice so that it toppled with him into the fire of hell?"[31] The building reformists allude to in this context is the edifice of the family. The soundness of its structure assures the soundness of society's structure. It is for this reason that Islam defines more precisely the role of the marriage partners: the male is to provide, the female to build a home and educate the young in the ways of Islam. The tendency in the West is to misconstrue the separate roles of the sexes, which is not seen by Muslims as denigrating the position of women, but rather of complementing that of the male in cementing family ties.

Biologically, it is argued that marriage and the family are an imperative of nature, an inescapable product of sexual mating ordained by God and a requisite for producing offspring. But more importantly, to reformers, the family provides the psychological framework for expressing and experiencing those feelings that serve, by extension, to cement society at large; namely ties of closeness, compassion, and collaboration in an intimate milieu that only a well-cohering family can provide, and through which the personality desired by Islam is shaped. Moreover, it is in those early years of child rearing that the mother's responsibility assumes a significant role. For such reasons, Islam insists that the faithful should marry morally upright women, well versed in the teachings of the faith, much of which is learned in those formative years at home. True faith acquired in those critical years leads to the humanistic development of the child as it progresses through life to the state of adulthood. Modern authors preaching an Islamic reinvigoration for the family treat the function and role as one from one end of the Muslim world to another without distinction as to race, color, or traditional backgrounds. The aim is to strengthen the ties of close dependence in the family so they might transfer to society at large and solidify it. The uprightness of society can only be gauged by the uprightness of its parts, or the individuals that constitute it. Ibn Taymīyah, the fourteenth century Islamic "fundamentalist," stated that the welfare of man cannot be achieved except through social coherence because of the need of one person for another. And those who harken back to the teachings of their spiritual forefathers argue that only a reinforced Islam can provide the impetus and the means for social solidification.

In conclusion, it can be said that the current trends in the world of Islam point clearly to a growing role for those who preach a renewal of faith as the *sine qua non* of a reinvigorated society sufficient unto itself both spiritually and materially. It would be a serious mistake to assume that Islamic activism represents today anything but a vital force for progress to nearly a billion people who do not feel comfortable in any but the inherited traditions of Islam. It is indeed for them a way of life which, from all indications, they do not intend to forsake for any other model.

CHAPTER 16

Perspectives on Activist Islam

IT IS IMPORTANT to avoid the extremely controversial issues concerning the subject of Islam and various erroneous perceptions. These issues are inconsistent in diagnosing what the West views as a manifest problem spreading from Muslim societies to infect non-Muslim societies that have always tended to look down on Islam and Muslims as "the other." If we were to look at these perceptions and attempt to provide some cogent answers, we would have to consider the long record of hostility characterizing the West's attitude toward both. We need not go back beyond nine hundred years to attempt a diagnosis of the ingrained suspicions and acts of hostility manifested by Christian societies of Europe toward Islam until the mid-twentieth century, and by the United States since then. The United States has replaced the erstwhile European colonizers of Muslims and has been branded as the promoter and supporter of neocolonialism by foisting the state of Israel on the Arab Muslim heartland and sustaining it with overwhelming military power, and by sustaining in places of authority unpopular Muslim rulers who have been more inclined toward self-service than public service.

What Are the Perceived Notions?

First and foremost is the notion that Islam is innately given to acts of violence in support of political goals or in expressing disaffection. This is commonly described in the West, especially by the electronic and published media that has been invariably, if not uniformly, hostile toward Muslims because Muslims refuse to acknowledge Israel's right to exist where it has been established. This is the hostility that the West all too often displays by labeling Islam's unfriendly acts as terrorism. Hence the ancillary notion that Islam promotes terrorism, and, when terrorist acts first occur, they are quickly attributed to Muslims before the facts are determined. A good example in point was the bombing of the Federal Building in Oklahoma City in 1995. Muslims in that community were harassed and terrorized by the media, and when the facts were in, no attempt was made to apologize for having falsely accused and labeled innocent citizens who had been arrested on mere suspicion.

Another incident worth mentioning concerns the relationship between the United States and those it had enlisted in the service of recruiting fighters for Afghanistan during the mounting campaign to oust the Soviets from that country. Shaykh ʿUmar ʿAbd al-Rahman, well-respected and highly regarded by many pious Muslims, most of whom support the agenda of Islamic revival, had been instrumental in recruiting thousands of Muslim fighters for Afghanistan, found himself and those he had recruited without a cause once the Soviets were ousted. Embittered by the fratricidal slaughter that replaced the Soviet-Afghan war, some of these fighters underwent a spiritual polarization that led them to experience the world in uncompromising terms. The capitalist West grew more sinister, while Islam became a shining beacon of truth and justice. They saw Shaykh ʿUmar as a spiritual master who held the key to their salvation and selected those teachings that best served their frustrations. The subsequent trial of Shaykh ʿUmar was interpreted by many as a deal between Egypt's President Mubarak, who was tired of Shaykh ʿUmar's agitation against his rule, and the United States government, which did not like Shaykh ʿUmar's incendiary words to the Afghan fighters residing in this country. The outcome of the trial aroused extreme anger among Muslim militants, who threatened further acts of violence against the United States.

Does this evidence of radicalization in Islam point to sanctioning acts of violence and conducting militant policies toward Muslims? If so then as one author put it, the West must bear some measure of responsibility for the development of the new radical form of Islam, "which in some hideous sense comes close to our ancient fantasies." Today, many people in the Islamic world reject the West as ungodly, unjust, and decadent. As the same author adds, "We constantly produce new stereotypes to express our apparently ingrain hatred of 'Islam'."[1]

The Domestic Factor

It would be misleading to attribute the rise of radical Islam solely to hatred of the West, nor to treat it as a homogeneous movement. First and foremost, the espousal of an activist and militant form of Islam is often in response to local conditions and to a genuine conviction by the overall body of concerned Muslims that the *ummah*, or community of believers, is in dire need of reform, indeed, of radical change, owing to the distortions of the governing norms sanctioned in Islam by their own ruling elements and spokesmen of their society. The response is based on local perceptions of societal ills attributed to misapplication of tenets of Islam, hence the difference from town to town, village to village. Strong Christian villages in upper Egypt have come under attack by Muslim extremists on the grounds that they endorse those in power who misuse Islam. They deprecate it as a tool or an instrument for replacing unjust laws that stifle freedom of expression and disenfranchise large segments of Egyptian society, for fear that should they be enfranchised, they might replace them by the free exercise of the ballot. Algeria is a case in point. Under strong domestic and foreign pressures, the ruling element dominated by the military agreed to hold free elections in 1992. But when it became clear that the Islamic Salvation Front was going to emerge as the clear winner with over 62 percent of the votes in the first round of balloting, pressured by both France and the United States, the military canceled the next round and denied the Islamists the potential victory they would have earned by the democratic process. The aftermath of such blatant tampering in the electoral process has been written in blood, those of some sixty thousand, mostly innocent people with the military sponsoring special hit squads to brutalize those who had voted for the Islamists, and the Islamists retaliating against those elements, largely secularists, who feared the potential conversion of a secular socialist society into an Islamic state should they gain control via the ballot. The West was not about to tolerate an outright Islamic government anywhere for fear that it would clearly be hostile towards it, as the Iranians proved to be.

Misuse of "Fundamentalism"

It has become almost axiomatic in the West to equate violence with "fundamentalism" without defining the underlying precepts of the term both in its original Christian definition and the Muslim understanding of the term. As one observer noted, "Western commentators often use—or misuse—terms taken from Christianity and apply them to Islam. One of the most commonly used is fundamentalism."[2] The closest the two perceptions come together is in the broad conception that both believe in the fundamentals of the faith as articulated in their respective holy books—the Bible and Qurʾān. But to Muslims, fundamentals are anchored in addition to the Qurʾān in the Traditions of the Prophet Muḥammad and in the structure of the earliest Islamic society that was perceived as reflecting the true intentions of Muḥammad and his followers in establishing that wholesome order that best reflected the true teachings of the faith in its pristine stage of development. No violence was mentioned as a tool for achieving change. The violence that ensued in the decades following the Prophet's death was motivated by political rivalries over leadership of the Islamic *ummah* or community of believers. To the extent the term is confined to reflecting the centrality of the Qurʾān and the Traditions, every practicing Muslim might be termed a fundamentalist. But one does not get that impression when one turns to the American media, written and electronic, where fundamentalism is automatically equated with fanaticism bordering on violence. "In the Christian context it is a useful concept. In the Muslim context it simply confuses because by definition every Muslim believes in the fundamentals of Islam. However, even Muslims differ in their ideas about how, and to what extent, to apply Islamic ideas to the modern world."[3] The Wahhābi school, dominant in Saudi Arabia, believes in a strictly literal interpretation of the Qur'ān and would approximate thereby the Christian fundamentalist's interpretation of the Bible.

Fundamentalism is not a new phenomenon, nor is it exclusively Islamic. The name "fundamentalist" was coined in the 1920s by American Protestants who argued that the text of the Bible has to be applied literally, and to designate those "doing battle royal for the Fundamentals." Also figuring in the name was *The Fundamentals*, a 12-volume collection of essays written between 1910 and 1915 by sixty-four British and American scholars and preachers.[4] Muslim fundamentalism is similar to the extent that advocates invoke both the text and the meaning of their sacred book as well as the model life of the Prophet Muḥammad. Muslim fundamentalists attribute the weakness of Muslim states to the loss of real faith and religious behavior. They blame Western values for having corrupted the true practice of Islam and argue for the return to the "real Islam" observed in the first half century of its birth. The problem is that the real society they aspire to revive and emulate did not truly exist, given the violence it experienced, first at the hand of the Khārijites, the first militant sect of Islam, which broke with Ali, son-in-law of the Prophet for his having compromised his caliphate, and the civil wars over leadership two and a half decades after the death of the Prophet.

The transformation of the inherent definition of the term fundamentalism in its Christian context and grafting it on Islam is the work, in the views of one observer, of the U.S. foreign policy establishment.[5] This presumption was driven home to me when I was called upon to confer with scholars of Islam in Saudi Arabia in 1993 and one boldly addressed me saying: "Now that communism is no longer the enemy, do you plan to target Islam next, to create a rallying cause for those who see in Islam a menace and a threat?" It was difficult to explain that U.S. policy under Presidents Bush and Clinton attempted to make a distinction between orderly political opposition and militant extremism. Both presidents committed themselves to contain Islamic extremism, as already evident in their imposing an embargo on Islamic Iran, and to address its causes, not to target Islam indiscriminately.

The cause of extremism with recourse to violence has been attributed by experts to the lack of economic, educational, and political opportunities, which can be defeated only by addressing the causes on which it thrives.[6] Islamic scholars do not subscribe to the views of the extremists who seek to justify the recourse to violence by having recourse to Qurʾānic verses. Indeed, some activist scholars argue that extremism is a misunderstanding of Islam, and that people who advocate violence wrongly interpret the scriptures. One of the contradictions is for a Muslim to brand a fellow Muslim a *kāfir* (apostate) to justify a holy war against him, as happened in the case of Ayatollah Khomeini of Iran accusing Saddam Hussein of Iraq of infidelity to justify an illegal *jihād* against him during the protracted war between the two countries. One can find in the Qurʾān evidence to refute the argument of the extremists to justify recourse to violence. Leading Islamic scholars, including those of the Azhar University itself, have condemned such arguments as un-Islamic.

Patterns of Islamic Responses

Patterns of Muslim activists' responses to established political order in the world of Islam fall under three headings: the first is to attempt to achieve actively *revolutionary ascendancy*, Iran being the clearest case in point, with the Sudan being a close second, where, with the first Islamists succeeding in gaining complete political and legal control of the government, and with the second, near such control. The emphasis is on revolutionary means and the use of force, not in the pursuit of peaceful democratic methods, to gain ascendancy. The second approach of Islamic activists is *revolutionary resistance* to the regime in place. Examples of this approach are the struggle of Islamists in Algeria when denied the fruits of initial electoral victory, the strong resistance by Islamic Jihad in Egypt to their government, and of Hamas in Palestine to the Palestinian Authority and the Israeli occupation. Resistance in such cases is the result of the conviction held by extremists that the regimes are too entrenched and unresponsive to popular needs and demands as to be undone only by militant resistance alone. The third response of Islamic activists to political order is *accommodation.* We have examples of this in the Muslim Brotherhood of Egypt, which has avoided militant expressions in reacting to unpopular government policies; in Pakistan, where the policy has been to achieve results by persuasive and nonviolent forms of pressure, which has led to some success recently in the government's willingness to consider the Islamic *Sharīʿah* as the basic source of all legislation; and in Jordan where the late King Hussein tolerated increasing numbers of Islamists in government counsels.

Explaining Islamic Activism

If by Islamic activism we understand a process whereby the tenets of the faith are observed in their true teachings and context, then we might argue that there have always been periods in Islam's history where the return to the basic sources of the faith was advocated by certain groups, usually as a way to solve the social or political problems caused by a decadent and "un-Islamic" society.[7] The earliest active effort of this kind is that of the eighteenth-century Wahhābi movement in Arabia, which led to the birth of Saudi Arabia, a product of reformed Islamic traditionalism and conservatism, yet a present-day leader in accepting Western influence and modernization anchored in a secular tradition. Another interesting observation to make is that in the course of industrialization, national-liberal and socialist movements played the most powerful role in the fight for independence in the middle of the twentieth century. Most of the Arab and Islamic states that came into being as separate political entities, with a few exceptions, did not anchor their new polities and constitutions in Islam.[8]

However, Islamist movements were not dead, although they were not yet strong enough to redress the affront to the dominant faith, i.e. Islam, as these newly created states opted for imitating the West in most of its aspects—social, economic, cultural, and political. A concise analysis of Islamic activism is to be found in an important U.S. government publication that brought numerous experts on the subject together for a series of seminars.[9] The link between religious revival and political reform is a common theme in Islamic history. During periods of decline, reformers sought to reawaken religious devotion. Loss of faith and the subversion of the ideals of Islam were taken to be the cause of social ills.[10] Reformers never ruled out the use of force to attain these ends. This is all the more obvious when the Qurʾān enjoins against injustice and tyranny on the part of the governing authorities who refuse to step down from leadership and persist in their oppressive ways. Islam has zero tolerance for violations of fellow Muslims' rights; does not preach the turning of the other cheek, and even mandates the removal of an oppressor by force if necessary. Such precepts reinforce the extremists' attitude toward unpopular regimes.

One can attribute in another vein the rise of activism to Muslim resentment of and reaction to European colonial rule and the humiliation inflicted thereby on a proud Islamic entity that had enjoyed centuries of military and political preeminence. In the Arab states it was Arab nationalism and Arab socialism as advocated by Abdul Nasser that sought to combat vestiges of colonial rule and the ideology that came with it, which was deemed offensive and destructive of pristine Islamic values as embodied in the *Sharīʿah*, Islam's fundamental law and constitution. Activists were able to gain support because of the centrality of the religion in the daily life of its adherents and its determinative role in shaping individual and collective identity. Even Nasser invoked Islam to support his more secular vision of society. So did Saddam Hussein in his last-ditch attempt to rally a broad segment of the Muslim world to his cause on the eve of, and during, Desert Storm.

"Whether the appeal to Islam is the result of a genuine desire for social justice or a cynical manipulation of religion for political gain, it remains [nevertheless] a potent tool for mobilizing popular support."[11]

Islamic activism succeeded those failed Arab and Iranian nationalisms as the weapon of choice to bring about much-needed social and political amelioration in their respective societies. Activists have tapped into the same anti-Western sentiment associated with the failed aforementioned secular nationalisms and have used a deep sense of humiliation and frustration among Muslim peoples to advance their cause. They argue forcefully for a return to Islam as the true alternative to Western models of social organization and development. It could be said that Islamic activism has become a "potent ideology of popular dissent."[12] In the words of a brilliant analyst of Arab history, Islam provided an effective language of opposition to Western power and influence, and those who could be accused of being subversive to them; to governments regarded as corrupt and ineffective, the instruments of private interests, or devoid of morality, and to a society which seemed to have lost its unity with its moral principles and direction.[13]

Watersheds for Islamic Activists

Partisans of reform in an Islamic context can be classified either as orthodox, subscribers to a sociopolitical Islam that fits comfortably in its modern environment, and Islamists, believers in turning the clock back to the time of Islam's inception. The sociopolitical partisans consider the traditional ways of interpretation binding and thus accept that Qur'ān and Sunnah (Traditions) have to be interpreted. They agree that the status quo has to be preserved while fundamentalists insist on implementation. Islamists aim at establishing an Islamic order by reintroducing the *Sharīʿah*, which will have its role in governing each sector of private and public life. This situation would not have happened were it not for the colonial era of domination and the regimes that it left behind, which triggered the rise of Islamism.

Recent political triumphs have reinforced the conviction that Islam is a viable ideology. Most significant of these triumphs is the ousting of the regime of Shah Muhammad Pahlavi by Islamists led by the Ayatollah Khomeini and its replacement in rapid order by an Islamic state guided by the Islamic *Sharīʿah*, reinforced by a plebescite, and by parliamentary institutions as proof that activist Islam does not preclude the democratic process.

The triumph of Islamism in Iran has served as a beacon guiding other would-be emulators elsewhere in the Islamic world. The most notable of Islamic triumphs is the ouster of the Soviet Union from Afghanistan led by a motley fighting conglomeration of rival tribes united only by their common devotion to Islam and its ideals. With such noteworthy triumphs, it is not difficult to understand why activists can appreciate the power of religion and of the mosque as the rallying place for action.

Islamists may vary in their organizations and methods. However, they hold in common an awareness of the political utility of religion and the need to transform society in accordance with their interpretation of Islamic principles and how they perceive their responding to present needs in keeping up with world changes and to meet whatever challenges such changes might present to the body of Muslims. They also hold in common the conviction that social ills plaguing their societies are the result of the irreligious and secular nature of their governments. Hence, to redress this problem necessitates a return to religion as the sole organizing principle of society.

According to such a rationale, Islam becomes a dynamic and activist political ideology that must acquire state power in order to implement its social, economic, and political agenda. Unlike the beliefs of Muslim modernists, or even of conservatives, Islamic activism is seen primarily as a political rather than a religious or intellectual tool for change. Once perceived primarily as a political tool, recourse to militancy, even to violence to achieve the desired ends by the extremists among Islamists, becomes inevitable.

Can Violence Be Avoided?

Were we to consider the case of Sudan, we would discover that the National Islamic Front there, guided by Ḥasan al-Turābi, its ideologue, espouses the policy of total Islamization of government and society without regard to the strong minority non-Muslim elements of the South. This already has occasioned a protracted civil war. Hence, if not direct, at least indirect, violence becomes the outcome of what modernists might term the inherent undemocratic nature of Islamism in that, if it should triumph, minorities living among the faithful would have to revert to the status of *dhimmis* or millets (under erstwhile Islamic hegemonic rule—Arab and Ottoman) with a status that recognized equality only within such social structures and not with the dominant element, the Muslim.

Westerners fault the Islamists for insisting on the return to a strictly theocratic structure, although not all Muslim advocates of reintegrating state and faith favor a strict theocratic structure. Both Pakistan and Indonesia provide good examples of this. In Pakistan the Jamaat-i Islami explicitly endorsed a constitution modeled on British parliamentary democracy as consistent with its teachings. It contained enough references to the Qur'ān and Sunnah to appease the Jamaat, but fell far short of what the activists sought.

In Indonesia the critic of an exclusivist theocratic version of Islam is Abduerahman Wahid, dubbed a leader of the neo-modernist group of Muslims who represent majority opinion in criticizing the government and those who would use Islam for political purposes, favoring instead a pluralistic interpretation of Islam and democratic politics. The question to be resolved is: Can the neo-modernists, who also base their rationale on the interpretation of the sacred texts of Islam, provide an alternative to the recourse to violence as advocated by extremists, who interpret such texts to justify their methods? In other words, should violence be the only means to their ends?

Questioning the Need for Violence

When judged in the full context of Islamic activism today, those who have had recourse to violence represent only an extreme minority of Muslims, who by their ruthless and violent methods have gained for themselves the suspicion of the non-Muslim world, which questions their readiness to honor democratic norms of international standard behavior respecting human rights. Undoubtedly, those who equate Islam with terrorism take their cue from the practices of extremists who out of desperation have lashed out against the United States for its alleged biased behavior in parts of the Muslim world. A good example of such violence recently is that of Osama Bin Laden who leads a small but well-financed cabal of followers who have risen to opposition following the landing of U.S. troops on Arabian soil to stage war against a Muslim nation. His group is ideologically committed to vanquishing Western influence in the Islamic world. He found sanctuary among the Taliban of Afghanistan who enforce "a draconian caricature of Islam that has been widely condemned by Muslims—including the Iranian government—as 'extremists'."[14] According to Norton, the "challenge" of Islam has been a persistent preoccupation for policy makers since the fall of the shah of Iran in 1979.[15]

The Muslim Brotherhood founded by Hasan al-Banna in Egypt in 1928 advocated peaceful methods to bring about social and educational reform in keeping with true Islamic tenets. They soon gained a following in the neighboring Arab countries of Jordan, Sudan, Syria, and Iraq. They were apolitical at first, but within less than a decade they gravitated toward advocating the establishment of an Islamic state as the only means of bringing about their slated reforms. This change of position eventually put them on a collision course with secular authorities and the revolutionary government of Nasser. Al-Banna was denied a position in Parliament to which he had been elected twice but forced to resign to avoid the shedding of blood in the inevitable violent collision between his angered followers and their autocratic government.

The recourse to violence out of frustration for not being able to avail themselves of a democratic process and to gain an official voice in the governing process was unavoidable. The anger of the Muslim Brethren was compounded by the fact that they had supported the young officer corps to power only to experience their betrayal in the end.[16] They fought bravely in the 1948 first Arab-Israeli war and turned against the regime when they were subjected to persecution in the aftermath of the revolution of 1952. Nasser outlawed the Brothers, imprisoned a number of their leaders, and executed Sayyid Quṭb, the articulator of Islamic fundamentalist doctrine, for his alleged complicity in the failed attempt to assassinate him.

Nasser's crackdown on the Brothers emboldened those who had favored a militant course of action to undo tyrannical rule. Indeed, the Islamic Jihad movement that stemmed from that was to be the instrument for the assassination of Nasser's successor, Anwar Sadat, in 1981 for his alleged betrayal of Islamic principles as they perceived them when he made peace with Israel in 1979. They chartered a course to violence in the pamphlet entitled by them "The Neglected Duty," which gave sanction to those persons legitimately engaged in a *jihād* of survival against illicit rulers to employ unconventional methods, including deception and killing.[17] This policy of doing whatever it takes to achieve "legitimate" ends has been pursued by Hamas, an offshoot of the Muslim Brothers, operating principally out of Gazza, whose leaders do not consider themselves restricted by any tactical consideration other than the one that would ensure the fulfillment of their goals. Self-sacrifice in the carrying out of a deadly mission is considered the gateway to the ultimate goal of every aspiring Muslim—a direct ticket to paradise.

Sadat brought on his own destruction when shortly after coming to power in 1970 he unleashed the Islamic movement and even encouraged the establishment of Islamic groups on university campuses and in various professional associations and trade unions in an effort to stem the imminent threat to his regime posed by the leftist-Nasserist power centers. He even styled himself the head of believers, thus helping to promote further the atmosphere of religiosity that had been gaining strength since the disastrous 1967 war with Israel. "In fact, the more Sadat stressed the religious theme and the more he associated his state with religion, calling it 'the state of science and faith,' the more he became vulnerable to the Islamic opposition… his initial policies, aimed at containing the leftist-Nasserist threat, eventually gave rise to a far greater Islamic challenge with the blossoming of the radical fundamentalist organizations as they expanded recruitment and training."[18] Indeed, his successor, Muhammad Hosni Mubarak acknowledged that Sadat was responsible for the formation of the Islamic groups; he was badly advised and he made a great mistake.[19]

Clearly Nasser and Sadat's harsh policies became instrumental in the proliferation of radical militant groups that evolved from the more peacefully inclined Muslim Brethren during its inception. Nearly two dozen such groups emerged in the span of a decade, major among them being the Islamic Liberation Party, Jamāʿat al-Takfīr wa ʿl-Hijrah (Apostasy and Flight), the Jihad Organization, and al-Jamāʿah al-Islāmīyah (Islamic Group), all of which charted a course of violence against the state and its upholders, with the exception of the original Ikhwān (Brethren) who still favored peaceful means for achieving the changes advocated by the activists.[20] Unlike them, the new, younger fundamentalist groups pursued a course of violent confrontation with the state, attracting unfavorable attention both internally and externally since the mid 1970s.

The intellectual fountainhead and inspiration of the radical Islamic movement in and out of Egypt was Sayyid Quṭb. He elaborated an ideology of resistance (*jihād*) against authority based upon his doctrinal interpretation of existing conditions of Muslim societies as vitiated by *jāhilīyah* (pre-Islamic ignorance or paganism) and their rulers as *kuffār* (infidels, or apostates), stating that "all those in the society who partake in this stage of affairs are in the category of apostates. Quṭb's conception of *takfīr* (apostacy or declaring someone non-Muslim), and *jihād*, which sanctions the overthrow of corrupt rulers by force, established a dangerous precedent for future radical fundamentalists to follow."[21]

Related to the theme of *jāhilīyah* is the fundamentalists' opposition to nationalism and their positing that contemporary *jāhilīyah* is linked to the onset of nationalism, and its twin, the secular nation-state, in the world of Islam, whose model is the European nation-state. "Because the secular nation-state is also a product of nineteenth-century European colonialism, it is built around a national political identity, which contravenes the older, Muslim-based community identity."[22]

From the very beginning, Islam labored to abolish all the pagan connotations of nationalism, such as race, language, ethnicity, and tribe, and to establish a universal Muslim *ummah* (community) based upon religious identification. The *ummah* established by the Prophet Muḥammad was based on faith not on kinship. Membership in the *ummah* and participation in public affairs were defined by religion, not by ethnic, national, or tribal considerations. Under the political Islam advocated today by Islamists, religion is to serve as the primary source of political identity and loyalty. "To Muslim fundamentalist thinkers of all kinds, the underlying strength of an Islamic order is its universality—the bond of religion is the heart of community solidarity. Contrariwise, nationalist particularism is the negation of Islamic universalism and breeds secularism and decline."[23]

The universality of the activists' demands is spurred to some extent by the theory advanced by Abu ʿl -ʿAlā Mawdúdi, who insisted that the message of Islam as revealed in the Qurʾān is not nationality-based, nor is it the province of any specific national group. In his words, "it is an ideological Qurʾānic-based state that transcends race and nationality."[24] He believed that Islam and nationalism are antithetical and that there can be no accommodation between the two as some Muslim reformers would advocate, since accommodation would carry in it the seeds of the most dangerous Western import, secularism.

Virtually all Islamic fundamentalist groups seek to reestablish Islam as the foundation of a just political and social order to replace existing corrupt, un-Islamic systems. Those of Egypt, Jordan, Palestine, Algeria, Lebanon, and Iran would not shun the resort to violence. Only the Jamaat of Pakistan have not to date advocated violent means to achieve such goals. They all see Western-style democracy as alien to Islam since, in an Islamic entity, God and his legislation do not govern man-made laws. They are also united in opposition to those aspects of modernity, especially social modernization, that they find inimical to Islam, a belief system deemed superior to Western materialism. Most important, they all maintain it is the duty of Muslims to reject the secular state and even resist it. The political elite in an Islamic state, they argue, should be Muslims not only in name, but also in practice. Thus, challenging the status quo is a given for activist Islamist groups who see this the means toward the establishment of a truly Islamic order.[25]

The Challenge to Western Hegemony

An equally menacing challenge for those who would invoke Islam as a weapon of resistance is that of the dominant imperialist and colonial country or countries of the West, which have not only penetrated the Islamic countries of the Middle East economically and politically, but buttressed by military and technological superiority, have sought to exercise influence in very significant cultural areas as well. As Norton puts it, "the source of the dissonance between official Washington and the Muslim world resides in the Middle East, where only 25 percent of all Muslims live." He further states that the United States government does not view Islam or Muslims in adversarial terms, except when Muslims engage in terrorism or seek to undermine U.S. objectives in the Middle East. Nevertheless, the United States and its policymakers are viewed with skepticism by most Muslims in and out of the Middle East, especially when elements hostile to the Islamic world seek "to paint those who simply oppose its polices with the brush of extremism."[26] Nor are they convinced by Vice President Gore's speeches in Malaysia that the United States is seeking only to promote freedom and democracy in the Muslim world rather than primarily stability and control to promote and protect its influence.

The principal mode of resistance adopted, however, by the affected Muslim elements has been more religious and cultural than violent extremism. Accordingly, one can discern several types of Muslim responses to what they term Western dominance and imperialism. One of the most obvious has been preaching from the pulpit of the mosques by fiery Islamists who argue that Christians and Jews have been hostile to Islam from its very inception, citing for specific examples the Crusades in medieval times and Zionist occupation of Muslim land (Palestine in modern times). Khomeini argued that the struggle between the West and political Islam was more than a struggle between Western imperialism and Islam as a religion. They refer to the dictum of the Qurʾān which states: "Never will the Jews or the Christians be satisfied with thee unless thou follow their form of religion."[27] In Khomeini's words:

> "if you pay no attention to the politics of the imperialists and consider Islam to be simply the few topics you are always studying and never go beyond them, then the imperialists will leave you alone. Pray as much as you like; it is your oil they are after—why should they worry about your prayers? They are after our minerals, and want to turn our country into a market for their goods. That is the reason the puppet governments they have installed prevent us from industrializing, and instead, establish only assembly plants and industry that is dependent on the outside world."[28]

The United States, thus, wittingly or not, has become the country most hated by Islamic activists on two counts: first, its support of unpopular and oppressive regimes in Muslim countries treated as client states (Egypt, Kuwait, Algeria), and second, buttressing Israel's intransigence in its ongoing violation of international laws adversely affecting the interests of Palestinians. In the eyes of Muslims and Arabs, the United States ever since the formation of the state of Israel, has followed a consistent policy of excessive cordiality and favoritism toward Israel. They would argue that Arab oil has contributed heavily to the enrichment and growth of the Western economy, but that oil has been used to help Israel in such a way that the legitimate interests of the Arab and Muslim states have not only been disregarded but adversely affected. Even President Nixon himself, a staunch defender of Israel's policies under the guidance of Henry Kissinger, came around to recognizing in due course the pitfalls of his one-sided policy when he stated, "The Arab-Israeli conflict poisons our relations with the Muslim world...Israel's occupation of Arab lands undercuts our ability to cooperate with countries with modernist, pro-Western leaders. Israel's occupation of Arab lands—and particularly its increasingly harsh treatment of the Palestinians—polarizes and radicalizes the Muslim world."[29]

Islamists fear the political and economic domination of the United States, together with its ongoing cultural penetration. They do not draw much solace from the likes of Huntington of Harvard who seeks to apply his "Clash of Civilizations" model to the Muslim world, arguing that the West is destined to clash with Islam, thus reinforcing the adversarial elements in the U.S. government that plan policies and strategies toward the Muslim world. Indeed, they have embraced the thesis of Willy Claes, then secretary general of NATO, in the mid-1990s, that the Islamic challenge is the major threat confronting the West. "Despite official denials from Washington, even moderate Muslim intellectuals believe that the Huntington thesis defines U.S. policy."[30] If this trend is not checked, they fear that eventually Islam, like Christianity, will be secularized and will become a personal and private religion.

The economic dynamism of the West would lead to more Islamic countries following the Egyptian model of 'infitāḥ' (opening up the land to Western economic penetration) and to the modeling of their economies along capitalist lines supported by the middle class and the bureaucracies.

In countries such as Saudi Arabia, an avowedly Islamic state, and Pakistan, aspiring to become one, middle class, military, and civilian bureaucracies have been endeavoring to insulate their industrial and banking systems from some of the traditional Islamic ideas relating to interest and the role of the public sector in Muslim societies.

The situation is different in the Islamic Republic of Iran where the influence of sociopolitical Islam is stronger. Westernization has been viewed, particularly by the dominant clerical circles, as the "degradation of Islamic and oriental identity, the negation of all previous values and the acceptance of a new personality according to the prevailing values in Western civilization."[31] The central purpose of sociopolitical Islam, it is argued, is to mobilize the power of the masses to wrest political and economic control from the West. This implies clearly that sociopolitical Islam cannot play an accommodative or subordinate role to Western hegemony as Saudi Arabia and Pakistan do.[32]

Islamists, however, have not fully realized the long-range threat to Islamic value systems posed by the hegemonic dominance of the materialist West spearheaded by the United States, which is out to serve its own economic and political interests in the world of Islam, even if it necessitates catering to tyrants as the expeditious way to gain results. Intellectuals have alleged that in their recourse to the Qur'ān for guidance, Islamists have not always come up with defined prescriptions and regulations to confront specific situations in their social context. Islamic thinkers are accused of not exploring links between ideas and certain economic and class structures, nor do they make any distinction between ideas and prescriptions or regulations independent of changing social or class structures as they cling to the immutability of their articulated Islamic ideas.

Others would argue that such an allegation does not reflect justly on the work of such noted Islamic thinkers as Mawdūdi, Sayyid Quṭb, or Khomeini, who formulated their ideas or concepts in response to Western challenges. The fallacy of their approach, it is argued by Muslim intellectuals, lies in their dismissing the Western challenge as *jāhilīyah* and capitalism and Marxism as being animated by materialism and almost indistinguishable. Khomeini, on the other hand, did see the greater danger of Western capitalism, but he and his followers failed to make clear how capitalism "had the continuing capacity to penetrate Islamic ideological frontiers and even corrode the very core of Islamic society."[33]

The Islamic movement in Egypt has been designated by the Western media and observers as a fundamentalist movement, posing a major threat to all regimes in Egypt, particularly to Sadat's and Mubarak's, the two staunch endorsers of U.S. policies, economic, and political objectives. Hence, the need they felt to devise some form of strategy for containing or co-opting a movement like the one represented by the Muslim Brethren. Academics and strategists in the West saw it as a security dilemma caused by dislocation and psychological malaise in a society undergoing rapid social change. Others, such as the structuralists, opined that the phenomena of the Brethren resulted from a reactionary consequence of the blockage by the world market forces of Egypt's development efforts.[34]

Sociopolitical Islam: An Alternative?

There are critics of the posture taken by Islamists of the "fundamentalist" variety who see in their preaching and acts of violence a negation of true Islamic principles. In Egypt, for example, the leftist author and critic Jalāl Amīn claims that the religious movement they represent and the militancy associated with it do not come to grips with certain basic social and economic problems and provide no solution to the people in terms of getting rid of backwardness and oppression. In his opinion, "the religious movement in Egypt has been unable to understand what the socioeconomic situation is. It replaces reality by the vision of a past that is no longer relevant. It tries to escape from the pains of this world into a magic world. It uses a toy gun similar to the one used by children to fire at this world... such a gun may scratch but does not kill anyone; [it] may cause noise but does not change anything."[35]

Some rationalists wonder how egalitarianism and justice as embodied in Islamic fundamentals can overcome existing and formidable social and power structures. Democracy, in their thinking, could emerge in other societies only when economic and capitalist development could dissolve or overcome feudal structures of the landed gentry. The question is: Should Muslim leaders with the help of Islamic ideas accelerate the process of social change and human development? Intellectual leaders who cling to the notion that ideas can triumph over interests will have to wait until Muslim societies find a way to develop and strengthen their social and political institutions if they are to withstand the challenges of the West. Secular Muslims believe this can be done by allowing some form of participatory democracy; the nonsecularists do not believe in its feasibility as long as puppet governments do not find it in their interests to do so, hence, the inevitable recourse to violence to undo the injustice and lack of social equality that continue to plague Islamic societies dominated by dictators.

In the eyes of some Islamists, the replacement of a secular regime is not enough by itself. They believe this would have to be followed up by a systematic attempt to set up a polity that satisfies the needs of the deprived population in rural and urban areas, as attempted by the revolutionary regime in Iran. The Islamic regime in that country made an earnest effort to introduce certain structural changes, such as bringing basic industries under state control, and land reforms and other measures to bring about income redistribution that could not all be implemented before the war with Iraq broke out.

In his seminal work, *The Failure of Political Islam*, Olivier Roy argued poignantly the case of how fundamentalists to date have failed to create the society they advocate. As other critics have pointed out, Muslim society needs to know what sort of mediating mechanisms are necessary to translate Islamic ideas into appropriate behavior, and how to do so. It has been suggested that if some sort of Islamic democracy could come to prevail, the role of the party in such a system should be less than an electoral instrument and more of a social service organization. A Muslim society, in which a great majority of the people are motivated intensely by religious considerations, may perhaps agree to accept such changes if they are couched and communicated in Islamic terms.

As for those who keep complaining about Western dominance and how Islam should resist and even overcome such dominance by creating an Islamic society, they have not to date, with the possible exception of Iran, produced an effective model of an Islamic polity. "Many Muslims also claim that an Islamic political system is vastly superior to the Western democratic system but among the billion Muslims that exist in this world, an Islamic society based on social justice and Islamic democracy has yet to come into being."[36] As one observer noted, "Islamic 'fundamentalism' lacks intellectual—and hence moral—foundations appropriate for the present age...It is all passion and no insight, all cause and no programme." He then goes on to postulate that

> If "Islam" is to be an organizing principle for society and state (?) today, it better acquire some moral content that is universalist and appealing to the "secularised" man of today who has been exposed to the full fury of the nihilistic science and technology and all their attendant ideologies. It would also mean giving cogent reasons for rejecting the global reign of consumerist gadgetry and electronic toys! I am afraid that "fundamentalism" has done Islam a disservice by giving the illusion that the solution to our "malaise" is merely to summon the will, whip all the Muslims into line and create a permanent ontological, even moral, divide between Muslims and others.

He further postulates that Muslim "fundamentalists" may also have capitally (sic) misread the Prophetic paradigm as the establishment of the Islamic state. It may be in keeping with the reading of Sunni Islam's jurisprudence, but the modern Shīʿite version postulated by Khomeini is equally irredeemably statist, legalistic, authoritarian, and exclusivist in his opinion. Viewing the Prophetic model as "eternal jihad," as "permanent revolution," as the Maoists would have expressed it, is neither ineluctably militant and violent, nor exclusively political and legalistic.

Since Muslims are a truly global community without a given center, they must develop a global, universalist, or "ummatic" (communal) consciousness and turn this lack of political cohesion to their advantage. As the same author, Parvez Mansour, bluntly puts it: "An Islam which is a global community (or a network of civil societal institutions) and possesses a universalist moral agenda is for me a more attractive form of Islam than any fiqhi (juridical) state, Mawdudite or Khomeinite! Raising the global consciousness of the individual Muslim and infusing it with a universal morality is the most important task of Islamic intellectualism. Unfortunately fundamentalists have failed us in this task."[37]

It has been argued that "Khomeini's theory of Islam is that it is primarily a sociopolitical order derived entirely from divine sources and not in any respect the product of cultural exchange." Accordingly, the accompanying theory of Islamic government is based on the premise that it is possible to replace the degenerate remnants of Islam found throughout the contemporary Muslim world with a genuine Islamic order. It is presumed thereby that if an Islamic system is properly constructed and administered, it will be just and perfect in every sense because it will be underpinned by the *Sharīʿah,* run by the clerics and devoid of contaminating attributes and influences. These theories show why Western traditions subsumed under the heading of "democracy" have no place whatsoever in his conceptual framework.[38]

Were we to analyze the theoretical structure that most Islamic fundamentalists employ today to justify their aims, we would discover three flawed arguments. First, their presenting Islam as principally a political doctrine, thus obscuring its spiritual and humanistic attributes, which are at the foundation of Islam itself. Second, imposing and maintaining an ostensibly pristine sociopolitical order by authoritarian means, which ignores the universal frailties of human nature and renders it "axiomatically incapable of dealing with the problem of power, the perennial tendency of those who have it to abuse it if they are not prevented by institutionalized restrictions." Third, "the rejection of Islamic civilization's eclectic origins is not only historically inaccurate but precludes the utilization of Western political traditions that could have provided safeguards against monopolization of power and violations of human rights."[39]

If sociopolitical Islam is to provide a viable alternative, then its programs and policies must exemplify human development. This will enable it to score two impressive gains over Islamic fundamentalism for winning public support. The first will yield greater social discipline and public support in Muslim states for strengthening their cohesiveness and rendering them strong in order to enable them to mount an effective response to Western dominance. The second, at the broader international level where a battle is taking place to win minds, by promoting human development, an Islamic system will present itself as a viable rival to Western social and political systems.[40]

In conclusion, it is not appropriate to proceed beyond the realm of speculation at this time since neither Islamic fundamentalism nor sociopolitical Islam have run their full course of demonstrating the feasibility of their respective assertions as to the ideal solution for Islamic societies. Nevertheless, it is safe to assume that if the world of Islam is to find its proper place in a rapidly evolving world, adjustments must be made and these must flow from the mainspring of Islam's fundamental beliefs buttressed by the sense of equity and justice that characterizes and underlies its humanistic and tolerant nature.

Footnotes

1. An Introduction to Islam

1. Cited by C. Snouck Hurgronje in his *Mohammedanism* (New York: G. P. Putnam's Sons, 1916), pp. 20–21.

2. G. Weil, *Mohammed der Prophet, sein Leben und seine Lehre* (Muḥammad the Prophet, his Life and his Teachings), Stuttgart, 1843.

2. The Setting in Arabia

1. ʿAbd-al-Malik ibn-Hishām, *Sīrat Rasūl Allāh,* trans. Alfred Guillaume: *The Life of Muḥammad* (London: Oxford University Press, 1956), p. 41.

2. (Through the French.) From the Arabic root "*ghaza*: to conduct a foray."

3. Literally "the days of the Arabians," more immediately in reference to the intertribal wars ensuing from anywhere a personal insult to dispute over cattle and water holes or the sportiness of it.

4. Muḥammad had a strong antipathy for the poets whom he accused of being inspired by the *jinn*; the Arabic term for poet "*shāʿir*" stands for "he who senses," by extrasensory means.

5. Some of the finest Arab poetry dates to this period. For a collection of the *Muʿallaqāt* (the suspended ones) see A. Arberry, *The Seven Odes*, Cambridge: University Press, 1957.

6. W. R. Smith, *Religion of the Semites* (New York: Meridian Library, 1959), p. 2.

7. Technically, "[the period of] ignorance" or barbarism, which is in reference to Arabia and its inhabitants in the era when they were not guided by Allah, the Qurʾān and His Messenger Muḥammad.

8. Al-ʿUzzah was one of the most venerated pagan female deities; even Muḥammad made her an offering when he was a boy. She is the Arab equivalent of the Greek Aphrodite or Venus.

9. Al-Lāt or *al-Ilāhah* (the goddess) was the popular object of worship in the environs of al-Ṭāʾif, about sixty miles east of Mecca.

10. "Manāh" derives her name from *manīyah*: allotted fate; she was the goddess of destiny, and her sanctuary was situated mainly between Mecca and Medina.

11. Exodus 3:1, 18:10–12.

12. For details consult Henri Lammens, *Les chrétiens à la Mecque à la veille de l'hégire: l'Arabie occidentale avant l'hégire* (Beyrouth: Imprimerie Catholique, 1928), pp. 12 *seq.*

13. Such traditions were preserved by ibn-Rustah, *al-Aʿlāq al-Nafīsah*, ed. De Goeje (Leyden, 1892), pp. 192 and 217.

14. Cf. *Sūrahs* 2:140, 5:14, 15.

15. "The wandering Arabs are more hard in disbelief and hypocrisy, and were likely to be ignorant of the limits which Allah hath revealed unto His messenger." (Qurʾān 9:97).

16. These convictions were shaped mostly by animistic practices. C. Snouck Hurgronje, *Mohammedanism* (New York: G. P. Putnam's Sons, 1916), p. 36.

17. Eric R. Wolf, "The Social Organization of Mecca and the Origins of Islam," *Southwestern Journal of Anthropology*, Vol. 7, No. 4 (Winter, 1951), p. 338.

18. Julius Wellhausen, *Reste arabischen Heidentums* (2nd ed.; Berlin, 1897), pp. 218 *seq.*

19. Same as Mandeans, or the so-called Christians of St. John, to whom the Qurʾān refers as peoples possessing scriptures.

20. Known also as *Majūs* or Zoroastrians. They too were treated as "Scripturaries" by Muḥammad and thus spared the ill-fate of the pagans.

21. Julius Wellhausen, *Skizen und Vorarbeiten* (6 vols.; Berlin: Reimer, 1884–99), Vol. III, p. 88.

22. Leone Caetani, *Annali dell' Islam*, Vol. I (Milan: Hoepli, 1905), p. 148.

23. Frants Buhl, *Das Leben Muhammeds*, trans. H. H. Schaeder (Leipzig: Quelle and Meyer, 1930), pp. 36 *seq.*

3. Muḥammad the Prophet

1. Frants Buhl, *op. cit.*

2. For a detailed account based on original sources of the known facts of his life consult Sir Wm. Muir, *The Life of Mohammad* (Edinburgh: John Grant, 1923), pp. 13 *seq.*

3. Qurʾān 96:1–5.

4. The term by which pre-Islamic monotheists were known.

5. Qurʾān 10:95.

6. Qurʾān 74:1–5.

7. Qurʾān 94:1.

8. Literally "he who senses," i.e. the unknown, by some extra-sensory power ordinarily attributed to the person who is in "league" with the *Jinn.*

9. Qurʾān 17:22.

10. Qurʾān 17:18.

11. Qur'an 49:11.

12. Qur'an 49:13.

13. Ibn Hishām, *op. cit.*, p. 119.

14. Qurʾān 41:4.

15. Qurʾān 41:6.

16. Qurʾān 22:52.

17. The three female deities were regarded by pagan Arabs, who deplored female offspring, as the daughters of Allah; hence the reference to "unjust division."

18. Qurʾān 53:21–23.

19. There are 17 references in the Qurʾān to demands made by the Qurayshites for a sign or a miracle.

20. Qurʾān 22:42–44.

21. It was officially established by the caliph ʿUmar in the year 639, as beginning with Muharram of the year 622.

22. Arabic "*Hijrah*" does not

mean "flight," as the misconception seems to prevail, but rather "a series of migrations."

23. Ibn Hishām, *op. cit.,* p. 342; R. A. Nicholson, *A Literary History of the Arabs* (Cambridge University Press, 1956), p. 158. See also R. B. Serjeant "The Sunnah Jāmiʿah" for additional details.

24. For details, see Ibn Hishām, *op. cit.*, pp. 231–34.

25. L. Caetani, *op. cit.*, Vol. I, p. 389.

26. Qur'ān 22:38–40.

27. Qur'ān 2:190–91.

28. Qur'ān 3:13.

29. Qur'ān 8:17.

30. Qur'ān 9:12.

31. Qur'ān 9:18.

32. Qur'ān 49:10.

33. Qur'ān 110:1–3.

34. Qur'ān 9:29.

35. Qur'ān 9:30–32.

36. Ibn Hishām, *op. cit.*, p. 651 (translation modified).

37. Notably al-Aswad, a Yemenite chief, a man of great wealth and sagacity who won over his tribesmen, forced himself on a number of neighboring towns killing Shahr, Muḥammad's governor at Ṣanʿāʾ who had gained the conversion to Islam of the Persian colony there and was killed by them in retaliation. The other two pretenders, Tulayḥah and Hārūn, or Musaylimah as he is better known, were not suppressed until after the Prophet's death, during the caliphate of Abu Bakr (632–34).

4. Muḥammad the Man

1. Qur'ān 2:136.

2. Qur'ān 5:3.

3. M. J. DeGoeje, "Die Berufung Mohammed's," in *Nöldeke-Festschrift* (Giessen, 1906), Vol. I, p. 5.

4. Wm. Muir, *op. cit.*, pp. 329 *seq.*

5. Qur'ān 3:102-105.

6. Sam. v. 13; I Chron. iii, 1–9, XIV, 3.

7. Kings 11:3.

8. 2 Chron. 11:21.

9. In the Battle of Badr, Khumays was killed and his wife, Ḥafsa, daughter of his loyal supporter and the future caliph ʿUmar, was widowed. At first she was offered to ʿUthmān, another future caliph, but he declined, then to Abu Bakr, Muḥammad's father-in-law, but he refused also. She settled for Muḥammad.

10. *Sūrah* 33:37.

11. These insinuations resulted from the 19th-century infatuation with scientifically superficial theories of medical psychology and the theories of those who applied them in their search for some scientific explanation based on such admissions as Muḥammad being in a semi-conscious and trance-like state with occasional loss of consciousness when he received revelations.

12. Tor Andrae, *Mohammed: The Man and his Faith*, trans. Theophil Menzel (New York: Harper Torch Book Series, 1960), p. 51.

13. Guillaume, *Islam* (Pelican, 1961 reprint), p. 28.

14. Qur'ān 2:136.

15. Qur'ān 3:144.

16. Qur'ān 33:40.

17. Qur'ān 2:113.

18. Qur'ān 2:120.

19. Qur'ān 2:121.

20. Qur'ān 5:57.

21. Qur'ān 5:59.

22. Qur'ān 5:51.

23. Qur'ān 22:35–36.

24. R. Bosworth Smith, *Mohammed and Mohammedanism* (London, 1889), p. 341.

25. Preserved by Ibn Hishām, *op. cit.*, p. 151; trans. and cit. P. K. Hitti, *History of the Arabs* (7th ed.; London, 1960), p. 121.

26. *Sūrah* 17: 22–37.

27. From "*Sūrat al-Nisā'*," Qur'ān 4:2 *seq.*

28. Qur'ān 17:38.

29. Qur'ān 17:39.

30. J. H. Hottinger, *Historia Orientalis*, 2nd ed., Zürich, 1651.

31. Published in London in 1730; cit. Tor Andrae, *op. cit.*, p. 173.

32. *Le Coran traduit de l'arabe précédé d'un abregé de la vie de Mahomet* (Paris, 1752), Vol. I, p. 221.

33. Hurgronje, *op. cit.*, pp. 23–24

34. Cited by Tor Andrae, *op. cit.*, p. 175.

5. Foundations of Islam: The Qur'ān

1. *Sūrah* 43:4–5.

2. See Toby Lester, "What is the Koran?" in *The Atlantic Monthly* (January 1999), pp. 43–57.

3. It is only in the 9th *Sūrah* that it does not occur.

4. *Sūrah* 56:95; 69:1.

5. *Sūrah* 2:164, 255.

6. *Sūrah* 69:40–41.

7. Qur'ān 26:224–226.

8. R. A. Nicholson, *op. cit.*, p. 159.

9. Qur'ān 113:1–3, 5.

10. Qur'ān 114: 1, 4–6.

11. Nicholson, *op. cit.*, p. 166 (with minor alterations).

12. H. A. R. Gibb, *Mohammedanism* (2nd ed.; Oxford University Press, 1953), p. 41.

13. Qur'ān 112:1–4.

14. Qur'ān 5:74.

15. Qur'ān 82:1–5.

16. Theodor Noldeke, *Geschichte des Qorāns*, ed. Fr. Schwally (Wiesbaden, 1961 reprint), Vol. I, pp. 53 *seq.*

17. See Julian Obermann's "Islamic Origins" in *The Arab Heritage*, ed. N. A. Faris (Princeton, 1946), pp. 58–120.

18. The alphabet lacked vowel symbols and even symbols to express emphasis. It also expressed several consonants by the same character. Were it not for dots, which did not exist at the time the Qur'ān was codified but added later according to a fixed order, and in reference to the present form of these symbols the same symbol could mean B, T, Th, N, or Y at the beginning and in the middle of words, where F, Q and W could also be readily confused for each other.

19. Published in Cairo, 1321 A.H. (1903).

20. Ed. Nassau-Lees, Calcutta, 1859.

21. Ed. H. G. Fleicher, Leipzig, 1846–48.

22. Hitti, *op. cit.*, p. 126.

23. Published for the first time in 1930, reprinted by Mentor numerous times since then. It is the version utilized mostly in this work.

6. The Fundamentals of Islam: Beliefs

1. R. A. 'Azzām, *The Eternal Message of Muḥammad*, trans. Caesar E. Farah (New York: The Devin-Adair Co., 1964), 3rd printing, Cambridge, 1993. p. 35.

2. Qur'ān 3:19.

3. Qur'ān 22:78.

4. Qur'ān 3:3.

5. Qur'ān 6:84–90.

6. Qur'ān 3:64.

7. Arabic "*Umm al-Qurah*," title by which Mecca became known.

8. Qur'ān 6:91–93.

9. Qur'ān 5:3.
10. Qur'ān 25:2.
11. A. A. Galwash, *The Religion of Islam* (2nd ed.; Cairo: I'timād Press, 1945), Vol. I, p. 139.
12. Qur'ān 112:1–4.
13. Qur'ān 7:54.
14. Qur'ān 16:3–12.
15. Qur'ān 13:9.
16. Qur'ān 6:59.
17. Qur'ān 3:26–27.
18. Qur'ān 7:180.
20. Qur'ān 76:8–9
19. *al-Maqṣad al-Asna* (2nd ed.; Cairo, 1324 A.H.), pp. 12 *seq*.; al-Baghawi, *Maṣābīḥ al-Sunna* (Cairo: Khayrīyah, 1900), Vol. I, pp. 96–97.
20. Qur'ān 59:23–24.
21. Qur'ān 4:124.
22. Qur'ān 11:52.
23. 'Azzām, *op. cit*., p. 60.
24. Qur'ān 85:22.
25. Whence the English "genii."
26. Qur'ān 17:23–39.
27. Qur'ān 82:19.
28. Qur'ān 20:102.
29. Qur'ān 69:13–18.
30. Qur'ān 20:109.
31. Qur'ān 3:10.
32. Qur'ān 18:50.
33. Qur'ān 42:22.
34. Qur'ān 76:12–15, 19, 21–22.
35. Qur'ān 78:23–26,
36. Qur'ān 10:27–38.
37. Qur'ān 4:48.
38. Qur'ān 4:56.
39. Qur'ān 42:40.
40. Qur'ān 10:108.
41. Qur'ān 54:49.
42. Qur'ān 3:145.
43. Qur'ān 87:2–3.
44. Qur'ān 9:51.
45. Qur'ān 15:21.
46. Qur'ān 25:2.
47. Reprinted from the official magazine of al-Azhar; Galwash, *op. cit*., p. 221.
48. Reproduced from al-Azhar's official publication; Galwash, *op. cit*., p. 222.
49. Qur'ān 16:90.
50. Qur'ān 6:163–164.
51. Qur'ān 2:155–157.
52. Qur'ān 18:30.

7. The Fundamentals of Islam: Obligations

1. Qur'ān 2:277.
2. Qur'ān 76:8–9.
3. Qur'ān 3:31.
4. Qur'ān 3:32.
5. Qur'ān 46:15.
6. Qur'ān 17:23–24.
7. Qur'ān 25:63.
8. Qur'ān 4:36–37.
9. Qur'ān 107:1–3.
10. Qur'ān 2:177.
11. Qur'ān 4:36.
12. Qur'ān 4:2.
13. Qur'ān 4:8.
14. Qur'ān 4:10.
15. Qur'ān 4:135.
16. The fundamental law of Islam, its constitution.
17. Qur'ān 5:8.
18. Qur'ān 5:8.
19. Qur'ān 4:58.
20. Qur'ān 6:153.
21. Qur'ān 51:19.
22. 'Azzām, *op. cit*., p. 91.
23. Qur'ān 9:34–35.
24. Qur'ān 2:275–276.
25. Qur'ān 59:8–9.
26. Qur'ān 49:10.
27. Qur'ān 9:71.
28. 'Azzām, *op. cit*., p. 80.
29. Qur'ān 6:33.
30. 'Azzām, *op. cit*., p. 75.
31. *Ibid*., p. 77.
32. Qur'ān 49:13.
33. Qur'ān 9:71.
34. Qur'ān 3:104.
35. 'Azzām, *op. cit*., p. 54.
36. Cited by L. V. Vaglieri, *An Interpretation of Islam*, trans. from

Italian by A. Caselli (Washington, D.C., 1957), p. 38.

37. Qur'ān 3:31.

38. Qur'ān 7:156.

39. Qur'ān 17:82.

40. Qur'ān 3:159.

41. Qur'ān 9:128.

42. Qur'ān 36:46.

43. Qur'ān 17:26–27.

44. Tor Andrae, *op. cit.*, p. 80.

45. From Arabic *masjid* or "place of prostration," transcribing in a literal sense an essential component of the prayer ritual.

46. The day is called "*al-Jum'ah*" (the "congregation"), named for this particular ceremony.

47. Qur'ān 62:9–10.

48. Qur'ān 17:78.

49. Mecca.

50. Jerusalem.

51. Qur'ān 4:43.

52. Vaglieri, *op. cit.*, p. 46.

53. At the beginning of his stay in Medina Muḥammad had chosen Jerusalem as the *qibla* of Islam but with the submission of Mecca he made it the center instead.

54. Fully illustrated by E. W. Lane, *Manners and Customs of the Modern Egyptians* (London, 1895), pp. 89–93.

55. Ameer 'Ali, *The Spirit of Islam* (London, 1952), p. 165.

56. Lane, *op. cit.*, p. 90.

57. Vaglieri, *op. cit.*, p. 45.

58. *Ibid.*, p. 46.

59. Qur'ān 29:45.

60. Qur'ān 24:56.

61. Qur'ān 57:18.

62. Qur'ān 9:60.

63. Qur'ān 2:183.

64. Qur'ān 2:184.

65. It is probable that the fast was formally instituted during Muḥammad's second year at Medina (624) when the corrected lunar year was in use and Ramaḍān, the ninth month, always fell in the winter when days were shorter. Then Muḥammad a few years later decreed the use of the uncorrected lunar year, which system has prevailed ever since.

66. Qur'ān 2:187.

67. Qur'ān 2:184.

68. Qur'ān 2:187.

69. Qur'ān 3:97.

70. M.Gaudefroy-Demombynes, *Muslim Institutions* (London, 1954), p. 99.

71. Refers to Muḥammad's nocturnal ascent to the Seventh Heaven.

8. Solidarity Through Institutional Unity

1. Developed out of legislation based on the Qur'ān and Traditions. See below, pp. 160–61.

2. Their caliphate was centered on Damascus and lasted trom 661 to 750.

3. Ruled from Baghdad, 750–1258.

4. Literally "someone who comes between."

5. At one time, in the tenth century, there were three independent caliphs, at Cairo, Cordova, and Baghdad.

6. A variety of what may be termed "ethnic nationalism."

7. During the caliphates of the 'Abbāsid al-Mutawakkil (847–61) and the Fāṭimid al-Ḥakam (996–1020) certain extra-legal discriminations occurred.

8. Sanctioned by the Ḥanafite, one of the four principal schools of jurisprudence in orthodox Islam.

9. Principally sanctioned by the Mālikite school of jurisprudence.

10. A sort of dowry paid to the bride's father or guardian for her benefit and use should she be widowed or divorced.

11. The formal "demand" in marriage or "engagement" after preliminary investigations and negotiations had taken place.

12. Literally when the "appointment for consummation" is to be held, or wedding day.

13. A specific type of school called *maktab, kuttāb* where the Qur'ān and related subjects are taught.

14. Someone who has committed the text to memory.

15. The other three are: Māliki, Ḥanafi and Ḥanbali.

16. Their centers of study were invariably their meeting places known as *ribāṭ, khanaqāh, takīyah* (tekke) and *zāwiyah.*

17. Known in Turkey as Büyük Bayram, and in certain parts of the Arab World as al-ʿĪd al-Kabīr or ʿĪd al-Qurbān. See above, p. 149.

18. Known also as al-ʿĪd al-Ṣaghīr (the little feast) and Küçük Bayram.

19. Muḥarram, Ṣafar, Rabīʿ al-Awwal, Rabīʿ al-Thāni, Jumāda al-Awwal, Jumāda al-Thāni, Rajab, Shaʿbān, Ramaḍān, Shawwāl, Dhu'l Qaʿdah and Dhu'l Ḥijjah.

20. Qur'ān 2:276.

9. Heterodoxy and Orthodoxy

1. For a detailed treatment of the philosophical and religious views of this important sectarian movement see Elie Salem's *Political Theory and Institutions of the Khawārij.* (Bibliography).

2. For the line of descent in order of their Imāmate: ʿAli (d. 661), al-Ḥasan (d. 669), al-Ḥusayn (d. 680), ʿAli Zayn al-ʿAbidīn (d. ca. 712), Muḥammad al-Bāqir (d. 731), Jaʿfar al-Ṣādiq (d. 765), Mūsa al-Kāẓim (d. 799), ʿAli al-Riḍa (d. 818), Muḥammad al-Jawād (d. 835), ʿAli al-Hādi (d. 868), al-Ḥaṣan al-ʿAskari (d. 874), Muḥammad al-Muntaẓar (al-Mahdi) ("disappeared" 878).

3. Adam, Noah, Abraham, Moses, Jesus, Muḥammad, and Muḥammad al-Tāmm, son of Ismāʿīl.

4. Included among others Ishmael, Aaron, Peter and ʿAli.

5. For details consult M. A. al-Shahrastāni, *Kitāb al-Milal wa-'l-Niḥal,* ed. Rev. W. Cureton (*Book of Religious and Philosophysical Sects, Parts I and II*) (London, 1842), pp. 145 *seq.* and W. Ivanow, *A Guide to Ismaili Literature,* London, 1933.

6. Hitti, *op. cit.,* pp. 443–444.

7. See L. Massignon, "Karmatians," *Encyclopedia of Islam,* Vol. II (Leyden and London, 1927), pp. 767–772.

8. We have an interesting description of them by Marco Polo, who passed through the region shortly after its destruction in his *The Book of Ser Marco Polo, the Venetian,* trans. Henry Yule (2nd ed.; London, 1875), Vol. I, pp. 46–49.

9. P. K. Hitti, *The Lebanon in History* (New York: St. Martin Press, 1956), pp. 261–262.

10. In reference to the fez-like cap they wear.

11. H. A. R. Gibb, *op. cit.,* p. 99.

12. Full Title: *Kitāb al-Jāmiʿ al-Ṣaḥīḥ* (The book of the verified compendium), ed. for the first time by L. Krehl and T. W. Juynboll (Leyden, 1862). It actually lists 7275, of which 3275 are repetitions.

13. *Kitāb al-Sunan* of Abu Dā'ūd (817–888) (ed. Cairo, 1863; Lucknow, 1888; Delhi, 1890); *al-Jāmiʿ al-Ṣaḥīḥ* of al-Tirmidhi (d. ca. 892); *Kitāb al-Sunan* of Nasa'i (830–915) (ed. Cairo, 1894), and the *Kitāb al-Sunan* of ibn Māja

(824–866) (ed. Delhi, 1865 and 1889). These have been reprinted with annotations in Cairo, Damascus and elsewhere.

14. It includes an introduction to the "Science of Tradition," edited for the first time in Calcutta, 1894.

15. Guillaume, *op. cit.*, pp. 97–98.

16. G. Bergstrasser, *Gründzuge des Islamischen Rechts*, ed. Joseph Schacht, cited by H. A. R. Gibb, *op. cit.*, p. 106.

10. Formalism and Free Expression

1. For details consult A. de Vlieger's *Kitāb al-Qadr*, materiaux pour servir a l'étude de la doctrine de la predestination dans la theologie musulmane, Leyde: E. J. Brill, 1903.

2. Known also as the "Imām of al-Ḥaramayn."

3. *Mantiq al-Tayr* C.S. Nott's English translation from the French translation of Garcin de Tassy. Boulder: Shamabala, 1954.

4. This is extensively treated by Abu Hāmid al-Ghazāli in his *Kasr al-Shahwatayn*. English translation and annotation by Caesar E. Farah under the title *Curbing the Two Appetites* (food and sex). Minneapolis: Bibliotheca Islamica, 1992.

5. Cited by Margaret Smith in her *Readings from the Mystics of Islam*. London: Luzac, 1972, p. 11.

6. Gibb, *op. cit.*, p. 135.

7. Louis Massignon, *La Passion d'al-Ḥallaj: martyr mystique de l'Islam* (Paris, 1922), Vol. II, p. 518.

8. Al-Ḥujwīri, *Kashf al-Mahjūb*, new ed. R. A. Nicholson (London: Luzac, 1959), p. 363.

9. *Ibid.*

10. D. B. MacDonald, *Development of Muslim Theology* (New York, 1903), pp. 238 *seq.*

11. R. A. Nicholson, "Mysticism," in *Legacy of Islam*, ed. Sir Thomas Arnold and Alfred Guillaume (Oxford University Press, 1960), p. 222.

12. Guillaume, *op. cit.*, p. 149.

13. Hitti, *op. cit.*, p. 587.

14. For debates over ibn ʿArabi's views see Alexander D. Kynsh's *Ibn ʿArabi in the Later Islamic Tradition.* Albany: State University of New York Press.

15. Translation by Margaret Smith in her *Readings*, p. 97.

16. See J. P. Brown, *The Darwishes or Oriental Spiritualism* (Oxford, 1927) for further details.

17. Founded by Aḥmad al-Badawi (d. 1276), and known sometimes as Aḥmadīyah, with two other offshoots in Egypt: Bayyūni and Dasūqi orders, popular in the lower confines of the Nile Valley.

18. From an unpublished manuscript, Madeleine F. Habib, "A Nakshbandi Session," p. 3.

19. For a sampling of Sufi literary genres see Caesar E. Farah's "The Prose Literature of Sufism" in *The Cambridge History of Arabic Literature*, Young, Latham and Sergeant (eds.). (Cambridge University Press, 1990), pp. 56-75.

11. "Medievalism" and the Dawn of "Renaissance"

1. Translated into French by B. Michel and M. Abdel Razik, Paris, 1925. Translated into English by I. Musāʿad and N. Cragg with the title *The Theology of Unity*, Arno Press, 1980.

2. John Esposito, *Islam, the Straight Path*, London: Oxford University Press, 1988, pp. 123–124.

3. *Ibid.*, p. 124.

4. First published in London, 1922.

5. Guillaume, *op. cit.*, p. 160.

6. Published for the first time in London, 1934.

7. H. A. R. Gibb, *Modern Trends in Islam* (Chicago, 1950), p. 60.

8. *The Reconstruction of Religious Thought in Islam* (London, 1934), p. 54.

9. Maḥmūd Aḥmad, *Ahmadiyyat or the True Islam* (Calcutta, 1924), p. 32.

10. M. Aḥmad in *Review of Religions* (Feb. 1952), p. 8. Cited by H. J. Fischer, *Aḥmadiyyah* (Oxford, 1963), p. 45.

11. C. C. Adams, *Islam and Modernism in Egypt* (London 1933), p. 129.

12. M. Aḥmad, *Ahmadiyya Movement* (London, 1924), p. 46.

13. *Review of Religions* (expresses the Qādiyāni view) (March, 1952), p. 40, cited by Fisher, *op. cit.*, p. 59.

14. Charles M. Remey, *A Series of Twelve Articles Introductory to the Bahá'i Teachings* (Florence 1925), p. 29.

15. *Ibid.*, p. 145.

16. *Ibid.*, p. 146.

12. Islamic Resilience

1. J. M. Gullick, "Indigenous Political Systems of Western Malays," London, 1965, as cited by Hussin Mutalib, *Islam and Ethnicity in Malay Politics*. Oxford University Press, 1990, p. 13.

2. Hussin Mutalib, *Islam and Ethnicity in Malay Politics*. Oxford Universtiy Press, 1990, p. 10.

3. Denys Lombard, "Islam and Politics in the Countries of the Malay Archipelago," in Oliver Carré (ed), *Islam and the State of the World Today* (translation). New Delhi: Manohar, 1987, pp. 140–141.

4. Mutalib, p. 23.

5. *Ibid.*, p. 236

6. Mohamed Suffian Hashim, "The Relationship Between Islam and the State of Malaya," *Intisari, I/1* (1962), p. 18.

7. Mutalib, p. 156.

8. M. Ali Kettani, *Muslim Minorities in the World Today*. London & New York: Mansell, 1986, p. 57.

9. Oliver Carré (ed), *Islam and the State of the World Today* (translation). New Delhi: Mahonar, 1987, p. 237.

10. Justice M. Van Koref, "Some Social and Political Aspects of Islam in Indonesia," *The Islamic Review*, "Working," July 1957, p. 3.

11. Anthony H. Johns, "Indonesia, Islam and Cultural Pluralism," in John Esposito (ed), *Islam in Asia. Religion, Politics and Society*. Oxford University Press, 1987, p. 203.

12. Clifford Geertz, *The Religion of Jawa*. The Free Press of Glencoe, 1960.

13. Johns, p. 203.

14. *Ibid.*, p. 207.

15. *Ibid.*, p. 208.

16. *Ibid.*, p. 209.

17. B. J. Boland, *The Struggle of Islam in Modern Indonesia*. The Hague, 1981, as cited by Johns, p. 209.

18. Full account of the marriage law by Katz and Katz in "The New Indonesian Marriage Law," *American Journal of Comparative Law 23:4*, Fall 1975, as cited by Johns, p. 218.

19. For distribution by region, see Kettani, p. 139.

20. *Ibid.*, p. 140.

21. *Ibid.*, p. 141.

22. *Ibid.*, p. 149.

23. The term presumably derives from Bilal, the first muezzin of Islam, first called upon by the prophet Muḥammad himself to perform this task.

24. Kettani, p. 150.

25. *Ibid.*, pp. 137–138.

26. Lela Garner Noble, "The Philippines, Autonomy for the Muslims," in Esposito, p. 98.

27. *Ibid.*, p. 101.

28. From *Straits Times*, June 26, 1974, as cited by Noble, p. 105.

29. Kettani, pp. 16–18.

30. *Ibid.*, pp. 154–155.

31. Chen Yuan, *An Outline History of the Propagation of Islam in China*, 1928, cited by Gao Wangzhi's study of Chen's History of Religions (paper presented August 1980 at Winnipeg), p. 17.

32. Pertaining to the history of the Yuan Dynasty. Cited by Gao Wangzhi, *ibid.*, p. 17.

33. *Ibid.*

34. Jin Yi Jiu, "The Koran in China." Paper presented at a symposium on the history of religions, Winnipeg (August 1980), pp. 4–8.

35. Yang I-fan, *Islam in China*, Hong Kong, 1957, p. 15.

36. *The Agrarian Reform Law of the People's Republic of China*. Peking: Foreign Languages Press, 1953, pp. 2, 6.

37. Such as his *On the People's Democratic Dictatorship, on New Democracy, the Chinese Revolution and the Chinese Communist Party*. Yang I-fan, *op. cit.*, p. 54.

38. *Jen Min Jih Pao*, August 5, 1952 and *Kwangming Jih Pao*, September 24, 1952.

39. *Kwangming Jih Pao*, May 25, 1955.

40. Ma Chien, translator, *Kelan Jing*. Sanghai: Commercial Press, 1952, Vol. I, p. 1.

41. *Sūrah* 16:78.

42. *Kelan Jing*, pp. 11–12.

43. *Sūrah* 10:37.

44. *Kelan Jing*, p. 30.

45. *Sūrah* 58:22.

46. *Hong Kong Ta Kung Pao*, November 22, 1944.

47. Asa Bā Faqīh, an Indonesian Muslim who visited Muslim places in China and reported his findings in his *A Muslim Visits China*, Singapore, 1955.

48. Interview with Abdul Wahab Bashir, "Muslim Plight Under Beijing Exposed," *Arab News*, January 19, 1993.

49. Kettani, p. 57.

50. *Ibid.*, pp. 58–59.

51. Bashkiria, Tataria, Daghestan, Udmurtia, Tchuvachia, Mordovia, Tchechen-Ingush, Mary, Kabard-Balkar, and Northern Ossets.

52. Adighia and Karachai-Tcherkess.

53. Southern Ossets.

54. Uzbekistan, Turkmenistan, Tadjikistan, and Kirghizia.

55. Azerbaidjan.

56. For details and statistical tables focusing on the demographic distribution of Muslims in the former USSR, see Kettani, pp. 62–66.

57. Jean-Paul Roux, *L'Islam en Asie*. Paris: Payot, 1958, p. 237.

58. *Ibid.*, 246.

59. Alexandre Benningsen and Chantal Lemercier-Quelquejay, "Islam in the Soviet Muslim Republics," in Olvier Carre (ed), *Islam and the State of the World Today* (translation). New Delhi: Mahonar, 1987, pp. 140–141.

60. Kettani, p. 64.

61. Sheikh R. Ali, "The Muslim Minority in the Soviet Union," *Current History*, April 1980, p. 186.

13. Islamic Dynamism

1. M. Ali Kettani, *Muslim Minorities in the World Today*. London & New York: Mansell, 1986, p. 160.

2. Dean S. Gilliland, *African Religion Meets Islam. Religious Change in Northern Nigeria.* University Press of America, 1986, pp. 19–20.

3. Pierre Rondot, *L'Islam et le Musulmans d'Aujourd'hui*. Paris, 1960, Vol. II, pp. 37–38.

4. P. Azam, "Les limites de l'Islam africain," *L'Afrique et l'Asie* (January, 1948), p. 45.

5. J. N. D. Anderson, *Islamic Law in Africa*. London, 1954, p. 219.

6. J. Richard-Molard, *Afrique Occidentale Française*. Paris, 1949, pp. 87 *seq*.

7. P. Alexandre, "L'Islam Noir," *Marchés tropicaux du Monde* (October 12 and 19, 1957), pp. 2386–2387.

8. For additional details on the current status of Islam in Africa see Jon Kraus, "Islamic Affinities and International Politics in Sub-Saharan Africa," *Current History* (April 1980), pp. 154–58, 182–84.

9. E. Psichari, *Terres de soleil et de Sommeil*. Paris, 1923, pp. 262 *seq*.

10. The practice is especially evident among the Lebou. See Rondot, *op. cit.*, p. 43.

11. M. Chailley, *Aperçu sur l'Islam en A.O.F.*, unedited papers of a conference held at Dakar in 1959, cit. Rondot, *op. cit.*, p. 45.

12. E. D. Morel, *Nigeria, Its People and Its Problems*. London, 1911, pp. 216–217.

13. G. Haines (ed). *Africa Today*. Baltimore, 1955, p. 95.

14. John L. Esposito, *Islam, the Straight Path*. Oxford University Press, 1988, p. 121.

15. Beverlee Turner Mehdi, *The Arabs in America 1492–1977*. New York: Oceana Publications, 1978, pp. 1–2. See also Allen D. Austin (ed), *African Muslims in Ante-Bellum America*. New York: Garland, 1984, for additional details.

16. "Islamic Ideals in North America," in Earle Waught, Baha Abu-laban, Regula B. Qureshi (eds), *The Muslim Community in North America*. Edmonton: University of Alberta Press, 1983, p. 260.

17. Kettani, p. 192.

18. Yvonne Haddad, *The Muslims of America*. Oxford University Press, 1991, p. 3.

19. Edward Said, *Covering Islam*. London: Rutledge & Kegan Paul, 1981.

20. Gutbi Mahdi Ahmed, "Muslim Organizations in the United States" in Haddad, *The Muslims in America*, p. 16.

21. "MSA and Family Builds in the U.S.," *Arabia: The Islamic World Review*, May 1983, p. 63.

22. For their role in spreading the word see Larry Poston, *Islamic Daʿwah in the West: Muslim Missionary Activity and the Dynamics of Conversion to Islam*, Oxford University Press, 1992.

23. S. Mazhar Hussain, *Proceedings of the First Islamic Conference of North America*. New York: Muslim World League, 1977.

24. Yasin T. al-Jibouri, *A Brief History of the Islamic Society of Georgia, Inc.* Atlanta: Islamic Society of Georgia, n.d., p. 2.

25. Ismāʿīl al-Farūqi, *Islamization of Knowledge: General Principles and Workplan*. Washington, D.C.: International Institute of Islamic Thought, 1982, p. 61; cited by Larry A. Poston, "Daʿwa in the West" in Haddad, *The Muslims in America*, p. 133.

26. Cited from Robert D. Crane's *Preparing to Islamize America.* Reston, VA: International Institute of Islamic Thought, 1987 p. 10. In Haddad, p. 133.

27. Poston, *op. cit.*, p. 98.

28. Gutbi Mahdi Ahmed, "Muslim Organization in the United States" in Haddad, *The Muslims of America*, p. 18.

29. Some allege that Fard was an alias for a Syrian Druze peddler with whom Elijah Poole (his prior name) was in contact.

30. Elijah Muḥammad, *Fall of America* (Chicago: Muhammad Temple of Islam No. 2, 1973); *Message to the Black Man* (Chicago, No. 2, 1965); and *Supreme Wisdom: Solution to the So-Called Negro Problem* (Chicago: University of Islam, 1957). These preachings shaped his perceptions of Islam.

31. Renamed Sister Clara Muḥammad Schools.

32. Gutbi Ahmed, *op. cit.*, p. 19.

33. Malcolm X speech to Harvard University Law School Forum in 1960.

34. H. Tahir, "Black Muslims-Islam and America," *Action*, June 26, 1972.

35. Wārith al-Dīn, *As the Light Shineth from the East* (Chicago, 1980), and *Lectures of W.D. Muḥammad* (Chicago, 1978).

36. Eric Lincoln, "The American Muslim Mission in the Context of American Social History," In Earl H. Waught et al (eds), *The Muslim Community in North America.* Alberta: University of Alberta Press, 1983, p. 224.

37. *Ibid.*, p. 20.

38. Louis Lomax, *When the Word is Given.* Cleveland & New York, 1963, p. 87.

39. Jan Jaap de Ruiter, "Language and Religion: Moroccan and Turkish Communities in Europe" in *ISIM Newsletter* 1/98, p. 28.

40. For details see T. Gerholm & Y.G. Lithman (eds.), *The New Islamic Presence in Western Europe.* London, 1988.

41. Herman de Ley, "Muslims in Belgium: Enemies from within or Fellow-Citizens?" in *ISIM Newsletter* 1/98, p. 32.

42. For more on the Muslims of Southeast Europe see Alexandre Popovic's "Islam and the State in the Countries of South-Eastern Europe" in Carré, *Islam and the State*, pp. 108–123.

43. Additional details in Kettani's *Muslim Minorities*, pp. 35–43.

14. Islam in Transition

1. Violette Graff, "The Muslims of India" in Olivier Carré, *Islam and the State of the World Today* (translation). New Delhi: Mahonar, 1981, p. 195.

2. Syed Shahabuddin and Theodore Wright Jr., "India, Muslim Minority Politics and Society" in John Esposito (ed), *Islam in Asia. Religion, Politics and Society*, Oxford University Press, 1987, p. 155.

3. *Ibid.*, p. 158.

4. M. Ali Kettani, *Muslim Minorities in the World Today.* London & New York: Mansell, 1986, p. 121.

5. Freeland Abbott, *Islam and Pakistan.* Cornell University Press, 1968, p. 181.

6. Mawlāna Mawdūdi, *Islamic Law and Constitution.* Khurshid Ahmad, ed. Karachi, 1955, p. 56.

7. Keith Callard, *Pakistan, a Political Study.* London: Allen & Unwin, 1957, p. 230.

8. Marc Gaborieau, "The Polit-

ical Roles of Islam in Pakistan" in Carré's *Islam and the State of the World Today*, p. 187.

9. Kettani, pp. 141–142.

10. *Ibid.*, p. 144.

11. *Ibid.*, p. 147.

12. *Ibid.*, pp. 144–148.

13. Magnus & Naby, p. 139.

14. Olivier Roy, *Islam and Resistance in Afghanistan*. Cambridge University Press, 1986, p. 31.

15. *Ibid.*, p. 68.

16. *Ibid.*, p. 75.

17. Ashraf Ghani, "Afghanistan, Islam and Counterrevolutionary Movements" in Esposito's *Islam in Asia*, p. 87.

18. Rabbani came from a Ṣūfi background. He was considered a modernist *alim* who has pursued Islamic studies at Ankara and Cairo, graduating from the Azhar. In him converged the three ingredients: classical culture (follower of mystical poet Jami), spiritual orthodoxy (reflecting his Ṣūfi background), and politicized Islam (legacy of Afghani and Mawdūdi).

19. Godfrey Jansen "Who Started the Gulf War" in *Middle East International* (May 15, 1987), pp. 15–16, as cited by Joyce N. Wiley in *The Islamic Movement of Iraqi Shi'ahs*, Boulder & London: Lynne Rienner, 1987, p. 2.

20. Bakir, Al-Sadr, *Islamic Political System* (translated by M. A. Ansari). Karachi: Islamic Seminary, 1982, p. 36.

21. Citations from a number of other authorities by Feride Acar, "Islam in Turkey" in Canan Balkir & Allan M. Williams (eds), *Turkey and Europe*, London & New York: Pinter Publishers, 1993, p. 220.

22. Paul Dumont, "The Power of Islam in Turkey" in Carré's *Islam and the State of the World Today*, p. 77.

23. *Ibid.*, pp. 91–92.

24. Acar, p. 222.

25. For more on his role in modern Sudanese Islamic politics see Abdelwahab El-Affendi, *Turabi's Revolution, Islam and Power in Sudan*. London: Grey Seal, 1991.

26. John Esposito, "Sudan" in Shireen T. Hunder (ed), *The Politics of Islamic Revivalism*. Indiana University Press, 1988, pp. 195–196.

27. El-Affendi, p. 171.

28. *Ibid.*, p. 171.

29. *Ibid.*, p. 173.

30. Youssef M. Ibrahim, "Arabs Anxiously Accuse Iran of Fomenting Revolt" in *The New York Times*, December 21, 1992.

31. Impression of this author after a week's visit with educators, journalists, and officials in April 1992, all of whom raised the same point. Their suspicion is further reinforced by recent revelations that the informant in the World Trade Center episode was an Egyptian serving as "agent provocateur" presumably for both the U.S. and Egypt to provide the grounds to incarcerate Muslim militants working to end Mubarak's dictatorship.

32. Mohammad Arkoun, "Algeria" in Shireen T. Hunter (ed), *The Politics of Islamic Revivalism*, p. 172.

33. "Ben Bella's Bid for Islamic Leadership," *Arabia, the Islamic World Review* (February, 1981), p. 31.

34. Norma Salem, "Tunisia" in Shireen T. Hunter (ed), *The Politics of Islamic Revivalism*, p. 153.

35. *Ibid.*, p. 160.

15. Current Trends

1. Sadeq el Mahdi, "Iran: the Message of Revolution," in *Arabia, the Islamic World Review*, February 1981, p. 29.

2. *Ibid.*

3. Daniel Pipes, "This World is Political, The Islamic Revival of the Seventies," *Orbis*, Spring 1980, p. 29.

4. *The Middle East and North Africa 1979–80*. London: Europa Press, 1979, p. 166.

5. Pipes, *op. cit.*, p. 39.

6. Article 8 of its Covenant.

7. For more on their role in the resistance movement, see Fredrick R. Hunter, *The Palestinian Uprising*. University of California Press, 1993.

8. R. H. Dekmejian, "Islamic Revival in North Africa and the Middle East," *Current History*, April 1980, p. 172.

9. From published seminars by M. Tozy on the subject of "Politics and Religion in Morocco, Synthesis or Hierarchization?" delivered in 1980 before the Faculty of Law, Casablanca.

10. For details see *Minbar al-Islam*, year XXXVI, Nov. 1978, a publication of the Ministry of Religious Endowments, Cairo.

11. M. al-Bahīy, "Islamic Society, Owners and Workers Together," in *al-I'tiṣām*, July 1976, pp. 14 *seq*.

12. Citations from the *Manchester Guardian* in "Sādāt wa ʾ-Muʿāraḍāt fī Miṣr" (Sadat and Opposition in Egypt), in *al-Sharq al-Awsat* (The Middle East), London, September 5, 1981, p. 6.

13. Ahmed Abdallah, "Egypt's Islamists and the State, from Complicity to Confrontation," *Middle East Report*, issue dedicated to *Political Islam*, No. 183 (Vol. 23, no. 4, July–August, 1993), p. 29.

14. Louis Duprée, "Islam, Design for Political Stability," *The Christian Science Monitor*, February 1980.

15. Ali Sharīʿati, *On the Sociology of Islam* (English translation by Hamid Algar). Berkeley: Mizan Press, 1979, p. 121.

16. *Ibid.*, p. 42.

17. See "al-Islām wa ʾl-tajdīd" (Islam and Renewal), by M. S. Jalāl, *Minbar al-Islām* (The Platform of Islam), year XXXIX/8 (1401/1981), pp. 19–25.

18. *Qurʾān* (Pikthall translation): LI:20–21.

19. ʿAbd al-Fattāḥ Salāmah, "Kayfa ḥarrara ʾl-Islām al-ʿaql" (How Islam Liberated the Mind) in *al-Sharq al-Awsat*, Oct. 6, 1981, p. 13.

20. *op. cit.*, p. 43.

21. *Ibid.*, p. 49.

22. Encyclopedic edition, p. 471.

23. Sayid Mujtaba Rukni Musawi Lari, *Western Civilization Through Muslim Eyes*, translated by F. J. Goulding. Houston, Texas: Free Islamic Literatures, Inc., 1974, p. 25.

24. Mohammad Abdel Moneim Khamis, "Les relations humaines recommendées par l'Islam," *Minbar al-Islām*, XXXIX/11 (1401/1981), p. 135.

25. XVI:90.

26. Khadija J. Asad, "The Role of Women in the History of Islam," *Invitation*, Vol. 11, no. 2 (April 1993), p. 1

27. Fatima Mernissi, *Beyond the Veil*. New York, London: John Wiley & Sons, 1975.

28. *Ibid.*, viii

29. Jane I. Smith, "The Experience of Muslim Women,

Considerations of Power and Authority" in Hadda et al (eds), *The Islamic Impact*, p. 90.

30. For how women feel and react under pressure see Bouthaina Shaaban, *Both Right and Left Handed, Arab Women Talk About their Lives*. Indiana University Press, 1988, 1991.

31. IX:109.

16. Perspectives on Activist Islam

1. Karen Armstrong, *Muhammad — A Biography of the Prophet*, San Francisco: Harper-Collins, 1993, pp. 42–43.

2. Akhbar Ahmed, *Living Islam, From Samarkand to Stornoway*, New York: Facts on File, 1984, p. 18.

3. *Ibid.*, p. 19.

4. See entry by Paul Merritt Bassett in *Grolier's Academic American Encyclopedia* under "Fundamentalism."

5. For details see Leon T. Hadar's *The Green Peril: Creating the Islamic Fundamentalist Threat.* The author is a university professor and former bureau chief for the *Jerusalem Post.*

6. Robert Pelletreau, "Resurgent Islam in the Middle East" in *Middle East Policy* 3, no. 2 (August 1994), p. 3.

7. Johanna Pink, "Some Facts about Fundamentalism" in *One Europe Magazine*. Bonn, 1999.

8. *Ibid.*

9. Entitled "Islamic Activism and U.S. Foreign Policy," by Scott W. Hibbad & David Little, published by the Endowment of the United States Institute of Peace, Washington, D.C., 1997.

10. John Esposito, *The Islamic Threat; Myth or Reality*. New York: Oxford University Press, 1992, pp. 119–20.

11. *Islamic Activism*, p. 11.

12. Muhammad Faour, *The Arab World after Desert Storm*. Washington, D.C.: United States Institute of Peace, 1993, p. 55.

13. Albert Hourani, *A History of the Arab Peoples*. Cambridge, Mass.: The Belknapp Press of Harvard University Press, 1991, p. 452.

14. Augustus R. Norton, "Rethinking U.S. Policy toward the Muslim World" in *Current History* (February 1999), p. 52.

15. *Ibid.*

16. For details see the seminal authoritative work by R.P. Mitchell entitled *The Society of the Muslim Brothers*. Oxford: Oxford University Press, 1969.

17. Cited by John Kelsay in his *Islam and War: A Study in Comparative Ethics*. Louisville: Westminster, 1993, p. 104.

18. Mahmud Fakhsh, *The Islamic Challenge in the Middle East: Fundamentalism in Egypt, Algeria and Saudi Arabia*. Westport, Connecticut and London: Praeger, 1997, pp. 45–46.

19. For more, see David Butler, "Mubarak Haunted by Egypt's Past" in *Middle East Economic Digest* 26 (March 1993): 2.

20. Fakhsh, p. 45.

21. *Ibid.*, p. 47.

22. Ira M. Lapidus, "The Golden Age: The Political Concepts of Islam," in *Annals of the American Academy of Political and Social Science*, no. 524 (Nov. 1992): 21.

23. Fakhsh, p. 10.

24. See his *Manhaj al-Inqilāb al-Islāmi* (The Course of Islamic Transformation) (Beirut: Mu'assasat al-Ris-lah, 1975), p. 8.

25. Faksh, p. 17.

26. Norton, p. 52.

27. Sura 12, verse 20.

28. Hamid Algar, trans., *Islam*

and Revolution: Writings and Declarations of Imam Khomeini. Berkeley: Mizan Press, 1981, p. 39.

29. Daniel Pipes and Adam Garfinkel (eds), *Friendly Tyrants: An American Dilemma*, New York: St. Martin's Press, 1991, p. 220.

30. Norton, p. 53.

31. Cited by Khalid Bin Sayeed in his *Western Dominance and Political Islam: Challenge and Response*. Albany: State University of New York Press, 1995, p. 26.

32. *Ibid*., p. 22.

33. *Ibid*., p. 33.

34. William R. Baker, "Afraid for Islam: Egypt's Muslim Centrists between Pharaohs and Fundamentalists," in *Daedalus*, vol. 120, no. 3 (Summer 1991), pp. 43 seq.

35. See his *Miṣr fi Muftaraq al-Ṭuruq* (Egypt at the Crossroads). Cairo: Dār al-Mustaqbal al-ʿArabi, 1990, p. 138.

36. Sayeed Bin, p. 151.

37. See his "Reservations about Fundamentalism," *Salaam Discussion Forum [Help]* posted on the Internet; http://www.ramadhan./com/discussion/fasting; messages/15html.

38. Alan R. Taylor, *The Islamic Question in Middle East Politics*. Boulder and London: Westview Press, 1988, p. 105.

39. *Ibid*., pp. 105–106.

40. Sayeed Bin, p. 153.

Glossary

A

ʿ*abd*—servant, term applies to worshiper of God.

adab—the science of proper upbringing; in literature it relates to "belles lettres."

ʿ*ādah* (ʿ*adāt*)—customary practices usually local (see ʿĀdāt) having sanctity of law.

ʿ*Ādāt*—corpus of law deriving from custom and usage, legislation of secular heads.

"afkhar al-umam"—"noblest of nations"—Arab conception of his ancestry.

"ahl al-dhimmah"—peoples, i.e. Christians and Jews, whose protection was enjoined by the Qurʾān.

"ahl an-Sunnah wa-ʾl-Ḥadīth"—literally "the people of Sunnah and Ḥadīth," official title of those adhering to orthodox Islam.

"ahl al-tawḥīd wa-ʾl-ʿadl"—literally "the people of unitarianism and justice," title applied to the rationalists Muʿtazilites.

ajāwīd—title given to the most pious members of the Druze sect.

akhund—Chinese version religious instructor.

al-Amīn—"the trustworthy," name by which Muḥammad was known

al-asmāʾ al-ḥusna—"the nicest names," ninety-nine, attributes of God.

"al-Baqarah"—"the Cow," second chapter of the Qurʾān.

al-ʿĪd al-Kabīr—see ʿ*Īd al-Aḍḥa* (below).

al-ʿĪd al-Ṣaghīr—see ʿ*Īd al-Fiṭr* (below).

al-Ikhwān al-Muslimūn—The Muslim Brethren, militant lay society applying the strict tenets of Islam to present living.

al-Ilāh—"the deity," a variant of "Allah."

"al-ʿImrān"—"the Family of ʿImrān," third chapter of the Qurʾān.

al-Islām—see *Islām.*

al-Jamʿīyah al-Islāmīyah—"The Islamic Society."

al-Jazīrah—"the Island," i.e. the Arabian peninsula.

"al-Kawthar"—"the Abundance," Chapter CVIII of the Qurʾān.

al-Kitāb—"the Book," i.e. the Qur'ān.
al-Khulafā' al-Rāshidūn—"The Orthodox Caliphs": first four successors of Muḥammad.
Allah—God.
Allāhu akbar—"God is great"—begins ritual prayer.
al-Mukarramah—"The Highly Honored," appellation reserved to Mecca.
al-Murābiṭūn—a dynastic power heavily tinged by Ṣūfism that ruled North Africa and Spain ca. 1061-1147.
al-Muwaṭṭa'—the corpus of Tradition compiled by Mālik ibn-Anas.
"al-Naṣr"—"The Succor," Chapter CX of the Qur'ān.
"al-Nisā'"—"The Women," fourth chapter of the Qur'ān.
al-Raḥim—"The Most Merciful," a quality of God.
al-Raḥmān—"The Merciful," a quality of God.
al-Sā'ah—"The Hour," a term applied to the "hour of reckoning" with God.
"al-salāmu 'alaykum wa raḥmatu 'l-Lāh"—terminal point in the ritual prayer, recited by the worshiper, literally: "[May] peace [be] with you and the mercy of God [also]."
al-shahādah—see *Shahādah* (below).
al-Shayṭān al-Kabīr—"the Great Satan," also stele at Mina where a pilgrim casts his seven stones.
al-Tābi'ūn—plural of al-Tābi', term applied to a follower of the Prophet's companions.
al-'Urwah al-Wuthqa—title of al-Afghāni's important work on a revitalized political Islam.
'amalah—plural of *'āmil.*
amān—safety of person and possession decreed by the Muslim community for foreign residents.
'āmil—an official who supervised the collection and distribution of tithe.
amīr al-mu'minīn—"commander of the believers," title by which caliph was also known.
amīr al-umarā'—literally "prince of princes," title first given to Seljuk Sultans by 'Abbāsid caliph.
amr—"decree," i.e. command of Allah.
"ana al-Ḥaqq"—literally "I am the truth," famous utterance of al-Ḥallāj that cost him his life.
Anṣār —"Companions" of Muḥammad, his followers among the Medinans.
Anṣār Allah—formal title whence *"Naṣārah,"* or Christians derive.
'aqaba—steep slope, such as at beginning of road to Muzdalifa from Mina.
'aqd al-nikāḥ—formalization of the marriage vows.
'āqil—someone in full control of mental faculties; also singular of *'Uqqāl* (see below).
'aql—mind, intelligence; the "universal mind" to the Ismā'īlis.
'aṣabīyah—strong "clannish spirit" popular in pre-Islamic Arabia.
"ashhadu anna la ilāha illa 'l-Lāh"—formula by the proper utterance of which one becomes a Muslim.
'aṣr—period of sunset, time of one of the ritual prayers.
ayatullah—literally "miracle of God," title by which leading mullas of Shi'ite Iran are known.
"Ayyām al-'Arab"—period in pre-Islamic Arabia characterized by strong internecine wars.

B

bāligh—see *'āqil.*
Baqā'—Ṣūfi version of "indwelling in God."

bāṭini—esoteric, hidden or inner meaning of Allah's word in the Qur'an.
bayān—rhetoric as a discipline of study.
Bayān (The)—*Expositor*, principal source of doctrine of the Bahā'i sect.
Bayt al-Lāh—"House of God."
bid'a—"innovation," heresy, extra legal interpretations of Shar'ī law when *ijtihād* technically ceased.
birr—"beneficence."
"Bism'l-Lāhi Allahu akbar"—"In the name of God; God is great."
Büyük Bayram—Turkish term for *'Id al-Aḍḥa*.

D

dā'i—a missionary of the esoteric sects of Islam—Assassins, Druze, Ismā'īli.
dā'i al-du'āt—grand master of the order of Assassins, literally "missionary-in-chief."
Dā'i al-Kabīr—title granted the head of the order of Assassins.
Dār al-Ḥadīth—Seminary for the study of the corpus of Traditions.
dār al-ḥarb—territory outside the boundaries of Islam where wars of jihād were permissible.
dār al-Islām—lands of Islam where technically no war was permissible.
Dār al-'Ilm—school for the study of the "religious sciences."
darwīsh (dervish)—initiate of a Ṣūfi order.
da'wah—summon to the faith.
dhimmis—see *ahl al-dhimmah* (above).
dhu-'l-Ḥijjah—Muslim month when the formal pilgrimage to Mecca is staged.
dīn—term applied to the sum total of a Muslim's faith.
dīyah—"blood money," compensation for spilled blood to avoid retaliation in kind.
du'ā—"invocation," or supplication.

E

El—head of the pantheon among early Semites, particularly Canaanites and Hebrews.

F

fanā'—Ṣūfi "passing away in God," the mystical union of the soul with God.
faqīh—Islamic jurist.
faqīr (fakir)—a poor man, one in need; also a member of a Ṣūfi order, a dervish.
farḍ—canonically imposed duty or obligation of faith.
"Fātiḥah"—opening chapter of the Qur'ān.
fatwa—an opinion of a mufti on an issue of canonical law.
fidā'i—"self-sacrifier," he who did the killing for the Assassins.
fidya—expiatory alm rendered in compensation for a missed canonical obligation.
fi sabīl-'l-Lāh— "for the sake of Allah": a good deed to be counted on Jugdment Day.
Fiqh—the corpus of Islamic jurisprudence.
fuqahā'—plural of *faqīh* (above).
fuqarā'—singular of *faqīr*.
fuṭūr—the meal which breaks the period of the fast, usually at sunset. Cf. *suḥūr*.

G

Ghulāh—extremist Shī'ite who believes Allah mistakenly chosen Muḥammad for the prophetic role which He intended to 'Ali.

Ghusl—full ablution ceremony involving the entire body.

H

ḥadath—a type of defilement which would invalidate the ritual prayer.

ḥadīth—"sayings" of Muḥammad.

Ḥadīth—corpus of the sayings of Muḥammad, the man.

ḥāfiẓ—he who has committed to memory the verses of the Qur᾿ān.

ḥājib—term applied to the chamberlain; official position under ʿAbbāsids.

Ḥājj—one who has performed the pilgrimage to Mecca.

ḥajj—formal pilgrimage, usually in dhu-᾿l-Ḥijjah between the 7th and 10th of the month.

ḥalaqah—a "circle" of students or disciples of a given teacher or "master."

ḥanīf—title by which pre-Islamic monotheists were known.

ḥarām—canonically forbidden.

ḥaram—hallowed area, especially around the monuments of Mecca.

Ḥanīsh—same as in English; term from which "assassin" is said to have derived.

ḥuffāẓ—plural of *ḥāfiẓ*.

ḥujjah—those who propagandize for the Ismāʿīli doctrines.

ḥulūl—Ṣūfi term for the stage of "indwelling with God" after *fanā᾿* takes place.

I

ʿibādāt—acts of worship necessary for the discharge of the devotional rites of Islam.

Ibāḍis—sect of Islam, stemmed from moderate elements among the *Khawārij*.

Iblīs—the Devil.

ʿĪd al-Aḍḥa—feast of sacrifice on the 10th of dhu-᾿l-Ḥijjah commemorating the ritual started by Abraham.

ʿĪd al-Fiṭr—major feast heralding the end of the month of Fast (Ramaḍān).

ʿĪd al-Qurbān—same as *ʿĪd al-Aḍḥa*.

ifāḍah—quick march to Mina after the *wuqūf* at Muzdalifah on the ninth day of pilgrimage.

iḥsān—"right-doing" or proper conduct, a moral duty enjoined by Islam.

ijāzah—permission grantd by the master to the disciple to repeat his discourses elsewhere.

iʿjāz al-Qur᾿ān—"miraculousness of the Qur᾿ān," argument for it not being created in time.

Ijmāʿ—principle in jurisprudence of legislating by consensus of those in the community who knew Islamic dogma.

Ijtihād—individual interpretation of the tenets of the faith, a principal of jurisprudence.

Ikhwān al-Ṣafā᾿—Brethren of Purity, Ismāʿīli society that flourished in Medieval Islam.

Il—pre-Islamic title of head of pagan pantheism.

Ilāh—see *al-Ilāh*.

Imām—spiritual guide of the Shīʿite sect.

imām—head of the community and/or leader in the congregational prayer among Sunnis.

imām khaṭīb—the person who delivers the *khuṭbah* (see below) at the Friday noon prayer.

īmān—beliefs, i.e. of the religion, or faith.

Injīl—Gospel.

in shā᾿-al-Lāh—"God willing."

iqāma—call to prayer repeated at the beginning of the prayer ritual.

ʿirḍ—"honor."

ʿishāʾ—"evening meal," time of the fourth ritual prayer of the day.
Islam—literally "submission," i.e. to Allah.
isnād—the chain of transmitting *ḥadīth.*
istiḥsān—deducing a legalistic principle on the basis of prudence.
istiṣlāḥ—principle of jurisprudence whereby a legal principle may result from considering the welfare of the Islamic community at large.
iʿtazala—"to secede"; see *Muʿtazilah.*
Ithna ʿAsharīyah—"Twelvers," title of the principal Shīʿite sect who believe in the twelve Imāms.
iʿtidāl—"erect posture," first and third steps in the ritual prayer.
izār—seamless white cloth wrapped around lins to knee level by the pilgrim performing the ḥajj.

J

Jahannam—Hell.
Jāhilīyah—"Times of Ignorance," Arabia before it received the revelations of Allah.
jāʾiz—canonically permissible deed.
jāmiʿ—"mosque," Muslim house or worship.
Jamʿīyat al-Daʿwa wa-ʾl-Irshād—"Society for Propagation and Guidance."
janābah—great defilement necessitating the *ghusl* before the ritual prayer is to be rendered.
jihād—striving on behalf of the faith, known also as the "holy war."
jinn—"spirits," two types: evil and helpful.
jiwār—protection granted an outsider in pre-Islamic Arabia usually the result of dwelling in the ḥaram of a sanctuary.
Jizyah—tribute tax paid by non-Muslims enjoying the protection of the Muslims.
julūs—"sitting on base of heels." sixth and eighth steps in the ritual prayer.

K

kabīrah—major unpardonable sin.
kāfir—term for infidel, non-believer.
kalām—Muslim dialectics.
khalīfah—"caliph," successor to Muḥammad's secular authority.
khalwah—secluded place where the Druze sect holds its religious meetings.
khātimah—the seal, end or last, i.e. Muḥammad's prophethood.
Khawārij—first puritanical albeit militant sect of Islam.
khīrqah—special robe of investiture for an initiate of a Ṣūfi order.
khiṭbah—declaration of intent on marriage.
khuṭbah—sermon delivered by the imām in the mosque to the congregation, usually at the Friday congregation.
khuṭbat al-naʿt—an eulogy sermon following a fixed formula.
khuṭbat al-waʿẓ—sermon oriented towards pious exhortations.
kiswa—vesture covering the Kaʿbah, draped annually, presented in recent times by the sovereign of Egypt.
kuttāb (kātib) al-sirr—scribe-confidents, official positions in the Islamic administration under the ʿAbbāsids.
kuffār—plural of *kāfir.*
kursi—chair, in reference also to Allah's throne in Heaven.

L

"la ilāha illa ʾl-Lāh—"there is no god but God," first prayer of *Shahādah.*
lawḥ maḥfūz—tablet upon which the

Qur'ān is preserved in the Seventh Heaven.

lughah—language.

M

madhāhib—plural of *madhhab*.

madhhab—juridical rite to which a Sunni Muslim may adhere.

Madīnah—Medina, second holiest city in Islam.

Madīnat al-Rasūl—"City of the Prophet" or Medina.

madrasah—originally school of canon law.

maghrib—"sunset."

Maghrib—West North Africa.

maḥmal—palanquin, used to bear the kiswa annually at pilgrimage time to the Ka'bah.

mahr—form of dowry, a normal condition involved in a contract of marriage.

makrūh—canonically frowned upon deed.

malā'ikah—"angels."

Manār—*Lighthouse*, official publication of the Salafiyah.

manāsik al-ḥajj—ful ceremony of performing the pilgrimage.

mandūb—recommended not imposed act of faith.

Maqām Ibrāhīm—A monument in Mecca consisting of a sacred stone on which Abraham allegedly stoold while building the Ka'bah.

maqṣūrah—enclosure inside the mosque for prayer out of sight.

ma'rifah—Ṣūfi "knowledge of the Creator": gnosis.

Masjid al-Ḥarām—sacred mosque inside the ḥaram near the Ka'bah in Mecca.

maṣlaḥah—concept of "public good" or "general welfare."

maṭāf—ellipsoidal roadway surrounding the Ka'bah on which the pilgrim circumambulates the Ka'bah.

Matāwilah—title by which the Shī'ites of Lebanon are known.

mathal—"example," theologically: parable.

Mathnawī—also *Masnavi*, title of al-Rūmi's classical composition of Ṣūfi poetry.

mawāli—"clients": converts to Islam dependents of Muslim Arab aristrocracy under Umayyads.

mawāqit—see *mīqāt* (below).

Mawlid—Muḥammad's birthday, occasion of feasting.

maẓālims—legal category of "wrongs."

Miḥna—inquisition set up by the caliph al-Ma'mūn to enforce Mu'tazilite views on doctrine.

miḥrāb—niche in the mosque pointing to the direction of Mecca.

mīqāt—prescribed station on the approach to Mecca for performing preliminary rites in preparation for rendering the pilgrimage.

Mi'rāj—Muḥammad's nocturnal journey to the Seventh Heaven.

mubāḥ—see *jā'iz* (above).

mufti—juriconsult, interpreter of Islamic law among Sunnis.

Muhājirūn—"Emigrants," i.e. those who went to Medina from Mecca with Muḥammad.

mujāhid—he who exerts himself on behalf of the faith, particularly in a jihād.

mujāhidūn—plural of *mujāhid*.

mujtahid—religious spokesman and interpreter of dogma of the Shī'ite sect.

mujtahīdun—plural of *mujtahid*.

mulk—dominion, territorial possession, symbol of secular power.

Munāfiqūn—Hypocrites, a Medinan party tolerated by Muḥammad.

Muntaẓar—awaited Imām of the Shī'ites.

murabu—African religious leader with Ṣūfi connections.
murīd—Ṣūfi novice.
murū'ah—pre-Islamic Arab concept of "manliness."
musaḥir—determiner of the time to begin the fast at dawn. Cf. *muwaqqit.*
muslim—"one who submits."
Muslim—He who officially adheres to the faith of Islam.
mustaḥabb—see *mandūb* (above).
mut'ah—contracting temporary marriages, sanctioned by the Shī'ites.
muṭawwi'—Saudi missionary, an enforcer of religious injunctions in practice.
Mu'tazilah—Important school of rationalists of the ninth century championing "free will."
Muwaḥḥidūn—plural of *Muwaḥḥid*: a Unitarian.
muwaqqit— "time setter," reminds the faithful in Ramaḍān when to start the fast.

N

nabi—"prophet."
nadhīr—"warner."
nafs—ego, soul, the "universal soul" to the Ismā'īlis.
naḥw—science of grammar, specifically syntax.
na'l—piece of leather sole strapped to bottom of feet by the pilgrim performing the ḥajj.
Naṣārah—Christians.
niṣāb—minimum value set on products of the soil for determining the amount of the poor-due.
nīyah—declared number of "bowlings" in prayer by which validity is determined.

Q

qara'—"to read," "to recite" verbal root of Qur'ān.
qibla—direction of prayer in Islam, i.e. Mecca.
Qiyās—principle of jurisprudence, derived by use of analogical deduction.
Qur'an—the "Bible" of Islam.
Quṭb—"Pole of the World" to the Ṣūfis, or the top-ranking saint of the hierarchy.
qu'ūd—same as *julūs.*

R

raḥmah—"mercy."
Raḥmān—"Most Merciful," an attribute of God.
rak'āt—plural of *rak'ah*, each stands for a full prayer cycle.
rasūl—"messenger."
ra'y—personal opinion or judgment exercised by the jurist in deriving a principle enjoying legal sanctity.
razzia—term for "foray" or "raid" from Arabic *ghaza.*
ribāṭ—Ṣūfi monastery.
ridā'—seamless white cloth draped around the shoulder by the pilgrim performing the ḥajj.
Risālat al-Tawḥīd—"The Epistle on the Unity of God," title of 'Abduh's important work.
rūh—"spirit."
rūh al-qudus—"holy spirit."
rukū'—kneeling in obeisance during ritual prayer.

S

sabbiḥ—"praise!" i.e. the Lord, God!
ṣadaqah—voluntary non-statutory alm rendered for the sake of acquiring merit with Allah.
sadd bāb al-ijtihād —"closing the gate of ijtihād" or ending personal exertion in the interpretation of doctrine.
ṣaghā'ir—minor sins which can be expiated.
Ṣaḥīḥ—"Verified," i.e. *ḥadīth*; title of

Bukhāri's compilation of traditions.

ṣaḥn—great open space or courtyard of the mosque.

saj'—rhymed prose.

sakīnah—calm, tranquility: result of the mystic beholding the Creator.

Salafīyah—"Reformed Traditionists," a "modernist" movement started in Egypt in this century.

ṣalla-'l-Lāhu 'ala Sayyidina Muḥammad—"May Allah cause His prayers [to descend] on our lord Muḥammad," intercession for him in the ritual prayer.

ṣalāh—ritual prayer, ordained five times a day.

Ṣalāt al-'Īd—formal prayer at termination of the month of fasting.

ṣalat al-jum'ah—Friday noon prayer performed usually in congregation.

Sanat al-Wufūd—"Year of the Delegations" in 631 when representatives from all of Arabia came to Mecca and pledged allegiance to Islam and Muḥammad.

Ṣawm—legal fast, basic prerequisite of the faith.

Shahādah—the process of reciting the testimonial which initiates one into Islam.

shahīd—someone killed fighting for the faith.

shā'ir—literally "he who senses," term applied to "poet."

Shar'ī—pertaining to *Sharī'ah*.

Sharī'ah—Fundamental Law of Islam: its "constitution."

Shawwāl—tenth month of the Muslim calendar, follows Ramaḍān.

shaykh—same as "sheik," or chief, head, leader of a tribe or Ṣūfi order.

Shaykh al-Islām—chief official spokesman for Islam, formal office in the administration of the Ottoman Turks.

Shayṭān—"Satan."

Shī'at 'Ali—"partisans of 'Ali," fourth caliph, who formed a distinct sect (Shī'ite).

shi'r—"poetry."

shirk—associating other deities or "partners" with the worship of Allah.

shuhadā'—plural of *shahīd*.

shu'ūbīyah—form of "ethnic nationalism."

ṣubḥ—morning time.

Ṣūfism—title by which Islamic mysticism is known.

suḥūr—meal at dawn at start of peri-of of fast. Cf. *fuṭūr*.

ṣujūd—"prostration," high point of ritual prayer.

sulṭān—literally: "possessor of ultimate authority," official title of Turkic heads of dynasties.

sunnah—conduct of Muḥammad as a man.

Sunnah—corpus of the Traditions.

sūq—market place, center of trading and social gatherings.

Sūrah—chapter heading of the Qur'ān.

T

Tābi'—see *al-Tābi'ūn*.

tafsīr—exegesis, i.e. Qur'ān.

taḥallul al-ṣaghīr—state of partial desanctification begun by pilgrim after 'Īd al-Aḍḥa.

ṭahārah—"magnification," i.e., of Allah, in prayer.

takbīr al-iḥrām—stage in the ritual prayer when its highest point of sanctity is achieved.

tanzīl—process of "sending down" the revelations of the Qur'ān from heaven.

taqīyah—"dissimulation," formally sanctioned by Shī'ism.

tāqlīd—"imitation" of precedents established by the ulema.

ṭarīqah—path followed by the Ṣūfis to achieve gnosis.

tāslīm—reciting the formula "May peace and the mercy of God be with you!"

ṭawāf—process of circumambulating the Kaʿbah during pilgrimage time.

ṭawāf al-ifāḍah—circumambulation of the Kaʿbah, last act heralding the end of the pilgrimage.

tawḥīd—in mystical terms: unity with God; in orthodox terms: proclaiming the unity of God.

Tawrāt—Torah.

tazakka—purifyuing the self-spiritually, absolving oneself in the eyes of God.

taʿziyah— "consolation" procession, staged annually by Shīʿites in commemoration of the death of Ḥusayn, the Prophet's grandson.

tekke—place where Ṣūfi orders, like the Bektāshis, held their *dhikr*.

U

ʿUlamāʾ—English "ulema" plural of *ʿālim*; refers to collective body of those knowledgeable in Islamic beliefs and dogma.

ummah—community of Muslims.

ʿUmra—lesser pilgrimage.

ʿUqqāl—collective body of Druze leaders having access to the sect's secrets, i.e. doctrines.

ʿushr—the fixed amount of the legal tithe (*zakāh*), literally "one-tenth."

W

"wa anna Muḥammadan rasūlu ʾl-Lāh"—"and that Muḥammad is the messenger of God"—second part of the *Shahādah*.

wājib—see *farḍ* (above).

waqf—"mortmain."

wuḍūʾ—limited ablution in preparation for prayer.

wuqūf—"station before Allah," most important phase of the pilgrimage ceremony, held on the ninth day.

Y

Yawm al-Dīn—"Day of Judgment."

Yawm al-Qiyāmah—"Day of Resurrection."

Yhwh—Semitic prototype for "Jehovah," God of Kenite tribe of Sinai adopted by Moses.

Z

ẓāhir—apparent or literal meaning of Qurʾān's as opposed to the *bāṭini*.

ẓuhr—noon, time for the third ritual prayer of the day.

zakāh—statutory alms of a portion of wordly possessions in expiation of what a Muslim retains.

zakāt al-fiṭr—statutory alms offered on the day ending the month of fasting.

Recommended Reading

The following is a useful list of important titles dealing with the various subjects treated as available in English and other Western languages:

1. Jāhilīyah Arabia

Lammens, Henri. *Le Berceau de l'Islam, L'Arabie occidentale à la veille de l'Hegire*. Rome, 1914. Classical study of Arabia on eve of Islam.

______ . *La Mecque à la veille de l'Hegire*. Beyrouth, 1924. Valuable reference for knowledge of Mecca and society at birth of Islam.

O'Leary, D. L. *Arabia before Muḥammad*. London, 1927. Compact but scholarly study of the peninsula and its pre-Islamic values.

Philby, H. St. J. B. *The Background of Islam*. Alexandria, 1947. Useful study by an expert on Arabia.

Shahid, Irfan. *The Martyrs of Najrān*. Brussels, 1971. Authoritative study of the organized Christian community of Arabia.

Smith, W. R. *The Religion of the Semites*. 3rd ed. London, 1927; Meridian, 1956, 1957, 1959. Classical study of the religious beliefs of the Semites in and out of Arabia.

2. General Works on Islam

Ali, Syed Ameer. *The Spirit of Islam*. London, 1922, 1923, 1935, 1946, 1949, 1952, . . . A penetrating Muslim modernist's treatment of Islam as a socioreligious force.

Arnold, Sir Thomas. *The Preaching of Islam*. London, 1896, 1913, 1930; Lahore, n.d. A classical study on the spread of Islam.

______ , and Guillaume, Alfred (ed.). *The Legacy of Islam*. Oxford University Press, 1942, 1944, 1945, 1947, 1949, 1952, 1960. A series of authoritative articles on Islam as a socioreligious and cultural force.

ʿAzzām, A. R. *The Eternal Message of Muḥammad*. Translated by Caesar E. Farah. New York 1964, 1965,

London 1980, Cambridge 1992. A Muslim's view of Islam in the modern world, challenging and illuminating.

Cragg, Kenneth and Speight, Marston. *Islam From Within, Anthology of a Religion*. Belmont, California: Wadsworth, 1980. Useful collection of essays from original writings on religion and issues.

______ . *The House of Islam*. Belmont, California: Wadsworth, 1975.

Donner, F.M. *The Early Islamic Conquests*. Princeton, New Jersey: Princeton University Press, 1981.

Faruqi, I.R. al-. *Islam*. Niles (Ill.): Argus, 1979.

Gibb, Sir H. A. R. *Mohammedanism*. Oxford University Press, 1949. 1950; 2nd ed. 1953; Galaxy Book, 1962. Penetrating study of Islam.

Guillaume, Alfred. *Islam*. 2nd ed. reprint. Pelican Book, 1961. A useful general study of Islam.

Hamidullah, M. *Introduction to Islam*. 5th ed. enlarged. Chicago, Illinois: Kazi Publications, 1981. A Muslim viewpoint of faith, society, law and perceptions of non-Muslims.

Haneef, S. *What Everyone Should Know About Islam and Muslims*. Chicago, Illinois: Kazi Publications, 1982.

Hodgson, Marshall, *The Venture of Islam*, 3 vols. Chicago, Illinois: University Press, 1974. Provocative interpretive study of Islam in its broadest range.

Jeffrey, Arthur. *Islam: Muḥammad and His Religion*, New York, 1958. A study of Islam from original sources translated and cited.

______ . *A reader on Islam: Passages from Standard Arabic Writings Illustrative of the Beliefs and Practices of Muslims*. The Hague: Mouton, 1962.

Rahman, Fazlur. *Islam*. 2nd ed. Chicago, Illinois: University of Chicago Press, 1979.

Rosenthal, Franz. *The Classical Heritage of Islam*. Translated from German by Emile and Jeremy Marmorstein. Berkeley and Los Angeles, California: University of California Press, 1975. Excellent collection of essays on various aspects of Islamic civilization from original sources.

Williams, John A. (ed.). *Islam*. New York, 1961; paper ed. 1963. A handy compact study based on translations from original sources.

______ . *Themes of Islamic Civilization*. Berkeley, California and London: University of California Press, 1971. Fine collection of essays from original sources on God, community, government, Jihād; and the Muslim's conception of the "Will of God."

3. Life of Muḥammad

Buhl, Frants. *Das Leben Mohammeds*. Translated by H. H. Schaeder. Berlin, 1930. Standard Western study of Muḥammad's life and work.

Haykal, M. H. *The Life of Muḥammad*. 8th ed. English translation by I. R. A. al-Fāruqī. North American Trust Publications, 1976. Based on original sources.

Ibn-Hishām. *The Life of Muḥammad*. Translated by Alfred Guillaume. Oxford University Press, 1955. The standard original account with useful notes.

Ibn Ishaq. *The Life of Muḥammad*. Translated by A. Guillaume. Oxford University Press, 1967.

Jeffrey, A. (ed.). *Islam: Muḥammad and His Religion.* New York: Liberal Arts Press, 1958.

Muir, Sir William. *The Life of Mohammad.* Rev. ed. Edinburgh, 1923. Detailed and thorough, from original sources.

Rodinson, M. *Mohammed.* Translated by Anne Carter. New York: Vintage Books, 1974.

Schimmel, A. *And Muḥammad Is His Messenger.* Chapel Hill, North Carolina: University of North Carolina Press, 1985.

Watt, W.M. *Muḥammad: Prophet and Statesman.* Oxford University Press, 1961.

4. The Qurʾān

Ali, A. Y. *The Koran: Text, Translation and Commentary.* Washington, D.C.: American International Printing Company, 1946.

Arberry, A. J. *The Holy Koran.* London, 1953. Contains helpful introductory material.

______ . *The Koran Interpreted.* London: Allen & Unwin, 1955; New York: Macmillan, 1964.

Baljon, J. *Modern Muslim Koran Interpretation.* Leiden: E.J. Brill, 1961.

Bell, R. *Introduction to the Qurʾān.* revised ed. W.M. Watt. Edinburgh University Press, 1970.

______ . *The Qurʾān.* 2 vols. Edinburgh, 1937–39. One of the best translations, attempts a critical arrangement.

Blachère, R. *Introduction au Coran.* Paris, 1947. Standard on history of Qurʾān.

Cragg, K. *The Event of the Qurʾān: Islam in its Scripture.* London: Allen & Unwin, 1971.

Dawood, N. J. *The Koran.* Baltimore, Maryland: Penguin Books, 1961. Attempts a chronological arrangement.

Irving, T. B. (translator and commentator). *The Qurʾān.* Brattleboro, Vermont: Amana books, 1985. First American edition. Facile reading. Well referenced for subject matter and easy access.

Izutsu, T. *God and Man in the Koran: Semantics of the Koranic Weltanschauung.* Tokyo: Keio Institute of Cultural and Linguistic Studies, 1964.

______ . *Ethico-Religious Concepts in the Qurʾān.* Montreal: McGill University Press, 1966.

Jansen, J. J. G. *The Interpretation of the Koran in Modern Egypt.* Leiden: E. J. Brill, 1974.

Jeffery, Arthur. *Materials for the History of the Text of the Koran.* Leyden, 1937. Handy for a critical study of the Qurʾān.

______ . *The Qurʾān as Scripture.* New York: Russell F. Moore, 1957.

Maududi, Abu Ala. *The Meaning of the Qurʾān.* Lahore: M. Ashraf, 1967.

Nöldeke, Th. *Geschichte des Qurʾāns.* 2nd ed., 3 vols., 1961 reprint. Leipzig, 1909–38. Classical study of Qurʾān.

______ . *Remarques critiques sur le style et la syntaxe du Coran.* Translated by G. H. Bousquet. Paris, 1953. Excellent study on composition and style of the Qurʾān.

Pickthall, M. M. *The Meaning of the Glorious Koran.* Mentor Religious Classic 10th printing 1963. Eloquent, true to spirit and meaning of the Arabic.

Rahman, Fazlur. *Major Themes of the Qurʾān.* Minneapolis: Bibliotheca Islamica, 1980.

Sell, Edward. *The Historical*

Development of the Qur'ān. London 1909. Old but still useful for understanding the background.

Stanton, H. U. W. *The Teaching of the Qur'ān.* London, 1919. Summarizes the essence of Qur'ānic doctrine.

Tisdall, W. St. Clair. *The Original Sources of the Qur'ān.* London, 1911. Opinionated but helpful for understanding Qur'ānic derivations.

5. Islamic Doctrine

Abduh, M. *The Theology of Unity,* translated by K. Cragg & I. Musa'ad. New York: Humanities Press, 1966.

Ali, M. Muḥammad. *A Manual of Ḥadīth.* Lahore, n.d. A selection of Traditions translated from the Arabic of al-Bukhāri annotated.

Azami, M. M. *Studies in Early Ḥadīth Literature.* 2nd ed. Indianapolis, Indiana: American Trust Publications, 1978.

Bokhari. *Les Traditions Islamiques.* Translated by O. Houdas and W. Marçais. 4 vols. Paris, 1903–14. Ultimate recourse for the verified *Ḥadīth.* English edition by Kazi. Chicago.

Gardet, Louis and Anawati, M. M. *Introduction à la théologie musulmane.* Paris, 1948. Discusses the evolution of theology from a Thomiste point of view.

Goldziher, I. *Introduction to Islamic Theology and Law.* Translated by A. and R. Hamori. Princeton, New Jersey: Princeton University Press, 1981.

______ . *Muhammedanische Studien.* Vol. II. Halle, 1890, 1961. Excellent source of study on Ḥadīth.

Guillaume, Alfred. *The Traditions of Islam.* Oxford, 1924. Kayat, 1966. Useful study based in part on Goldziher's work.

Juynboll, G. H. A. *The Authenticity of the Tradition Literature.* Leiden: E. J. Brill, 1969.

Macdonald, Duncan B. *Development of Muslim Theology, Jurisprudence and Constitutional Theory.* 1903 reprint. New York. Standard work in English on the subject.

Margoliouth, D. S. *The Early Development of Mohammedanism.* London, 1914. Helpful study of the formulation of Islamic doctrine.

Siddiqi, M. Zubayr. *Ḥadīth Literature.* Calcutta University, 1961. Origin, development, special features and criticism. Useful source of reference.

Smith, J. I. & Haddad, Y. Y. *The Islamic Understanding of Death and Resurrection.* Albany, New York: SUNY Press, 1981.

Tritton, A. S. *Muslim Theology.* London, 1947. Useful reference to various aspects of doctrinal development.

Wensinck, A. J. *The Muslim Creed.* Cambridge, 1932. Critical study of the rise of the orthodox view.

6. Institutions and Practices

Arnold, Sir T. W. *The Caliphate.* Oxford, 1924. Still the best on relating the development of the caliphate.

Calverley, E. E. *Worship in Islam.* Madras, 1925. Excellent exposé of the articles of faith.

Coulson, N. J. *A History of Islamic Law.* Edinburgh University Press, 1964.

Farah, Madelain. *Marriage and Sexuality in Islam.* Translation of al-Ghazzali's "Etiquette of Marriage" from his IHYA. Sums up Sunni-Ṣūfi concepts, official and authoritative in a theological context.

Fyzee, A. A. A. *Outlines of Muhammadan Law*. 3rd. ed. Oxford University Press, 1964.

Gaudefroy-Demombynes, Maurcie. *Muslim Institutions*. Translated by J. P. Macgregor. London, 1954. Relates principal institutions of Islam from original sources.

Gautier, Émile F. *Moeurs et coutumes des musulmans*. Paris, 1955. Useful study of Muslim customs.

Lammens, Henri. *Islam: Beliefs and Institutions*. Translated by Sir E. Denison Ross. London, 1929. Indispensable source of reference.

Lane, E. W. *The Manners and Customs of the Modern Egyptians*. London, Everyman's, 1954. Illustrated first-hand observation of Muslim institutions in practice.

Levy, Ruben. *An Introduction to the Sociology of Islam*. 2 vols. London, 1933. Standard for sociological development of Muslim institutions.

Qaddawi, Y. al-. *The Lawful and the Prohibited in Islam*. Indianapolis, Indiana: American Trust Publications, n.d.

Schacht, Joseph. *An Introduction to Islamic Law*. Oxford, 1964. The standard reference.

Sharīʿati, Ali. *On the Sociology of Islam*. Translated by Hamid Algar. Berkeley: Mizan Press, 1979. Important statement on critical issues confronting Islam in assessing modern views of society and man's role therein.

Ṭabaṭabāʾi, Hossein M. *An Introduction to Shīʿi Law*. London: Ithaca Press, 1984. A bibliographical study preceded by an outline of Shiʿi law.

Taleghani, Sayyid Mahmud. *Society and Economics in Islam*. Translation of the Ayatollah's writings and declaration and writings by R. Campbell. Significant contribution to understanding of Shīʿite perception of economics, *jihād* and martyrdom, and education in a modern revolutionary context.

Tritton, A. S. *Islam: Belief and Practices*. London, New York, 1951, 1957. Practical and helpful.

von Grunebaum, Gustav. *Muhammadan Festivals*. New York, 1951. Comprehensive on the subject.

7. Formalism and Intellectualism

Abdouh, Mohammed. *Rissalat al tawhid, Exposé de la religion musulmane*. Translated by B. Michel and M. Abdel Razik. Paris, 1952. Classical treatise on true Islam by an outstanding modernist.

de Boer, T. J. *The History of Philosophy in Islam*. London, 1933. Valuable brief account.

de Vaux, B. Carra, *Les Penseurs de l'Islam*. 5 vols. Paris, 1921–26. Invaluable source of reference for Muslim thinkers of different schools.

Donaldson, D. M. *Studies in Muslim Ethics*. London, 1950. Standard work on the subject.

Makdisi, George, "Ashʿari and the Ashʿarites in Islamic Religious History," in *Studia Islamica*, Vols. XVII (1962), pp. 37–80 and XVIII (1963), pp. 19–40.

Watt, W. M. *Free Will and Predestination in Early Islam*. London: Luzac, 1948. Excellent study, valuable reference.

______ . *The Formative Period of Islamic Thought*. Edinburgh University Press, 1973.

______ . *Islamic Philosophy and Theology*. Edinburgh University Press, 1962. Comprehensive, useful.

______ . *Muslim Intellectual: A Study of Al-Ghazali*. Edinburgh 1963. Most informative and intriguing study of the man and his environment.

Wolfson, H.A. *The Philosophy of the Kalam*. Cambridge, Massachusetts: Harvard University Press, 1976.

8. The Sects and Religious Life

Abd el-Jalil, J. M. *Aspects interieurs de l'Islam*. 2nd ed. Paris, 1952. Valuable insight by one who knows Islam.

Bousquet, G. H. *Les grandes pratiques rituelles de l'Islam*. Paris, 1949. Cultic practices, including the mystical approach.

Chittick, W. C. (ed. & trsl.). *A Shi͑ite Anthology*. Albany, New York: SUNY Press, 1981.

Donaldson, D. M. *The Shi͑ite Religion*. London, 1942. Thorough but not critical.

Hitti, P. K. *The Origins of the Druze People and Religion*. New York: Columbia University Press, 1928. Beirut, 1964. Authoritative and revealing.

Hodgson, Marshall G. (Translator). *The Order of the Assassins*. The Hague, 1955. Collection of translations of various authors; most complete on the subject.

Hussain, J. M. *The Occultation of the Twelfth Imām*. London: The Muhammadi Trust, 1982.

Jafri, J. H. M. *The Origins and Early Development of Shi͑i Islam*. London: Longman, 1979.

Lewis, B. *The Origins of Ismā͑ilism*. Cambridge, 1940. A basic work on this important sect.

Macdonald, D. B. *The Religious Attitude and Life in Islam*. Chicago, 1912. Excellent insight into Islam at work.

______ . *The Religious Attitude and Life in Islam*. New York: AMS Press, 1970.

Momen, Mojan. *Shi͑ite Islam*. New Haven: Yale University Press, 1985.

Rauf, M. Abdul. *Islam: Creed and Worship*. Washington, D.C.: The Islamic Center, 1974.

Sachedina, A. *Islamic Messianism*. Albany, New York: SUNY Press, 1981.

Salem, Elie A. *Political Theory and Institutions of the Khawārij*. Baltimore, Maryland: The Johns Hopkins Press, 1956. An important study for understanding the first sect of Islam and its historical impact.

al-Ṭabāṭaba'i, M. Ḥusayn, *Shi͑ite Islam*. Translated by Seyyed Hossein Nasr. State University of New York Press, 1977.

9. Mysticism

Affifi, A. E. *The Mystical Philosophy of Muhyid Din ibnul-Arabi*. Cambridge, 1939, 1964. Courageous attempt to reduce a difficult subject to order.

Arberry, A. J. *An Introduction to the History of Ṣūfism*. London: Longman, 1942.

______ . *Ṣūfism: An Account of the Mystics of Islam*. New York: Harper Torchbooks, 1970

Baldick, J. *Mystical Islam*. New York: New York University Press, 1989.

Birge, J. K. *The Bektashi Order of Dervishes*. London, 1937.

Detailed full treatment of the order, history and doctrine.

Brown, J. P. *The Darwishes or Oriental Spiritualism*. Ed. H. A. Rose. Oxford, 1927. Useful reference for Ṣūfi organization and observances.

Burckhardt, T. *An Introduction to Ṣūfi Doctrine*. Translated by D.M. Matheson. Lahore: Muhammad Ashraf, 1959.

Dermenghem, Émile. *Vies des saints musulmans*. Paris, 1942. Special study of beatified leaders of the Ṣūfi orders.

Gilsenan, M. *Saint and Ṣūfi in Modern Egypt: An Essay in the Sociology of Religion*. Oxford: Clarendon Press, 1973.

Ling, M. *What is Ṣūfism?* Berkeley, California: University of California Press, 1977.

Massignon, Louis. *Essai sur les origines de lexique technique de la mystique musulmane*. Paris, 1922, 1954. Ultimate recourse for Study of Ṣūfi origins.

______ . *The Passion of al-Hallaj: Mystical Martyr of Islam*. Translated by H. Mason. 4 vols. Princeton, New Jersey: Princeton University Press, 1983.

Nicholson R. A. *The Mystics of Islam*. London, 1914, 1963 reprint. Best single study on the subject.

Schimmel, Annemarie. *Mystical Dimensions of Islam*. Chapel Hill, North Carolina: The University of North Carolina Press, 1975. An authoritative work that conveys the humanistic and literary dimensions of Ṣūfism in its fullest historical and geographical range.

Smith, Margaret. *Readings from the Mystics of Islam*. London 1950. Excellent selections fully illustrative of the subject.

Trimingham, J. S. *The Ṣūfi Orders in Islam*. Oxford University Press, 1971.

Watt, W. M. *The Faith and Practice of al-Ghazali*. Oxford, 1952. Insight into a leading theologian's attitude towards his faith.

10. Relation to Christianity and Judaism

Andrae, Tor. *Der Ursprung des Islams und das Christentum*. Uppsala, 1926. Authoritative study on common origins of Islam and Christianity.

Bell, R. *The Origin of Islam in Its Christian Environment*. London, 1926. Relates the impact of Syrian Christianity on Muḥammad.

Cragg, Kenneth. *The Call of the Minaret*. New York, Oxford, 1956. Interesting study in contrast between Christianity and Islam.

Jomier, J. *The Bible and the Koran*. Chicago, Illinois: Henry Regnery, 1967.

Kateregga, B. D. and Shenk, W. *Islam and Christianity*. Grand Rapids, Michigan: William B. Eerdmans, 1980.

Katsh, Abraham I. *Judaism in Islam*. New York, 1954. Biblical and Talmudic backgrounds in Sūrahas 2 and 3 of the Qurʾān.

Parrinder, G. *Jesus in the Qurʾān*. Oxford University Press, 1973.

Rosenthal, Erwin I. J. *Judaism and Islam*. London, New York, 1961. Attempt to show Islam's dependenee on Judaism.

Sweetman, J. W. *Islam and Christian Theology*. 3 vols. London, 1945–55. Useful but necessitates caution, contains much information on the sects.

Watt, W. M. *Islam and Christianity Today*. London: Routledge and Kegan Paul, 1983.

Weil, Gustav. *The Bible, the Koran and the Talmud*. New York, 1863. Dated but still valuable as a study in comparison.

11. Islam in the Modern World

Adams, C. C. *Islam and Modernism in Egypt*. London, 1933. Authoritative study of Afghāni, ʿAbduh and the Salafiyah.

Allen, H. E. *The Turkish Transformation*. Chicago, 1935. Impact of modernism on Islamic tradition in Turkey.

Amīn, ʿUthmān. *Muḥammad ʿAbduh*. Translated by Charles Wendell. Washington, D.C., 1953. Important work on a significant element in Islamic modernism.

Anderson, J. N. D. "Recent Developments in Sharīʿa Law." Nine articles in *The Muslim World*. October 1950 to 1952. Standard reference for transformations in Sharīʿah laws.

Arberry, A. J. and Landau, R. (eds.). *Islam Today*. London, 1943. Series of articles on Islam in recent times.

Azzam, Salem (ed.) *Islam and Contemporary Society*. Longmand: Islamic Council of Europe, 1982. Doctrine, civilization, economic force, aesthetic values, universalism, and human rights from an Islamic perspective.

Bennigsen, A. and Lemercier-Quelquejay, C. *Islam in the Soviet Union*. New York and London: Fredrick A. Praeger, 1967. The most useful single volume on the subject.

Boisard, Marcel A. *L'Islam Aujourd'hui*. UNESCO, 1985. Significant essays on Islam and Muslims in the conscience of the West, science and technology, education, and economic development.

Bousquet, G. H. *L'Islam maghrebien*. Paris, 1943, 1955. Revealing study of Islam in West North Africa.

Enayat, Hamid. *Modern Islamic Political Thought*. Austin: University of Texas, 1982. How Islam's traditional heritage has affected development of modern ideas. Good treatment of Sunni-Shīʿi differences.

Fisher, Humphrey J. *Aḥmadiyyah*. Oxford, 1963. Most comprehensive to date, slanted to the movement in Africa.

Gibb, H. A. R. *Modern Trends in Islam*. Chicago, 1947. Penetrating speculative study, critical and valuable.

______. *Whither Islam*? London, 1932. Treats Islamic trends in North Africa, Egypt, India and Indonesia.

Gouilly, Alphonse. *L'Islam dans l'Afrique occidentale française*. Paris, 1952. Commendable source of reference for Islam in West Africa.

Hartmann, R. *Die Krisis des Islam*. Leipzig, 1928. Critical study of Islam's confrontations in the modern world.

Hitti, P. K. *Islam and the West*. Princeton, Anvil, 1962. Fascinating expertly presented study of foci of contact.

Hurgronje, C. Snouck. *The Achehnese*. 2 vols. Leyden, 1906. Definitive study of Islam as a socioreligious force in Indonesia.

I-fan, Yang. *Islam in China*. Hong Kong, 1957. Brief but most revealing.

Kettani, M. Ali. *Muslim Minorities in the World Today*. London:

Mansell, 1986. Unique attempt to study status of Muslim minorities around the world and their efforts to overcome handicaps and safeguard values.

Lincoln, C. Eric. *The Black Muslims in America*. Boston, 1962. Attempt at objective study of a movement in flux.

Lomax, Louis E. *When the Word Is Given* . . . New York, 1963. Emotional, penetrating and revealing study of the "Black Muslims."

Miller, W. M. *Bahaism, Its Origin, History, Teachings*. New York, 1931. Useful one volume reference.

Monteil, Vincent. *Essai sur l'Islam en U.R.S.S.*, volume for 1952, *Revue des Éstudes Islamiques*. Paris, 1953. Factual, objective and commendable.

Rondot, Pierre. *L'Islam et les musulmans d'aujourd'hui*. 2 vols. Paris, 1958–60. Critical and penetrating.

Roux, Jean-Paul. *L'Islam en Asie*. Paris 1958. Compact useful study of Islam in most countries of Asia.

Ruthven, Malise. *Islam in the World*. Oxford University Press, 1984. Prophet Muḥammad's paradigm, law and disorder, spiritual renewal, and challenges from the West.

Smith, Wilfred Cantwell. *Islam in Modern History*. Princeton 1957; Mentor, 1959, 1961, 1963. Challenging controversial study of Islam in the state of flux.

le Tourneau, R. *L'Islam contemporain*. Paris, 1950. Lucid exposé of Islam today.

Trimingham, J. S. *A History of Islam in West Africa*. Oxford, 1962. Valuable source of data, an updated study.

Wilson, S. G. *Modern Movements among Moslems*. New York, 1916. Outdated but valuable to the historian.

12. Renewal and Activism

Abd-Allah, U. F. *The Islamic Struggle in Syria*. Berkeley, California: Mizan Press, 1983.

Akhavi, Sharough. *Religion and Politics in Contemporary Iran*. Albany, New York: SUNY Press, 1980.

Algar, Hamid (translated). *Islam and Revolution: Writings and Declarations of Imām Khomeini*. Berkeley, California: Mizan Press, 1981.

______ . *The Roots of the Islamic Revolution*. London: The Muslim Institute, 1983. Brief anthology embodying views of Ayatollah Khomeini, Ali Sharīʿati, and others on inducement to revolution based on dialogue with author.

Antoun, R. T. and Hegland, M. E. *Religious Resurgence, Contemporary Cases in Islam, Christianity & Judaism*. Syracuse, New York: Syracuse University Press, 1987.

Arjomand, S. A. (ed.). *From Nationalism to Revolutionary Islam*. Albany, New York: SUNY Press, 1984.

______ . *The Turban and the Crown: The Islamic Revolution in Iran*. Oxford University Press, 1988.

Ayoob, Mohammed (ed.). *The Politics of Islamic Reassertion*. New York: St. Martin's Press, 1981.

Benard, C. and Khalizad, Z. "*The Government of God*": *Iran's Islamic Republic*. New York: Columbia University Press, 1984.

Burke, E., III and Lapidus, I. M. (eds.). *Islam, Politics, and Social Movements*. Berkeley, California:

University of California Press, 1988.

Cudsi, A. S. and Dessouki, A. E. H. *Islam and Power*. London: Croom Helm, 1981.

Daweesha, Adeed (ed.). *Islam in Foreign Policy*. Cambridge, Massachusetts: Cambridge University Press, 1983.

El-Affendi, A. *Turabi's Revolution: Islam and Power in the Sudan*. London: Grey Seal, 1991.

Esposito, J. L. (ed.). *Islam and Politics*. 3rd ed. Syracuse, New York: Syracuse University Press, 1991.

______ . *The Islamic Threat*. Oxford University Press, 1993.

______ . *Voices of Resurgent Islam*. Oxford University Press, 1983.

Fischer, M. M. J. *Iran: From Religious Discourse to Revolution*. Cambridge, Massachusetts: Harvard University Press, 1980

Gellner, Ernest (ed.). *Islamic Dilemmas: Reformers, Nationalists, and Industrialization*. Mouton, 1985. Anthology of essays focusing on Islamic adaptations to the modern world and the impact thereof.

Haddad, Y. Y., Haines, B. and Findly, E. (eds.). *The Islamic Impact*. Syracuse, New York: Syracuse University Press, 1982.

Hamidullah, M. *Muslim Conduct of State*. 7th ed. rev. Lahore: Muhammad Ashraf, 1977.

Hasan, M. K. *Contemporary Muslim Religio-Political Thought in Indonesia: The Response to "New Order Modernization."* Kuala Lumpur: Dewan Bahasa dan Pustaka, 1980.

Jansen, G. H. *Militant Islam*. New York: Harper & Row, 1979. One of earliest effective analyses of militant forces and their causes, and the underpinning rationale.

Keddie, Nikki. *An Islamic Response to Imperialism: Political and Religious Writings of Sayyid Jamal ad-Din 'al-Afghani'*. Berkeley and Los Angeles, California: University of California Press, 1972.

Lambton, A. K. S. *State and Government in Medieval Islam*. Oxford University Press, 1981.

Lapidus, Ira M. *Contemporary Islamic Movements in Historical Perspective*. Berkeley, California: University of California's Institute of International Studies, 1983. Provides background explanations of current movements commanding world attention.

Malik, H. *Sir Sayyid Ahmad Khan and Muslim Modernism in India and Pakistan*. New York: Columbia University Press, 1980.

Mardin, S. *Religion and Social Change in Turkey*. Albany, New York: SUNY Press, 1989.

Pipes, D. *In the Path of God: Islam and Political Power*. New York: Basic Books, 1983.

Piscatori, J. (ed.). *Islam in the Political Process*. Cambridge, Massachusetts: Cambridge University Press, 1983, 1984.

________ . *Islam in a World of Nation States*. Cambridge, Massachusetts: Cambridge University Press, 1986.

Siddiqui, Kalim (ed.). *Issues in the Islamic Movement*. London: The Open Press, 1983. An angry Islamic response to disaffection in Iran's neighboring countries.

Sivan, E. *Radical Islam: Medieval Theology and Modern Politics*. New Haven, Connecticut: Yale University Press, 1985.

Vatikiotis, P. J. *Islam and the State*. London: Croom Helm, 1987.

Weiss, A. M. (ed.). *Islamic Reassertion in Pakistan: Islamic Laws in a*

Modern State. Syracuse, New York: Syracuse University Press, 1986.

Wright, R. *Sacred Rage: The Crusade of Modern Islam*. New York: Simon & Schuster, 1985.

13. Women and the Family

Abd al-Ati, H. *The Family Structure in Islam*. Plainfield, Indiana: American Trust Publications, 1977.

Abdul Ghani, Mufti M. *Rights of Husband and Wife*. Delhi: Dini Book Depot, 1981.

Azari, Farah, ed. *Women of Iran*. London: Ithaca Press, 1983.

Esposito, John L., *Women in Muslim Family Law*. Syracuse, New York: Syracuse University Press, 1982.

Fernea, E. W. and Bezirgan, Q. B., eds. *Middle Eastern Women Speak*. Austin, Texas: University of Texas Press, 1987.

______ . *Women and the Family in the Middle East*. Austin, Texas: University of Texas Press, 1985.

Keddie, N. R. and Beck, L., *Women in the Muslim World*. Cambridge, Massachusetts: Harvard University Press, 1978.

Mernissi, Fatima, *Behind the Veil*. New York and London: John Wiley & Sons, 1975.

Minai, Naila. *Women in Islam*. New York: Putnam, 1981.

Nashat, Guity, ed. *Women and Revolution in Iran*. Boulder, Colorado: Westview Press, 1983.

Shaaban, Bouthaina, *Arab Women Talk About their Lives*. Bloomington, Indiana: Indiana University Press, 1988; Midland, 1991

Smith, Jane, ed. *Women in Contemporary Muslim Societies*. Lewisburg, Pennsylvania: Bucknell University Press, 1980.

14. Muslims Around the World

Abbott, F. *Islam and Pakistan*. Ithaca, New York: Cornell University Press, 1968.

Abugiedeiri, el-T. *A Survey of North American Muslims*. Indianapolis, Indiana: Islamic Teaching Center, 1977.

Akiner, Shirin. *Islamic Peoples of the Soviet Union*. London: Kegan Paul, 1983.

Aossey, Y. Jr. *Fifty Years of Islam in Iowa 1925–1975*. Cedar Rapids, Iowa: Unity Publishing Co., n.d.

Banuazizi, A. and Weiner, M. (eds.). *The State, Religion, and Ethnic Politics: Afghanistan, Iran, and Pakistan*. Syracuse, New York: Syracuse University Press, 1986.

Bennigsen, A. and Lemercier-Queleuejay, C. *Islam in the Soviet Union*. London: Pall Mall Press, 1967.

Binder, L. *Religion and Politics in Pakistan*. Berkeley, California: University of California Press, 1961.

Carré, O. (ed.). *Islam and the State in the World Today*. New Delhi: Manohar Publications, 1987.

Dekmejian, R. H. *Islam in Revolution: Fundamentalism in the Arab World*. Syracuse, New York: Syracuse University Press, 1985.

Dessouki, A. E. H. (ed.). *Islamic Resurgence in the Arab World*. New York: Praeger, 1982.

Esposito, J. L. (ed.). *Islam in Asia: Religion, Politics and Society*. Oxford University Press, 1987.

______ . (ed.). *The Iranian Revolution: Its Global Impact*. Miami: International University Press, 1990.

Gilliland, D. S. *African Religion Meets Islam: Religious Change in Northern Nigeria*. University Press of America, 1986.

Gowing, P. G. and McAmis, R. (eds.). *The Muslim Filipinos*. Manila: Solidaridad Publishing House, 1974.

Haddad, Y. Y. (ed.). *The Muslims of America*. Oxford University Press, 1991.

______ . and Lumis, A.T. *Islamic Values in the United States*. Oxford University Press, 1987.

Hooker, M. B. (ed.). *Islam in Southeast Asia*. Leiden: E.J. Brill, 1983.

Israeli, R. and Johns, A.H. (eds.), *Islam in Asia*. Jerusalem: Magnes Press, 1984.

Magnus, H. & Naby, Eden. *Afghanistan: Mullah, Marx, and Mujahid*. Westview Press, 1998.

Majul, C. A. *Muslims in the Philippines*. Quezon City: University of the Philippines Press for the Asian Center, 1973.

Martin, B. *Muslim Brotherhoods in Nineteenth-Century Africa*. Cambridge, Massachusetts: Cambridge University Press, 1977.

Metcalf, B. D. *Islamic Revival in British India, 1860–1900*. Princeton, New Jersey: Princeton University Press, 1982.

Means, G. "The Role of Islam in the Political Development of Malaysia" in *Comparative Politics* 2 (1969), pp. 264–84.

______ . *Muslim Communities in Non-Muslim States*. London: Islamic Council of Europe, 1980.

Mutalib, Hussin. *Islam and Ethnicity in Malay Politics*. Oxford University Press, 1990.

Noble, Lela G. and Shuker, A. "Muslims in the Philippines and Thailand" in their edition of *Ethnic Conflict in International Relations*. New York: Praeger, 1977.

Poston, L. *Islamic Da'wah in the West: Muslim Missionary Activity and the Dynamics of Conversion to Islam*. Oxford University Press, 1992.

Ratnam, K. J. *Communalism and the Political Process in Malaya*. Kuala Lumpur: University of Malaya Press, 1965.

Roy, O. *Islam and Resistance in Afghanistan*. Cambridge, Massachusetts: Cambridge University Press, 1986.

Trimingham, J. S. *Islam in the Sudan*. London: Frank Cass, 2nd impr. 1965.

______ . *The Influence of Islam upon Africa*. London: Longman and Beirut: Librairie du Liban, 1968.

Waugh, E., Abu Laban, B. and Qureishi, R. *The Muslim Community in Noth America*. Edmonton: University of Alberta Press, 1983.

Wiley, J. *The Islamic Movement of Iraqi Shi'as*. Boulder and London: Lynne Rienner Publishers, 1992.

15. Islamic Modernism and Reform

Ahmad, Aziz, *Islamic Modernism in India and Pakistan, 1857–1964*. Oxford University Press, 1982

Commins, D. D. *Islamic Reform: Politics and Social Change in Late Ottoman Syria*. Oxford University Press, 1990

Donahue, J. J. and Esposito, J. L. (eds.). *Islam in Transition: Muslim Perspectives*. Oxford University Press, 1982.

Haddad, Y. Y. *Contemporary Islam and the Challenge of History*. Albany, New York: SUNY Press, 1982

Hoballah, M. F. *Islam and Human Tenets*. Washington, D.C.: The Islamic Center, n.d.

______ . *Islam and Modern Values*. Washington, D.C.: The Islamic Center, n.d.

Hosseini, I. M. *The Muslim Brethren: the Greatest Modern Islamic Movement*. Beirut: Khayat, 1956.

Hunter, S. T. (ed.). *The Politics of Islamic Revivalism*. Bloomington, Indiana: Indiana University Press, 1988.

Iqbal, M. *The Reconstruction of Religious Thought in Islam*. 2nd ed. London, 1934; Lahore: M. Ashraf, 1968.

Kerr, M. H. *Islamic Reform: The Political and Legal Theories of Muhammad Abduh and Rashid Rida*. Berkeley, California: University of California Press, 1966.

Levtzion, N. and Voll, J. O. *Eighteenth-Century Renewal and Reform in Islam*. Syracuse, New York: Syracuse University Press, 1987.

Mawdudi, S. Abul Ala. *A Short History of the Revivalist Movement in Islam*. Lahore: Islamic Publications, 1973.

Mitchell, R. P. *The Society of the Muslim Brothers*. Oxford University Press, 1969.

Nasr, S. H. *Traditional Islam in the Modern World*. London and New York: Kegan Paul International, 1987.

Noer, Deliar. *The Modernist Muslim Movement in Indonesia*. Singapore: Oxford University Press, 1973

Rahman, Fazlur. *Islam and Modernity*. Chicago, Illinois: University of Chicago Press, 1982.

Smith, W. C. *Modern Islam in India*. London: Gollancz, 1946.

Voll, J. O. Islam, *Continuity and Change in the Modern World*. Boulder, Colorado: Westview Press, 1982

16. Orientalism

Hudson, M. and C. and Wolfe, R. G. (eds.). *The American Media and the Arabs*. Washington D.C. Georgetown University, 1980.

Hussein, A., Olson, R. and Qureshi, J. (eds.). *Orientalism, Islam and Islamists*. Amana Books, 1984.

Said, E. *Covering Islam*. London: Routledge and Kegan Paul, 1981.

______ . *Orientalism*. New York: Vintage Books, 1978.

17. References

The Encyclopaedia of Islam. 4 vols. Leyden, 1913–1938; new edition in preparation. A must for those interested in all aspects of Islam.

The Shorter Encyclopaedia of Islam. Leyden, 1953, Cornell reprint. Emphasis on religion and canonical law.

al-Faruqi, I. R. and L. L. *The Cultural Atlas of Islam*. New York: Macmillan Inc., 1986. A blend of history, religion, and legacy, well-illustrated.

Hitti, P. K. *History of the Arabs*. 10th ed. New York: St. Martin's Press, 1974.

Hodgson, Marshall, *The Venture of Islam*, 3 vols. Chicago, Illinois: University Press, 1974. Sweeping integral treatment of historical Islam.

Holt, P. M., Lambton, A. K., and Lewis, B., eds. *The Cambridge History of Islam*. Cambridge University Press, 1978.

Savory, R. M. (ed.). *Introduction to Islamic Civiliation*. Cambridge University Press, 1976.

Schacht, J. and Bosworth, C. E., (eds.). *The Legacy of Islam*. 2nd ed. Oxford: Clarendon Press, 1974.

INDEX